Tim Morris Don Petcher

Science & Grace

GOD'S REIGN IN THE NATURAL SCIENCES

CROSSWAY BOOKS

A PUBLISHING MINISTRY OF
GOOD NEWS PUBLISHERS
WHEATON, ILLINOIS

Science & Grace

Published by Crossway Books
a publishing ministry of
Good News Publishers
1300 Crescent Street
Wheaton, Illinois 60187

Cover design: Jon McGrath

Cover photo: Getty Images

First printing 2006

Printed in the United States of America

Library of Congress Cataloging-in-Publication Data

Morris, Tim, 1961–
Science and grace : God's reign in the natural sciences / Tim Morris and Don Petcher.
p. cm.
Includes bibliographical references and index.
ISBN 978-1-58134-549-0
ISBN 1-58134-549-6 (tpb)
1. Religion and science. I. Petcher, Donald N., 1952– . II. Title
BL240.3.M67 2006
261.5'5—dc22 2005023917

VP 16 15 14 13 12 11 10 09 08 07 06
15 14 13 12 11 10 9 8 7 6 5 4 3 2 1

Contents

Preface

WHY SHOULD ANOTHER BOOK on science and Christianity be written when there are already so many out there? To answer this question we must give some historical explanation from our own experiences and also answer some additional questions. In teaching our students at Covenant College about the relation between science and Christianity, we have found many excellent resources for how science has affected Christianity, and how Christianity has in turn helped to shape science. But we also wanted to inform the students of how our underlying convictions, and in particular our theological convictions, relate to the way we view the world we study and the way we view our own participation in the scientific endeavor. However, we were unable to find a one-volume source that addresses these issues in a way that speaks both to the evangelical mind-set and also to the subtlety of the issues involved without compromising what we hold to be fundamental theological truths. So eventually we set out to write such a book.

Why would this kind of book benefit God's people? It seems to us that in terms of connecting modern science with Christian faith, many Christians think no further than the creation/evolution debate. And while this is an important area for Christian thinking and involvement, science and Christianity issues go much deeper. As God's people we all have responsibilities before God to use the Scriptures to continuously assess each culture in which we live rather than to passively let the culture shape our perspectives. Modern science is a cultural achievement that has demonstrated many successes, mostly for the good of mankind. But modern science also has its down side, and partly as a consequence, in the Postmodern world science has come under suspicion in various ways. Not only has science been knocked off its pedestal of being the source for objective truth in the world, but science is also seen by many as a potent enabler of evil. As Christians we ought to be grateful for benefits of the science of our age, and we need to oppose its misuse, but we also need to be aware of the potential it holds for setting up "idols of thought" or "idols of the mind." As idols always do, these science-related idols oppose God's gospel of grace in various ways. Some of these ways are more obvious and direct, but many others are quite subtle. Thus a main focus of our book is to suggest ways that God's people can think faithfully about science in terms of the gospel and so avoid idolatry.

What particular readership did we have in mind as we wrote? An author's answer to this question can provide important clues as to the specific usefulness of the book for various kinds of readers. Based on our experiences with Christian college students, we originally set out to address evangelical Christians who have some familiarity with science and Christian faith issues and who are interested in ideas that may help refine their Christian perspective on science. We believe such readers will find the way we frame these issues in the book helpful in stimulating their own thinking. There is plenty here for those who are interested in the move from a Modern to a Postmodern cultural backdrop and what its effects may be on science and the church. And while we do not deal systematically with the specifics of the creation/evolution controversy, plenty of material here finds application in that debate.

But in addition to this original intended readership, as we wrote we began to see a wider audience for whom the book might find some relevance. Because of the breadth of topics touched on here, we deal with many issues that are not limited to their application to science, but are relevant to many areas of a Christian's life before God. For example, in the early chapters our recommendations for ways of thinking about God's relation to His creation should be helpful to many Christians in evoking a greater sense of His wonder and glory as we ponder in new ways His ever-present grace in upholding the universe. And in a later chapter our recommendations for considering our responsibilities as "knowers" will find much wider application than just in the sciences. Likewise our chapter dealing with some of the specifics of Christian vocation in the sciences includes much that can be applied to other callings for God's people. Indeed, any

Christian who has ever wondered what relevance his or her "day job" has to the Kingdom of Christ would almost certainly run into similar issues as raised here in the context of science. What we present here is a strong antidote to the tendency in our day to separate our Sunday religion from our secular work week, as if God is only relevant when we are worshiping on Sunday, and the day-to-day grind of our weekly activities is unrelated to what we profess on Sunday. Readers who have felt this tension between Christian commitment and everyday work will find much to help and much to ponder in these pages.

Many factors have gone into the development of this book. Perhaps first and foremost, both of us are graduates of Covenant College, and from the time of our respective undergraduate days, we each have had a long-term interest in the relation between science and our Christian commitment. After graduate school in elementary particle physics for Don and cellular and molecular biology for Tim, both of us went on to do postdoctoral work in our respective fields before returning to Covenant to teach. Don joined the faculty in 1993 and Tim two years later. We thus first met in 1995, and after a few discussions it became evident that we each had similar interests in terms of working out a more robust and comprehensive understanding of science from a Christian perspective than we already had to that point. We also each had a similar desire to aid students and churches to better understand our dialog with the world concerning these issues and our participation as Christians in the cultural science in the face of the tensions that exist today.

Our first endeavor together was to create a course we called "Science in Perspective," designed to fulfill the core science requirement for those not majoring in science at Covenant. Our idea was to introduce students to the "hot topics" in science in their philosophical, theological, and historical context. We also wanted to present science as the multifaceted, wonderful, and wonder-producing enterprise we found it to be in our scientific work. In practice, science is not a bland, "detached, purely logical" enterprise that mechanically leads to truth, as it is often portrayed. Science is a wholly human enterprise with all the subtleties and foibles of any other human activity, and it provides many opportunities to bring Christian thinking and creativity to bear on its tasks.

Our major goal in teaching this course was to send our students out with a greater awareness of the subtlety of issues in order to equip them for better service to the church and for more productive dialog with the world. While teaching this course, we became aware of the Templeton Foundation's efforts to encourage a richer dialog between science and religion through promoting the teaching of courses jointly considering science and religion issues. We subsequently won one of the course awards offered by the Templeton Foundation in the Science and Religion Course Program, and this was the beginning of a very interesting chapter in our lives of attending conferences funded by the Templeton Foundation, culminating in our participation in the first Oxford Seminars on Science and Christianity hosted by Alister McGrath and John Roche at Wycliffe Hall, Oxford, for one month each summer from 1999 to 2001, also funded by the Templeton Foundation.

At the same time, and partly in the context of our projects for the Oxford Seminars, we were both pursuing our respective interests in science and Christianity, expressed in papers presented here at Covenant in the spring of 2000, leading to material included in this volume. Tim presented a pair of chapel talks entitled "Science and Grace," while Don presented a paper to the faculty entitled "Toward a Covenant Theology of Science." Don's paper followed up in part on some work presented in his 1996 talk "Scientific Law as Covenant Law" on the occasion of the dedication of Mills Hall, Covenant College's new science building. Tim's work as represented in his talk has helped to shape chapters 6 to 9 of the book, whereas parts of Don's paper informed our introductory chapter and laid the foundation for chapters 4 to 6. While participating in the Oxford seminars, we realized that our respective projects mutually supported and complemented one another, and sometime during the second year, we decided to join forces in the writing of the present work. A final and very helpful experience helping to shape our endeavor occurred in the summer of 2002 when we both participated in the Calvin College workshop, "Natural Science in the Calvinist Tradition," organized by

John Schneider and Davis Young and funded by Fieldstead & Company. This seminar was extremely valuable in helping us shape the material here as we dialogued with a variety of people and perspectives within the Reformed tradition.

Covenant College has afforded us a rich backdrop for pursuing our interests, with its openness to addressing any and all questions wherever they lead, in the context of a confessional commitment to the Bible and the Reformed tradition from its various backgrounds. Thus with the firm commitment that there can be no conflict between the Bible and God's creation, properly interpreted, we find ourselves connected to three distinct strands of the Reformed tradition. Our most direct link is to the Scottish Presbyterian tradition as derived through our denomination's past liaison to Old Princeton, with their strong commitment to sound doctrine, while at the same time taking science seriously. This is combined with the Dutch Reformed tradition with its strong cultural focus, which came in part through Francis Schaeffer and his connection to the college through denominational affiliation and through the L'Abri conferences held here in the late sixties and early seventies. Also a number of faculty members with a Dutch Reformed background have since joined the faculty, providing breadth in this direction. Third, our southern Presbyterian heritage adds emphases on piety, personal holiness, and the need to distinguish ourselves from the world, while at the same time maintaining a gospel immediacy within it. These three strands, with their different emphases on the theological, cultural, and pietistic aspects of genuine Christian faith and practice, have provided rich resources for our work. Thus the Reformed tradition has given us an essential systematic unity, and the diverse emphases of the three strands have helped illuminate the multiple facets of a faithful Christian response to the science of our day.

Although it will be clear to readers that the perspectives we present grow out of our own theological location in the Reformed Christian tradition as expressed above, we have tried to avoid Reformed "jargon" and have emphasized themes that should resonate across a variety of Christian theological traditions. What we present is not intended to be an argument for taking a Reformed perspective but rather an attempt to flesh out a particular version of that perspective with respect to science. To this end, rather than making primary reference to our confessional heritage at various points, we have framed our discussion by referring directly to Scripture. We do confess though that it seems difficult to us to make sense of all the Scripture we have used in a coherent picture unless God is sovereign over all areas of His creation, as Reformed doctrine has always emphasized, and we invite the reader to consider this prospect.

While it is our hope that our book is unique in its approach and the topics it addresses, the writing process has made us all too aware of what "the Teacher" warned about in Ecclesiastes so long ago: "Of making many books there is no end, and much study wearies the body" (Eccl. 12:12). The number of books relevant for and past opinions related to our subject is astounding, and we could not possibly do justice to all of them. We are also aware that "there is nothing new under the sun" (Eccl. 1:9); there are few genuinely new thoughts, and most ideas of the sort we discuss have likely been expressed by someone in the past. We hope we have faithfully represented the work of others when we were aware of that work. Also there are no doubt many cases where we have presented ideas without reference, when similar ideas have already appeared in past works of which we are yet unaware. If any of our thoughts fall into this category, we apologize and would be delighted to hear of such works and to give credit where it is due in future treatments. Further we are only too aware that our subject matter touches on a vast number of topics, many of which are well outside our fields of direct expertise. Although we have sought to obtain counsel from others who have expertise in these fields in order to fill such gaps, we no doubt have introduced numerous simplifications into such areas. We hope that such shortcomings will not detract from our main goal of edifying the evangelical churches by helping to broaden the horizons of our collective thinking in terms of modern-day science. We trust, by God's grace, whatever the inadequacy of this present effort, that the reader will in some way be blessed by our endeavor. Again we invite those who discern various shortcomings to provide feedback to help us develop our thinking further.

Finally we would like to remark that with two authors writing different parts of the book, the reader may notice the different styles of each author. We have not made a great effort to unify the style even though we each have substantially "bought in" on the contents of the whole manuscript. We have also endeavored to make the chapters reasonably self-contained so that the book need not be read in its entirety to make sense of each chapter. This inevitably has resulted in a certain amount of redundancy and some fairly lengthy chapters. For these things, again, we beg the reader's indulgence.

Acknowledgments

Many have helped in immeasurable ways in moving this book along. We first wish to prominently thank Sir John Templeton and the Templeton Foundation, without whom this work would not have come about. While Sir John may not agree with everything we write in these pages, we are indebted to him for the vision that realized that the world would be a better place if a more vigorous dialog were taking place concerning science and religion, and we wholeheartedly agree. His gracious philanthropy has set the stage for a much more nuanced discussion of this important tension in our lives than has been possible before, and to that we are indebted. May our effort add a small token to the ongoing dialog that has the potential to give God a greater glory in our midst. We are also greatly indebted to Covenant College, both for encouraging this type of endeavor and for support along the way: for sabbaticals, which each of us enjoyed during the course of the writing, for summer travel support and occasional course reductions, for development funds for book purchases and other expenses, and intangibly for the heritage that fosters this kind of scholarship.

In particular we want to acknowledge Professor Chuck Anderson from whom each of us had classes during our college years. Professor Anderson imprinted us at a formative stage with an appreciation for Christ and culture issues, and he played an essential role in developing our theological frame of reference for dealing with them.

Others who played an important role for one or the other of us in those early years of development include Francis Schaeffer, Os

Guinness, John Sanderson, Reg McLelland, Jerry Wenger, and Jack Lothers. We are grateful for Covenant College, a place with a tradition that encourages such investigations and that wholeheartedly strives to understand all things in view of the grace of God given us in our Lord and Savior, Jesus Christ.

We are also indebted to many individuals, both at Covenant and elsewhere, who have aided in the writing process in many different ways. We are indebted to Alister McGrath of Wycliffe Hall and John Roche of Linacre College, Oxford, for organizing the Oxford Seminars on Science and Christianity, to John Hedley Brooke for sponsoring Don's sabbatical in the fall of 2001 at Harris Manchester College, Oxford, and for many helpful discussions, and to John Schneider and Davis Young for organizing the Calvin College Summer Workshop on Natural Science in the Calvinist Tradition.

We also would like to acknowledge individuals who have aided by reading and commenting on parts of the manuscript and those who have especially encouraged us along the way. Particular thanks are due to Henry Krabbendam, who read every word and gave much valuable feedback. We would also like to thank Roy Clouser, Bill Davis, Edward B. Davis, Brian Fikkert, Richard Follett, Jeff Hall, Roger Henderson, Kelly Kapic, Roger Lambert, Bob Monroe, Niel Nielson, and Rebecca Pennington for reading and commenting on various parts of the manuscript (in some cases substantial parts). We would also like to thank our rather captive audiences of students in our Science in Perspective classes of spring 2003 and fall 2004, who, although required to read and respond to much of the manuscript, graciously took their role seriously in offering valuable suggestions toward the final draft.

Finally, we would like to express some more personal thanks. Tim would like to give special thanks to his wife, Lisa: Lisa, you are the most precious gift God has given me on this earth, and your love and encouragement over these years made completion of this project seem possible. Thanks as well to my children Emilie, Aubrey, Meredith, Joseph, and Caroline for your patience and understanding through what was a much longer process than anticipated. Thanks to my parents, Bob and Elaine Morris, for introducing me to my Lord at a tender age, for giving me a foundation in the Reformed tradition, and for nurturing my interest in the "big questions." I am also deeply grateful to God for the privilege of sitting under faithful preaching of the Word throughout my life. Thanks to those faithful preachers of the gospel who continuously confronted me with the reality and largeness of God's grace: Elmer Dortzbach, Tom Champness, Karl Ellis, Ed Hague, Mark Cushman, Jim Pickett, Mike Higgins, and Randy Nabors. Finally, I'd like to thank Don Petcher for his friendship, his optimism, for never running out of interesting ideas, for his great patience with my "longwinded" drafts, and for his unflagging enthusiasm for this project. I look forward to continuing "adventures with Tim and Don!"

Don would like to begin with thanks to the many pastors he has sat under over the years who have faithfully preached the Word: Particularly I would like to thank Paul Alexander, who first introduced me to the gospel of grace, and more recently Joe Novenson, who always refreshes me in portraying God's grace to us, Frank Hitchings, who never fails to convict and to encourage, and Bob Eckhardt, who always has insightful and reflective words to say both in the pulpit and out, even on matters of science. I would also like to thank Tim Morris for his perseverance, his everlasting optimism about deadlines, and the enduring grace that the Spirit has graciously given him that he has shown to me and others at every stage of the project. And last, but certainly not least, I would like to thank my wife, Ling Mei, and daughter, Evelyn, for many ways of support—Ling Mei for many stimulating discussions over the years that have undoubtedly, both consciously and subconsciously contributed to the ideas expressed here; Evelyn for understanding when Daddy could not do this or that because I had to work on "the book," and both for understanding when I have been away, sometimes for a month at a time, at workshops and seminars, and generally for picking up an extra share of the house and yard work while the book was in preparation. Ling Mei, you are my best friend, and I could hardly have asked for a more interesting person to spend my life with; Evelyn, by God's grace you are everything I could ask for in a daughter, and then some. I thank God for both of you. And, Tim, yes, more adventures!

Lastly, we thank Marvin Padgett, Ed Veith, and the entire Crossway editorial team for their patience with our slow pace and for their excellent editorial help. They have been a joy to work with at every stage. We especially thank Lila Bishop for her excellent copy editing and her flexibility in working with us in the editing process.

All quotes from the Bible are from the New International Version unless otherwise specified.

Section**One**

Science and Christian Belief in the Postmodern Context

Do not conform any longer to the pattern of this world, but be transformed by the renewing of your mind. Then you will be able to test and approve what God's will is—his good, pleasing and perfect will.

ROMANS 12:2

We demolish arguments and every pretension that sets itself up against the knowledge of God, and we take captive every thought to make it obedient to Christ.

2 CORINTHIANS 10:5

FROM ITS INCEPTION IN the Jewish context, Christianity has engaged countless cultures and in consequence countless varieties of ways of thinking about the world. Christians throughout the centuries have endeavored to follow Paul's instructions even as the "patterns of this world" have continuously changed. The history of ideas—the ebb and flow of ways of looking at the world—is thus not only a fascinating topic in its own right, but is extremely practical as Christians seek to "take captive every thought" in each age in each context in which they are called to live. In the context of Western culture, Christianity has engaged its culture under the oversimplified headings of "Premodern" and "Modern"—headings that paper over a great variety in patterns of thought and context. In Premodern Western culture—say, up to A.D. 1500—Christianity engaged both Greek and pagan European culture in various ways, significantly influencing and being influenced by both. As Modern culture grew out of the Premodern, Christianity was a participant in the birth and development of the major hallmark of the Modern age, science, and has influenced and been influenced by the scientific mind-set it helped to birth.

We now seem to be living in a time of transition from Modern to Postmodern, and how exactly Christianity will influence and be influenced by this transition remains to be seen. We do indeed live in very interesting times as believers as we seek to avoid the conformation that Paul warns of and be obedient to the commands to be transformed and to demolish godless pretensions. This is challenging. As Western Christians we are moving out of a Christianity mostly embedded in a Western Modern context for the last four hundred years, and in so doing we have "grown up" with modern science and are used to dealing with science in a Modern context. In addition, modern science grew up as Modernism grew—and came to prominence as perhaps the epitome of the Modern way of thinking. Science has never known a non-Modern backdrop for its operation. How exactly both science and Christianity will make this transition to the Postmodern context, both in their own right as well as in their continued relationship to one another, remains to be seen, but it seems to us that all of us living through this transition have responsibilities here, and in many ways this book is intended to inform and encourage believers in taking up these responsibilities.

In this first section of the book we begin to lay foundations for an extended discussion of science and Christian belief in this Postmodern context. In the first chapter, we lay out the context, contrasting the Modernist "warfare" metaphor between science and Christianity with the Postmodern relativistic attitude. We also lay out the problem that we Christians face in reassessing the entire landscape of science and religion in its new context, and we offer some metaphors of our own to aid in the big picture.

In the second chapter we briefly review the beginnings of modern science and then sketch the key realizations that led us as a culture from almost a blind faith in the power of rational and empirical scientific methodology to the Postmodern situation, which calls that faith into question in various ways. Ironically some of the reasons for questioning the extent of the Modern faith in science arise from science itself, and we highlight these. While Christians for the most part have found a generally Modern picture of things congenial to Christian faith, throughout the Modern period there have been specifically Christian criticisms raised against various aspects of the Modern project.

The third chapter in this section zeros in on various "dissenters" to the Enlightenment hope that science would be able to function in the modern world as the final arbiter of truth. These dissenters, all of whom would be recognized as evangelical Christians of one sort or another in our contemporary context, were critical of central elements of the Modern mind-set. Interestingly these dissenters raise issues that resonate in various ways with current Postmodern critiques of Modernism. This brief overview of the development of modern science and Christian critiques will provide some of the resources for considering our own expressions of Christian beliefs and beliefs about science as we go forward in the twenty-first century increasingly embedded in a Postmodern context.

Chapter**One**

The Need for a Theology of Science

Trust in the LORD *with all your heart and lean not on your own understanding; in all your ways acknowledge him, and he will make your paths straight.*

PROVERBS 3:5-6

MODERN SCIENCE WAS BIRTHED in a Western European culture dominated by Christianity, and right up until the nineteenth century most people would have considered it strange to think that there was a basic conflict between science and religion.[1] This situation shifted significantly during the nineteenth century as science came into its own as the signature of the "Modern" period; suddenly, in the view of some, a long-smoldering struggle between science and religion flared into a "hot" war! This conflict thesis continues to be popular to this day, many insisting that there is a basic competition between science and Christianity such that a high regard for one automatically translates into low regard for the other. There is also the widespread perception that the stakes in the conflict are extremely high indeed: either the very foundation of modern civilization on the one hand or the very truth of the Christian faith on the other. In the midst of the "war," however, peace initiatives have often been offered; perhaps the most prominent suggestion over the years has been that science and religion should be considered as just talking about different things. In this view, supposedly, science is limited to the "value-free facts" of nature, and religion is concerned only with human values—thus the two areas occupy separate, non-competing realms. So peace comes, not by conquest, but by simply straightening out the unnecessary confusion of categories.

While many of us at the start of the twenty-first century out of habit continue to view the relations between science and Christianity in the fairly straightforward war or negotiated peace terms, the reality is that the basic underpinnings of war and peace postures have been significantly altered. Developments in the philosophy of science as well as in science itself have increasingly blurred the boundaries between science and religious convictions in such a way that definitively establishing either lines of battle or lines of truce has become difficult. These developments have called into question the idea that science is or even can be a completely objective fact-finding activity carried out in isolation from "nonscientific" influences. While nature "out there" is still the same for everyone, it seems that the kinds of judgments scientists make in the course of their work have various components that do not themselves directly emerge from the logic rules and sensory data of supposedly objective scientific methodology. Science is increasingly seen as a fully human activity, involving a variety of social, cultural, and religious factors that go beyond mere reason and the senses. There seems to be no way to cleanly separate one's science from the whole of one's human experiences and convictions. In essence, the war and peace proposals were firmly planted in the Modernist mentality, which itself is now being called into question.

Yes, we now live in a cultural climate often referred to as "Postmodern." Somehow we have gone beyond the "Modernity" that so emphasized science as the bottom line for providing knowledge, leaving it behind to move on to a new phase of culture. The move from Modernism to Postmodernism is certainly one of the most significant stories of our time, and Christians have been struggling to find faithful ways to respond to this shift.[2] While some have gone too far in the Postmodern direction, most Christians rightly recognize dangers of Postmodern relativism. But many Christians, in their strong rejection of relativism, end up siding with Modernism by default. They find the reaffirmation of an ideologically neutral science a really tempting option, especially in view of the supposed "glory days" of seventeenth- and eighteenth-century natural theology, during which the power of science as an objective enterprise was harnessed in various ways to legitimate Christian belief. But the hope that a Modern science "cavalry" will ride to the aid of Christian belief in Postmodern times seems a vain hope indeed. While Christians rightly believe that the Postmodern "anything goes" relativism is on the wrong track, combating Postmodern relativism by simply reaffirming Modernist convictions about scientific objectivism is not the solution.

How should we respond to the developments of the twentieth century? Indeed, most evangelical Christians still feel that they are on a war footing with much of modern science, and the heat of the battle makes it difficult to reflect on a larger picture. Thus there is a great need to reassess the whole lay of the landscape that has brought us into the conflict era in the first place. Our approach in this book will be to step back for a time from the battle lines as they were drawn late in the Modern period.

We Christians, like all humans, inevitably absorb a variety of cultural elements into our worldviews, and the shift in the cultural backdrop in our time from Modern to Postmodern can serve to highlight elements of current "Christian" perspectives on science that upon further examination may turn out to be more reflective of Modern cultural perspectives than of biblical perspectives per se. The shift in our culture to Postmodernism has also forced to the surface many important questions that have long lain unattended and unrecognized in the Modern era and now call for Christian examination. These questions will force us to rediscover forgotten or devalued resources within our own Christian faith. These reassessment tasks call us to wander a bit through regions of history, philosophy, and theology that at first seem to lie far off from the urgency of conflicts on the front lines, but these "detours" are worth taking because they provide the vantage points we need to bring a revitalized Christian perspective to this important area of our cultural life.

Not only can a broad reassessment revitalize Christian understanding of science, but it can also give us something to say to a culture increasingly ambivalent about scientific knowledge. Science in our culture is simultaneously revered, feared, and reviled. The wonder of the human genome project, space probes, new and strange notions of deep space realities, and the marvels of information technology are widely heralded in the popular media. At the same time the "dark side" of science—drug companies that hide damaging data, the dangers of genetic manipulation and cloning techniques, and the horror of biological warfare—also makes big stories. In addition elements of cynicism and even ridicule tinge cultural attitudes toward science as people sneer at flip-flops in public health recommendations or put their faith and money into "alternative" medical approaches that are not supported by scientific research. A Christian perspective must be able to give an account in the culture for both the power of science as well as its limitations and distortions.

Trees, Roots, and Branches

Setting the stage for our project will require some major shifts in the instinctively Modern way we think about the categories of "science" and "theology" themselves. Some metaphors might be helpful here to illustrate the kind of shift we have in mind. In the Modern landscape right from the beginning, science and theology have been assumed to be two distinct trees of human knowledge. In this Modern mind-set, each tree is rooted in its own distinctive type of soil, each grows by different processes, and each bears its own sort of fruit. In the earliest articulations of a Modern approach to science, the two soils or sources of knowledge were understood to be "two books," the book of Scripture and the book of nature. In this view, the tree rooted in the book of Scripture grew through prayer, faith, and Spirit-guided reflection on the Word, bearing the fruit of Christian doctrine as its contribution to truth. The tree rooted in the book of nature grew by experimentation, reason, and public demonstration, bearing the fruit of scientific truth.

Working out how to best nurture this grove of knowledge has been a major concern of the Modern era. Some Moderns have encouraged certain branches from the two trees to grow toward each other and to intertwine in the belief that, though each tree is independently rooted, scientific knowledge and theological knowledge can and should mutually reinforce one another. Various natural theology proposals follow this pattern. Other Moderns have argued that the science tree is the only one in the end that passes muster as providing genuine knowledge, and that as the science tree grows and flourishes, the theology tree will wither under the shade of an increasingly complete canopy of scientific explanation. Classic forms of scientific naturalism follow this pattern. Still other Moderns have argued that the theology tree, although also valid, is so different from the science tree that to avoid confusion, it should be moved far away from the science tree, pruned to remove fact-oriented branches, and encouraged to flourish as a forum exploring human meaning and spirituality, while avoiding cross-pollination with the science tree. This is essentially the "peace initiative" mentioned earlier in the chapter, that science and theology address entirely different realms of human experience. More recently others have argued that the way forward would be to cut down the theology tree and to graft a branch from it into the science tree to bring proper scientific grounding and analytical rigor to bear on theological knowledge—to develop a kind of science-based spirituality. This describes the mind-set of a variety of proposals in the last few decades concerning nature-based spiritualities and "natural theism."

Although each approach offers a distinctive pattern for nurturing the trees of human knowledge, they all share the typically Modern assumption that a proper method exists by which humans can stand on the forest floor to act as independent and impartial judges of knowledge. This search for an impersonal objective guarantor of truth has been a major storyline of Modernism. The demise of Modernism was in part brought on by the realization that this search has failed, that humans can't really wield the chainsaws or the pruning shears, from the neutral vantage point of the forest floor because each has his own worldview. It turns out that each human is already inevitably sitting in the branches of some knowledge tree or other.

From Science *and* Theology to a Theology *of* Science

If none of the "two trees" scenarios will work out, then how should we proceed in thinking about the relationship between science and theology? A different tree metaphor may help to communicate the direction we are recommending in this book. Rather than starting with the separately growing trees of science and theology, we should start with a variety of trees, some with scientific branches emerging from their trunks. These trees are rooted in the most basic human convictions about who or what they ultimately trust—that is, all the trees in the forest are worldview/theological[3] trees. One's basic theology in this sense has to do with who or what he is ultimately living for and working in service of. Every human is trusting, is serving, someone or something, and from such basic heart commitments flow all of our knowing and ultimately all our doing. From a Christian perspective, whatever stands in the place of the God revealed in the Scriptures sets an all-encompassing religious trajectory for one's life, including the science one does and believes is valid. Every human has bought into some theological tree or other, and the science each does will in one way or another be impacted by the sap flowing into the science branch from its respective theological trunk. For Christians, therefore, the important questions do not have to do with how Christian theology will respond to an independently rooted and validated science tree but rather with what *kind* of science should grow from a Christian theological tree. These questions can best be addressed by developing what we call "a theology of science."

Rivers and Streams

But doesn't this kind of picture lead to relativism concerning science? This question perhaps can best be addressed by shifting metaphors. In the Modern mind-set, when one stepped into the scientific river, one left behind all human subjectivities, biases, and unproven assumptions that are a normal feature of ordinary day-to-day life. A thorough scrubbing in the scientific river would cleanse away those things that would distort the true reading of the natural world that is the goal of science. Once in the river and properly washed of biases, starting with the same facts and following the same objective rules of investigation and conclusion making, the judgment of each scientist was supposed to be the same. Thus the Modern picture: All participants leave behind their particularities and are carried along by a current generated and sustained by the objective rules of science itself.

The demise of Modernism significantly shifts this picture. Science is still a mighty river, and if one is to participate in the common project of science, one must step into the river. But we now know that this river is not able to wash away all biases in favor of a universal and objective scientific methodology. It is rather the flow of a complex cultural enterprise that arises from a confluence of various historical, cultural, and philosophical brooks and streams, each growing out of its own foundational religious commitments, including the stream of Christian theology and practice as well as the ancient Greek tradition. In the providence of God, the cultural project we call science has gradually become a mighty river in which different sciences have always been done and we believe can and should continue to flourish. Rather than different theological trees, in this metaphor we now have different theological tributaries, all flowing into the one large riverbed of science as mingling streams, each contributing its own insights. The constraining riverbed, signifying the "constraints of creation," the real world "out there," by God's grace keeps the whole enterprise of science on track, allowing common work between various streams. But the riverbed is wide enough to continue to hold all the various mingling streams within its boundaries. The various streams are then again clearly revealed when the river gets down to the delta of drawing implications from the commonly held conclusions of the wide river. Various delta channels flow in many directions, indicating a divergence of views concerning the implications of what we are all doing in common. Thus while all the different streams of thought engage together in the common river of cultural science, each will have very different ways of looking at what it is doing, and each may end with different claims when ultimate conclusions are drawn. So by God's grace, these different sciences can do various kinds of productive work together, but are ultimately different sciences in a very real sense. Therefore we Christians can and should work to do a science that arises from our own theology, and we should also contribute to and value the broader flow of cultural science, an understanding that we ourselves ground in our own Christian theological foundation as well.

Some Basic Elements of a Christian Theology of Science

So what exactly do we mean by a theology of science? It should be clear already that we do not mean by this a theology derived from science or a scientific methodological approach applied to theology. Rather we have in mind a view of science shaped by the "theology" that flows out of the basic religious commitments of one's heart, whatever they may be. For the Christian, the theology is derived from Scripture,[4] and the basic heart commitments might be expressed under two themes: an embrace of the gospel and a shunning of idolatry, the latter of which in its essence is anti-gospel. Therefore we will constantly be asking how our scientific understanding and activities are to be shaped by our Christian commitment to embrace the gospel and shun idolatry.

So what do we mean by "gospel"? The word *gospel* of course means "good news"; it is the good news that we in our rebellion as enemies against God have been loved by Him to such an extent that He took upon Himself in Christ the punishment that we deserve in order to restore us back to Him. More specifically, He has cancelled out the certificate of debt that we owed in our sinfulness, replacing our sinful record with a new and perfect record in Christ (Col. 2:13-14), He has given us the ability to serve Him by giving us a new heart (Ezek. 36:26), and He has prepared in advance good works for us to do (Eph. 2:10), and in so doing He has given us a new life. For "he who began a good work in you will carry it on to completion until the day of Christ Jesus" (Phil. 1:6).

In a real sense this brief description gets at the essence of the gospel, but in another sense it is only the tip of the iceberg. There are assumptions behind our description as well as implications that follow. For example, in our brief description, we have assumed that God is our Creator. We have assumed that we, as His creatures, have rebelled against Him and hence fallen from grace; indeed all of creation has participated in this fall. Likewise we have acknowledged that in our redemption in Christ, now we stand in His grace or favor, accepted into His family as servants of the loving Master. We also look forward to a coming kingdom in which His reign will be more visible, and we will serve forever. By "gospel" insofar as it pertains to science we must have this bigger picture in mind. The fact that the universe is a creation and that it has participated in the Fall with us and that we are redeemed servants all have implications for how we view the study of that creation, which is science. An exploration of this gospel will require that we examine the unity of all things under the rule of God, the relation of God to His creation, the place of humans in creation, the impact of the Fall on creation and on human activity in it, the implications of our new birth in Christ for human knowing and doing, the gospel call to be in the world but not of the world, and the significance of the present and coming kingdom of Christ. A theology of science will entail the exploration of these aspects of the gospel as they are presented in Scripture accompanied by an attempt to explicate the importance of each aspect of the gospel for the way we think about science and the way we participate in our culture in these Postmodern times.

Idolatry directly opposes the gospel. Idolatry at its root is always a denial of the gospel—a prideful placing of our trust in something other than God and His promises to faithfully rule and redeem. In the Old Testament are many words for idol, with various meanings, from man-made objects (Hab. 2:18) to those things that are worthless (Isa. 44:15-17). Shunning idols is also related to faithful covenant-keeping (Deut. 5:8) and to truthfulness (Ps. 24:4). But perhaps the most essential problem is that an idol points to the creature rather than to the Creator (Deut. 5:8), placing something created in the place of God. Thus it provokes God's righteous anger (1 Kings 16:12-13).

The apostle John in the New Testament places idolatry at the center of the cosmic contest between God and Satan:

> *We know that we are children of God, and that the whole world is under the control of the evil one. We know also that the Son of God has come and has given us understanding, so that we may know him who is true. And we are in him who is true—even in his Son Jesus Christ. He is the true God and eternal life. Dear children, keep yourselves from idols. (1 John 5:19-21)*

This passage puts the notion of idolatry in a larger context—the very struggle between the children of God and the children of the evil one—and relates this struggle to understanding, which for believers comes from Jesus Christ Himself. According to this passage, there are two basically distinct ways of looking at the world, one that we are to strive for and the other to be rejected. The one points us to the work and rule of Christ, that is toward His grace, and the other away from Christ. An inappropriate way of looking at science leads to pride; an appropriate way leads to repentance, humility, and dependence on the grace of God. A theology of science will help identify and repudiate scientific "idols of thought" and habits of mind that are idolatry-prone, and thus a faithful theology of science will help us resist the evil one. In this book we hope to give an account of a Christian theology of science rooted in and energized by the power and wonder of the grace of God revealed in Christ. It is our prayer that such an account will further excite and equip God's people to serve Him faithfully both as "producers" and as "consumers" of science in our contemporary culture.

Book Structure

Abraham Kuyper—the nineteenth-century Dutch theologian, scholar, and statesman—once said that in order for a worldview to be robust enough to provide an all-embracing set of principles to address all of life, it should be based on a principle able to provide special insight into three relations: man's relation to God, man's relation to man, and man's relation to the world.[5] All these relations are relevant for us in considering science along with one more: God's relation to the world. Although unintended, it is perhaps not coincidental that these four relations serve as general summaries of the major themes of our book. Thus the reader might understand our task in the book as addressing how Christianity indicates that these relations apply to the task of science.

Section one lays a foundation for our study by introducing issues relating to the Enlightenment hope for science and to the Postmodern move away from that hope, and it also raises various theological issues, by highlighting several historical "dissenters" from the Enlightenment view. In section two we will begin our study by investigating God's relation to the world and the idols one might avoid by understanding it appropriately. This section focuses primarily on the Trinitarian nature of God's involvement with His creation, the issue of miracles, and the question of what a scientific law is. Then in section three, we examine Christian involvement in science by focusing on the great commandment's directive to love God and neighbor. We explore the implications of this command for God's relation to man as we do our work before Him, for man's relation to the creation as we interact with God's universe in our scientific investigations, and for man's relation to man as we cooperate with others in our culture in scientific tasks.

It may also be helpful to give a quick chapter-by-chapter description. In chapter 2 we introduce the reader to highlights from the founding of modern science and the development of the Modernist picture of science as the pinnacle of objective human knowledge. We then focus on major developments both from science as well as in the culture at large that led to the shift to Postmodernism, and we explore some of the implications of this shift for views of science. In chapter 3, we then present a selection of dissenters from the Modernist view of scientific knowledge. Our dissenters, who raised their objections primarily for theological reasons, come from various ages and Christian traditions, but all would be sympathetic to the evangelical Christian worldview. This chapter allows us to provide important background for the issues we raise in subsequent chapters.

In chapter 4 we emphasize the centrality of the Trinity in creation as well as redemption, and we focus on the importance of an understanding of the purposes of the triune Creator as He brings His creation to its ultimate end, putting all things under Christ's feet. This naturally brings us to the theme of the Covenant of Grace, as foundation for chapter 5. In that chapter we trace the historical development of the mechanistic view of science and explain how this has deeply affected the way we look at God's involvement in the world and how we view miracles—in ways that are not theologically sound. Both these chapters serve as backdrop for chapter 6, where we outline what implications the theological investigations have for our understanding of "scientific laws" and some characteristics we might expect of them.

In chapter 7 we turn our attention to issues surrounding our way of thinking about the nature of the world, of history as God unfolds it, and of our roles as new creatures in Christ in the fulfillment of God's purposes. We make the case that we cannot conduct our science in isolation from our knowledge of who we are in Christ and what the universe is in the ultimate plan of God to reconcile all things to Himself in Christ. In chapter 8 we explore how human knowing should be considered in terms of human responses to God's revealing work, whether in Scripture or in Creation. Pleasing God in our knowing is to be our primary motivation in developing and judging scientific knowledge. Our task in science is to respond faithfully to His revelation in creation, and part of that faithful response is to take seriously the very words of Scripture. In chapter 9 we explore specific actions and activities involving science that should naturally grow out of the being and knowing convictions discussed in the previous two chapters. Our conduct of scientific work should show us to be submissive, attentive, and confident, yet humble stewards of the scientific gifts God has given us.

Chapter 10 addresses how we should conduct our science in the context of the scientific culture in the twenty-first century, given the dominant Christianity-versus-science mind-set of the twentieth century. Evangelical Christians seem to have stored up significant resentment toward the scientific culture, and the dominant voices within the scientific culture strongly protest explicit Christian criticism of scientific concepts. We argue that following God's example of bestowing favor and finding joy in His creation, we are to work for the good of the common human cultural task of science and find joy in it as well. Yet as God also judges sin and corruption in His creation, we must always be mindful that though we are called to be in the scientific cultural world, we are not to be of it. Thus we are to continually examine and repent for our own sinful motivations and corrupted ways of thinking, and we are to humbly but persistently play critical and prophetic roles in the scientific culture as well.

Finally we close with chapter 11 summarizing the present work and pointing toward issues for which our theological treatment of science has ramifications and concerning which further work is needed.

Chapter Two

Modern Science in a Postmodern World

Pride goes before destruction, a haughty spirit before a fall.
PROVERBS 16:18

IN THE FIRST CHAPTER we have argued for the need to step away from the supposed battlefront of the warfare image of science and Christianity in order to gain the larger bird's-eye view of how these two "realms" are fundamentally related. As we have said, this involves stepping back from the contemporary science and Christianity issues and digging into some history, philosophy, and theology, each of which is foundational for understanding the big picture. To set the stage, see this chapter as a quick introduction to "how we got here from there," that is, from the early beginnings of science to the Postmodern world. The story is basically one of explaining why modern science, in all its optimism from the early stages until right up to the present day, has fallen under the Postmodern skeptic's eye. To that end, this chapter could be considered in a nutshell the "rise and fall of the Enlightenment project" and reasons for the subsequent move to Postmodernism as they are related to science.

The story we wish to portray traces the development, not so much of the rise of the sciences, but of the kind of thinking that leads eventually to the Modern scientific approach to knowledge. We will see that the story is not a simple one, as if science started from a "primitive" beginning and then grew in sophistication as more and more data came in, always progressing in the right direction, to gradually shape the marvelous enterprise known as science today. There is in fact not one simple storyline; rather there are several parallel stories that overlap and converge, while along the way conflicts, tensions, and surprises play their part. And one of the chief ironies that is often missed is that in many ways developments in the sciences have been at the forefront in the arguments leading to a Postmodern perspective! In other words, while science can still be seen as a continuing and unfolding search for that which God has revealed to us through His creation, the very developments of science themselves have led us to reconsider many areas of our thinking, not the least of which is how we are to view science itself.

In this chapter, therefore, we start to lay some groundwork for a Christian understanding both of the success of science and of the conflicts concerning science that we experience in our age. We begin our framing of the big picture by taking a trip back in time to the era generally considered the gestation period of the Scientific Revolution when science as an enterprise had not yet come into its own and was still considered part of a centuries-long discussion in philosophy about how we can attain knowledge about the world. Then we provide some highlights of the eighteenth-century European movement that has come to be called the Enlightenment for its major role in the development of the Modern point of view. The Enlightenment held out great hope for the promise of science as an objective and universal source for all human knowledge, and the attempt to find a completely neutral rational and empirical method for obtaining certain truth is sometimes referred to as the "Enlightenment Project,"[1] a central theme in the Modern world.

However, the birth of the Enlightenment is not a straightforward story either, because even as the brave new world of Modernism was being born, the seeds of its demise were also being sown. So after setting the stage for the Enlightenment optimism and the rise of the Modern world, we will briefly trace five science-related developments that have contributed to the transition from Modern to Postmodern perspectives. They will be discussed in the ensuing sections as (1) some troubling philosophical conundrums, (2) the discovery of worldviews, (3) some surprises in modern physics, (4) corresponding developments in the philosophy of science, and (5) the subsequent renewed interest among historians to revisit questions of science and religion of the past. By the end of the chapter, we hope the reader will have come to see that the landscape for the objectivity of science is littered with enough minefields for us to recognize that a new map for understanding the relation between science and Christianity is ultimately needed.

Birth of the Enlightenment Project

The term "Enlightenment" is roughly associated with the eighteenth century as a time of coming out of the "dark ages" during which understanding was assumed to be lost.[2] However one assesses the medieval period, obviously something dramatic did happen at the time of the so-called Scientific Revolution. While some still think of this period as the "throwing off of the shackles of religion" to begin to enter into a more "enlightened" time, a more credible view supported by recent scholarship seems to be that several things occurred around that time that were all influential and mutually supported the development of modern science. Among these are the questioning of certain components of the received philosophical wisdom inherited from the Greeks and the theological positions derived therefrom,[3] and the emergence of the "voluntarist" position within theological circles.

The received classical doctrine, with direct connections to ancient Greek philosophy, asserted that a necessary God must create of necessity in a certain way. When the church opened the door to questioning the received wisdom, alternative views arose, such as voluntarism. Voluntarism is an assertion that God had the freedom to create and manipulate the world in whatever way He saw fit. This led to the obvious conclusion that in order to understand the world, one would have to study it. For if the world were not necessarily a certain way, mere logic and reflection could not provide definitive understanding.

An additional factor is that the Reformation helped to bring about a more open political climate that afforded a freedom to reassess traditional interpretations of Scripture. Other influences played a role as well, such as Renaissance developments in the world of art and architecture, in which the focus was increasingly on man, in contrast to the heavenly themes of the past. In that climate, certain men such as Tycho Brahe (1546-1601) and Galileo Galilei (1564-

1642) appeared, who put more focus on the investigation of the behavior of the universe directly than was customarily done in the generally accepted physics and cosmology of the time.

At the foundation of the Enlightenment lie two of the most important figures responsible for the Scientific Revolution, Francis Bacon (1561-1626) and René Descartes (1596-1650). While Bacon is widely credited as the "father of the scientific method," undoubtedly the more revolutionary figure was Descartes. Bacon made important contributions to the method of science, whereas Descartes had seminal influence on mathematics and on science itself, as well as making striking contributions to philosophy. For this reason, Descartes is often called the "father of Modern philosophy" and sometimes the "father of the Enlightenment." Bacon and Descartes provided the intellectual impetus for the two central pillars of modern science: empirical methodology and rational inquiry, thus establishing the familiar roles of reason and the senses as the "raw materials" for scientific inquiry.

Descartes lived as the pre-Modern medieval period waned, and new scientific discoveries were ushering in a new era of philosophical inquiry. The controversial thesis of a sun-centered solar system was published posthumously in *De Revolutionibus* by Nicolas Copernicus (1473-1543) in 1543, only about half a century before Descartes was born and barely a generation before the births of Galileo, Kepler, and Bacon. Indeed, Descartes, no doubt influenced by these newly emerging ideas of science including the work of Galileo and Kepler, proposed a "machine" picture of the universe, to which we will return.[4]

But for the moment we are primarily interested in his foundations for philosophy, perhaps most directly spelled out in his *Meditations on First Philosophy*. In that work Descartes tells us that at the foundation of his thought, he was disillusioned by the "highly doubtful nature" of his "edifice" of beliefs, based on a "large number of falsehoods [he] had accepted as true in his childhood."[5] After much thought, he tells us, "I . . . am finally compelled to admit that there is not one of my former beliefs about which a doubt may not properly be raised; and this is not a flippant conclusion or ill-considered conclusion, but is based on powerful and well thought-out reasons."[6] In search of a greater certainty, he set out to "demolish everything [of his own present system] completely and start again right from the foundations" in order to find a new, clear, and orderly method by which truth could be obtained. Impressed by Euclid's mathematics, he determined to model his system on the reasoning found in the "divinely implanted truths of mathematics."[7] Thus, using the "light of reason" alone, he hoped that mankind would be "propelled away from the dangers of the deliverances of the senses" to a certainty of truth that could not be doubted.

In order to establish this new science of knowledge, Descartes began to subject his reasoning to increasingly radical levels of doubt until he could find the "Archimedean point"[8] that could not be doubted. He finally found this Archimedean point in his awareness of his own existence. He could not doubt that he was in fact doubting, and therefore he concluded that he knew at least that he was "a thinking being." From this he went on to argue that he existed, that the God he had taken for granted in his previous system of thought also existed, and that thus we can have confidence in the existence of the world outside of us. His starting point is summarized in his famous dictum "*Cogito, ergo sum*" or "I am thinking, therefore I am," a deduction that, according to Descartes, is not from simply a logical argument, but from an intuition.[9]

While some of Descartes's techniques of doubt may seem humorous (for example, the rigor with which he maintained for the purposes of argument that he could not afford to believe that he had a body until proven so), the importance of his argument does not lie in the use of pure rational thinking alone, but also in his radical departure from the dominant philosophies of the time. Those philosophies entailed the tacit assumption that they were working out of a Christian framework, and therefore our existence depended on God's existence. The question of establishing God's existence rationally would in that context constitute more of an apologetic[10] exercise than a rational attempt to justify belief.

By contrast, Descartes sought his "Archimedean point" solely within himself in order to give himself confidence that he was on firm ground in his knowledge and could extrapolate from there. As is clear from his argumentation, he did not consider his experience to be trustworthy in a rigorous sense (although he would allow it as evidence) and that the only things he could in fact rely on infallibly were his logical deductions from undoubtable first principles. His methodology was clearly patterned after Euclidean geometry, which he counted as one of the great successes of rational thought. Philosophers nowadays refer to this approach to philosophy as an example of "foundationalism," an attempt to build the whole system on certain foundational axioms that can (supposedly) not be doubted and upon a procedure that would allow deductions from the foundations to further knowledge.[11]

We can hardly introduce Francis Bacon's accomplishments in a better way than to quote the important Enlightenment thinker, Francois-Marie Arouet de Voltaire (1694-1778), who ironically held the professing Christian in the highest esteem, even though we see Voltaire later as a leading proponent of the Enlightenment attempt to remove Christianity from science.

> This great man is the father of experimental philosophy. It is true, wonderful discoveries had been made even . . . in the ages of scholastic barbarity. . . . In a word, there was not a man who had any idea of experimental philosophy before Chancellor Bacon; and of an infinity of experiments which have been made since his time, there is hardly a single one which has not been pointed out in his book. He had even made a good number of them himself.[12]

In a nutshell Bacon's method, so over-extolled by Voltaire, was to recommend suspending any knowledge of purpose, or "final causes," and simply observe repeatedly and draw inferences. In contrast to Descartes, Bacon was apparently deeply skeptical of the ability of human reason alone to arrive at truth. For, he argued,

> The subtlety of nature is greater many times over than the subtlety of the senses and understanding. . . . The logic now in use serves rather to fix and give stability to the errors which have their foundation in commonly received notions than to help the search after

> truth. So it does more harm than good. . . . The syllogism consists of propositions, propositions consist of words, words are symbols of notions. Therefore if the notions themselves (which is the root of the matter) are confused and overhastily abstracted from the facts, there can be no firmness in the superstructure. Our only hope lies therefore in true induction.[13]

In other words, Bacon tells us that nature is more subtle than we can possibly imagine, and reason is only as good as the concepts or axioms it is based on. Furthermore, the bottom line for reason is not in the structure of logical arguments or syllogisms, and not even in the language that makes up these arguments, but in the very notions or concepts to which the language refers. These concepts, Bacon tells us, can easily be mistaken. Hence he argues that we must study nature empirically, directly using our senses, and build our scientific theories by induction or by taking more and more data until a general explanation for the data can be found.

It may seem as though Bacon's target was the rationalism of Descartes, but this is not the case. Indeed, Descartes's proposed system was not published until much later than the 1620 date of the *Novum Organum* (New Organon) in which the above quotes appear. On the contrary, Bacon's words were targeted at the Aristotelian science that dominated the day. The term "Organum" (instrument or tool) was used in Aristotle to refer to the tool of logic for science and scientific reasoning, and by that time the collection of Aristotle's works on the subject was known as the "Organon."[14] Thus Bacon is clearly setting his proposal over against Aristotle's method, which grounded science in logic and arguments from the supposed built-in purpose, or "final cause," of things.

In proposing his method to get at the truth, Bacon was not naïve about the difficulties and pitfalls associated with it. He goes on to say that man can set up "idols which beste man's mind," which he numbers at four. There are "Idols of the Tribe" (tradition), "Idols of the Cave" (in man's secret convictions), "Idols of the Market Place" (those gleaned from common interaction with others—perhaps to be taken as idols of culture), and "Idols of the Theater" (dogmas of philosophy and incorrect ways of demonstration).[15] While Bacon identifies these four classes of "idols of the mind," he is not against reason completely in his proposed scientific methodology. For he specifically states that while we should avoid both the extremes of the pure dogmatist (or rationalist) "spiders" that "spin out their own webs," we should also avoid the pure empiricist "ants" that "only heap up and use their store."[16] Thus while you may take a false turn by jumping too quickly to a conclusion from too few data, you will not get anywhere by merely collecting immense amounts of data without drawing any conclusions. Hence Bacon's method consisted of careful data gathering and then drawing inductive conclusions,[17] with the emphasis on proceeding slowly and carefully before drawing these conclusions. So while Bacon suggested a method for engaging in science, his method emphasized induction and the empirical rather than the deductive reasoning and the rational emphasis of Descartes.

In these two men we see the early beginnings of the "Enlightenment Project," by which we mean an attempt to define foundations for knowledge that would be certain and objective, based on the two "twin pillars" of scientific inquiry: reason and experience. Interestingly enough, despite the break from the Christianized Aristotelian past that these two men represent, both Descartes and Bacon were, at least in their own understanding, arguing from within a Christian framework. Evidence to this effect can be seen in Descartes's own emphasis on an argument for God's existence[18] or, in practical matters, in his basing his law of inertia on the immutability of God.[19] Bacon's science was largely motivated by the Christian theme of man's dominion over the creation for the good of humanity.[20] He also sometimes brought doctrines into his arguments concerning science, as is indicated by his use of the fact of creation to argue against an eternal universe.[21] In the words of Thomas Torrance,

> Far from leading to a neglect of nature, the distinction between Grace and nature directed Bacon to the pursuit of natural science as a religious duty, for he understood it to mean that God has kept the Godward side of nature hidden, that is, He has kept final causes or the ultimate law of nature 'within His own curtain,' but whatever

> is not-God is laid open by God for man's investigation and comprehension. It is therefore by keeping within the limits and ends of knowledge which God Himself has set in the creation of man, which faith makes clear to him, that man can fulfill his function as an interpreter of nature and build up his kingdom on *scientia*. This is man's right by creation, and by the Grace of God and it remains his right even if he has fallen from God, although the fall means that that kingdom can be acquired only by the sweat of his brow and laborious discovery in the actual investigation of nature itself.[22]

The Rise of the Enlightenment Project

Thus we see the Enlightenment Project emerging as an attempt to find a way toward certain knowledge through human faculties, those of reason and experience. On these perhaps overly human-centered but not antireligious foundations, how is it possible that little more than a century later, science would be billed as the means to lead humans out of "bondage" to religion. But this is exactly what we find. For despite the fact that both reason and experience are quite legitimate human faculties for the pursuit of knowledge, we see that all too quickly, putting these human faculties at the center led to a false confidence in our ability to obtain absolute knowledge, which provides the excuse to find God outmoded. For just a century later we find Voltaire, the man who extolled Bacon so highly, working on the famous *Encylcopédie* of all knowledge—edited by Denis Diderot (1713-1784) and Jean le Rond d'Alembert (1717-1783). This *Encylcopédie,* with contributions from many of the intelligentsia of the day, was based on the Enlightenment assumption that the "light of reason" had finally led people out of the medieval darkness of the "superstition" of religion.

The project was conceived in 1749 when some Parisian booksellers approached Diderot about helping with a translation of Ephraim Chambers's *Cyclopaedia* into the French language. Diderot convinced them rather to entrust him with an entirely new project, the *Encylcopédie.* Revealingly and somewhat ironically, the 1950 version of *Chambers's Encyclopedia*[23] says of this endeavor, "It would contain articles on all artistic and technical subjects, but under cover of a design apparently disinterested would be a means of demolishing the 'prejudices,' as Christian beliefs were then called. The leading authorities of the day were enrolled, and also the leading infidels."[24] Under the guise of unbiased truth, the *Encylcopédie* represents a very thinly veiled attack on the Christian religion.

The Marquis de Condorcet (1743-1794), one of the "encyclopedists," provides an example representative of this period, particularly in the nation of France. In his "Sketch for an Historical Picture of the Progress of the Human Mind" at the end of the century, he extolled Descartes, Bacon, and other major contributors to the Enlightenment Project and then summarized the accomplishments in this way:

> Up till now we have shown the progress of philosophy only in the men who have cultivated, deepened and perfected it. It remains for us to show what have been its effects on public opinion; how reason, while it learnt to safeguard itself against the errors into which the imagination and respect for authority had so often led it, at last found a sure method of discovering and recognizing truth; and how at the same time it destroyed the prejudices of the masses which had for so long afflicted and corrupted the human race.
>
> At last man could proclaim aloud his right, which for so long had been ignored, to submit all opinions to his own reason and to use in the search for the truth the only instrument for its recognition that he has been given. Every man learnt with a sort of pride that nature had not forever condemned him to base his beliefs on the opinions of others; the superstitions of antiquity and the abasement of reason before the transports of supernatural religion disappeared from society as from philosophy.[25]

Nothing is good enough for Condorcet short of eradicating religion from society. Clearly he had an axe to grind.

The seventeenth and eighteenth centuries saw a variety of other important developments in the growth of science and further support from the intelligentsia. Among these developments was the rise of mechanistic or machine-based conceptions of the natural world. Isaac Newton's (1642-1727) theory of gravity provided a major impetus in this direction. This theory met the need for an "explanation" for the heliocentric Copernican model of the universe[26] and unified motion near the earth with that of the heavens. This demystified the heavens[27] even beyond Galileo's observation of moons around Jupiter.[28] This was the beginning of a wholesale move toward mechanism, which proved to be very attractive in the face of the new science.

For as Colin Gunton tells us, Newton resisted the mechanistic philosophy for good theological reasons, but despite this resistance, later generations of Christians found the transformation of a mechanistic model of nature from just a picture to aid understanding to a full-blown mechanistic philosophy difficult to resist.[29] In this context, John Hedley Brooke raises the interesting question: "Would God's special providence, His watchful concern for the lives of individuals, not be jeopardized if all events were ultimately reducible to mechanical laws?"[30]

Nevertheless, as Brooke goes on to tell us, Christians did get on the mechanistic bandwagon, and ironically some of the scientists who did most to push the mechanistic philosophy were those such as Robert Boyle (1627-1691), who thought that the model enriched our view of God's action in the universe. But there was a hidden danger in this: "The clockwork analogies of Boyle and Descartes, though lodged in the theologies of nature that remained Christian in inspiration, were to appear perfectly at home when lodged in deistic philosophies—in the anti-Christian literature of the Enlightenment. For Voltaire, in the eighteenth century, the clockmaker God was to be an attractive alternative to the gods of established religions."[31] In other words, even though the mechanistic philosophy had sprung from Christian origins, and despite the good intentions of men like Boyle who attempted to use the mechanistic model as an apologetic for Christianity, the model also allows the possibility that the universe stands on its own. So it is easily taken over by a deistic philosophy in which God is only needed to start things off, or perhaps God could be dispensed with altogether. Another eighteenth-century scientist, Pierre Laplace (1749-1827), thought so.[32] Laplace was well known for his atheism[33] and also for his commitment to deterministic mechanism. One of his most well-known quotes illustrates his viewpoint:

> The present state of the system of nature is evidently a result of what it was in the preceding instant, and if we conceive of an Intelligence who, for a given moment, embraces all the relations of being in this Universe, it will also be able to determine for any instant of the past or future their respective positions, motions, and generally their affections.[34]

In this statement Laplace, who could be considered the archetypical deterministic atheist of the time, shows us how thoroughly the mechanistic philosophy can be taken to divorce ourselves from the "need" for God.[35]

In the eighteenth century, acceptance of the mechanistic philosophy also continued on other fronts. For example, the philosophy gained momentum when geologists began to adopt mechanistic explanations for the history of the features of the earth, with a new science of mechanistic geology emerging in the nineteenth century.[36] Mechanistic philosophy also began to move into biology in the late eighteenth century, culminating in Darwin's theory of evolution several decades later. So by the end of the nineteenth century, the mechanistic philosophy had become a dominant force in all areas of science.

Thus, building on the auspicious beginnings rooted in a basically Christian conception of the natural world, science developed in the eighteenth and nineteenth centuries around the mechanistic model. The continued successes of science in the nineteenth century led to a kind of arrogance toward the religion that was perceived to be no longer needed. Gradually amidst the successes of science and the perception that religion was somehow at odds with it, the idea arose that the best way to describe the relation between science and religion was one of warfare and that obviously science would ultimately triumph.[37] For example, J. W. Draper, a well-known English scientist, in 1875 characterized science and religion as "two contending powers, the expansive force of the human intellect on one side and the compression arising from traditional faith, and human interests, on the other."[38] Some twenty years later, A. D. White, in defense of the nonsectarian charter of Cornell University against sectarian opposition, wrote *A History of the Warfare of Science and Theology in*

Christendom. He ended his work by saying that there was "antagonism between the theological and the scientific universe and of education in relation to it."[39] This warfare model was particularly encouraged by Darwin's theory of evolution, which did bring its share of controversy to the church. The important thing here is that not until the late twentieth century did this warfare model come under renewed scrutiny. Ironically, it took the move to Postmodernism to provide the impetus for the warfare model's demise.

The Enlightenment Project Fails: The Move to Postmodernism

With science so firmly in the driver's seat in the late nineteenth and early twentieth centuries as the unique tool of truth and the only reliable purveyor of facts, how is it possible that just a half century later Thomas Kuhn could write his famous volume *The Structure of Scientific Revolutions*, likening the so-called scientific revolutions of the past to the religious notion of a "conversion experience"?[40] In this work he implied that science is not about truth or facts as much as it is about social construction. To put an exclamation mark upon the point, a decade or two after Kuhn published his seminal work, books about science were being written with titles such as *Physics as Metaphor*[41] and *Inventing Reality*.[42] In the next section we outline how such a surprising shift took place.

While we do not wish to present a full history of how we came from Modernism to the Postmodernism of today, we do wish to outline five important developments in this move that are related to science. As listed previously, these are (1) some troubling philosophical conundrums, (2) the discovery of worldviews, (3) some surprises in modern physics, (4) corresponding developments in the philosophy of science, and (5) the subsequent renewed interest among historians to revisit previous questions of science and religion.

1. Some Troubling Philosophical Conundrums

Already by the end of the eighteenth century, philosophers began to recognize the severity of problems in Enlightenment thought that presented major difficulties for scientific conceptualization and methodology. For example, Descartes in his mechanistic philosophy of the physical universe maintained that while animals were machines, humans were set apart in that they had souls—"the ghost in the machine" as more recent writers often refer to it.[43] If the universe is mechanistic, how does that account for a soul—a concept invested with major theological significance.

In another apparent dualism, John Locke (1632-1704) referred to a medieval distinction between the "substance" of things and their "accidents." The substance referred to the unchanging essence of a thing, whereas the accidents had to do with aspects that were not essential to its nature and could be different, such as color. Locke argued that the notion of substance was conceived to support the directly experienced accidents, but in fact we have no idea what it is.[44] This distinction raised significant questions about the ability of sense perception to penetrate the truth about what things were "in themselves," an issue later picked up by Immanuel Kant.

Meanwhile, a mortal blow seemed to be struck by David Hume (1711-1776), who, given the distinction between the mental experience of sense perception and objects in the world "out there," questioned whether we can know anything directly about origins of those sensations or the relation between the sensations and the objects at all.[45] In so doing, in some sense Hume seemed to be courageously pointing out that the scientific emperor in fact had no clothes. If we seriously question whether we are actually experiencing the thing we are perceiving, science is stillborn before it takes its first breath. Further Hume questioned a central explanatory and investigational rational tool of science, the cause-and-effect relationship. He pointed out the fairly obvious fact that one never "sees" a cause, even though one may see apparently related events take place.[46] How can we maintain that one thing can be said to cause the other without introducing a metaphysical principle from outside of science—something rigorous scientists were supposedly prohibited from doing?

Two important responses to Hume warrant pointing out at this stage. Thomas Reid and Immanuel Kant (1724-1804) were both contemporaries of Hume, and their responses to him could not have been more different. Hume's own countryman, the "Scottish Common Sense" philosopher Thomas Reid (1710-1796), recognized that Hume's skepticism was not only corrosive for Christian faith but also for science: "But can any ingenuous mind admit this skeptical system [of Hume] without reluctance? I truly could not . . . ; for I am persuaded that absolute skepticism is not more destructive of the faith of a Christian than of the science of a philosopher, and of the prudence of the man of common understanding. I am persuaded that the unjust live by faith as well as the just."[47] He goes on to say that all sorts of everyday behavior, including personal virtue, would appear to be ridiculous if all private belief would be laid aside. For example, Reid tells us that we do our daily labor in the belief that we will be paid for our efforts, and such attitudes as piety, patriotism, and friendship are all predicated on a belief that they make a difference to our lives and to society.

In his critique of Hume, Reid took issue with the very assumptions that Hume had adopted, denying his skepticism on the basis of common sense. The strength of Reid's position was not a mere naive denial of skepticism, however, but the insistence that a philosophy that did not at least correlate with commonsense experience was unacceptable. In Frederick Copleston's words, "It was his view that philosophy must be grounded in common experience and that if it reaches paradoxical conclusions which contradict common experience and conflict with the beliefs on which everyone, even skeptical philosophers, necessarily base their lives in practice, there must be something wrong with it."[48] To what paradoxical conclusions was he referring? In Reid's own words:

> [Hume] saw the absurdity of making every object of thought double, and splitting it into a remote object, which has a separate and permanent existence, and an immediate object, called an idea or impression, which is an image of the former. . . . According to this system we have no intercourse with the external world, but by means of the internal world of ideas, which represents the other to the mind.
>
> He saw it was necessary to reject one of these worlds as a fiction and the question was, which should be rejected? Whether all

mankind, learned and unlearned, had feigned the existence of the external world without good reason? Or whether philosophers had feigned the internal world of ideas, in order to account for the intercourse of the mind with the external?[49]

According to Reid, Hume rejected the wrong world. Thus Reid criticizes Hume and others on the basis that their philosophy leads to a denial of any experience of the real world in favor of a constructed world of ideas, even though everyone in actual life accepts and acts upon the commonsense notion that we actually experience the real world. Significantly here as well as for our later discussions, Reid also points toward an element of faith upon which common sense relies. For of skepticism he says, "I am resolved to take my own existence, and the existence of other things, upon trust; and to believe that snow is cold, and honey sweet, whatever they may say to the contrary. He must either be a fool, or want to make a fool of me, that would reason me out of my reason and senses."[50] And further he claims that this trust is not ultimately in his own senses or his own reasoning from his sensory experience, but is based on faith in God:

[T]he wise author of our nature intended, that a great and necessary part of our knowledge should be derived from experience, before we are capable of reasoning and has provided means perfectly adequate to this intention. For, first He governs nature by fixed laws, so that we find innumerable connections of things, which continue from age to age. Without this stability of the course of nature, there could be no experience; or, it would be a false guide, and lead us into error and mischief. If there were not a principle of veracity in the human mind, men's words would not be signs of their thoughts: and if there were no regularity in the course of nature, no one thing could be a natural sign of another. Secondly, He hath implanted in human minds an original principle by which we believe and expect the continuance of the course of nature and the continuance of those connections which we have observed in time past. It is by this general principle of our nature, that, when two things have been found connected in time past, the appearance of the one produces the belief of the other.[51]

Immanuel Kant did not agree with Reid's assessment,[52] and in the face of Hume's skepticism, he set out to reassess the issues entirely and in the process to "rescue" science. He does this in the "best" spirit of the Enlightenment:

> Enlightenment is man's release from his self incurred tutelage. Tutelage is man's inability to make use of his understanding without direction from another. Self incurred is this tutelage when its cause lies not in lack of reason but in lack of resolution and courage to use it without direction from another. *Sapere aude.* "Have courage to use your own reason!"—that is the motto of the enlightenment.[53]

Kant was convinced of the correctness of certain of Hume's critiques, and in his reassessment he further developed the dualism between the "things as we see them" and the "things in themselves." Kant wanted knowledge to be universal and scientific; he wanted to rescue Newtonian science from Humean skepticism; he wanted in short to maintain the Enlightenment pretense. But the way he accomplished these goals was quite radical. In taking Hume's critique of science seriously, he had to admit that we could not experience such things as cause and effect directly. However, he argued, we do have experiences, and we do base our science on cause and effect among other things; so evidently our minds order the world in a certain way. Thus Kant concluded that the basic notions of our experience were not necessarily "out there," but they were categories in our mind "in here," which are common to all humans. In that way Kant could rescue science but at a price. He had to abandon the notion that we actually apprehend things "in themselves"; so we can only know the experience of perception in our minds. Among these categories must be such Newtonian notions as absolute space that are elemental to our doing science.[54] Since the categories are asserted as universally valid for all people, our experiences are claimed to be universal, and while we may not be able to know the thing-in-itself directly, we at least have grounds for a universal science based on common human mental furniture. Kant's contribution is often referred to as a Copernican revolution in philosophy,[55] because he redirected the focus from an investigation with a passive mind of what is out there to that of an active mind shaping what we perceive. In his own words:

> Ancient Philosophy adopted an entirely inappropriate standpoint toward the human being in the world, for it made it into a machine in it, which as such had to be entirely dependent on the world or on external things and circumstances; it thus made the human being into an all but purely passive part of the world. Now the critique of reason has appeared and determined the human being to a thoroughly active place in the world. The human being itself is the original creator of all its representations and concepts and ought to be the sole author of all its actions.[56]

Rather than the mental sun revolving around the solid and fixed earth, it was the mental sun that grounded the movable earth by giving the earth solid existence in the "sun" of the human mind. Thus, according to Kant, in a certain sense we shape the reality around us rather than allowing it simply to testify to its own true nature.[57]

While these subtleties in philosophy may not be directly on the minds of scientists today or even on the minds of those practicing science at the time, they certainly set the stage for the aftermath of theoretical thought as well as provided a framework for the discussions about science for the next hundred years. One rather direct consequence of Kant's philosophy relates to his suggestion that science and religion are quite different; while science relates to our experience about the world, God is not the object of that kind of experience and therefore not the object of scientific investigation. Hence, according to Kant, religion must have alternate grounding. While knowledge of God is relegated to the category of "things in themselves" and therefore not knowable through experience, and while pure reason was limited to the realm of experience, his solution was that religion is concerned with "practical reason" that governs the realm of ethics. Thus he introduced a kind of dualism between science and religion that has affected the most common view of religious knowledge even to this day. While the unparalleled success of scientific inquiry in the twentieth century has allowed working scientists and popular perceptions of science to largely ignore these philosophical issues, the advent of the Postmodern age is bringing such issues to the fore with new urgency. So, while Kantian skepticism dominated the philosophical aftermath concerning science in the European scene, Reid's contribution has not been forgotten. For as we will see in the next chapter, commonsense philosophy played a larger role in the Anglo-American tradition that strongly affected the American evangelical posture toward science in the following century.

2. *The Discovery of Worldviews*

The notion of worldviews is very common today, so much so that practically every Christian college advertises that classes are taught from a "Christian worldview," and even secular universities acknowledge the importance of worldviews.[58] It may surprise some to realize that this is a relatively recent phenomenon. Indeed, in the 1950s and '60s the notion of worldview was hardly on the horizon in the United States until such men as Francis Schaeffer (1912-1984), who spent time in the European academic scene, popularized the idea here among Evangelicals.[59] However, as we will see in the next chapter, the idea had already taken root in certain Evangelicals in Europe by the late nineteenth century. Where did it come from?

Kant was in the Enlightenment tradition within which the notion of objective truth was the goal, and the tendency was to think that this was a reachable goal, with ultimately everyone agreeing on the outcome. While mainstream reactions to Kant went in many different directions,[60] it is in a fledgling minority that we find the notion of worldview developing. Names often associated with the emergence of the understanding of the role of the individual perspective in knowledge claims are Friedrich Schleiermacher and Wilhelm Dilthey with respect to interpretation, and Friedrich Nietzsche in philosophy.[61] As we shall see, in these men and others, during the nineteenth century, the important idea was born that in many respects our view of the world is shaped as much by our own personal convictions, which differ from person to person, as it is by reason or experience.

In other words, in the nineteenth century the "egocentric predicament" was discovered. That is, no person can claim to have a completely objective viewpoint, but each can only see from his or her own perspective, or worldview. In our day, this seems to be fairly obvious, but with the confidence in autonomous objectivity that accompanied Enlightenment thought, this was by no means apparent at the time.

One of the first to begin to come to grips with the problem was the theologian Friedrich Schleiermacher (1768-1834). On the one hand, Schleiermacher, who was influenced by the Romantic movement in Germany, was not happy with the Enlightenment focus on reason and experience alone, with its tendency to define theology as a reflection on rational thoughts about God. Nor did he like Kant's formulation of the nature of religion as primarily having to do with ethics. On the other hand, he also reacted against the orthodox tendency to see theology as a reflection on a collection of supernaturally revealed truths, which, as he saw it, confused the dogmas about God with God Himself. In answer to both of these, Schleiermacher suggested that religion stems from some deeper faculty within man than reason or dogma; it stems from our "feeling of dependence on the infinite,"[62] which according to Schleiermacher is a universal feeling among humankind.[63] This "feeling of dependency" he also referred to as "piety," something he wished to characterize as distinct from the science and morality focus of Enlightenment thinkers, as well as from dogmas as emphasized by the orthodox view.[64] In this move, Schleiermacher represents a revolution in theology foundational for all liberal theology since that time. Thus, on this view, religion is based not on reason or revelation, but rather on the experience of the believing subject.

The move also held much importance for the interpretation of the Scriptures. For, if religion is based on a "feeling of dependency," then in order to really understand the Bible in a way suitable for the present, we need to understand the role of "feeling" or psychological disposition in those who wrote and experienced the events recorded there.[65] Hence the Bible is not so much a systematic series of texts to be understood by studying the language and grammar, but rather a product of the authors of the times, who wrote in their own historical and psychological setting. In other words, in Schleiermacher the science of interpretation, or *hermeneutics,* was born. Because of this new focus on the subjective, Schleiermacher is sometimes called the "father of Modern theology" because this shift in theological method of emphasizing the human factors of interpretation has set the trend in liberal theology for the last two hundred years.

Clearly if one emphasizes the human element entirely at the neglect of the fact that God is behind the unfolding of the Scriptures, it is only one short step to relativism. But the importance of Schleiermacher's observation should not be underestimated; we do need to take into account an understanding of the author's perspective to better understand a text. In other words, we must not throw out the baby with the bathwater; there is important insight in realizing that no one comes to the biblical texts without partiality,[66] whether that partiality comes from the enlightenment of the Holy Spirit or by a desire to undermine God's claim over all of truth and knowledge. Hence, the understanding that interpretation depends in part on the individual is not only a hallmark of liberal theology, but has held tremendous importance for conservative theology as well. This observation does not lead inevitably to relativism. Indeed, Schleiermacher himself was rather optimistic that by his methods one could come rather close to re-creating the mind of the author, because both participated in human life that was in some sense universal.[67] However, over the next two centuries such optimism was not maintained in mainstream philosophy.

Within philosophy proper this emphasis came to full fruition in Friedrich Nietzsche (1844-1900), who considered everything to be perspectival. Born only forty years after the death of Kant, Nietzsche rejected the Enlightenment notion of truth and brought a deep skepticism to philosophy. In response to the search for universal truth in the Enlightenment Project, Nietzsche suggested that there are no universals; there are only particulars. Hence all knowledge can only be particular. Thus if we try to point to a universal meaning for a concept such as a dog or a leaf, we are just fooling ourselves; not all dogs are alike, nor are all leaves. For if we look closely enough in each case, we will find striking differences. So to define a universal category of "dog" or "leaf" is merely a human construct. Likewise, to Nietzsche, a universal construct such as a "law of nature" is not a property of nature but actually a human imposition on nature. In contrast to Kant who placed our knowledge in universal categories in the mind (the same for everyone), Nietzsche's denial of such universality suggests that all knowledge is purely an individual human creation. In fact, we have no access to reality, and there simply is no "true world" out there to be discovered.[68]

Nietzsche also rejected the Enlightenment concept of objective values as somehow transcending individual human circumstance,[69] arguing that our understanding both of truth and of value comes not from anything outside of us but from our own "will to power." In other words, there is no transcendent source for truth or values, and any assertion respecting these actually comes from our own desires rather than from anything external. It is this idea, that we as a culture have separated ourselves from the supposed transcendental, that Nietzsche refers to as the "death of God." According to Stanley Grenz, on the basis of such views, Nietzsche more than anyone else deserves to be called the "patron saint of Postmodern philosophy."[70]

Around the same time period, Wilhelm Dilthey (1833-1911) sought to apply the rigorous methods of science to history. But he found that this was not possible because no one perspective of history is universally adhered to by all. This led him to the notion that the interpretive task is embedded in the "horizon of history" in the sense that each of our points of view is shaped by our experience and tradition from the particular period of history in which we find ourselves.[71] Thus he "discovered" the notion of worldview (originally *Weltanshauung* in German, which is often translated as "world and life view"), a term that he is generally credited as being the first to use.

Each of these nineteenth-century figures led in some way to the undermining of the Enlightenment Project and to the move to Postmodernism. Even so, as Thomas Torrance points out, the full Postmodern shift had not yet been achieved:

> Scientific thinking involves a methodological abstraction from all subjective factors in its concern for strict impartiality and disinterestedness. However, when this rigorous scientific method came to

> be applied beyond the realms of mathematics and physics, e.g. to history by Dilthey, it soon became evident that there is no such thing as impartial science (*voraussetzungslose Wissenschaft*) although methodological impartiality maintained its place. The really great change has come about in our own day through the theory of relativity and quantum mechanics, when it became evident that the development of classical science had reached the point when there had to take place a considerable change in the whole structure of scientific consciousness.[72]

So by the end of the nineteenth century, the undermining of the Enlightenment Project was not yet complete but well underway. We leave this section with a twofold insight. First, we realize of course that Nietzsche went too far in abandoning any notion of universal truth in general, for among other things this view contradicts the Christian understanding of the God who exists and reveals Himself to us. However, we also cannot deny the important lessons learned from the realization that we cannot get outside ourselves to see things from an absolute point of view. Thus, the egocentric predicament teaches us that although there may be universal truth, it is at least a little more difficult to agree upon than we might have thought, and agreement won't come through reason and experience alone. This is the essential insight that helped lead to our understanding of the role of worldviews today. But there is still more that led to the undermining of the Enlightenment optimism concerning science as the way to objective truth. We next turn to the radical new physics that helped push us along on the road to Postmodernism.

3. Surprising Developments in Modern Physics

Meanwhile, as philosophy struggled to find an objective way to describe science so as to obtain objective truth, the successes within science continued unabated. Giddy with the successes in the physical and geological sciences in the eighteenth and early part of the nineteenth century, scholars began to apply the methods of science to all areas of study, even to the point of subjecting the origins of Scripture to scientific scrutiny. By the end of the nineteenth century the mechanistic view of the universe was fully entrenched in the scientific community, not only in physics and geology but also in other branches of science, including biology, thanks to Darwin's theory, and even in the human sciences. Such was the continuing drive for the sought-after scientific objectivity and certainty based on the power of mechanistic models constructed by reason and according to sense data.

Ironically though, Kant's supposed objective "categories of the mind," which are supposed to represent universal experience, eventually met challenges from the scientific arena as well. For example, one of Kant's categories was the notion of absolute space, represented by Euclidean geometry. For much of history, the geometry of Euclid was considered unique and self-evident; so it was assumed to be true about reality as well, and hence Newtonian physics assumed that space was described by this geometry. Therefore Kant had assumed that space and time as described by Euclidean geometry belonged to the categories with which we shape our experience.

The first challenge came when Nicolai Lobachevsky (1792-1856) and Georg Riemann (1826-1866) found alternative geometries, geometries that were internally consistent but distinctly different from Euclidean geometry.[73] At first these were viewed as merely curiosities, but just after the turn of the century, Einstein's relativity theory replaced Newton's absolute space with a relative spacetime. In other words, space and time get mixed up. Within Einstein's theory, notions such as length and duration proved not to be absolute quantities to be agreed upon by all observers but rather perspectival, depending on the reference frame from which they are measured. This means, for example, that two people moving with respect to one another will not necessarily agree on the order of events taking place. One person might say that two events happened at the same time, while another might insist that one of the events happened earlier than the other. The difference is real, a result of perspective that is related to the information traveling from event to observer.[74] This curious state of affairs results in the well-known twin paradox: One twin goes off in a rocket ship while the other remains on earth, and when the first returns, he is younger than his stationery sibling.[75] These notions are not mere speculation; they have been carefully tested in many experiments. Further, in Einstein's theory, the geometry of spacetime itself proved to be one of the non-Euclidean varieties, thus rendering Kant's supposed universal category of Euclidean geometry to be inappropriate for a description of the universe as a whole. If Kant could get this category wrong, even if there are universal categories of the mind, how can we trust that we have figured out what the appropriate categories are?

A couple of decades later, a second of Kant's categories, that of cause and effect, came under scrutiny in the development of quantum theory. In Newtonian physics the mechanistic philosophy seemed to pertain, and the notion of a particle seems clear; you could think of it as kind of like a tiny billiard ball, with a definite position and a definite velocity at any given time, potentially with relations in the form of forces with respect to other particles. Knowing the position and velocity of a particle, and all the forces involved, would allow you to predict the future trajectory of the particle precisely. It was on this basis that Laplace based his famous statement as quoted earlier, that knowledge of the position, velocity, and relations of every particle in the universe at a given time would allow one to predict the future, at least in principle.

In quantum theory, this can no longer be the case. Every so-called particle also has a wavelike nature. And just as a wave cannot be said to be in a definite location at a given time, so it is with a quantum particle such as an electron. Heisenberg's uncertainty principle tells us that if you know where a particle is, you cannot know exactly what its velocity is, or if you know its velocity rather precisely, you won't know its location. A more recent perspective is that an electron cannot be said to have both a definite position and velocity at a given time, because it is not a particle as we construe them to be in our minds, but it also has wavelike properties. While interpretations of quantum theory vary, all include some basic change in our fundamental understanding of reality. The most striking feature of the new physics is the loss of definiteness in predicting any particular outcome. Thus quantum theory, with its strange statistical description of the world, not only rudely undermined confidence in the strict cause-and-effect mechanistic universe, but also caused scientists to question whether the actual underlying events of any process could be described objectively at all.

Ironically if the commonsense categories of the mind that Kant thought so necessary were undermined, Reid's commonsense philosophy fares no better. For what we learn in the new developments of modern physics is that the absolute categories we need to describe the universe simply may not coincide with the common sense we build up from our relative experience. In the case of relativity, we do not directly experience speeds of everyday objects close to that of light, nor do we experience the sorts of behavior described by the quantum theory. Hence we are faced with the question: How reliable is our common sense when we are trying to ascertain absolute categories of the universe?

These developments inevitably had an adverse effect on philosophers who were trying to ground the methods of science in solid "foundational" criteria, which would inevitably lead to universally accepted objective truth. We turn to this topic in the next section.

4. Developments in the Philosophy of Science

In the face of the above developments within both philosophy and science, philosophers of science were forced to reconsider the traditional foundations upon which they presumed science was built. This eventually resulted in a loss of confidence in the ability to define precisely how knowledge that can be considered objective, universal, and certain is to be obtained through the scientific enterprise. In other words, they lost confidence in the ability to find a rigorous foundationalist view of science as leading to objective truth.

The early Baconian model of science had suggested that empirical observation along with induction would lead inevitably to hypotheses. Then the hypotheses could subsequently be tested—all this in an objective manner. But as philosophers began to recognize the subjective element in other areas of philosophy, i.e., through the discovery of worldviews, science was revealed not to be essentially different from other areas of human inquiry. For how is a hypothesis developed? Clearly creativity would have to play a role; the inductive method alone never leads to theories directly. There must be some creative "leap," and creativity certainly cannot be said to be merely objective.

Suppose then that we acquiesce and admit that creativity comes in at some level in order to form the hypotheses. Could we not still objectively test the hypotheses once we have them? But even this step comes into question, since in the inductive argument all you do is continue to amass data. Of course, as long as the data correlate with the hypotheses, you may consider your theory validated. But one data point that contradicts the theory would show it to be invalid, and how can you check all the possible circumstances? That would amount to an infinite number of experiments. Thus the notion arose that theories can never really be verified, but at least they can in principle be falsified.[76] But even this idea has its problems. There are subjective elements in the judgment as to whether a falsifying data point is indicative of the falsity of the hypothesis we think we are testing. Perhaps an error was made due to faulty equipment. Or perhaps some mistake was made in the understanding of the theories concerning the operation of the equipment used to test the hypothesis. How could one be sure? Subjective judgment calls are therefore needed to make the decisions as to what is to be trusted. Thus science depends on prior theoretical commitments in many ways.

Perhaps the nail in the coffin of foundationalist philosophy was driven in by Thomas Kuhn, who maintained that scientific revolutions are as much socially driven as they are driven by the data.[77] As you can see, the situation is rather complicated. The final conclusion is that worldviews, or at least subjective elements, matter, even in science.[78] This realization has invoked a number of new studies in the history of science as seen in the next section.

5. Renewed Interest Among Historians in Science-Religion Issues

Finally with the above developments behind them, late twentieth-century historians began to reexamine situations in the history of science from a more open perspective. Indeed, the issue of science and religion is now one presently being researched with great excitement among historians of science and others such as social historians. Why? Because, in short, in the move to the Postmodern world as outlined above, everything has changed in relation to this issue. What used to be considered "warfare" between science and religion has now become an interesting dialog of give and take, with much intricate interplay. Almost every recent text on the history of science now apologizes for our historian predecessors for their blindness in not seeing that presuppositions, or worldviews, have played an important part in how scientific theories are adopted. What used to be a simple (Modernist) thesis that science represents progress and that religion is detrimental to the practice of science now has become the thesis that science is not neutral (or science is "theory-laden," as is often said), and that the sorts of metaphysical claims that come from religion affect science at very fundamental levels in all those who practice it. The actual events of history have not changed, of course, but rather the change has come in the reassessment of the Modernist thesis. For along with Postmodernity came the freedom to open up old cases and ask new questions. When the answers began to come in, the Modernist cart was overturned.

Take, for example, the cases of Galileo Galilei (1564-1642) and of Giordano Bruno (1548-1600). The trial of Galileo is a well-known historical case, usually represented as a church trying to stick to old-fashioned ideas and hold back the progress of science. Bruno was burned at the stake supposedly because he supported the Copernican view of the solar system, and he is often referred to as a martyr for science. But after the new studies came in, neither case appears as simple as folk legend would have us believe. No, now the discussions between Galileo and the pope are seen with merits on both sides.[79] Galileo's evidence was not all that convincing to outsiders, especially given the limited ability to do the relevant experiments at the time, and indeed some of his scientific claims were even wrong.[80] Besides that, Galileo's claims about the solar system were merely descriptive; Newton had not yet provided the "law" or mathematical description of gravity that would be convincing to a broader intelligentsia that the earth moving around the sun is a simpler hypothesis than the other way around. Under these circumstances, the pope can be viewed as the one maintaining a proper skepticism in the face of as yet unsubstantiated claims. And what about Bruno? While it is no longer fashionable in the Western world to burn people at the stake for heresy, his execution was more for heresy than for his claims about science.[81] In both cases also, a certain belligerence on the part of the "persecuted" played a role.

Indeed, as John Hedley Brooke ably reveals in his book *Science and Religion*, much of history contains interesting episodes relevant to the relation between science and religion. Historians recognize now that the issues go back all the way to the origins of our Western traditions, even to the ancient Greek philosophers.[82] We will return to some of these topics in later chapters as they become relevant for particular issues, but for the time being we wish to add a few comments to further put our discussion in the Modern/Postmodern context.

The recent investigations in history such as concerning Galileo and Bruno tell us that an effort to remake the thinkers of those days in our own Modern image does not work. Whatever progress was made in the scientific revolution and the move to the Modern period, the men involved must still be seen as very much men of their times. Each is seen to have built on earlier ideas but to have also held earlier fallacies. Copernicus, the father of the new cosmology, for example, may have been influenced by the neo-Platonist notion that the sun, as the greater light, should have a central role as the heavenly body that most adequately represents God.[83] Bruno picked this up, believing that the church at the time was a corruption of an earlier undefiled religion associated with the Egyptians.[84] And Kepler's early work represented an interesting mixture of empirical methods and Platonism:

> Empiricism of a different sort was practiced by Kepler, who welcomed the astronomical data of Tycho Brahe as a means of confirming preconceived beliefs about the geometry of the universe. The data were vital, but so was the preconception that the planetary orbits [were circular and] could be inscribed within, and circumscribed without, the five regular Greek solids. It was an empiricism of a sort, but regulated by Kepler's fusion of a Pythagorean harmony with a Christian doctrine of creation.[85]

In the face of modern science, Kepler's use of the so-called perfect solids in his attempt to explain the distances between the orbits of the planets is astoundingly off the mark, even though his answers were reasonably close to the actual distances observed. But Kepler had a strong a priori commitment to the mathematical perfection of the orbits, which is why he assumed these orbits would be circular, and why he proposed that the spheres on which the circles were carried were circumscribed and proscribed around the perfect solids. Although Brahe's precise data led Kepler ultimately to abandon his commitment to the circular orbits, this story reveals that his methods were not purely those of the modern-day scientific ideal.

On the other side, there were at the time both physical and philosophical arguments in support of an earth-centered cosmology. For example, the dominant Aristotelian philosophy held that all beyond the moon was perfect and immutable, but the earth embodied corruption and change.[86] Therefore to place the earth out among the planets would make it co-equal with the perfect realm. This obviously would violate the Christian doctrines of sin, the Fall, and the great gulf between mankind and perfection when understood in this Aristotelian context.

In contrast to the idea that men were suddenly snapped out of ignorance into the "light," these examples illustrate the currently popular thesis that a more continuous development took place in the history of ideas. While in the supposed conflicts, such as that surrounding Galileo, good arguments were with the side of the fledgling science, they were also with the church, and the same goes for bad arguments. Perhaps more importantly, the examples also serve as a warning to the church. In John Hedley Brooke's words, "Certainly the Catholic Church had a vested interest in Aristotelian philosophy, but much of the conflict ostensibly between science and religion turns out to have been between new science and the sanctified science of the previous generation."[87] This provides an important warning for us. It is entirely possible for the arguments of the church to be based not on a proper interpretation of the revealed Word, but rather on a regurgitated version of the supposed knowledge that had already been accepted by those in the not too distant past. Or as John Cottingham says in his introduction to Descartes's *Meditations on First Philosophy*, "What is called 'common sense' in any age frequently turns out to be the half-digested remains of earlier philosophical theories."[88] Several examples of this have already been mentioned, such as the case of Bruno, and the case of Galileo and the church, and many others could be brought up.[89] As Brooke summarizes, "By speculating, for example, on the mechanism by which God reformed the solar system, [Newton] drew attention to the role of providence in nature—but at a price. Those who did not share his religious sensibilities would look at the mechanism and see no further."[90] In other words, your conclusions depend on how you look at the mechanical laws. Depending on your presuppositions, you might see a watchmaker, or alternatively you might see a mechanism that runs by itself.

Science in a Postmodern World

So although the Enlightenment Project had auspicious beginnings, and often with motivations that seemed very much in line with Christian commitments, the Project as envisioned by many has failed. The Modern pretense that autonomous human reason and objective method on their own can penetrate the ultimate truth and bring order and fulfillment to humans has been exposed as a false hope. Such is the message of the Postmodern world. Yet scientists in the Postmodern world continue to make progress in their scientific investigations, a progress that seems to be common to all, and in some sense independent of skeptical philosophies, strange physics, worldview considerations, and historical reassessments. What does this mean? Are the Postmodern critiques then just so much hot air? How can worldviews matter and yet science operate so successfully? How might Christians respond to this situation? We gradually develop some relevant perspectives on these questions in the chapters that follow, but we will begin in the next chapter by examining some objections various Christians throughout the Modern period have already made to the hegemony of Modernism. Each objection arose primarily from the theological convictions of these believers as they reacted critically to aspects of the Enlightenment Project.

One final thought we should keep in mind: This chapter's story makes it clear that well-meaning Christians at every age are also people of their times. We likewise are included in this category. So the question remains, what idols do we presently hold that come from our own blindness in relation to the culture in which we live? We hope that remaining chapters will help us all reflect on this question.

Chapter Three

A Christian Science?

Credo ut intelligam, non intelligo ut credam ("I believe that I may understand; I do not understand that I may believe.")

St. Anselm

What could be different about science when viewed from a Christian perspective? Isn't science simply neutral? Or does the fact that worldviews come into play in science mean that science done by Christians is or should be really something different from that done by non-Christians? In other words, should we expect separate approaches to science according to worldview—a "Christian science," a "humanist science," and a "materialist science," all different? What is science anyway, and if there are different approaches to science, what would their overlap be? The answers to these questions are not simple; we have already seen that in the previous two chapters and will revisit them in the chapters to come.

There is certainly much about science that cannot depend on worldviews, but there is also much that does. We, of course, expect that a study of God's creation, as science entails, should, in principle, always yield the same answers to all of our investigations. So there should be significant areas of agreement in science. But science is also dependent on human involvement, and therefore on the worldviews of the humans involved. And further, since science concerns itself with knowledge, and Christians claim to know things about the universe (e.g., that it is God's creation) that are not held in common with non-Christians, does that not mean that Christians should approach the investigations of science differently in some sense from non-Christians? The answer is yes; there are many issues in science that differ depending on one's basic convictions about the world. Therefore we need to ask the question, What issues unique to Christians are important for the investigation of science? In this chapter we begin to uncover answers to these questions by looking to the past to hear the voices of some who realized that there are alternatives to the Enlightenment Project when approaching science.

Let us begin by asking, Where were the Christian voices in the story of the rise and fall of the Enlightenment Project? One part of the answer, as we have already observed, is that the story as a whole takes place largely within a Christian backdrop, and many of the major players had Christian commitments. But part of the answer is also that there were Christian dissenters to the Modern story, and there were a variety of specifically Christian critiques of Modernist excesses related to science all along the way. In examining the question of whether there is a serious Christian science to be developed, in contrast to materialist science, say, it will be helpful to review several of these historical figures to get a handle on the specific critiques that they had of Enlightenment science, critiques based on their theological convictions and that also in some cases strikingly anticipated many of the Postmodern critiques of Modern science that are with us today. These dissenters come from a variety of Christian traditions, and all would be recognizable as Evangelicals today. We will briefly discuss the views of a reform-minded Catholic, Blaise Pascal (1623-1662), a Lutheran, Johann Georg Hamann (1730-1788), a Presbyterian, Charles Hodge (1797-1878), and finally Abraham Kuyper (1837-1920) and Herman Dooyeweerd (1894-1977), both from the Dutch Reformed tradition. We hope to raise a number of theological issues that continue to be relevant for us as we think about science today. Just as science developed from the seventeenth to the twentieth centuries, so has the critique developed, as we shall see. By the end, we will be left with a number of theological issues that will help set the stage for our own assessment of what a Christian view of science might be, beginning in chapter 4.

The major focal point of dissent seems to be the relation between faith and reason/knowledge. This is an old question, not unique to the Modern period, as is illustrated in the following quote from Philip

Schaff's *History of the Christian Church*, written in the late nineteenth century:

> Following Augustine, the Schoolmen [i.e., Scholastics, or late medieval scholars] started with the principle that faith precedes knowledge—*fides praecedit intellectum*. Or, as Anselm also put it, "I believe that I may understand; I do not understand that I may believe," *credo ut intelligam, non intelligo ut credam*. They quoted as proof text, Isa. 7:9: "If ye will not believe, surely ye shall not be established." Abaelard was an exception, and reversed the order, making knowledge precede faith; but all arrived at the same result. Revelation and reason, faith and science, theology and philosophy agree, for they proceed from the one God who cannot contradict himself.[1]

The distinction between Anselm's position of faith before reason and that of Abelard (1079-1142), who had it the other way around, is one that persists, at least subtly, even to this day. Our first two dissenters focus precisely on this distinction. To begin, we move forward from the late medieval period to the fledgling beginning of science, and we meet Blaise Pascal as a Cartesian critic.

Blaise Pascal, a Seventeenth-Century French Critic of Descartes

Pascal, a particularly early dissenter to Enlightenment thought, was a contemporary of Descartes. Pascal, a French Catholic like Descartes, is known for his advances in mathematics and physics as well as his deep Christian faith. In the words of Frederick Copleston, in his philosophy Pascal was not so much interested in defending the Christian faith as "showing how the Christian revelation solves the problems which arise out of the human situation."[2] He is well known in Christian circles across the board for his deep reflections on the Christian faith as published in his *Pensées*. There Pascal reveals a strong dislike for Descartes's rationalistic and mechanistic philosophy—in a nutshell: "Descartes [is] useless and uncertain."[3]

Why did Pascal feel this way? Evidently he thought that

Descartes's rationalism was leading philosophy on a road away from true faith in the Christian God and that his mechanistic conception of the universe was tantamount to deism. "I cannot forgive Descartes. In all his philosophy he would have been quite willing to dispense with God. But he had to make Him give a fillip[4] to set the world in motion; beyond this, he has no further need of God."[5] In a similar vein, Pascal faults Descartes for giving the "machine" model too much credence: "In general terms one must say: 'That is the result of figure and motion,' because it is true, but to name them and assemble the machine is quite ridiculous. It is pointless, uncertain, and arduous. Even if it were true we do not think that the whole of philosophy would be worth an hour's effort."[6] In other words, Pascal is saying that there is much more to reality than the machine analogy can provide.

Many of Pascal's criticisms have to do with the Enlightenment elevation of reason. He advocates a more balanced approach: "Two excesses: to exclude reason, to admit nothing but reason."[7] He believes that reason itself should lead us to a more humble posture than Descartes's philosophy suggests: "Reason's last step is the recognition that there are an infinite number of things which are beyond it. It is merely feeble if it does not go as far as to realize that. If natural things are beyond it, what are we to say about supernatural things?"[8] Ultimately, therefore, reason must include a submission to faith in that which is revealed by God: "Know then, proud man, what a paradox you are to yourself. Be humble, impotent reason! Be silent, feeble nature! Learn that man infinitely transcends man, hear from your master your true condition, which is unknown to you. Listen to God."[9] But there must nevertheless be a balance, for faith is not counter to reason. "If we submit everything to reason, our religion will be left with nothing mysterious or supernatural. If we offend the principles of reason our religion will be absurd and ridiculous."[10] "One must know when it is right to doubt, to affirm, to submit. Anyone who does otherwise does not understand the force of reason. Some men run counter to these three principles, either affirming that everything can be proved, because they know nothing about proof, or doubting everything, because they do not know when to submit, or always submitting, because they do not know when judgment is called for."[11] In the final analysis, our knowledge comes not only through reason, but also through the heart:

> We know the truth not only through our reason but also through our heart. It is through the latter that we know first principles, and reason, which has nothing to do with it, tries in vain to refute them. The skeptics have no other object than that, and they work at it to no purpose. We know that we are not dreaming, but, however unable we may be to prove it rationally, our inability proves nothing but the weakness of our reason, and not the uncertainty of all our knowledge, as they maintain. For knowledge, of first principles, like space, time, motion, number, is as solid as any derived through reason, and it is on such knowledge, coming from the heart and instinct, that reason has to depend and base all its argument. The heart feels that there are three spatial dimensions and that there is an infinite series of numbers, and reason goes on to demonstrate that there are no two square numbers of which one is double the other. Principles are felt, propositions proved, and both with certainty though by different means. It is just as pointless and absurd for reason to demand proof of first principles from the heart before agreeing to accept them as it would be absurd for the heart to demand an intuition of all the propositions demonstrated by reason before agreeing to accept them.
>
> Our inability must therefore serve only to humble reason, which would like to be the judge of everything, but not to confute our certainty. As if reason were the only way we could learn! Would to God, on the contrary, that we never needed it and knew everything by instinct and feeling! But nature has refused us this blessing, and has instead given us only very little knowledge of this kind; all other knowledge can be acquired only by reasoning.
>
> That is why those to whom God has given religious faith by moving their hearts are very fortunate, and feel quite legitimately convinced, but to those who do not have it we can only give such faith through reasoning, until God gives it by moving their heart, without which faith is only human and useless for salvation.[12]

As we move on, we will see that Pascal's very early criticism of the use of reason alone, as it was emerging in association with the rise of modern science, was almost prescient. He already understood that a humble posture should be taken before God when claims are made concerning Him and His creation, a stance we too would like to affirm. But we have the benefit of three centuries of hindsight; Pascal remarkably saw this important truth even in the fledgling stages of the Enlightenment. We will continue to see this same theme developed in the ensuing Enlightenment dissenters from later ages as well. In addition, Pascal's notion that knowledge does not come from reason alone, but also from the heart, is forward looking as well, a notion that is perhaps not even fully appreciated today.

Johann Georg Hamann, an Eighteenth-Century German Critic

Although Pascal was an early critic of the Enlightenment Project, he was certainly not the only one. Perhaps the Enlightenment's most thorough contemporary critic was Johann Georg Hamann (1730-1788). A contemporary of Kant, Hamann was a pious Lutheran with a sharp wit and critical mind.[13] Perhaps surprisingly, Hamann found an important reason for critiquing the Enlightenment Project in the skepticism of Hume. It was not Hume's skepticism as such that gripped Hamann, but his focus on the need for something behind reason that the Enlightenment had missed—that something being faith. According to Hamann, echoing Pascal a century earlier, belief is at the foundation of knowledge, and he refers to Hume favorably in this regard that belief is essential for knowing that things exist.[14] For example, Hume writes in his *Treatise on Human Nature:*

> Thus the sceptic still continues to reason and believe, even tho' he asserts that he cannot defend his reason by reason; and by the same rule he must assent to the principle concerning the existence of body, tho' he cannot pretend by any arguments of philosophy to maintain its veracity. . . . We may well ask, *What causes induce us to believe in the existence of body?* but 'tis in vain to ask, *Whether there be body or not?* That is a point, which we must take for granted in all our reasonings.[15]

Through declarations such as this, Hume gives a role to belief, as prior to reason, in accepting our own existence and that of the external world without rational proof. Hamann saw in this a welcome subversion of the Cartesian idea that knowledge comes through inductive reasoning. In his words, "Our own existence and the existence of all things outside us must be believed and cannot be determined in any other way," and "Belief is not the product of the intellect, and can therefore also suffer no casualty by it: since belief has as little grounds as taste or sight."[16] Although Hume was an unbeliever and an enemy of the Christian church, Hamann saw in him a kind of reluctant witness to the truth in spite of himself, such as Saul or Balaam.[17] Hamann then turned Hume's skepticism into a positive Christian affirmation, that faith is necessary and foundational for knowledge. To quote Isaiah Berlin on Hamann:

> . . . our most famous philosophers cut away the branch on which they are sitting, hide with shame, like Adam, their unavoidable and agreeable sin; they deny the brute fact, the irrational. Things are as they are; without accepting this there is no knowledge, for all knowledge reposes on belief or faith, *Glaube* (that is the transition that Hamann makes without argument), faith in the existence whether of chairs and tables and trees, or of God and the truth of his Bible, all given to faith, to belief, to no other faculty. The contrast between faith and reason is for him a profound fallacy. There are no ages of faith followed by ages of reason. These are fictions. Reason is built on faith, it cannot replace it; there are no ages that are not ages of both: the contrast is unreal. Irrational religion is a contradiction in terms. A religion is true not because it is rational but because it is face-to-face with what is real: modern philosophers pursue rationality like Don Quixote, and will in the end, like him, lose their wit.[18]

Thus like Pascal before him, Hamann saw the necessity of reason and of faith, but also the possibility for abuse and ultimately skeptical confusion if either is abstracted entirely from one another or from God.

> Reason is the source of all truth and all error. It is the tree of the knowledge of good and evil. Therefore both sides are right and both wrong, those who deify it and those who slander it. Likewise faith is the source of unbelief as well as of superstition. Out of one mouth proceeds both blessings and curses (James 3).[19]

Interestingly, Hamann follows up this line of thinking by pointing out that it is language, a gift that separates us from the rest of creation, that allows us to engage in this two-edged sword of reason.[20] Thus even though our self-expression as found in language is patterned after God's own self-expression in the Word (logos), no human reason is pure; it is always accompanied by our own blindness, as permeated by sin. Because of these criticisms, Hamann had a healthy suspicion of philosophy in general, declaring himself "close to suspecting that the whole of our philosophy consists more of language than of reason, and the misunderstandings of countless words, the personification of arbitrary abstractions . . . have generated an entire world of problems which it is as vain to try to solve as it was to invent them."[21] In a critique of rationalism that bears some resemblance to that of Bacon as quoted in the last chapter, Hamann warns against several features of the emerging Enlightenment philosophy, in Isaiah Berlin's words:

> "Only a *scholastic reason* divides itself into realism and idealism; a correct and authentic reason knows nothing of such imaginary divisions."[22] Analysis and synthesis are equally arbitrary.[23] The fault of all philosophers is to introduce arbitrary divisions, to shut their eyes to reality in order to build "castles in the air."[24] The language of nature is not mathematics—God is not a geometer. Conventional signs are needed, no doubt, but they are unreal. Words like 'cause,' 'reason,' 'universality' are mere counters, and do not correspond to things. The greatest error in the world is "to confuse *words* with *concepts* and *concepts* with *real things*."[25]

On this basis, Hamann says of Kant that the logical conclusion of Kant's critical philosophy would be to "break down into a series of vicious dualisms (form versus content, sensibility versus understanding, reason versus experience, nature versus freedom, the pure versus the practical, and so on)."[26] Kant's analysis did entail dualisms as we have seen in the previous chapter. For example, he cut a wedge between the phenomena of experience and the "noumena," "things in themselves" that were known to thought alone and could not be experienced, and he separated the two realms of "pure reason," which can make judgments concerning experience, and "practical reason," which does not make judgments but is important for behavior (ethics).

Hamann's main point in being critical is that Kant's system overvalues the formal character of knowledge; for Hamann there could be no such separation between reason and experience.[27] His attitude toward such rationalistic philosophies is well summarized in the following: "every systematiser must be expected to look on his system precisely as every Catholic looks on his true Church."[28] In other words, there is really a faith at the bottom of the commitment to the system, and this faith is not itself founded upon reason. Hamann is not the only one who made such criticisms, of course. But Hamann's critique is interesting to us because it came out of his Lutheran convictions that all creation is one; because it comes from the one God, it is unified. Therefore, the unity of faith, reason, and experience are grounded not in the unity of thought, but in the unity of reality itself.[29] This we know by faith, and thus with one stroke, according to Hamann, by faith we sweep away all dualistic philosophies that would tend to divide up God's creation in rational categories that cannot truly be held separate in reality. This is well illustrated in quotes from letters to his friend, Friedrich Heinrich Jacobi, where he uses the metaphor of divorce:

> It is pure idealism to divorce faith and sense perception from thinking. Togetherness [*Geselligkeit*] is the true principle of reason and language, by which our perceptions and conceptions are modified. This and that philosophy always divorce things which in no way can be separated. Things without relations, relations without things. There are no absolute [i.e., relationless] creatures, just as little as there is absolute certainty.[30]

> No philosophy can separate what God has joined together....[31]

Indeed since the time of the Reformation and even before, the unity of all creation has been a common theme, which has also helped develop an appropriate attitude toward science. But as we shall see, to avoid dualistic thinking, even if our faith encourages us to do so, is easier said than done.

Hamann's critique of dualisms extends to other areas as well. For example, Hamann sees these Kantian dualisms as underlying the attitude leading to a split between the natural and the supernatural. In W. M. Alexander's words:

> A world where, on the basis of a Kantian dichotomy, "phenomena" have relevance to men and "noumena" to God, in which history is the sphere of human action and human responsibility alone, and in which the problem can arise how any event in history can be divine; a world as a sphere so . . . removed from God that the presence of God is thought of as "supernatural," in which great energy can be expended pro and con on the problem of how God can intermittently "break into" a foreign domain—this kind of world Hamann does not recognize. Its problems are artificial constructs, straw men.[32] "Just as men often oppose their nature to their reason and will, and take their customary ways of acting for necessities, so even more often in philosophy they would oppose nature to their Creator and speak of 'supernatural works' and works 'contrary to nature'."[33]

Along with this separation, Hamann finds it ironic that philosophers such as Descartes often wish to prove the existence of God from within their philosophy: "For if they are fools who in their hearts deny the existence of God, it strikes me as yet more foolish that they want to prove him first."[34] As Alexander says of Hamann's attitude, ". . . a god produced in this fashion is not God. A demonstration of God is *prima facie* evidence that it is not God we are dealing with." We have some sympathy with these views, and we will return to the issues in later chapters. For now, let us move up one century, change continents, and meet our next dissenter.

Charles Hodge, a Nineteenth-Century American Evangelical

By the nineteenth century, the European scene was a mixture of optimism over the promise of Enlightenment science and skepticism concerning the real promise of the Enlightenment philosophy. With the French Revolution seemingly leading to anarchy, followed by the rise of Napoleon, there were grounds for skepticism even on the practical level.

By contrast, in America, where the American Revolution and aftermath had provided foundations for stability, an optimism concerning many aspects of the Enlightenment continued. The new world was not so much influenced by the Humean skeptical side of the Enlightenment, but rather found its intellectual roots in the more optimistic Scottish Common Sense philosophy of Thomas Reid, and a confidence in the Baconian empirical scientific approach to knowledge.[35] Through the Scottish philosophy, it seemed that this modern scientific approach could be reconciled with the two other important strands of American thought, "the self-evident" principles of the American Revolution and the faith and fervor of evangelical Christianity.[36] By the mid-nineteenth century, America had already gone through a broad-based Christian revival known as the Second Great Awakening, and the evangelical community was thriving. It is in this context that we find our third dissenter, Charles Hodge (1797-1878).

Princeton Seminary and its faculty played a major leadership role in the intellectual life of the evangelical Christian community in America throughout most of the nineteenth century and was also a substantial player in the intellectual and academic life of the nation as a whole. Princeton, like most other scholarly institutions of that era, was firmly entrenched in the Christian-friendly and optimistic American strand of Common Sense philosophy.[37] Of the Princeton theologians in the nineteenth century, there was no more visible nor influential scholar than Charles Hodge.

In contrast to Pascal and Hamann, Hodge was not overtly critical of the place of reason in Modern analysis per se. As most of his

American contemporaries, Hodge held Baconian scientific methodology in high esteem as a sure pathway to the truth about the world. On the basis of his Common Sense philosophical convictions, he seems untroubled by Hume's skepticism or Kant's dualistic responses to it. But he was no friend of the Enlightenment proper, as can be seen in his introduction to his *Systematic Theology*, where he lays foundations by discussing different methodologies of theology. Among these he describes the "Speculative Method," by which he means the accepting of certain principles *a priori* and using them to determine what is and must be.[38] The first category of speculative theology he calls the "Deistic and Rationalistic Form," which he describes as "that which rejects any other source of knowledge of divine things than what is found in nature and the constitution of the human mind."[39] This is the Enlightenment philosophy in a nutshell, that knowledge comes by reason and by experience alone. Hodge strongly rejects this approach to theology because it does not admit the Scriptures as an equally viable source of knowledge. However, in denying the foundations of the Enlightenment philosophy, he rather embraces its methods, in commending what he calls the "Inductive Method" of theology. A couple of quotes from his *Systematic Theology* illustrate this:

> [The Inductive Method] is so called because it agrees in everything essential with the inductive method as applied to the natural sciences.
>
> First, the man of science comes to the study of nature with certain assumptions. (1.) He assumes the trustworthiness of his sense perceptions. . . . (2.) He must also assume the trustworthiness of his mental operations. . . . (3.) He must rely on the certainty of those truths which are not learned from experience, but which are given in the constitution of our nature. . . . [Here Hodge discusses cause and effect.]
>
> Second, the student of nature having this ground on which to stand, and these tools wherewith to work, proceeds to perceive, gather and combine his facts. These he does not pretend to manufacture nor presume to modify. . . .
>
> Third, from facts thus ascertained and classified he deduces the laws by which they are determined. . . . [Here Hodge uses the theory of gravity as an example of deduction from the facts.][40]

This description sounds very much like a description for doing science. But Hodge has something else in mind. His data are not the data of nature, but the data of Scripture. In other words, the scientific method is also the appropriate model for doing theology.

> The Bible is to the theologian what nature is to the man of science. It is his storehouse of facts; and his method of ascertaining what the Bible teaches is the same as that which the natural philosopher adopts to ascertain what nature teaches.[41]

Hodge goes on then to outline the method of science as applied to what he considers the science of theology, which studies the data of Scripture, a method that parallels natural science at every point. He concludes the chapter by saying,

> The true method of theology is, therefore, the inductive, which assumes that the Bible contains all the facts or truths which form the contents of theology, just as the facts of nature are the contents of the natural sciences. It is also assumed that the relation of these Biblical facts to each other, the principles involved in them, the laws which determine them, are in the facts themselves, and are to be deduced from them, just as the laws of nature are deduced from the facts of nature. In neither case are the principles derived from the mind and imposed upon the facts, but equally in both departments, the principles or laws are deduced from the facts and recognized by the mind.[42]

Hodge repeats several places in the following chapter his conviction that the facts speak for themselves. For example, as he comes to his definition of theology, he leads with the following:

> So the facts of science arrange themselves. They are not arranged by the naturalist. His business is simply to ascertain what the arrangement given in the nature of the facts is. If he mistake, his system is false, and to a greater or less degree valueless. The same is obviously true with regard to the facts or truths of the Bible. . . . It is important that the theologian should know his place. He is not master of the situation. He can no more construct a system of theology to suit

> his fancy, than the astronomer can adjust the mechanism of the heavens according to his own good pleasure. As the facts of astronomy arrange themselves in a certain order, and will admit of no other, so it is with the facts of theology. Theology, therefore, is the exhibition of the facts of Scripture in their proper order and relation, with the principles or general truths involved in the facts themselves, and which pervade and harmonize the whole.[43]

Thus we see that while Hodge rejected certain aspects of the Enlightenment Project, he was no dissenter to the objectivity presumed by the Enlightenment philosophy. Theology was to be scientific in its methodology, and consequently in essence "laws of doctrine" would emerge from inductive analysis. Since facts of Scripture and the facts of nature both come from God, any laws properly inferred from either of them, whether in astronomy or theology, cannot be contradictory. If they seem so, we have erred in one or the other. So in view of his belief that science leads to reliable and objective knowledge, he maintained that we should remain open to the possibility that scientific discoveries might require us to change our interpretation of Scripture at some points.

> From [the fact that the Bible comes from the Holy Spirit] it follows that the Bible can teach no error, whether in reference to doctrines, morals, or facts; whether those facts be historical, geographical, geological or astronomical.
>
> In the second place, however, the *Princeton Review* has ever held and taught, in common with the whole Church, that this infallible Bible must be interpreted by science. . . .
>
> Science is not the opinions of man, but knowledge: and specially, according to usage, the ascertained truths concerning the facts of the laws of nature. To say that it contradicts facts is to say that it teaches error; and to say that it teaches error is to say it is not the Word of God. The proposition that the Bible must be interpreted by science is all but self-evident.[44]

He illustrates this with the reminder that for five thousand years the church understood the Bible to teach that the earth stands still, but this belief has been overturned by science. He goes on to raise the other side of the question: "Of course, this rule works both ways. If the Bible cannot contradict science, neither can science contradict the Bible."[45] Next he indicates that all scientific teachings of the past that contradicted the clear teachings of Scripture "have come to shame," and so we are to expect will those in the future.

Given his commitment to a scientifically executed theology and to a healthy reverence for the findings of science, Hodge was keenly interested both in science and its methodology, and in the relation between science and theology.[46] So naturally he kept abreast of the important scientific advancements of the day,[47] and is even said to have been a "respectable amateur" where science is concerned.[48] When Charles Darwin published *The Origin of Species by Means of Natural Selection* in 1859, it provoked a varied reaction from Evangelicals, indicating that Hodge was apparently not alone among Evangelicals in his reverence for science. As George Marsden puts it in referring to the American context:

> By 1859, Evangelicals, both scientists and theologians, thought they had discovered an impregnable synthesis between faith and reason. Scientific reason, the kind they most respected, firmly supported Christian faith. In principle they were deeply wedded to a scientific culture, so long as it left room (indeed, a privileged place of honor) to add on their version of Christianity.[49]

Even though Hodge did not react immediately to Darwin's theory when it was first published, he did eventually provide one of the more interesting reactions among evangelical thinkers in the United States at the time. After writing little concerning Darwin's theories for more than a decade after the publication of *Origin of Species*, he did include some discussion of Darwin in his *Systematic Theology* of 1872-1873. Then shortly thereafter, in 1874, he published a book-length monograph entitled *What Is Darwinism?* Why wait fifteen years to publish such a work? Perhaps it was a response to the increasing number of attempts to reconcile the Bible and biological science in evangelical circles.[50]

The remarkable thing for our purposes is that Hodge did not primarily attack Darwinism from an exegesis of Genesis as one might expect in view of the polarized creation/evolution debates today. Rather he approached the subject from within a broad scriptural and philosophical framework. Hodge began by asserting that Darwin's theory is a theory of the universe, of its origin and existence, and proceeded to outline points that a biblical view of the universe must entail. He then followed with outlines of alternative competing views as were prevalent in his day such as the pantheistic theory[51] and Herbert Spencer's philosophy.[52] He then summarized Darwin's own theory. Before coming to his own objections to the theory, in a lengthy section he engaged the thought of many of the proponents of evolution according to the principles of scientific reasoning. One section stands out in portraying his attitude toward what he was doing; we quote from it somewhat at length:

> It is very reasonable that scientific men, in common with lawyers and physicians and other professional men, should feel themselves entitled to be heard with special deference on subjects belonging to their respective departments. . . . But it is to be remembered that no department of human knowledge is isolated. One runs into and overlaps another. We have abundant evidence that the devotees of natural science are not willing to confine themselves to the department of nature, in the common sense of the word. They not only speculate, but dogmatize, on the highest questions of philosophy, morality, and religion. And further, admitting the special claims to deference on the part of scientific men, other men have their rights. They have the right to judge of the consistency of the assertions of men of science and of the logic of their reasoning. They have the right to set off the testimony of one or more experts against the testimony of others; and especially they have the right to reject all speculations, hypotheses, and theories which come in conflict with well-established truths. It is ground of profound gratitude to God that He has given to the human mind intuitions which are infallible, laws of belief which men cannot disregard any more than the laws of nature, and also convictions produced by the Spirit of God which no sophistry of man can weaken. These

> are barriers which no man can pass without plunging into the abyss of outer darkness.
>
> If there be any truth in the preceding remarks, then it is obvious that there can be no harmony between science and religion until the evils referred to be removed.[53]

In this passage we see Hodge defending his right to speak to the claims of scientists, based largely on a number of what he would suppose to be neutral grounds. Thus he complains that the scientists abuse their supposed authority over the march toward objective truth. He goes on to spell out the evils of which he speaks, being mainly of two sorts. First is their failure to recognize that there are other kinds of evidence of truth than just the senses, of which he mentions "consciousness" and "intuitions of the reason and conscience" as examples. Second is their inclusion of their own "speculations and explanations" on a plane as important as the "required facts." So in establishing his right to criticize, Hodge first argues that they all hold logic in common, but that scientists should be careful not to step too far outside the bounds of the established facts. This seems to be fair criticism.[54] Next, Hodge brings up his objections to Darwinism. While some of his objections are rather philosophical, such as his claim that there is no pretense that the theory can be proved, most are scientific arguments. For example, he spends quite a bit of time assessing the evidence for the "fixity of species," arguing that no clear distinction has been given between different related species and subspecies of the same species. In this he does not resort to biblical claims, but appeals directly to the then accepted science of the time. Finally his bottom line, which he calls "the grand and final objection," is that Darwin's theory is based on random mutation, and therefore there is no pretense of design or progress. Hence there is no sense of purpose in this theory. Among his concluding remarks, we find the oft-quoted passage:

> We have thus arrived at the answer to our question, What is Darwinism? It is Atheism. This does not mean, as before said, that Mr. Darwin himself and all who adopt his views are atheists; but it

> means that the theory is atheistic, that the exclusion of design from nature is, as Dr. Gray says, tantamount to atheism.[55]

So here we have an example of Hodge doing just what he had said he would; he criticizes the claims of science from the basis of the clear teaching of Scripture. In other words, he uses philosophical and theological "laws" inferred from the data of Scripture in order to critique a scientific theory. That is, we know from Scripture that creation, and indeed all of history, is purposeful, and it is God who has given it purpose. Thus a theory built on merely (not just apparently) random events is a theory that denies what we clearly know from other sources. It is significant here that in this passage Hodge quotes Asa Gray, a leading evangelical biologist of the day, who readily accepted the theory of evolution, provided the process was ascribed to God. So Hodge leaves the door open; while he clearly does not endorse evolutionary theory himself, his main target is the lack of purpose he judges to be inherent in the theory as proposed by Darwin, rather than the theory itself.[56]

So Hodge along with many of his contemporaries had a very optimistic view of the ability of the facts to speak for themselves both in Scripture and in nature, and the ability of the scientific method to bring out the truth. This optimism concerning an impartial science is certainly representative of the American culture at the time, where the notion of worldviews had not really begun yet to make its impression. By contrast, when Darwin's writing appeared on the scene on the European continent, both liberal theology and theological skepticism were in full swing as science continued its advance. Our next dissenter is Abraham Kuyper, a man who grew up in the liberal Dutch Reformed church, and, as we shall see, he learned the impact of worldview from a fairly early age.

Abraham Kuyper, a Late Nineteenth-Century Dutch Reformer

While not so well known in America until perhaps late in his life, Abraham Kuyper (1837-1920) was a formidable theological, academic, and political force in his own country of Holland and had important influences in wider Europe and on the Dutch immigrant churches in North America. Upon his visit to Princeton Seminary in 1898 to deliver the prestigious Stone Lectures, B. B. Warfield (1851-1921), a Princeton professor of theology and heir to Hodge as theological leader at Princeton, summed up Kuyper's accomplishments in the following way:

> For many years he has exercised a most remarkable influence in his own country. Leader and organizer of the antirevolutionary Party; editor-in-chief of *De Standaard*; founder, defender and soul of the Free University of Amsterdam; consistent advocate of spiritual freedom in the church, and of the rights of the confession and the principles of the Reformed truth, to which the Dutch people owe all that has promoted their greatness; teacher of religion who feeds thousands of hungry people with his instruction in *De Heraut*, his weekly, and whose lectures at the Free University have shaped a generation of theologians who are well versed in historical and systematic theology—in short, a power in Church and State. . . .[57]

Kuyper was born into the family of a minister in the Dutch Reformed State Church and grew up in the liberal environment of mid-nineteenth-century continental Europe, in the aftermath of the French Revolution and Napoleonic wars. He studied theology under the "grand master of Dutch Modernism," J. H. Scholten,[58] where he gained an appreciation for the Modernist movement in theology. However, early in his career, through reading the novel *The Heir of Redclyffe* by Charlotte Yonge,[59] he became convicted of his own pride, which brought him to his knees before God. In later years, reflecting on this experience, he realized that there are "two directions, two paths, open to everyone. Each has its own principle and in the systematic development from that principle, the one necessarily flows forth out of the other, . . . [marking] it as a life direction . . . starting from a . . . spiritual orientation of the human heart."[60]

This was a realization that began a lifelong focus on the clear distinction between the Modernist and the Christian worldviews. His thinking about this issue gained impetus when his former professor,

Dr. Scholten, began to deny that John himself wrote the Gospel called by his name, a fact he had formerly affirmed. The thing that particularly struck Kuyper was that by his own admission Scholten changed his mind because of a shift in worldview from a Platonic to an Aristotelian perspective. This candid admission made it clear to Kuyper that behind every scholar's work is a worldview that has important influence.[61] With this realization, Kuyper came to that understanding that is the basis of his dissenter status in our story and is central to his whole line of thinking: Faith at the root level of the heart's commitment precedes knowledge in every form. This difference in worldviews or "life systems,"[62] as Kuyper often calls them, is what ultimately separates Modernism from traditional Christianity, and Modern science[63] from Christian science.

In his 1898 Stone Lectures,[64] entitled simply *Lectures on Calvinism*, Kuyper focuses squarely on the contrast between the "life system" of historic Christianity as represented by Calvinism[65] and the life system of Modernism.

> Two *life systems* are wrestling with one another, in mortal combat. Modernism is bound to build a world of its own from the data of the natural man, and to construct man himself from the data of nature; while, on the other hand, all those who reverently bend the knee to Christ and worship Him as the Son of the living God, and God Himself, are bent upon saving the "Christian Heritage." This is *the* struggle in Europe, this is *the* struggle in America, and this also, is the struggle for principles in which my own country is engaged, and in which I myself have been spending all my energy for nearly forty years.[66]

For Kuyper, herein lies a basic *antithesis*[67] that is played out in all of life: two worldviews battling against each other, one on the side of God and the other in opposition. The combat is not one over mere facts, but it is a fight of principle against principle. Modernism, he tells us, is an all-embracing life system, based on the principle of the centrality of natural man. And what can successfully oppose Modernism? It must be an opposing life system governed by a central principle strong enough to embrace the whole unity of life and to guide further cultural development along the lines of its own principle. So Kuyper is more than a mere dissenter; he calls for a comprehensive replacement for the Modernist project. What can oppose a comprehensive system that puts natural man in the center? In Kuyper's view only a comprehensive system that unapologetically puts God in the center. And according to Kuyper, this is precisely what Calvinism does, a fact that can perhaps be summed up best in his oft-quoted statement, ". . . there is not a square inch in the whole domain of our human existence over which Christ, who is Sovereign over *all*, does not cry: 'Mine!'"[68] Thus Calvinism, in Kuyper's view, provides the foundational principle upon which to elaborate a comprehensive life system that can speak to all of culture, including science. With God fully at the center of all aspects of culture, no sacred/secular split down the middle of life can be allowed to exist, because "at every moment of our existence, our entire spiritual life rests in God Himself."[69] Thus armed with God at the center, Kuyper first offers a critique of Modernism and then provides some positive direction for Christians to view science anew.

Central to his critique, and in a remarkable foreshadowing of Postmodern perspectives, Kuyper explicitly denies the objectivity of a scientific enterprise based on reason and experience alone:

> If there were no other way open to knowledge than that which discursive thought provides, the subjective character which is inseparable from all higher science,[70] the uncertainty which is the penalty of sin, and the impossibility between truth and falsehood to decide what shall be objectively compulsory would encourage Skepticism to strike ever deeper root. But since an entirely different way of knowledge is disclosed to us by wisdom and its allied common sense, which, independent of scientific investigation, has a starting point of its own, this intuitive knowledge founded on fixed perceptions given with our consciousness itself, offers a saving counterpoise to Skepticism.[71]

Thus Kuyper points out that because of sin, our judgments may be impaired and can hardly be considered objective, and without some sort of underlying foundation, reason and experience cannot of themselves bring certainty. Hence they open the door to skepticism. He echoes some of the earlier objections of Pascal as well as later objections of Postmodernists; "wisdom" in this quote is presumably a reference to that which is obtained from God, and common sense presumably to that which is "simply known" from the heart without external mediation.[72]

If then reason and experience don't stand alone, some underlying faith commitments must be essential for doing science. Indeed, Kuyper indicates just this necessity and thus dissents from the reason-versus-faith convictions of Modernism:

> Notice that I do not speak of a conflict between faith and science. Such a conflict does not exist. Every science in a certain sense starts from faith, and, on the contrary, faith, which does not lead to science, is mistaken faith or superstition, but real, genuine faith it is not. Every science presupposes faith in self, in our self-consciousness; presupposes faith in the accurate working of our senses; presupposes faith in the correctness of the laws of thought; presupposes faith in something universal hidden behind the special phenomena; presupposes faith in life; and especially presupposes faith in the principles, from which we proceed; which signifies that all these indispensable axioms, needed in a productive scientific investigation, do not come to us by proof, but are established in our judgment by our inner conception and *given with our self-consciousness.*[73]

Here Kuyper points to faith as an inescapable foundation for doing science, and in so doing he lists those common areas that all human investigators presuppose in their work: a functioning selfhood, a reflecting mind, our physical senses, the laws of logic, objects of investigation, existence of something universal behind the particular phenomena, etc. It is clear, then, that for Kuyper, faith is not blind; rather it is considered "merely as the means or instrument by which to possess certainty, and as such needs no demonstration, but allows none,"[74] thus echoing Pascal and Hamann. These areas of faith apply to both the natural and the "spiritual" sciences, i.e., to both the hard sciences and to the humanities. This is not so different from Hodge's observation: There are things about science that must be accepted in common. The question is: On what basis do we accept them? Hodge calls these principles "assumptions," which could be considered self-evident and seem associated with reason, whereas Kuyper points behind the scenes to the necessity of a faith involved, in the sense of holding to presuppositions that are taken for granted.

> . . . it is a matter of pre-assumption that there is a God, that a creation took place, that sin reigns, etc., we grant this readily, but in the same sense in which it is pre-assumed in all science that there is a human being, that that human being thinks, that it is possible for this human being to think mistakenly, etc., etc. He to whom these last named things are not presuppositions, will not so much as put his hand to the plough in the field of science . . .[75]

But if the foundation for science ultimately rests upon faith commitments, given the list of ones that must be held in common for any scientific investigation, what does this mean about the impact of other basic faith commitments that are not the same for everyone? Not every foundational faith element is held in common. In particular, the rift between the Modernist and the Christian will become evident at a foundational point concerning the very nature of the scientist and the world he studies.

> Truly the entire interpretation of science, applied to the cosmos as it presents itself to us now, and is studied by the subject "man" as he now exists, is in an absolute sense governed by the question whether or not a disturbance has been brought about by sin either in the object or in the subject of science.[76]

Thus the issue is not one between faith associated with religion and a "neutral" science; rather it is between two different faiths, the one Christian, the other with naturalistic assumptions:

> . . . the conflict is not between faith and science, but between the assertion that the cosmos, as it exists today, is either in a *normal* or

> an *abnormal* condition. If it is normal, then it moves by means of an eternal evolution from its potencies to its ideal. But if the cosmos in its present condition is *abnormal*, then a *disturbance* has taken place in the past, and only a *regenerating* power can warrant it the final attainment of its goal. This, and no other is the principal antithesis, which separates the thinking minds in the domain of Science into two opposite battle-arrays. [77]

In other words, an antithesis also runs through science, depending on the extent to which we adopt principles of Christianity or principles in opposition. Of this Kuyper says, "But of necessity we must accept this hard reality, and in every theory of knowledge which is not to deceive itself, the fact of sin must henceforth claim a more serious consideration."[78] This leads to an inevitable conflict resulting from the fundamental antithesis between truth and a lie:

> The fatality of the antithesis between falsehood and truth consists in this, that every man from his point of view claims the truth for himself, and applies the epithet of "untrue" to everything that opposes this. Satan began by making himself as the speaker of truth. ... If this concerns a mere point of detail, it has no further results, but if this antithesis assumes a more universal and radical character, school will form itself against school, system against system, worldview against worldview, and two entirely different and mutually exclusive representations of the object, each in organic relation, will come at length to dominate whole series of subjects.[79]

Kuyper goes on to comment that

> the notion that science can settle this dispute is of course entirely vain, for we speak of two all-embracing representations of the object, both of which have been obtained as the result of very serious scientific study.[80]

Thus, at the root two different kinds of people, the regenerate and the unregenerate, are doing two different kinds of science, science in a fallen world or science in a natural world continually evolving. This is a kind of warfare image, but from a quite different perspective than the so-called warfare image between faith and science propagated in the late nineteenth century, and Kuyper was well aware of that.

> And the fact that there are two kinds of people occasions of necessity the fact of two kinds of human life and consciousness of life, and of two kinds of science; for which reason the idea of the unity of science, taken in its absolute sense, implies the denial of the fact of *palingenesis* [i.e., regeneration], and therefore from principle leads to the rejection of the Christian religion.[81]

Kuyper goes on to say, "Not faith and science therefore, but *two scientific systems* or if you choose, two scientific elaborations, are opposed to each other, *each having its own faith*."[82] So in contrast to the Christian starting point, the naturalistic assumption of a "normal" process of development from past to present denies two essential things for understanding science, those being regeneration and revelation:

> All prosecution of science which starts out from naturalistic premises denies the subjective fact of *palingenesis*, as well as the objective fact of a special revelation, which immediately corresponds to this.[83]

Thus from Kuyper's point of view, those who insist that there is only one science deny the reality of sin, and consequently of two aspects of God's grace in working against our fallenness: God's power in revealing himself to rebellious people (revelation) and God's power to change us by creating in us a new heart (regeneration or *palingenesis*). Ignoring these facts will result in a distorted science. But since the unregenerate inevitably ignore these facts in their science, we must acknowledge that two different sciences are in play. Faulty foundations will inevitably have their consequences in how scientific facts are interpreted.

> To believe that an absolute science . . . can ever decide the question between truth and falsehood is nothing but a criminal self-

> deception. . . . The antithesis of principles among Theism, Pantheism and Atheism dominates all the spiritual sciences [i.e., human sciences from psychology to theology] in their higher parts, and as soon as the students of these sciences come to defend what is true and combat what is false, their struggle and its result are entirely governed by their subjective starting point. In connection with the fact of sin, from which the whole antithesis between truth and falsehood is born, this phenomenon presents itself in such a form that one recognizes the fact of sin, and that the other denies it or does not reckon with it. Thus what is normal to one is absolutely abnormal to the other. This establishes for each an entirely different standard. And where both go to work from such subjective standards, the science of each must become entirely different, and the unity of science is gone.[84]

So in the end Kuyper's warfare thesis is even more radical, more intractable than any science-versus-religion warfare model a Modernist could imagine. But Kuyper didn't just leave in the wake of his radical antithesis a fractured humanity with scientific endeavors hopelessly mired in sin, with no hope or incentive to work together on scientific tasks. Kuyper did find grounds for the two kinds of people to work together, ultimately by the grace of God:

> This must be emphasized, because it is in the interest of science at large, that mutual benefit be derived by both circles from what is contributed to the general stock of science. What has been well done by one need not be done again by you. It is at the same time important that, though not hesitating to part company as soon as principle demands it, the two kinds of science shall be as long as possible conscious of the fact that, formally at least, both are at work at a common task. . . . The formal process of thought has not been attacked by sin, and for this reason *palingenesis* works no change in this mental task.
>
> There is but one logic, and not two . . . [this one logic] contributes in two ways important service in maintaining a certain mutual contact between the two kinds of science.
>
> In the first place, from this fact it follows that the accuracy of one another's demonstrations can be critically examined and verified, in so far at least as the result strictly depends upon the deduction made.

> By keeping a sharp watch upon each other, mutual service is rendered in the discovery of logical faults in each other's demonstrations, and thus in a formal way each will continually watch over the other. And on the other hand, they may compel each other to justify their points of view over against one another.[85]

Kuyper grounded these areas of commonality and hope that some common productive work could be done even across the antithetical divide in the Calvinist doctrine of *common grace*.[86] In the words of S. U. Zuidema:

> Common grace checks the operation of sin and the curse on sin, and in principle makes possible again the unfolding of creation's potentialities and the development of the creature. It fosters this unfolding, nourishes it, strengthens it. It makes for a "grace-endowed nature";[87] nature remains nature . . . but common grace curbs the destructive operation of sin and postpones the curse on nature; in fact, in the realm of the temporal and the visible it even enables people to do the good, the moral good, the civic good, opening up the possibility of progress in the life of creation. Thus, next to the stemming of sin and curse, common grace in Kuyper's view also operates for "progress": it serves and promotes cultural development and progress, and makes these possible.[88]

Thus, according to Kuyper, because this grace is common to all, it allows valid insights to be made by those who are not believers in Christ:

> Everything astronomers, or geologists, physicists or chemists, zoologists or bacteriologists, historians or archaeologists bring to light has to be recorded—detached of course from the hypothesis they have slipped behind it and from the conclusions they have drawn from it—but every fact has to be recorded by you, also, as a fact, and as a fact that is to be incorporated as well in your science as in theirs.[89]

Furthermore, common grace allows for the possibility of, or even calls for, Christian participation in culture and such activities as science:

> Common grace . . . is the area where Christian scholarship, Christian politics, Christian social action and individual Christian activity are to be developed. Common grace provides the platform, as it were, on which all these cultural tasks are to be acted out. Common grace is the presupposition of the possibility of Christian cultural activity. Common grace makes the activity born of particular grace possible. Common grace makes the antithesis, makes *Pro Rege* [for the King] action possible.[90]

However, that does not mean that we can go all the way with unbelievers in doing science. Kuyper always maintained a balance between the antithesis of worldview warfare and the measure of unity enabled by common grace.

It's important to understand that in Kuyper's view only those systems robust enough to address all of human relations can establish themselves as driving forces of history and culture. Among these he numbers paganism, Islamism, Romanism (i.e., Catholicism), Modernism, and Calvinism, and he holds that each system will have a coherent but different understanding of all of life's relations,[91] which has allowed stable civilizations to be fostered under the tenets of each system.

In relation to this, let us mention one final important point about Kuyper's critique of the Enlightenment philosophy; echoing the strong criticisms of Hamann against Kant's dualistic thinking, Kuyper criticized strongly the Enlightenment idea that there was somehow a break between subject and object, or knower and known, that results in dualism. Instead, Kuyper argued for an "organic unity"[92] of all creation, and of all knowledge as obtained both from special revelation (Scripture) and from general revelation (nature). This follows, according to Kuyper, from the commitment that God ought to be our starting point for knowledge when we approach science:

> And since the object does not produce the subject, nor the subject the object, the power that binds the two organically together must of necessity be sought outside of each. And however much we may speculate and ponder, no explanation can ever suggest itself to our

> sense, of the all-sufficient ground for this admirable correspondence and affinity between object and subject, on which the possibility and development of science wholly rests, until at the hand of Holy Scripture we confess that the Author of the cosmos created man in the cosmos as micro-cosmos "after his image and likeness."
>
> Thus understood, *science* presents itself to us as *a necessary and ever-continued impulse in the human mind to reflect within itself the cosmos, plastically as to its elements, and to think it through logically as to its relations; always with the understanding that the human mind is capable of this by reason of its organic affinity to its object.*[93]

Thus Kuyper saw in the organic unity of all creation a basis for the Christian's involvement in the sciences, and this notion led him to work out his extensive doctrine of common grace that we have mentioned above.

To summarize, we see Kuyper as perhaps the most comprehensive Christian critic of the Enlightenment philosophy of his time, with many positive contributions toward how Christians should view the enterprise of science. With his staunch adherence to orthodox theology and his avid support for the grounding of science as an appropriate Christian endeavor, he was led to see deeply into the problems involved. Thus he laid out for us a clear contrast between the way believers approach science as opposed to how unbelievers do so, while at the same time pointing the way for understanding how we can work together in view of God's grace, both special and common. While many of Kuyper's views are profound, they were also often only suggestive and remained to be worked out by the next generation. Our final dissenter is perhaps the most prolific of such next generation scholars, Herman Dooyeweerd.

Herman Dooyeweerd, a Twentieth-Century Christian Philosopher

Herman Dooyeweerd (1894-1977) grew up in a home where Kuyper's work was looked on with favor,[94] and he attended the Free University of Amsterdam, the school Kuyper played a large role in founding.

Thus Kuyper had much influence on him. While Dooyeweerd initially studied law, acquiring a Ph.D. in that subject in 1917, he was much motivated by Kuyper's many interesting contributions to thought, and eventually he became interested in philosophy, in working out a broad philosophical foundation for the sciences in general.[95] While Dooyeweerd went on to develop his fairly comprehensive system of philosophy that he saw as firmly grounded in Calvinist principles, we wish to emphasize rather his assessment of theoretical thought through which he found a powerful way to address the difficulties in Enlightenment philosophy from the standpoint of Christianity.[96] In so doing, Dooyeweerd clarified some important aspects of how to think Christianly about science and society, which will help us in our own investigations.

Let us begin with Dooyeweerd's observation that the notion of antithesis is not something merely philosophical that was invented by Kuyper himself. For "anyone who lives the Christian religion and understands the Scriptures knows that."[97] This antithesis is expressed simply in the difference between those who serve the Spirit of God and those who serve the spirit of an idol;[98] either we are for Christ, or we are against Him. Thus, Dooyeweerd cautions, this antithesis *has to do with the everyday life and experience of each one of us* and is therefore not merely theoretical but very practical. Although scientists may wish to "escape from themselves," they cannot in reality escape from "the deepest root of their life," which arises from deeply held convictions of the heart as to whom they serve.[99] For, because our allegiance to one side or the other of the antithesis flows from convictions of our inner spirit, it is of necessity religious and involves our innermost foundational motives.[100] According to Dooyeweerd,

> The true religious antithesis is established by the revelation found in God's Word. We come to understand this revelation when the Holy Spirit unveils its radical meaning and when it works redemptively at the root of our fallen existence. The key to God's revelation is the religious ground motive of Holy Scripture. This motive sums up the power of God's Word, which, through the Holy Spirit, not only reveals the true God and ourselves in unmeasurable depth but con-

> verts and transforms the religious root of our lives, penetrates to life's temporal expressions, and redemptively instructs us. The biblical ground motive . . . consists in the triad of creation, fall, and redemption through Jesus Christ in communion with the Holy Spirit.[101]

Here Dooyeweerd speaks of the "religious ground motive of Holy Scripture," which we come to understand through the working of the Holy Spirit in us to open our eyes when we are born again. This "ground motive"[102] or "basic driving force" for the Christian arises out of the truths of God's Word, which Dooyeweerd summarizes as "creation, fall, and redemption through Jesus Christ in communion with the Holy Spirit," which is often summarized nowadays as "creation/fall/redemption." As a basic driving force in our hearts, the ground motive should be thought of as more than simply a set of rational assumptions; it is the fundamental driving force out of which all of life flows: "The biblical ground motive is not a doctrine that can be theologically elaborated apart from the guidance of God's Spirit."[103] So it is not merely theology in a narrow sense, but rather it involves deeper convictions of the heart, perhaps even unexpressed. Thus it is prior to any theoretical considerations or rational systems.

If we live our lives then according to the Christian ground motive, we should think of it as living existentially in the light of God the Creator in His good creation, in the reality of the Fall, in the grace of our redemption in Christ, in fellowship with the Holy Spirit, and in service to the King. It is therefore not to be thought of as merely a theoretical reality but also as a practical and existential reality. While a ground motive is therefore not to be identified with an elaborated worldview associated with a set of rational commitments, it can give rise to one. For example, the Christian ground motive gives rise to a Christian commitment to the principles of Christianity.

Furthermore, a spirit is operative in the ground motive, whether it be the Spirit of God or some other "spirit of the age." And because this spirit is operative on the foundational level of our heart's convictions, we are its servants, not its rulers. In other words, the spirit is bigger than individuals. As the "spirit of the age," we can think of it as representing the underlying social convictions that establish the sort of community life one finds in the culture. Thus a religious ground motive is not merely personal, but it is communal.[104] And everywhere Christians find themselves, there will be competing ground motives; the Holy Spirit at work in the hearts is accompanied by the draw of the cultural "spirit of the age," whatever it may be.

What other ground motives are there? According to Dooyeweerd, in the history of the Western world from ancient times until the time of his writing, there are three others, and all three are dualistic. In each of these other cases, much as in earlier dualisms we have seen, the dualism is expressed in taking two complementary parts of creation and setting them off against each other as opposites. The first ground motive Dooyeweerd identified is the pre-Christian one found in Greek antiquity, relating to a dualism between form and matter, or principles of order and that which is to be organized. The form principles give order to the matter of this world so that it is formed into particular things, e.g., planets, oceans, land masses, trees, horses, humans, and so on. In other words without the forms, the matter would be nothing but chaos. For this reason Plato, for example, called the forms "gods." Even though matter exists every bit as independently as the forms, he favored the form side of his dualism because it is what accounted for order, intelligence, beauty, and goodness in the cosmos, as opposed to the less desirable "chaos." (Thus Platonic philosophy tends to favor one side of the dualism over the other, with the Forms as the perfect and their material reflections as imperfect copies of the original.) This form/matter ground motive played a large role throughout the medieval period, right up to the modern times and strongly affected the early church.

The second ground motive, historically, is the Christian ground motive, which became fully revealed in the Incarnation. As we have seen, Dooyeweerd summarizes this ground motive as "creation, fall, and redemption through Jesus Christ in communion with the Holy Spirit," or just "creation/fall/redemption." In the Christian ground motive, all creation, that which is other than God, depends on God alone, with only Christ as the mediating factor (Col. 1:17). In early medieval history, this Christian ground motive commingled with the form/matter ground motive in the lives of people at that time, and, according to Dooyeweerd, a third dualistic ground motive grew out of the synthesis—the Scholastic ground motive of nature/grace as espoused by Thomas Aquinas.

This view accepted the form/matter account of nature and took God's revelation to concern only "super-nature," i.e., God, the soul, heaven, angels, and so on. This ground motive holds that nature can be known by reason, and reason is the same for everyone, while only those who have received grace can have faith in the revealed truths. Since theories about nature are matters of reason not faith, they are common to all and therefore unobjectionable, so long as they don't contradict any revealed truths. Thus within this ground motive the vast majority of theories of nature are considered religiously neutral. We see this ground motive lingering on in our present times in a tendency to separate things that are "natural" or secular, and things that are sacred or spiritual. The separation of reason as natural/neutral/objective and faith as requiring grace is therefore related to this ground motive.

Finally, according to Dooyeweerd, as humanism and scientism began to change the issues, in the new secularism the Modernist ground motive of nature/freedom emerged. This ground motive sees nature in a variety of ways but always as law-governed, and therefore struggles to make room for human freedom. Its problem is how human thought and choice can be free when all explanations of nature depend on finding the laws that determine it. After all, are not humans parts of nature too? Some thinkers working within this framework have leaned heavily on the nature side and given up on human freedom, conceding that *everything* is determined by laws. Others, however, have tried to turn the tables and save human freedom by making nature depend on us![105] This latter ground motive still dominates much of the dialog surrounding science and the human enterprise.[106]

Within his explanation of ground motives, we see how Dooyeweerd clearly distinguishes himself as a dissenter from the Enlightenment philosophy. Reason is not neutral as the Enlightenment philosophy would purport, but rather is controlled by the ground motive(s) involved. Indeed, according to Dooyeweerd, the logical aspect of creation is only one of many aspects; so to take it as the absolute arbiter of truth is to elevate reason above its proper place before God as His creature and servant. Such an improper elevation of reason occurs whenever, supposedly on the ground of reason, a theory elevates one (or more) aspects of creation and takes it (them) to be what all the rest of creation depends on. But taking any aspect as independent and making the rest of creation to depend on it is the same as taking this aspect of creation to be divine; it is a substitute for God. Moreover, any such deification of aspects of creation would permeate not only philosophy but scientific theories as well. Thus the theories of science cannot help but reflect the religious beliefs of those who hold them, and this is the reason why there are varying interpretations of any theory depending on the religious standpoints involved. Therefore the result of elevating the logical or rational aspect of reality results in an idolatry—a deification of some aspect of creation—resulting in a limited and distorted understanding rather than an appropriate understanding of all of reality. This potential idolatry is important to understand when approaching science.[107]

Now as we have seen, according to Dooyeweerd, the religious antithesis is absolute; it represents the struggle between light and darkness; it is the one true dualism. But, echoing Hamann's critique of Kant, the dualisms of the three dualistic ground motives are false separations of creation. This gives rise to Dooyeweerd's notion of "dialectic," in which the mind can create a false dualism by "the logical opposition of what belongs together in reality." In faulty dualistic thinking, two "polar opposites" or "poles" that are both part of the same reality are artificially held in opposition. To illustrate, Dooyeweerd uses the example of rest and motion.[108] There is no notion of rest if we do not have the idea of motion, and vice versa. These two notions are not absolutes in themselves, but each takes its meaning relative to the other. They are two sides of the same coin. They therefore are unified when one considers the whole picture. Thus these two concepts stand in dialectical relation to one another. They are relative opposites.

According to Dooyeweerd, the notion of dialectic is intimately related to all the dualistic ground motives mentioned above; in Greek philosophy we would not have a concept of universals without the particulars of everyday life and trying to make sense of how they all fit together.[109] Likewise in the Scholastic ground motive of sacred/secular, the sacred takes its meaning in contrast to the secular, and vice versa. How would we have the notion of secular if we did not have the opposing idea of sacred? Similarly with form versus freedom, we do not know how to understand freedom without asking the question: "Freedom from what?" The form often turns out to be a controlling influence such as a law, as for example a judicial law of society or a law of nature.

Now within the framework of antithesis and dialectic, Dooyeweerd provides us with an understanding of a kind of idolatry. First let us remind ourselves that according to Dooyeweerd, the antithesis between light and darkness is not relative but absolute. The two sides cannot be brought together. Either we serve God, or we are in rebellion. But recall his critique concerning the logical aspect. According to Dooyeweerd, as we have emphasized earlier, theoretical thinking is not the place to find absolutes; so no absolute starting point can be found there. Only religion, with its focus on deity, has a place for the absolute.[110] Anything created is relative to God, without any absolute in itself. Now the basic problem of idolatry is whether man acknowledges the true God as divine or takes something in creation to play that role. If the latter, then man begins to worship something in created reality rather than the creator. In other words, man takes something relative (relative to God) and makes it absolute, i.e., absolutizes or deifies it (puts it in the place of God). "By deifying what is created, idolatry *absolutizes* the relative and considers self-sufficient what is not self-sufficient."[111] Now when something is *absolutized*, or held to be absolute when it is actually relative, then its relative opposite must also come into play. Then either the relative opposite becomes a competing absolute, or one side is elevated and the other is suppressed. Thus, for those who do not acknowledge the true God, but look for the divine within the cosmos by absolutizing one pole or the other, a false opposition is set up, or in a sense competing "gods" are in play. "The result," says Dooyeweerd, "is a religious dialectic: a polarity or tension between two extremes within a single ground motive." In other words, the two "poles" of the dialectic break apart;

they are no longer seen as two sides of the same coin, but two competing absolutes, both vying for deification. Because they are held as absolute, there is nothing "bigger" to subsume them in their proper relative relation. So, according to Dooyeweerd, all the religious ground motives of Western history that compete with the Christian ground motive are born in the absolutization of one of two poles of a relative dualism, and thus represent idolatry. Each dualistic ground motive is therefore based on the dialectic. So says Dooyeweerd:

> Because it is religious, the religious dialectic tries desperately to rid itself of this corelativity. Without ceasing, it drives thinking and the practice of life from pole to pole in the search for a higher synthesis. In this quest it seeks refuge in one of the antithetical principles within the ground motive by giving it religious priority. Concomitantly, it debases and depreciates the opposite principle. But ambiguity and brokenness of the dialectical ground motive do not give it access to reconciliation in a truly higher unity; reconciliation is excluded by the ground motive itself. In the end a choice must be made.[112]

All of this can be done quite without realizing it. The point is that the absolutization of something created has made it impossible to resolve the issue theoretically. A ground motive has been born based on the deification of something created. Something created, therefore, is put in the place of God, resulting in the restlessness of idolatry. There is therefore only one way out—to repent and to put our faith in the true God.[113]

Further, Dooyeweerd emphasizes that once a ground motive is introduced into history, it continues to compete with the others for the hearts of people. In this context he speaks of another type of religious dialectic that arises out of an attempt to synthesize the Christian ground motive with another. This results in an attempt to "mutually adapt divine revelation and idolatry." When so doing, the religious antithesis is watered down; it may be recognized in the sphere of faith and religion, but other areas of life may be considered neutral and unaffected by the religious antithesis.[114]

What does all this have to do with science? Throughout his discussion, Dooyeweerd refers to science in the context of theoretical thinking. Of course, from what has been said above, he maintains that a religious ground motive, playing the role of a sort of "gut level" instinct, is prior to any theoretical thinking, and hence theoretical thought can never be considered neutral. In this sense he agrees with Kuyper's doctrine of two sciences, or perhaps more, as many as there are ground motives. But the major point is that life and the issues of the heart are always tangled up with theory; there is no taking a vacation from the motives of the heart.

Further, Christians are not exempt from faulty thinking just because we are Christians. Without realizing it, any of us can be affected by other ground motives and cultural forces merely because we have been brought up in a communal way of thinking in our society. In other words, the real religious antithesis does not allow us to simply separate one people against another and be done with it. Rather it affects the attitudes of our own hearts, and we need the Spirit of God to help us to see when non-Christian ground motives have had an impact on our own thinking, to enable us to repent and to strive to see revelation truly, as He desires us to see.

Looking Ahead

After hearing from five dissenters from the Enlightenment philosophy, what have we learned that we need to take with us into the following chapters? First, from both Pascal and Hamann, we learned the need to reconsider the role of faith in relation to reason, a theme that was also picked up by Kuyper and Dooyeweerd. Such dissents at least provide the very important warning that we should not take Enlightenment claims of the neutrality of reason, and therefore of science, without reconsideration. Yet even that small suggestion changes the whole posture of how we are to approach science. For we must explore the fact that what we know and how we appropriate our knowledge is related to what we believe. Along these lines, Kuyper went so far as to say that two different sciences proceed out of the two distinct faiths of Enlightenment humanism and Christianity. Here we have met the religious antithesis that all of us Evangelicals know so well, both personally in our struggle against sin and communally in some aspects of the so-called culture wars.

Dooyeweerd adds to this by bringing up the important point that all theoretical thought is grounded in the heart, for "out of [the heart] are the issues of life."[115] In his analysis, in a sense Dooyeweerd completes from a Christian perspective the discovery of worldviews discussed in the last chapter that led to a questioning of the Enlightenment principles within mainstream philosophy, confirming that worldviews are important for considering science. Or perhaps more deeply focused, whatever is at the foundation of our faith commitments does affect our approach to science! This brings us back to our theme in the previous chapter. By now, in our Postmodern world, even the secular philosophers have recognized the role of worldviews or faith commitments as important in contributing to our final scientific conclusions, and for convincing philosophical reasons. From our vantage point we should not be surprised. After all, we are finite creatures; so there is something relative about our own starting point; we can only see from our own perspective. To that, we add that we are also sinful creatures, again bringing focus to the antithesis. If we Christians understand this, do we not appear somewhat foolish to maintain that there is only one rationality upon which all conclusions are based? Where axioms differ, rational argumentation cannot bring us together, especially when passions are involved. In this Kuyper was right. Far better for us to admit the importance of our faith commitments and develop our view of science from there, than to pretend that we all have the same starting point. Then we can admit our own faith commitments to others and compare notes from the "bottom up," rather than having to pretend that we are all on common ground and then arguing about the conclusions alone.

Knowing the role that worldviews play, but also recognizing the progress of much of science that we do hold in common, in some sense, every worldview now has a responsibility to give an account for the success of science, while also maintaining the principles inherent in that worldview. This is our task from a Christian standpoint, and from that standpoint clearly our foundational principles are to flow out of the Christian ground motive of creation/fall/redemption, and our fundamental commitments built on this, which are largely theological. Therefore, as we have stated in the first chapter, our starting point for understanding science must be theology. In other words, for the Christian, the first task in understanding science is to formulate what we have called there a theology of science.

In the present chapter we have also come across several theological doctrines and ideas relevant to science. For example, after hearing from Kuyper, we can no longer think about science without thinking about Christ as King over all creation. This also invokes the doctrine of the nature of God as Trinity and the fact that He is working out His purposes in history, relating to the doctrine of providence. Clearly therefore another important theme in Kuyper and in Dooyeweerd, along with the doctrines of creation, the Fall, and redemption, is the doctrine of the final consummation to which God's providence will lead. Hence to Dooyeweerd's creation/fall/redemption ground motive we must add the notion of consummation, or the final putting of all things under Christ's feet. Thus in order to understand science aright, we must have an eye toward God's final purposes in what He is doing in history. We are to be consciously aware that it is His story to be worked out for His ends, as we all play our parts.

Having been confronted with the notion that antithesis is fundamental in our consideration of science, this naturally gives rise to the important question: Are we really doing something different from unbelievers when we do science? This is the issue of Kuyper's "two sciences." If the answer is yes, this leads to the obvious follow-up question that we raised in the introduction: If we do really participate in two different sciences, then how do Christians and non-Christians work together to make progress in the cultural science? Kuyper's answer to this question was grounded in common grace. All people, whether believers or not, have been given gifts and talents with which to investigate God's creation and learn from it. This will be an important part of our approach as well when we consider how, in very general ways, God's favor rests on all mankind. However, we cannot separate this favor from the redemptive work of Jesus Christ. To this end, we close this chapter with a cautionary observation from Dooyeweerd concerning Kuyper's notion of common grace:

> *In all of this it is imperative to understand that "common grace" does not weaken or eliminate the antithesis (opposition) between the ground motive of the Christian religion and the apostate ground motives* [italics his]. Common grace, in fact, can be understood only on the basis of the antithesis. . . . The religious root of common grace is Christ Jesus himself, who is its king, apart from whom God would not look upon his fallen creation with grace. . . . For if one tries to conceive of common grace apart from Christ by attributing it exclusively to God as *creator*, then one drives a wedge in the Christian ground motive between *creation* and *redemption*.[116]

In other words, common grace can only be understood correctly if we view the whole story of Christ's work. Christ is both creator and redeemer, and these cannot be separated. Thus Dooyeweerd here fully embraces Kuyper's edict; there is no realm where Christ is not King, no realm that Christ does not call "Mine!," and he insists that the edict also pertains to common grace. The sun rising and setting on all mankind is therefore a grace to all mankind, rooted in the Redeemer of the world, not something merely to be associated with creation alone.[117]

We will return to many of the themes introduced in this chapter as we develop our own perspective of science in the following pages—as we seek to respond faithfully to the contemporary scientific culture by identifying potential and actual idols to avoid in our thinking about science. In the next section, we will start with a consideration of God's relation to His creation and how this affects our understanding of His actions within it. As we begin our investigation of theology and science, we must recognize that it is all from grace and that all grace is to be found in and through our Lord Jesus Christ.

Section Two

Jesus Christ, the Lord of Creation

He made the earth by his power; he founded the world by his wisdom and stretched out the heavens by his understanding. When he thunders, the waters in the heavens roar; he makes clouds rise from the ends of the earth. He sends lightning with the rain and brings out the wind from his storehouses.

JEREMIAH 51:15-16

I pray also that the eyes of your heart may be enlightened in order that you may know the hope to which he has called you, the riches of his glorious inheritance in the saints, and his incomparably great power for us who believe. That power is like the working of his mighty strength, which he exerted in Christ when he raised him from the dead and seated him at his right hand in the heavenly realms, far above all rule and authority, power and dominion, and every title that can be given, not only in the present age but also in the one to come

EPHESIANS 1:18-21

DO YOU EVER FIND YOURSELF looking at a rainbow or a sunset and thinking, *Wow, what a glorious creation God has made?* But then suppose you step back and think about the laws of physics that describe that same rainbow and sunset. Doesn't considering the same phenomena as "merely" the way light refracts through droplets of water or is dispersed by the atmosphere take the awe away? Doesn't it all seem a little cold and mechanistic? Where is God? When we think about the world in this way, God begins to seem far off from the "machine" of nature that runs according to these "natural laws."

If the universe is truly "governed" by laws of nature that exist apart from God, then it does seem to be just a big machine that runs on its merry way without His intervention, except perhaps from time to time to perform an occasional miracle. Of course, there is God's spiritual involvement with us, but that we typically take to be very different from any involvement in the physical world. Thus we typically live in a kind of a tension between a mechanistic physical universe in which God rarely, if ever, is observed, and the knowledge, and indeed the experience, that we should praise him for the particular workings of that physical universe. If we take God's role to be primarily "spiritual," we set up a dualism that only considers God's power at work in our hearts and forgets about the power with which He upholds His creation. In other words, God is only the God of redemption and not the God who also upholds the creation He redeems. The mechanistic idea of the universe tends to do that to us.

Are these the correct ways to think? Or in other words, are these the appropriate habits our minds ought to have with respect to God's creation? Or are we engaging in mental idolatry of some kind? The basic question raised here is: How is God related to His creation? That question actually raises at least two related issues. The first is, how can God be said to be both "in heaven" and also intimately involved with His creation? Or in the usual philosophical terminology, how can He be said to be a transcendent being—separate, above, and apart from His creation—and at the same time an immanent presence upholding His creation? A second and closely related issue is, how can it be that God acts intimately and on a daily basis in sustaining His creation when we see the creation as operating apparently "on its own," according to "natural laws," just as a machine operates? The first of these is the question of "transcendence and immanence"; the second is that of how/where we see divine action in the world. This latter question is also related to how we view miracles and their relation to other ways God acts in His created universe, such as in the laws of nature.

In this section we attempt to shed some light on these questions.

In chapter 4 we begin by asking how God can be transcendent and yet imminently involved in His creation. This leads us to a focus on God's Trinitarian nature, and the mystery of the Trinity then extends to the mystery of creation. Out of this focus naturally flows God's covenant with His people, through the mediator Jesus Christ. We find that the persons of the Trinity have roles in the covenant of redemption similar to those they have in creation. This leads us in chapter 5 to consider the issue of divine action in relation to natural laws and miracles. Here we investigate God's covenant with His creation and find God's covenant faithfulness as a basis for understanding both laws and miracles.[1] Finally, armed with the appropriate theological categories, in chapter 6 we return to the question: What is a natural law?

Chapter Four

In the Name of the Father, Son, and Holy Ghost

Creation proceeds from the Father through the Son and in the Spirit, so that in the Spirit and through the Son it may return to the Father.

HERMAN BAVINCK

SCIENCE INVOLVES A STUDY of the creation made by a God who reveals Himself. In other words, what we scientists study is a creation, and it is created by a God we know about from His own self-revelation, which comes most clearly through His Word. Therefore a fundamental starting point in discovering how we are to view science is to first ask what the Bible teaches us about God and in particular about the relation God has to His created world. We know from a number of passages from Scripture that God continues to sustain or uphold His creation, that He is intimately involved in it in some way. But we also know that God is not His creation; the creation is something separate from the Creator. It is easy to find a tension here. How can God be *immanently* involved in His creation and at the same time be *transcendent*, or above all that He has made? This is a tension that, as we will see, leads some down the road to making God a part of creation, i.e., pantheism, and others up the path of removing God altogether from present involvement in the world, e.g., deism. Rather, we would like to argue that God is both transcendent and immanently involved with creation, and the key to understanding this is His Trinitarian nature and the Trinitarian involvement of that nature with creation.

Creation and Trinity in History

Because of such obvious verses as Colossians 1:16-17, where we are told of Christ, "all things were created by him and for him. He is before all things, and in him all things hold together," the importance of the Trinity in the doctrine of creation has always been acknowledged in theology. However, this doctrine has not played a major role in the history that led us to the mechanistic conception of reality we spoke of in chapter 2, because somehow the role of the Trinity in the relation of God to His creation seems to have been largely overlooked. The mechanistic view we saw in chapter 2, that leans toward making creation an independent entity that "runs on its own," dominated the nineteenth century and does still to some extent dominate our conception of nature today, as we will elaborate on in the next chapter. But this view did not always dominate; in earlier times very different mental models of the universe were held. Nevertheless, Colin Gunton suggests that there may be a reason for the lack of connection between the Trinity and God's relation to His creation that stems from the earliest times of theological history.[1] Apparently we barely missed a continuing influence of an early and promising formulation of a Trinitarian view of creation, given by Irenaeus (A.D. 120-202), already in the second century, which would have pointed the way for a better understanding of God's relation to His creation. However, according to Gunton, this formulation was largely ignored shortly thereafter in favor of a concept more suited to the later move to mechanism.

As with most philosophical problems, the early Greek philosophies have had a large effect on our current thinking, and this case is no exception. Even from the early patristic period, church fathers drew from Greek ideas to address the question, at least indirectly, and this, according to Gunton, had a detrimental effect on the theology of creation. The Platonic view, focusing on the existence of a world of "Forms"[2] or "universals" that were believed to embody the perfect versions of the "particulars" we encounter in everyday experience, was very influential among the early church fathers. Plato speaks of "the One" as the originator of the Forms, but he assigns the role of "Maker" of the universe to the so-called Demiurge, also referred to as Father.

Both of these have eternal status, as does chaotic matter. Thus in Plato there is a kind of threefold ontology of eternal and independent principles: Universal Forms, Demiurge, and material. These are not all equally supreme, however; the Forms are higher than the material, and the Demiurge is in the middle. The task of the Demiurge then was to form the chaotic matter into order, using the Forms as blueprints.[3] Nevertheless, with all being eternal, matter in some sense participates in, or is part of, the divine,[4] suggesting a kind of pantheism. The Demiurge does play the role of a mediator between the world of Forms and the material world, but this mediator, as a lower being than the One, hardly represents a suitable model for the Trinitarian concept of creation. Later Plotinus (A.D. 205-270) extended this view of creation to the notion of a chain of being, with the One on top and formless matter on the bottom. In between, closest to the One is "Mind" (*nous*), which is "eternal and beyond time, but contains within it an element of plurality and multiplicity."[5] Next comes the "Soul" (*psyche*), which contains higher and lower elements oriented to the Mind, and to "Nature" (*physis*) respectively. Human souls participate in both the Mind and Soul, and hence represent a juncture between the world of intelligence and the world of sensibility. Since Plotinus considers the human soul as eternal, its embodiment as material represents a lowering of man from a more perfect to a lesser existence.

Gunton argues that the neo-Platonic thought of Plotinus, along with his dualistic view of soul as good and matter as evil, made its way into early Christian views of cosmology through many of the church fathers.[6] Thus Plato's influence through later writers, in focusing on a dualistic view of the universe and the hierarchy of being, eventually led early church fathers to lose sight of the Trinitarian or Christological emphasis in creation that could have been the focus had they followed early teaching by Irenaeus, who had already pointed to the importance of the Trinity in formulating a view of creation in close relation to redemption:

> As is well known, Irenaeus frequently says that God creates by means of his two hands, the Son and the Spirit. This enables him to give a clear account of how God relates to that which is not God:

> of how the creator interacts with his creation. The second aspect reveals the other side of this same reality, the freedom of God in relation to the created universe. Because God creates by means of his own Son and Spirit, he is unlike the deities of the Gnostics and the One of neoplatonism in that he does not require beings intermediate between himself and the world in order to achieve his ends. That is, because the Son and the Spirit are God, to create by means of his two hands means that God is himself creating. This is accordingly a theology of mediation which breaks through Hellenic doctrines of degrees of being. There do not, on this account, need to be intermediate beings between God and the world, because the Son and the Spirit mediate between the divine and the created.[7]

Similarly, Athanasius (A.D. 297-373), in his case against the Arian heresy,[8] argued that the agency of the Son in creation proves that He is not a creature.[9] Basil of Caesarea (c. A.D. 330-379), in following up the implications of the doctrine that God created the world out of nothing through Christ,[10] concluded, according to Gunton, "against the assumptions of almost the whole of the ancient world, that there are no degrees of being: that is to say, that everything created has the same ontological status."[11] Although Athanasius echoed similar themes, Gunton says that "the odd, if not tragic, thing about the history of the doctrine of creation is that, with few exceptions, Basil was not heeded in the ancient world."[12] He goes on to tell the story of Augustine's (A.D. 354-430) "definitive but deeply problematic" doctrine of creation in which his stress is on God's will rather than the Christological emphasis on the personal love of God toward His creation, or in effect, the covenantal relation of God to His created world through Christ. According to Gunton,

> [Augustine's] understanding of divine action becomes abstract and essentially at variance with the spacious movement of the author of Genesis. If God is omnipotent will, as Augustine seems to believe, he must create all things instantaneously.[13]

John Calvin (1509-1564), an important scholar of the Reformation, was heavily influenced by Augustine, and although we do see the Trinity in his discussions on creation,[14] it does not have the prominent emphasis in comparison to redemption that it perhaps deserves. If we mainly emphasize God's sovereignty and His providence as is often associated with this theological tradition, we may miss how immanently present and personally involved He is in His creation! With the Trinitarian focus, on the other hand, comes both of these important ideas.

Trinitarian Theology and Creation

To begin to glimpse the mystery of the involvement of the Father, Son, and Holy Spirit in all their creative power, let us start at the beginning:

> *In the beginning God created the heavens and the earth. Now the earth was formless and empty, darkness was over the surface of the deep, and the Spirit of God was hovering over the waters. And God said, "Let there be light," and there was light. (Gen. 1:1-3)*

Compare this with the first chapter of John:

> *In the beginning was the Word, and the Word was with God, and the Word was God. He was with God in the beginning. Through him all things were made; without him nothing was made that has been made. In him was life, and that life was the light of men. The light shines in the darkness, but the darkness has not understood it. . . . The true light that gives light to every man was coming into the world. He was in the world, and though the world was made through him, the world did not recognize him. He came to that which was his own, but his own did not receive him. Yet to all who received him, to those who believed in his name, he gave the right to become children of God—children born not of natural descent, nor of human decision or a husband's will, but born of God. The Word became flesh and made his dwelling among us. We have seen his glory, the glory of the One and Only, who came from the Father, full of grace and truth. (John 1:1-5, 9-14)*

Many commentators will point out the obvious parallels between this passage in John 1 and Genesis 1. Presumably John had the earlier text in mind when he wrote these introductory words, and he intended to further clarify its meaning in relation to Jesus the Christ. For in Genesis, Moses talks of God creating the world through speaking, whereas John tells us that all things were made through Christ, who is said to be the Word (logos) of God.[15] In Genesis, when the earth was "formless and empty," God spoke and light came into the world. The exact same language is used of the coming Messiah in Jeremiah 4:23: "I looked at the earth, and it was formless and empty; and at the heavens, and their light was gone." In John the true Light has already come in the person of Jesus, and will come again, replacing the created lights of Genesis 1 that anticipated Him: "The city does not need the sun or the moon to shine on it, for the glory of God gives it light, and the Lamb is its lamp" (Rev. 21:23).

John adds to the Genesis passage, elucidating the meaning of the prophets that what originally was God making a covenant or an agreement with His chosen people has now become the incarnation of Jesus as the Messiah, who came to reveal God's glory to the whole world. With Christ's coming, we have now seen this glory-presence, a concept that parallels the glory-presence of God appearing in the cloud in the Exodus (see Ex. 16:10; 24:16). This passage is therefore telling us at least two things important for our present line of inquiry. First, it draws together God's workings in creation with His carrying out His promises associated with the covenant, and second, it ties Jesus into those workings, as set up long ago through the prophets. In other words, God's Covenant of Grace with His people cannot be separated from His relation with His creation, and second, the Trinitarian nature of God is vitally important for understanding both. Jesus, the Mediator, stands quite literally between the Father and His covenant with His creation in all ways!

How is this covenant relation of God to His creation borne out? Is it only a spiritual relation, or does it include all that we are as created beings? The first hint is already recorded "in the beginning." "In the beginning God created the heavens and the earth. Now the earth was formless and empty, darkness was over the surface of the deep, and the Spirit of God was hovering over the waters" (Gen. 1:1-2). Meredith G. Kline argues that the presence of the Spirit at the beginning, when compared with other subsequent images of the covenant God made with His creatures, is an indication that right from the beginning, God's creation was a part of His covenant. In Kline's words:

> In the interpretive light of such redemptive reproductions of the Genesis 1:2 scene, we see that the Spirit at the beginning overarched creation as a divine witness to the Covenant of Creation, as a sign that creation existed under the aegis of his covenant lordship. Here is the background for the later use of the rainbow as a sign of God's covenant with the earth (Gen. 9:12ff.). And this appointment of the rainbow as covenant sign in turn corroborates the interpretation of the corresponding supernatural light-and-clouds phenomenon of the Glory (the rainbow character of which is explicit in some instances) as a sign of the Covenant of Creation.[16]

This language, according to Kline, anticipates a number of covenant-related events that come later: God's presence in the glory-cloud in the wilderness during Moses's time, the descending of the Spirit as divine testimony to God's Son, the angel in Revelation 10:1ff., a glory-figure as clothed in a cloud and accompanied by a rainbow, an angel who "swore by him who lives for ever and ever, who created the heavens and all that is in them, the earth and all that is in it, and the sea and all that is in it, and said, 'There will be no more delay! But in the days when the seventh angel is about to sound his trumpet, the mystery of God will be accomplished, just as he announced to his servants the prophets'" in proclaiming the fulfillment of the promise of the covenant. All these symbols that accompany the later proclamation of the covenant are there at the beginning of creation! Thus already in the first chapter of Genesis we begin to see a broad picture develop of the covenant relation God establishes with His people, and this covenantal relationship flows naturally out of His Trinitarian involvement with His creation. Before returning to the doctrine of the Trinity, let us elaborate on the notion of covenant.

A covenant is a formal, solemn, and binding agreement between two parties. While O. Palmer Robertson tells us in his book *The Christ of the Covenants* that some do not think there is a single definition of the word that encompasses all its uses in Scripture, Robertson settles on the following definition, which he claims to be broad enough to be all-encompassing:

> A covenant is a *bond in blood sovereignly administered.* When God enters into a covenantal relationship with men, he *sovereignly* institutes a life-and-death bond. A covenant is a bond in blood, or a bond of life and death, *sovereignly* administered.[17]

Covenant is a very deep biblical theme that, as the Scriptures unfold, is seen to embody the gospel. God has made a covenant with His people, beginning with Noah, clarified through Abraham, and developed through the prophets, ultimately to reveal that God would not only require righteousness from us (that we cannot fulfill), but that He would provide that righteousness Himself in His Son Jesus Christ and also provide the payment for our failure to fulfill our part of the bargain through Christ's death (blood) and resurrection. In so doing He would make us a new creation, in giving us a new heart. This is God's Covenant of Grace, or His Covenant of Redemption, with us. But what Kline is telling us is that God's acts of redemption are not only those particular acts of miracles, resurrection, and salvation, but all of creation must be included, sometimes as signs, sometimes as the everyday backdrop upon which His covenant faithfulness plays itself out. As we shall see in the next chapter, this covenant faithfulness is played out in various ways: partly through God's faithfully upholding the "laws of nature," partly through the so-called miracles (e.g., flood/rainbow, crossing of the Red Sea, promises of blessings in grain and new wine, feeding of the five thousand, and of course, the Resurrection), and also it plays out in human hearts (e.g., regeneration of some, hardening of others such as Pharaoh).

Creation and Covenant

Do the Scriptures really teach that God's covenant involves His workings in creation in a direct covenantal way? We have already seen a hint of God's covenant with His creation in Genesis 1, but in the story of Noah, this covenantal relation becomes a little clearer:

> *The LORD smelled the pleasing aroma and said in his heart: "Never again will I curse the ground because of man, even though every inclination of his heart is evil from childhood. And never again will I destroy all living creatures, as I have done. As long as the earth endures, seedtime and harvest, cold and heat, summer and winter, day and night will never cease." (Gen. 8:21-22)*

In this passage God "said in his heart" or promised to Himself the beginnings of the grace He is to show to His chosen people. This is revealed in two parts: First, He expresses grace to His creatures not to destroy them as in the Flood, no matter how sinful they are. But second, concerning His creation, God promises to insure a constancy of behavior—"day and night will never cease," and in so doing, He ensures also that man can expect the regularity of the creation. In the next chapter of Genesis, God reveals directly to Noah the nature of this covenant relation He has established with His creation and with man:

> *Then God said to Noah and to his sons with him: "I now establish my covenant with you and with your descendants after you and with every living creature that was with you—the birds, the livestock and all the wild animals, all those that came out of the ark with you—every living creature on earth. I establish my covenant with you: Never again will all life be cut off by the waters of a flood; never again will there be a flood to destroy the earth." And God said, "This is the sign of the covenant I am making between me and you and every living creature with you, a covenant for all generations to come: I have set my rainbow in the clouds, and it will be the sign of the covenant between me and the earth. Whenever I bring clouds over the earth and the rainbow appears in the clouds, I will remember my covenant between me and you and all living creatures of every kind. Never again will the waters become a flood to destroy all life. Whenever the rainbow appears in the clouds, I will see it and remember the everlasting covenant between God and all living crea-*

tures of every kind on the earth." So God said to Noah, "This is the sign of the covenant I have established between me and all life on the earth." (Gen. 9:8-17)

Note that this covenant specifically involves what we would usually call the "laws of nature" in the behavior of the sun, moon, waters, and light forming a rainbow. This covenant relation becomes much clearer in Jeremiah, after the full-blown Covenant of Grace is revealed. The first such passage says,

"The time is coming," declares the LORD, *"when I will make a new covenant with the house of Israel and with the house of Judah. It will not be like the covenant I made with their forefathers when I took them by the hand to lead them out of Egypt, because they broke my covenant, though I was a husband to them," declares the* LORD. *"This is the covenant I will make with the house of Israel after that time," declares the* LORD. *"I will put my law in their minds and write it on their hearts. I will be their God, and they will be my people. No longer will a man teach his neighbor, or a man his brother, saying, 'Know the* LORD,*' because they will all know me, from the least of them to the greatest," declares the* LORD. *"For I will forgive their wickedness and will remember their sins no more." This is what the* LORD *says, he who appoints the sun to shine by day, who decrees the moon and stars to shine by night, who stirs up the sea so that its waves roar—the* LORD *Almighty is his name: "Only if these decrees vanish from my sight," declares the* LORD, *"will the descendants of Israel ever cease to be a nation before me." This is what the* LORD *says: "Only if the heavens above can be measured and the foundations of the earth below be searched out will I reject all the descendants of Israel because of all they have done," declares the* LORD. *(Jer. 31:31ff.)*

In this passage there is a clear intertwining of God's dealings with nature and with His people. In fact, He appeals to the certainty of His faithful upholding of His decrees governing nature in order to assure His people that the New Covenant will surely be enacted. For who would doubt that the heavens will move along the same way tomorrow as they have today. This regular behavior had, of course, long since been experienced by the hearers. To appeal to such a reliable fact would make the covenant promise of redemption that much greater a certainty in their minds. But at the same time, God is emphasizing that He is also responsible for the ongoing sustenance of the motion of the heavens, and this is something that we can rely on, only because of His faithfulness. Two chapters later in Jeremiah, God uses this comparison again to indicate who is working out the covenant:

> *This is what the LORD says: "If you can break my covenant with the day and my covenant with the night, so that day and night no longer come at their appointed time, then my covenant with David my servant—and my covenant with the Levites who are priests ministering before me—can be broken and David will no longer have a descendant to reign on his throne. I will make the descendants of David my servant and the Levites who minister before me as countless as the stars of the sky and as measureless as the sand on the seashore." (Jer. 33:20-22)*

The logic goes like this. Because we are unable to thwart God's covenant with creation, the implication is that no more could we thwart His determination to bring all His elect to repentance. Thus are the laws of creation no more or less sure than the laws of redemption. And these laws of creation are sure precisely because God has covenanted to make them sure as a part of His carrying out His own purposes.

If the laws that govern creation are covenantal in nature, we should expect that a study of the nature of God's covenant should give us insight into the character of the laws of creation. Yet at the same time we must not miss Jeremiah (chapter 31) echoing the book of Job in saying that God's wisdom in His establishing and working out His purposes in creation is unfathomable to us:

> *"Where were you when I laid the earth's foundation? Tell me, if you understand. Who marked off its dimensions? Surely you know! Who stretched a measuring line across it? On what were its foot-*

> *ings set, or who laid its cornerstone—while the morning stars sang together and all the angels shouted for joy?" (Job 38:4-7)*
>
> *"Can you bind the beautiful Pleiades? Can you loose the cords of Orion? Can you bring forth the constellations in their seasons or lead out the Bear with its cubs? Do you know the laws of the heavens? Can you set up [God's] dominion over the earth? Can you raise your voice to the clouds and cover yourself with a flood of water? Do you send the lightning bolts on their way? Do they report to you, 'Here we are'?" (Job 38:31-35)*

By implication, all of creation, though mysterious to us in many ways, answers directly to God who upholds it. This anticipates the themes of the next two chapters: We should not expect the world to act entirely predictably as a big machine; we should expect that it holds surprises for us that we will never entirely uncover and comprehend.

A Triune God of Creation and Redemption

To further elaborate on the nature of God's covenant relation to His creation, we observe that there are a number of parallels between God's covenant with His creation and the Covenant of Grace, in which we see the three persons of the Trinity playing similar roles. Obviously we see God the Creator, as the guarantor and effecter of the Covenant of Grace. He is the one who brought about the creation and guarantees its continuance. God's speech brings about action: "The Mighty One, God the LORD, speaks and summons the earth from the rising of the sun to its setting" (Ps. 50:1 ESV). All that He says comes to pass:

> *As the rain and the snow come down from heaven, and do not return to it without watering the earth and making it bud and flourish, so that it yields seed for the sower and bread for the eater, so is my word that goes out from my mouth: It will not return to me empty, but will accomplish what I desire and achieve the purpose for which I sent it. You will go out in joy and be led forth in peace;*

the mountains and hills will burst into song before you, and all the trees of the field will clap their hands. (Isa. 55:10-12)

This passage again ties the obedience of creation to the certainty of God's word being carried out, which we see now as relating to His Word—that is, Jesus. In both the covenant with creation and the Covenant of Grace, there is one mediator, the Word of God. Evidently these are not to be viewed as two separate covenants, but one, with the same mediator acting in both roles. Let us look further at the role of the Son. In Colossians we read:

For he has rescued us from the dominion of darkness and brought us into the kingdom of the Son he loves, in whom we have redemption, the forgiveness of sins. He is the image of the invisible God, the firstborn over all creation. For by him all things were created: things in heaven and on earth, visible and invisible, whether thrones or powers or rulers or authorities; all things were created by him and for him. He is before all things, and in him all things hold together. And he is the head of the body, the church; he is the beginning and the firstborn from among the dead, so that in everything he might have the supremacy. For God was pleased to have all his fullness dwell in him, and through him to reconcile to himself all things, whether things on earth or things in heaven, by making peace through his blood, shed on the cross. (Col. 1:13-20)

In this passage we read again that all things were created in Christ, but there is more. He is God's image and firstborn over all creation. Thus in His incarnation, he actually took on the material of the creation in His human body to reveal God to us. What a glorious mystery! In this passage also we find that not only was the world created through Him, but it is also sustained or held together through Him and that through His death and resurrection He is destined to have supremacy over all things; all things are to be reconciled to Him. Elsewhere we read that God has put all things "under his feet" (1 Cor. 15:27; Eph. 1:22; Heb. 2:8). Christ has a destiny; He is given a kingdom that consists of all things. And due to the intimate interconnection between the created world and the spiritual reality in these passages, they cannot be separated. Thus the created world has a destiny, being played out in history, according to God's will, carried out through Christ the mediator, who also has been given supremacy. We have a picture of Christ's ongoing sustenance of the physical universe as God's purposes are being brought to pass, with the ultimate goal of establishing a kingdom. In Hebrews is a passage that further clarifies this relation of Christ's sustaining role in creation to His mediatorial role in redemption:

> *In the past God spoke to our forefathers through the prophets at many times and in various ways, but in these last days he has spoken to us by his Son, whom he appointed heir of all things, and through whom he made the universe. The Son is the radiance of God's glory and the exact representation of his being, sustaining all things by his powerful word. After he had provided purification for sins, he sat down at the right hand of the Majesty in heaven. (Heb. 1:1-3)*

We have thus far said much of God the Father and of Jesus Christ the Mediator, but what of the Holy Spirit? We are typically well aware of the role of the Spirit in salvation. He is the one who enters us and opens our eyes to the gospel, who witnesses to us in our inner being. He is the comforter who dwells in us; He is the presence of God in us, thereby giving us life. What is the role of the Spirit in creation? Our only mention of the Spirit so far has been in Genesis 1 where He appears "hovering over the waters." The doctrine of the Spirit in creation does not appear to be so clearly spelled out, but there are other hints. For example, in Psalm 104 we read, "When you hide your face, they are terrified; when you take away their breath, they die and return to the dust. When you send your Spirit, they are created, and you renew the face of the earth" (Ps. 104:29-30). Here the psalmist is speaking to God concerning animals; he obviously associates the coming of the Spirit with their creation, not only of life but their whole being. He also speaks of renewal, which is a form of beautification. In the book of Job Elihu associates the Spirit of God with creation and "the breath of the Almighty" with life:[18] "The Spirit of God has made me; the breath of the Almighty gives me life" (Job 33:4). "If it were his intention and he withdrew his spirit and breath, all mankind would perish together and man would return to the dust" (Job 34:14-15). The concept of the Spirit as life-giver also occurs in other passages such as Isaiah 32:15, John 6:63, and Romans 8:2, 6, 11. So the Spirit is not only the giver of spiritual life but also of physical life. We therefore cannot separate our redemptive existence from our created existence.

Perhaps even more important in relation to the doctrine of creation is the fact that the Spirit of God is sometimes referred to as the Spirit of Christ (Rom. 8:9; 1 Peter 1:11), the Spirit of Jesus (Acts 16:7), and the Spirit of Jesus Christ (Phil. 1:19). Thus the Spirit represents the presence of Christ in the world, even as Christ is seated at the right hand of God the Father. There is only one conclusion: The Spirit of God is active as the Spirit-presence of Christ in His work of sustenance in His creation. As John Calvin says in his *Institutes:* "For it is the Spirit who, everywhere diffused, sustains all things, causes them to grow, and quickens them in heaven and in earth."[19]

A picture therefore emerges for Trinitarian involvement in creation that is rather analogous to the redemption picture, with the Father as creator/dispatcher, the Word as mediator/sustainer, along with His Spirit as the presence of God in creation. Thus the Father creates through the Son, who sustains the creation with the presence of the Spirit, who orders and gives it life.[20] The Spirit also renews or beautifies creation, as He does in the redemptive activity of sanctification. The presence of all that is beautiful can be attributed to Him, even as He makes us who have rebelled into His royal priesthood. Herman Bavinck echoes this general sentiment in his book *In the Beginning:*

> The outgoing works of God are indivisible though it is appropriate to distinguish an economy of tasks in the Godhead so that the Father is spoken of as the first cause, the Son as the one by whom all things are created, and the Holy Spirit as the immanent cause of life and movement in the universe.[21]

Certainly the Trinitarian nature of God presents a mystery to our minds because God is three in one in such a way that one person can be seen as representative of another. This truth is captured well by Meredith G. Kline in his book *Images of the Spirit*, where he discusses the Trinity's roles in creation with particular emphasis on the relation of the Spirit to the presence of God:

> What Genesis 1:2 identifies as Spirit, Hebrews 1:2, 3 identifies as Son; God is one. Hebrews 1:2b attributes to the Son the creation of the world (John 1:3; Colossians 1:16ff.). Then, before the sustaining, directing role of the Son in divine providence is dealt with in Hebrews 1:3b, he is identified as the image and glory of God, "the effulgence of his glory and the very image (*charaktēr*) of his being" (v. 3a). This description of the likeness of the Son to the Father does not refer to the eternal ontological reality of God apart from creation but to the revelation of the Father by the Son in creation.[22]

And further:

> In creating all things, the Word of God who was in the beginning thus proceeded forth from the Spirit of God—as did also the incarnate Word and the inscripturated Word. We are confronted again with this mystery of the Son's identity with the Spirit and his personal distinctiveness and his procession from the Spirit in the figure of that Angel associated with the Glory-cloud and called "the Angel of the Presence" (Isa. 63:9ff.; Exod. 32:2, 12-15).[23]

Kline thus argues for the presence of the Spirit of God in creation as both a creating power and a "presence-paradigm" for creation. The creation is then to become the stage upon which God reveals Himself for who He is, in the unfolding of history. Thus creation and redemption are intimately tied together as one whole, with God the Trinity at work in both, as creator, as mediator, and as enabler of the promises of the covenant. To this Kline adds that the "Glory-Spirit was present at the beginning as a sign of the *telos* of creation, as the Alpha-archetype of the Omega-Sabbath that was the goal of creation history."[24] Our purpose, of course, is to consider the ramifications for our view of science, which we will return to in subsequent chapters. We close this chapter with a broader look at some issues involved when considering how we view God's creation in general. We note the importance of Trinitarian theology for avoiding heresy as well as inappropriate habits of the mind.

The Trinitarian Character of God's Covenant with Creation

What might we gain, and what inappropriate habits of the mind do we stand to cast off, with a better understanding of this doctrine of the Trinity in creation? We must first recognize that a Trinitarian God is usually considered a mystery to our minds. How can one being be three persons? But perhaps this is not the right question; God's mysteries are not for us to figure out rationally but to accept by faith and to learn from. In this vein, numerous authors have pointed to the Trinity as a deep ontological model for our understanding of our own context. Metaphysically, this formulation gives us a picture of the one and the many; God is three in one, particulars of a universal; and His creation bears this imprint everywhere.

For example, when a marriage takes place, we are told that the two become one. Their relationship is supposed to be one of selfless love as modeled by the Trinity. Also the church is one and yet many, and the notion of *koinonia*, or "fellowship," as experienced in the church body is to model the selfless love shared by the three persons of the Trinity.[25] In both cases the appropriate model demands that each individual has freedom, but each gives up that freedom willingly when appropriate for the health of the couple or community.[26] On the more mundane level, everywhere we look we see many in one—grass blades in a lawn, parts in a car, bricks in a wall, etc. No wonder the philosophers have spent so much time on the problem of the one and the many.[27] It is everywhere!

What does all this have to do with science? The question before us that relates to science, however indirectly, is: What is the relation of God to the world? The answer to this question affects the answer to the more directly related question: How do we view the world? If we follow the Augustinian line as described above, we end up with a tension between a transcendent God "out there" and not so personally related to His creation. This view lends well to the mechanistic view of creation of the nineteenth century as we will see in the next chapter. In its extreme form, this view leads to deism, which holds that God just created the world and set it in motion but no longer has much, if anything, to do with it.

By contrast, if we favor the other side, we might postulate a God so immanently involved in His creation that He begins to lose His transcendence. This second view in its extreme form leads to pantheism, the view that God actually is the universe, or at least to panentheism, that the universe is *part of* God. This latter view, which stems from Hegelian "immanence philosophy,"[28] has had a resurgence lately in the "openness of God" movement, which sees the universe as evolving and sees the free will of man as contributing to this, thereby creating our own destiny. If our destiny is as yet undetermined, and the world is part of God, then the future of God is also as yet undetermined. Hence on this view He must be considered to be "open" to different options, and hence God is evolving with the universe.[29]

Clearly, both of these are to be avoided. The interesting thing is that they arise from emphasizing one side or the other of a dialectic, that of immanence and transcendence.[30] Perhaps the most natural formulation of the relation of God to the world from a human point of view is to think in a dualistic fashion—that God is "up there," and his creation is "down here," and He somehow governs it "from afar." This leads to a natural tendency to think that the "scientific laws" we observe in this orderly creation are somehow built in, a part of creation. Alternatively, one might think that God mediates His action in the world through some other part of reality, such as the laws of nature as separate created entities. On this view, law becomes very much like Plato's Demiurge, a lesser being that could also be thought to enjoy eternal existence or could be thought to have been created.

A more appropriate understanding comes from reflecting on the Trinitarian theology of creation. For consider the basic picture, as in the words of Herman Bavinck, that "Creation proceeds from the Father through the Son and in the Spirit, so that in the Spirit and through the Son it may return to the Father."[31] With this understanding, we realize that God is not the world, but He is in the world;

yet He is also not in the world. He is appropriately transcendent in the role of the Father and yet immanent in the Spirit, with Christ the mediator making it unnecessary for an additional category of created reality to enforce or embody the "law," whether thought of as built in to the present world or external to it as go-between. Jesus the Christ is the only go-between that we need! Again, the Christ of redemption cannot be separated from the Christ of creation, and the Trinitarian involvement in both remains a wonderful but satisfying mystery.

Thus just as at the time of the Arian controversy, the doctrine of the Trinity continues to be important to ward off various types of heresy today. In recent times, Cornelius Van Til expressed this in his discussion on unity and plurality in "The Defense of the Faith":

> The persons of the Trinity are mutually exhaustive of one another. The Son and the Spirit are ontologically on a par with the Father. It is a well-known fact that all heresies in the history of the church have in some form or other taught subordinationism. Similarly, we believe all 'heresies' in apologetic methodology spring from some sort of subordination.[32]

Perhaps the same could be said for a theology of creation. Van Til goes on to speak of the importance of this doctrine in creation in a little deeper philosophical setting where he echoes Gunton on Basil as quoted earlier:

> All aspects [of creation] being equally created, no one aspect of reality may be regarded as more ultimate than another. Thus the created *one* and *many* may in this respect be said to be *equal* to one another; they are equally derived and equally dependent upon God who sustains them both. The particulars or facts of the universe do and must act in accord with universals or laws. Thus there is order in the created universe. On the other hand, the laws may not and can never reduce the particulars to abstract particulars or reduce their individuality in any manner. The laws are but generalizations of God's method of working with the particulars. God may at any time take one *fact* and set it into a new relation to created law. That is, there is no inherent reason in the facts and laws themselves why

> this should not be done. It is this sort of conception of the relation of facts and laws, of the temporal one and many, embedded as it is in that idea of God in which we profess to believe, that we need in order to make room for miracles. And miracles are at the heart of the Christian position.
>
> Thus there is a basic equality between the created one and the created many, or between the various aspects of created reality. On the other hand, there is a relation of subordination between them as ordained by God. The "mechanical" laws are lower than the "teleological" laws. Of course, both the "mechanical" and "teleological" laws are teleological in the sense that both obey God's will. So also the facts of the physical aspect of the universe are lower than the facts of the will and intellect of man.[33]

Van Til here anticipates much of what we want to emphasize in the next two chapters. In a nutshell, he is saying that the Trinity gives us philosophical grounds for understanding the richness of creation and also its relation to God. The so-called laws we speak of are only expressions of the regularities we observe that are subservient ultimately to the purposes (teleology) of God. Thus God's freedom to work miracles apart from these laws is firmly planted in the relation of subordination of the whole created order to the God who sustains it. These themes will emerge much more clearly in what follows.

Van Til goes on to relate this subordination of the physical facts and laws of nature to the so-called cultural mandate given in Genesis: "God blessed them and said to them, 'Be fruitful and increase in number; fill the earth and subdue it. Rule over the fish of the sea and the birds of the air and over every living creature that moves on the ground'" (Gen. 1:28). The "facts and laws" of those things in subordination to man are hence lower than the "facts and laws" of our will, in our task to subdue them and have dominion over them. "In order to subdue it under God, man had to interpret it . . .," thus linking the cultural mandate with the practice of science. Thus our subordinate freedom becomes an important theme for understanding science as an appropriate task for our engagement. This theme arises in section 3.

Finally Colin Gunton adds some insights as to the use of the

Trinitarian view of creation in our thinking about God. The first is the concept of relation and freedom in the Trinity. Gunton argues that one of the central aspects we see in the Godhead is that the persons of the Trinity are in relation to each other, but this relation is not static, but dynamic, and indeed there is freedom with each person of the Trinity. For otherwise how could we be told that the Son freely laid down His life for us.[34] This gives the Godhead a certain internal freedom that is quite unlike the "necessary" God of the medieval philosophers[35] we will meet in the next chapter. And it is this internal freedom out of which God freely creates all things. The relational character of God, according to Gunton, also provides the basis for the relational character of the creation, in relation to Him.

To summarize this chapter, the Trinitarian theology of Scripture opens up a rich set of possibilities for our thinking about God's relation to His creation. First, we do not need to be caught in tension between the two dialectical poles of God's immanence or nearness in creation and His transcendence over creation; for God is both/and through the mediatorial role of the second person of the Trinity, Jesus Christ. Second, we do not have to view creation either as a deterministic world of material with everything "built in," or as a world of autonomous freedom from God; the very sustaining presence of Christ through His Spirit allows a view of considerable richness concerning God's relation to His creation. We have also seen that the focus on Christ's mediatorial role leads naturally to the doctrine of God's covenant faithfulness to His creation, a doctrine that will be important in the next two chapters, where we see that it has definite consequences for how we view the notion of "law of nature." We will return to this topic in chapter 6. But first, in the next chapter, we will consider the important question of miracles and the tension between God's freedom and the mechanistic view of the universe.

Chapter Five

Supernatural Laws and Natural Miracles

Jesus said to the servants, "Fill the jars with water"; so they filled them to the brim. Then he told them, "Now draw some out and take it to the master of the banquet." They did so, and the master of the banquet tasted the water that had been turned into wine. He did not realize where it had come from, though the servants who had drawn the water knew. Then he called the bridegroom aside and said, "Everyone brings out the choice wine first and then the cheaper wine after the guests have had too much to drink; but you have saved the best till now."

JOHN 2:7-10

Creation and Miracles

Picture yourself at the wedding where Jesus performed this His first public miracle. Suppose you were one of the onlookers when the jars were brought to Him. What would you have been thinking as you watched the drama play out? Obviously that this incident was out of the ordinary would not have escaped your notice. Now suppose aside from the curious nature of what had happened, you were disposed to think in terms of what was actually going on under the surface, say, in terms of physics and chemistry. In your mind's eye, how would you account for what you had seen?

To be sure, your ponderings would drastically depend on your worldview. If, for example, you had no great appreciation for the notion of physical laws as strict regularities in nature, such as may have been the case of a first-century observer, you probably wouldn't even have thought in terms of the action "violating" something, such as a "law of nature," even though you would have recognized that something was out of the ordinary. Or alternatively, suppose you were used to thinking in terms of everyday occurrences being attributable to "occult" properties. Then you might have assumed that "spirits" were involved.

By contrast, if you were steeped in nineteenth-century mechanism, with the image that the universe runs according to definite mathematical laws like a machine, you would probably have thought that what had happened violated the way the universe normally works. Perhaps you then might have suspected trickery before accepting the miraculous.

Now let's suppose you were one who took this a bit further—that you went so far as to insist that science had shown your notion of the mechanical universe to be the true nature of things. Then you might even have insisted that the feat must have been a trick and that in reality there must be some underlying explanation within the bounds of the mechanical laws of physics and chemistry. Particularly, if you had only heard of the miracle, such as in reading the text of the Gospel, or having it told to you by a third party, you would likely have denounced it as impossible. All of these have been prominent ways to react to this miracle recorded in John, by various people and at different times in our history, and in a certain sense, they are all still with us today. See how easily extra-biblical ideas can creep in! The question for us is: Do any of these views help us to understand how we Christians ought to think?

In order to recognize that something miraculous occurred, on the one hand we need a contrast; we must be familiar with the notion of what is usual or "natural" in order to identify what is not. But on the other hand, if God is to be seen as the sustainer or upholder of the usual laws of nature at all times, as well as the worker of miracles, why do we think of them as so distinct, so as to ascribe them to different realms? Why do we think of God's regular activity as "natural," and when He surprises us, we think of it as "supernatural"?

Perhaps we can find one reason for this in the terminology we use. Consider the term "law of nature." The language is that of the legal profession. It suggests that behind the laws, there should be a legislator of some sort, for where do the laws come from? People of different worldviews would take this somewhat differently, of course. From the point of view of a materialist, someone who believes that there is nothing beyond the material world, the term may be taken as misleading; the word *law* would function more as a metaphor merely for some built-in properties of the universe rather than to point to any actual behind-the-scenes legislator. That is, if the assumption is that there really is no legislating God, and matter is all there is, then *law* can only refer to "the way things behave" with nothing more behind it.

A mechanist, who may not be a strict materialist but who assumes nature to operate along the lines of a machine metaphor, may have a legislator in view, but only to solve the philosophical problem of origins. This legislator could thus be the god of deism, the one who merely played the role of starting things off in the beginning, with no subsequent meaningful interaction with the universe since. Indeed, as we have seen, the historical move from Christian mechanism to deist mechanism is a very easy one to make. In the deist's view the notion of *law* merely describes the way things work, much the same as for the materialist, with the only exception that there was an intelligence who established the laws in the first place.

For the Christian, however, the word *law* takes on a richer meaning. From the previous chapter, we know that the Trinitarian God as the legislator behind the scenes continues to uphold the universe, "sustaining all things by his powerful word" (Heb. 1:3). The central question then is: How can we have a view of God's interaction with His creation that establishes the validity of the regularities or laws of nature that can be scientifically studied, while at the same time it upholds God's freedom to act apart from these laws? Or in other words, *how* does God interact with the universe in this sustenance? Did He create the universe with built-in laws so that it carries on of its own accord, so to speak, unless he intervenes in a miraculous way? In other words, are the laws a part of the universe? Or is God more intimately involved in the day-to-day "operations" of the universe so as to be equally involved in the regularities or laws as He is in the miracles? The default position of most of us is probably closer to the former view. By virtue of our place in history and our cultural experience, we tend to think of the universe as standing on its own, with built-in laws. And since that is the case, the natural tendency is to think of miracles as something God does by breaking in, suspending the laws momentarily, and doing something different. How we came to this view has a long history, a history that will prove helpful for us to understand how our present habits of the mind on these subjects have emerged. So before returning to the direct question of how we ought to think about such things, we would like to take a little historical excursion.

The "Two Powers" and the Move Toward Mechanism

As we have seen in the last chapter, the early church doctrine of creation narrowly missed the chance to be framed in the context of God's Trinitarian relation to His creation, but was rather shaped by an emphasis on the doctrine of God's will. In this brief analysis we will first see how this doctrine strongly affected the thinking of the church concerning God's relation to his creation up through the Scholastic period. Subsequently we will see how the issues changed during the rise to mechanism and how an already existing dualistic view of God's action was ready and waiting to be adapted to the new problem, the tension between God's free action in the world (miracles) and the mechanistic laws that so controlled modern scientific thinking.

God and Creation in the Medieval Church

While the specific theme of God's covenant faithfulness as a way of understanding His relation to creation was not so directly formulated in early church history, it does have a long and important connection with the doctrine of God's will in relation to His providence. In particular, as William Courtenay puts it, in the medieval period, the question that needed solving was, "How can one affirm the full freedom and omnipotence of God, debtor to no one, and simultaneously affirm the dependability of the orders of nature and grace, especially the certitude of the rewards of grace and salvation for those who perform meritorious acts in a state of grace?"[1] In other words, how can God be so free as to possibly be capricious, and yet we can in fact rely on His faithfulness? This question, though not identical to our own, has a similarity in its dialectic polarity. While Courtenay has the questions of special grace primarily in mind, we would like to focus on the side that the same dilemma presents for God's relation to His creation.

The early wrestlings with this doctrine were apparently due to Augustine. He distinguished between "capacity" and "volition," the first relating to what God can do and the second to what He actually does. Is God capable of doing things that He does not wish to do? Augustine's answer was in the affirmative, but he offered reasons for God's not doing them. Some actions would thwart the fulfillment of His divine plan; some would deny justice.[2] In his book *The Consolation of Philosophy*, Boethius (A.D. 475-525) added to Augustine's formulation the idea that God as the supreme good was not capable of doing evil.[3] Courtenay then picks up the story in A.D. 1067, with a conversation between Peter Damian (A.D. 1007-1072) and his fellow cardinal Desiderius[4] (1027-1087) over the meaning of a passage in Jerome (c. A.D. 347-420). The question: Could God restore the virginity of a maiden once it had been lost?[5] In essence, the question is: Could God change the past? Jerome said no. This raises the question: Are there really things God cannot do?[6] Desiderius suggested that God's omnipotence should not be thought of as God's power to do anything at all, but rather His power to do what He wills. So something He cannot do is just something He does not wish to do. But Damian was not happy with this formulation; if God can only do what He wills, then this limits Him. Surely there is a realm of possibility for God to act beyond what He actually chooses to do.[7]

While Damian accepted the criteria that God neither wishes nor is able to wish what is evil, essentially the same criteria as given by Augustine and Boethius, Anselm (A.D. 1033-1109) found it lacking.[8] Anselm recognized that in this formulation, statements about what God could not do often precluded what He could know, or in other words threatened His omnipotence. For God certainly knows of evil, as found in His creatures, even if He does not author it. So in contrast to Damian's list of things God could not do, such as lie and act unjustly, Anselm suggested that He could not be corrupted; nor could He make false something that is true. This last statement implies for Anselm that, as opposed to Damian, God cannot go against His own past will. In his later work, *Cur deus homo*, Anselm resolves a potential tension in his picture through an appeal to the Incarnation. As he argued, in order to do something, one must have the will to do it, not merely the ability. Thus ability never results in action without will. Now God in Christ had a human nature, and part of a human nature is the ability to sin. So although the divine nature did not have the ability to sin, the human nature could in principle sin, if Christ had the will to do so. This is needed for Christ to have been fully human and tempted in all things, yet without sin. However, according to Anselm, Christ in His human nature needn't have the will to sin or even the ability of the will to sin.[9] So Anselm made a further distinction between an action necessitated from outside and an action necessitated from within, thus rendering the latter a free decision. This notion of freedom of self-determination in God is, according to Courtenay, related to covenant:

> In developing the latter concept, Anselm put forward a notion of self-imposed necessity or causality that operates through promise and covenantal obligations. When someone, of his own free will, promises to fulfill some vow or act in a particular way, we can describe this fulfillment of his promise as a necessary action on his part even though it is done without compulsion and of his own free will.[10]

Courtenay goes on to say,

> For Anselm, the only thing that binds or forces God to act in particular ways is the necessity that results from God's promises, reinforced by the consistency of the divine nature and will and by God's integrity and sense of honor owed to himself and to those to whom the promise is made.[11]

Thus by the end of the eleventh century, while they differed on particulars such as whether God could change the past, Anselm and

Damian had come to agree that God acts by choice rather than necessity and that omnipotence meant not arbitrary power, but power to do what is in keeping with His nature.[12] Within the century, these two notions came to be called God's absolute power (*potentia absoluta*) and His ordained power (*potentia ordinata*). Albertus Magnus (A.D. 1193-1280), one of the first to adopt this distinction, explains the two concepts as follows: "The absolute power pertains to things concerning which there is no divine pre-ordination; the ordained power . . . to those things which have been pre-ordained or disposed by God."[13] In other words, the absolute power refers to the vast array of things that God could in principle do (including those He actually does do), and the ordained power to those things that He actually chooses to do, these being in keeping with His covenant promises with Himself and to His creatures. It is important to note that in this formulation, God's absolute power was seen to contain His ordained power; they were not two realms. In this sense, the absolute power should not be considered as having anything to do with divine action per se, but only with divine freedom.[14] What God does is only associated with what He ordains, but this of course is also part of His divine freedom. Hence God's absolute power subsumes His ordained power. That is to say that He has freedom to ordain or not to ordain, which is identical with His freedom to act or not to act.

A Shift in Medieval Thought

In the twelfth and thirteenth centuries a profound development occurred. The main catalyst was the rediscovery of many of the ancient Greek works, which were introduced into Latin during these centuries for the first time. In particular, most of Aristotle's works had been lost until this time. Two important figures, Albertus Magnus and his student Thomas Aquinas (A.D. 1225-1274), took it upon themselves to understand these newly discovered works of Aristotle so as to ascertain their relation to Christian theology. Aquinas, who was particularly impressed by the breadth and depth of thought in Aristotle, largely endorsed the Aristotelian system, making every effort to synthesize it with Christianity. However, in the year 1277, only three years after Aquinas's death, Etienne Tempier, the bishop of Paris, condemned as contrary to the Christian faith 219 philosophical propositions related to Aristotle's teaching. The condemnations[15] were focused at the extreme rationalism in Aristotle's system as a whole, but the interesting thing for our story is that many of these condemnations had to do with propositions relating to a limitation of God's freedom in His absolute power (*potentia absoluta*). According to Aristotelian logic, God could not do anything "illogical," a notion that to Aristotle was identical with impossible. For example, it was said that God could not move the whole universe over to another place and leave a vacuum behind, because the notion of a vacuum was deemed illogical and therefore impossible. Even God could not violate logic.[16]

While Tempier's point in the condemnation was to emphasize God's freedom and omnipotence over and above the limitations placed on Him by Aristotelian thinking,[17] it opened the door for speculating broadly about how God might have created the universe. For example, now the possibility of void space became ponderable because it was no longer considered simply illogical. By the fourteenth century Nicole Oresme (c. A.D. 1320-1382) used this very notion to suggest that the cosmos may be surrounded by void space.[18] Many have argued that, to a greater or lesser degree, this newfound freedom to think in new directions that were no longer encumbered by Aristotle's notion of the illogical or impossible played a role in the rise of modern science three centuries later.

Undoubtedly spurred on by this freedom, or in essence because the issue of God being limited was no longer a problem, during the next two centuries, an interesting shift in usage concerning God's two powers began to take place. Only a few decades after the condemnation, Duns Scotus (c. A.D. 1265-1308) was using the notion that God acts *de jure*, or according to law, in relation to His ordained power, but He can act *de facto*, apart from the law, in His absolute power.[19] A contemporary, William of Ockham (c. A.D. 1280-c. 1349), who for the most part took the meaning of the two powers in the same way as Aquinas, began to "slip" into sometimes using the ordained power for a slightly different focus, such as "in accordance with the laws ordained or instituted" or "in accordance with the common course of nature," emphasizing the action of God rather than His will.[20] Two things are of note. First, the notion that God's ordained power represented all His actual action slipped into a dualism between the ordinary action and the extraordinary, each pertaining now to different categories of God's action. So a cleavage in God's action had taken place. His action was no longer entirely accounted for by His ordained power but originated in His absolute power as well. Second, the notion of law began to be associated with the ordained power as a sub-category of His total action. By the end of the fourteenth century,

> Pierre d'Ailly (1350-1420), one of the leading scholastics and churchmen of his day, could insist that [Ockham's usage] conveyed a "more proper" (*magis proprius*) understanding of the ordained power than did the older usage that limited God *de potentia ordinata* to being able to do "only those things which he himself ordained that he would do." Hence, in his own very frequent usage of the distinction d'Ailly does not hesitate to illustrate the operation of God's power by involving the analogy of the king's absolute power, and he is prone to speak of God as acting "naturally" when he acts in accordance with his ordained power, and as acting "supernaturally or miraculously" when he acts by his absolute power, breaching thereby "the common law" or "common course of nature."[21]

Thus the original focus on God's ordained power as a subset of his absolute power gave way to a separation between the two; His ordained power included now only the ordinary workings of nature, whereas His absolute power also became a power wherein God worked in the realm of miracles. Apparently the original question concerning the two powers had been forgotten; so they came to serve another purpose. Two centuries later, this new focus had become the norm. By that time Francisco Suárez (A.D. 1548-1617), an older contemporary of Galileo, had replaced d'Ailly's "more proper" with the phrase "more usual," and he often used the term "ordinary power" (*potentia ordinaria*) in place of ordained power (*potentia ordinata*).

Even Martin Luther picked up on this theme, using the terms "absolute" and "extraordinary" on the one hand as opposed to "ordained" and "ordinary" on the other.[22]

Mechanism vs. Miracle: Modern Science Comes of Age

Not surprisingly did the meaning behind the usage of the "two powers" change from the twelfth to the sixteenth century. For the issues during the later period were entirely different from those of the former. In original inception, the issue was whether there were limitations on what God could or could not do. With His freedom fully vindicated in the thirteenth century, that question was no longer at issue. But during the following centuries, with the rise of modern science and the focus on laws of nature, there was more reason to stress God's "ordinary" activity, as opposed to the contrasting notion of miracle. So evidently the already existing notion of the two powers was conveniently co-opted to describe this new separation. In some sense, science was forcing miracle out of the realm of nature and into another category; with God's absolute power becoming now a description of action, not only of possibility.

As we move into the seventeenth century, the tendency toward a mechanistic philosophy became stronger. As we have already seen in chapter 2, the mechanistic philosophy became irresistible to Christians and non-Christians alike, some using it to support their Christian convictions, others using it to rebel against Christianity. Francis Oakley suggests that this story is important for another reason. As we look back on the development of modern science, particularly in the seventeenth century, we see authors, such as the early mechanist Robert Boyle, defending Christianity alongside their writings on their discoveries of science, but this practice gradually was abandoned. From our point of view today, in Oakley's words:

> The story of the relationship between science and religion in the seventeenth century was, in its most fundamental aspect, the story of the progressive exile of the sovereign God of Abraham, Isaac, and Jacob to the remote and inaccessible post of First Cause—the First Cause to which eighteenth-century deists were to accord a thin and

sanitized respect and their atheistic colleagues to dismiss as an embarrassing redundancy or a comic obsolescence.[23]

From such a vantage point, the writings of the likes of Boyle have often been attacked as attempting an "'arbitrary and artificial reconciliation' of irreconcilable religious and scientific positions."[24] The notion is that scientists of Boyle's day must have lived in a terrible tension between the "old outmoded Christian principles" and the "modern scientific" vision of the world acting as a great machine "according to mechanistic laws."[25] But, seen in the light of the richer historical background and tradition in which Boyle finds himself, another interpretation is much more natural. For among the things that Boyle tells us are:

> God is "the supreme and absolute lord" of creation, who "established those rules of motion, and that order among things corporeal which we are wont to call the laws of nature."[26] He points out that "the laws of motion, without which the present state and course of things could not be maintained, did not necessarily spring from the nature of matter, but depended upon the will of the divine author of things."[27] He insists that this "present course of things"—which he refers to also as "the ordinary or usual course of things" and as "the instituted order"[28]—can be invalidated by God, who, being omnipotent, can "do whatever involves no contradiction."[29] He concludes that "though some modern philosophers have made ingenious attempts to explain the nature of things corporeal, yet their explications generally suppose the present fabric of the world and the laws of motion that are settled in it."[30]

This language does not sound like a defense against modern-day accusations, but it rather sounds for all the world like the language of his predecessors. Hence, what may seem to be a weak defense to a nineteenth-century skeptic, sounds to a believer of any age the proclamation of the truth as it has been handed down to us throughout the history of the Christian tradition. What is Oakley's warning here? Beware of Whig interpretations of history.[31] To pretend that there was a tension between Boyle's methodological commitment to working within the mechanistic philosophy of the day and his convictions that God upheld the universe at all times was to read back into history a modern attitude. We should realize though that history is not the only thing to color a perspective. Two people at the same time in history can hold radically different views about the very same phenomena. This is why John Brooke points out in his book *Science and Religion*, "Whereas in France, the materialist La Mettrie would claim that the study of nature made only unbelievers, the contrary claim of Robert Boyle, that one could only be an atheist if one had *not* studied nature, was the more common sentiment in the English speaking world."[32] The point is that La Mettrie was practically a contemporary of Boyle. To have such a strikingly different attitude cannot be accounted for by the science alone. Evidently the predominant worldview operating in France at the time was decisively different from that in England.

It seems that the detractors of religion in every age will be able to formulate a naturalistic account of nature, and this is no less true in our day.[33] Ultimately it takes the Holy Spirit to open the eye of faith to see beyond the materialist world. No doubt, the mechanistic philosophy has provided refuge for those who wished to deny God in the seventeenth century, just as Darwin's theory has done so two centuries later. Therefore when, in 1670, Henry Stubbe proclaimed, against the Royal Society in London, that the "concept of a mechanical, geometric universe threatened the primacy of God in the creation,"[34] even if he was a fraud,[35] he was no doubt correct in that if one accepts the mechanist view as a *metaphysical* conviction, then there is little room for miracle. This leads us back to ask what lessons we are to learn from our story.

We started out by asking whether we could find a view of nature that would both ensure God's sovereign upholding of the universe and also ensure the validity of science—that is, that the laws of nature are in some sense "real." In our somewhat lengthy historical diversion, what have we learned? To emphasize a few things, let us recount the high points. First, we saw that in the medieval period, a two-pronged dilemma arose, largely due to the adoption of certain assumptions inherited from Greek philosophy. In particular, some of the claims of Greek logic assumed as indubitable had to be ultimately thrown out.

In that dilemma, God's providence, including both nature and miracles, was pitted against His freedom. This dilemma dissipated when the scriptural sword of God's Word overcame the cords of Aristotelian logicism. As the scene changed, a new dilemma arose, this time from contrasting the claims of Christianity to the Modernist mechanistic science. In this case, one far more familiar to us, the view that nature is an autonomous machine of cause and effect clashed with its dependence upon God. This dilemma finds the regular workings of nature pitted against the very idea of miracle. In both cases, the dialectic based on the dualism between form (God's providence, laws of nature, determinism) and freedom (God's freedom, miracles) comes into play. In both cases then, the cultural worldview of the time caused a tension with the principles of Christianity. However, the latter dilemma seems still to be with us in our habits of thought today, perhaps lingering as a false dilemma from a bygone era.

In the present-day post-mechanist view of things, the laws of physics as regularities of the universe are taken for granted. While these laws are no longer typically viewed as mechanistic in the sense of nineteenth-century determinism—quantum theory has upset all that—nevertheless, in our culture we certainly have a tendency to think of the laws as mechanistically embedded in the universe in some way, even if they are taken as statistical in nature.[36] We are accustomed to thinking in this way largely because of the success of our modern-day science. Consequently, with this habit of the mind, miracles must constitute a suspending or a violating of the laws. Our tendency then is to want to split God's actions up into two categories just as our late medieval brethren did; on the one hand, He is preserving or sustaining the universe in some sense through the "laws of nature." On the other hand, He is free to violate these laws, thereby performing "miracles." But is this a faithful way to think?

Law, Miracle, and Providence

There is another point of view, the point of view from providence.[37] From this angle, the laws, as well as the miracles, are viewed as part of God's providence as He works out His purposes for His creation.

Perhaps the issue might be made clearer if, rather than focusing on law, we focus on miracle instead. Assuming God as legislator, we can ask the question: What, if anything, would be different about His relation to the universe during the time a miracle occurred? Would we say that He stopped legislating, that He violated His own law in any meaningful sense? No, rather we ought to say that He is equally upholding the universe as always, but at the moment the miracle occurred, He (as legislator behind the scenes) decided to govern in a way somewhat out of the ordinary. In other words, the issue is not one of whether a law is abrogated but rather: What was the goal of the legislator in governing in the way He did? It is not that there is a law that exists somehow outside of God that can be disobeyed; it is rather that God, who is above all created laws, has a point to make or a purpose to fulfill every so often by employing His power to change the way things work at that moment. Regardless of whether the normal pattern that we call law occurs, or something different that we call miracle occurs, God bears the same relation with His creation in either case. In both cases He continues to sustain and uphold the universe in His faithful providence.

Thus both law and miracle are part of God's providential workings in the world, though all within His ordained power in the medieval parlance. Law characterizes His regular providence as a backdrop for miracle, which one might consider his special providence. Without the regular workings of providence, we would not be able to distinguish that which is different. Consider by contrast an imaginary world patterned after the beliefs of ancient Greeks, who had many gods (Zeus, et. al.), with all the gods acting willy-nilly according to their own interests and possibly capriciously. At the same time, they believed in fate as a blind force behind everything, to which even the gods were subject. In such a world, no one would know what to expect, precisely because we could not rely on any notion of consistent regularity based on God's love commitment to us. If things really were like that, not only would we find difficulty in carrying out a reasonably stable life, but also we would not be able to recognize when something out of the ordinary occurred. If everything is out of the ordinary, everything is ordinary.

Aren't we glad that we live in a world governed by one faithful God! His faithful providence thus serves (at least) two important purposes. First, we are able to live a relatively predictable life, without constant and completely unpredictable upheaval. This is a matter of common grace to all, whether we recognize it or not. Second, the regularity serves as a measure against which we can judge those things that are out of the ordinary. In this way, God can clearly reveal Himself and has revealed Himself. And of course He has a definite purpose in doing so—to point the way to His only unique Son, Jesus Christ.

So from the point of view of "nature," a miracle may look drastically different from a regular experience—something "supernatural." But from the point of view of providence, a miracle seems to be just another outworking of God's purposes.

Providence and Idols of the Mind

If we further try to analyze the situation, we easily arrive at two possibilities, both of which are fairly close to historical positions on miracles. On the one extreme, emphasizing the view from providence, one thinks of everything that happens as merely what God wills at any given moment, thus not allotting nature any real autonomy itself. On this view there is by definition no distinction between miraculous divine activity and normal divine activity insofar as God is concerned, because He is responsible for everything that happens. In a sense, on this view God is recreating at every moment in a sort of "continuous creation"; there is no real cause and effect. This view has been known historically as "occasionalism," since it is said that everything that happens is an occasion for God to act as His sovereign will decides.[38]

On the other extreme is the notion that nature has a real autonomy within which the laws of nature operate, in some sense independent of God, but (if the view remains within orthodoxy) that God is free to intervene with miracles if He so desires. This view fits quite well with the mechanistic view of nature; the notion is that because God is rational, He orders the universe in a deterministic and mathematical way, and therefore a "real" cause-and-effect progression is asserted. In this case, the miracle must be seen as a special or "supernatural" intervention, quite distinct from the laws of nature, a view sometimes called "supernaturalism." Among people who take the very words of Scripture seriously, both of these emphases seem to be fairly prevalent and are often set off against each other.[39] But there is an obvious tension here; one view seems to destroy the integrity of God's creation, but the other seems to give it too much autonomy. In pursuing this line of reasoning, we are actually getting ourselves caught in a philosophical conundrum, pitting seeming opposites against each other. In other words, there is a dialectic operative here also. The problem is very similar to others in theology, such as the relation of God's sovereignty to man's freedom, which have caused similar divisions in church history.

The question then arises: Must we have such an either/or perspective? What should we think about these different ways of dualistic thinking? Let's start with the observation that the issues "occasionalism" and "supernaturalism" flow out of the second of the two-pronged dilemmas above between sovereignty and freedom, which is not entirely an appropriate way to think. If we think in terms of the dualistic picture, several pitfalls await us. Occasionalism appears to move to the one pole of the dialectic—that of God's sovereignty—at the expense of losing for creation any independent existence. Supernaturalism appears to give too much independence to creation, endowing it with powers of its own in the cause-and-effect laws of nature, making it necessary to separate God's action in the world into two categories, those of nature and miracle. In the extreme, we may tend to move more radically to either one pole or the other of the dialectic, denying a separate reality to creation on the one hand (akin to pantheism), or denying God's continual upholding of creation on the other (akin to deism). But as we have asserted in chapter 3, such dialectical thinking should be avoided.[40]

Nor does it seem that the actual positions espoused by those who take Scripture seriously entirely embrace such dialectical thought. For the so-called supernaturalist does not deny that God is upholding all aspects of creation at every moment, for this would be a denial of several very clear passages of Scripture such as Colossians 1 and Hebrews 1.[41] And the so-called occasionalist does not deny that there are regularities or laws of nature that can be discovered and used for reliable predictions under normal circumstances and that are suitable for scientific investigation.[42]

In pitting God's sovereignty against nature's freedom, perhaps we have been asking the wrong question. Indeed, our brief study in Scripture about the relation of God to His creation and our excursion in history point us in a different direction. The lesson to be learned is that rather than worrying about God's absolute control or about nature's autonomy, we should focus on God's providential workings within His covenant faithfulness to His people, working for His own ultimate purposes to bring about His chosen ends. The doctrine of providence ensures a focus on God's upholding of "all things by His powerful word" (Heb. 1:3), and the doctrine of the covenant ensures that God acts in a faithfully uniform way with regard to the everyday workings of creation. What of the universe? This doctrine establishes the universe as God's creation, separate from but subservient to Him. Thus we can assert that God is fully operative, and also creation is fully operative in all that occurs.[43] Beyond this we need not go. Philosophical speculation has its place, of course, but whenever we try to go behind the metaphysical scene of what God has revealed, we will eventually reach limits, and this is to be expected. As Pascal warns us, we should not presume to go beyond our abilities to comprehend.

> All things have come out of nothingness and are carried onwards to infinity. Who can follow these astonishing processes? The author of these wonders understands them: no one else can.
>
> Because they fail to contemplate these infinities, men have rashly undertaken to probe into nature as if there were some proportion between themselves and her.
>
> Strangely enough they wanted to know the principles of things and go on from there to know everything, inspired by a presumption as infinite as their object. For there can be no doubt that such a plan could not be conceived without infinite presumption or a capacity as infinite as that of nature.[44]

In other words, we should not try to penetrate the impenetrable! However, fortunately such penetration is unnecessary for what we are commanded to do—that is, to glorify God in our thoughts and actions and to enjoy Him and His good gifts. Perhaps at this point we should heed a warning from the scientific-minded Robert Boyle:

> In Boyle's eyes, it is a mark of ignorance as well as presumption for us mortals "to talk of God's nature and the extent of his knowledge as of things that we are able to look through and measure." Whenever we speak of God and his attributes "we ought to stand in great awe," hence not speak irreverently of his divine essence without considering the "immense distance betwixt God and us" nor without a deep and real sense of the "immeasurable inferiority of our best ideas to the unbounded perfections of our Maker."[45]

The mind of man cannot resolve a dialectical tension through reason alone.[46] But it is not possible for us to understand the mind of God, finite and sinful as we are. In doing our science, let us remember our place. So although we may not be able to find the answers to all metaphysical questions we might ask, our heart's faith response can still embrace the whole with awe and reverence toward God our creator.

What we need therefore is a richer view—a view that encompasses both God's providence in its proper place and yet also establishes the trustworthiness of the laws of nature God has placed in His creation, thereby establishing also the validity of science. For this richer picture, let us return to God's covenant with creation that we have already seen in the last chapter.

Covenant, Law, and Miracle

We thus have arrived at a twofold perspective regarding knowledge within a covenantal understanding. On the one hand, we should expect some general principles to emerge from our general knowledge of the covenantal relation with creation, the regularities that we consider as laws. (We will address this more fully in the next chapter.) But on the other hand, we should not expect knowledge in an absolute sense nor in complete details about these so-called laws. Only God can know His purposes absolutely and exhaustively. This truth demands therefore a humble posture on our part where science is concerned. So the doctrine of the covenant provides a foundation for the validity of science, while at the same time keeping science in its place. Undergirding God's covenant relation with His creation is what we might call a radical sustenance, in which His creation depends on Him at every moment for its being, but yet it exhibits regularities according to His covenant faithfulness.

Finally we return to God's purposes being worked out in creation as the emphasis for understanding His actions in the world. Colin Gunton provides us with some interesting insights. First he reminds us that the goal or purpose of creation is an eschatological one,[47] or in other words, the goal is one related to the consummation, the final summing up of all things in Christ. This means that before God created, He already had in mind the ultimate goal or purpose to which He would bring His creation, which He partially reveals in His covenant promises.

Eschatologies can make two errors with respect to creation that a Trinitarian view of creation seeks to avoid. On the one hand, in the tradition of neo-Platonic thought, it is possible to consider the goal of eschatology to be to save us from the material world rather than to sum up all things, including the creation, in Christ. This spiritualizing of the eschaton (i.e., end times) has its roots in the Greek notion that matter is evil and spirit is good.

The Trinitarian view clearly emphasizes the role of the Spirit in all of creation, thus accounting for God calling it good in the beginning (Gen. 1:31). On the other hand, some treat the original creation as an ideal, to which we are to be restored, rather than to focus on the coming kingdom as being something very much richer and better than that from which we started. The Trinitarian focus keeps the work of Christ prominently before us so that we will not forget that He is bringing us to heights we would not have reached without his mediatorial intervention, and the covenant gives us the confidence that this goal will be realized. We are also reminded that creation, including our own involvement, is a work in progress, through Christ, in the

Spirit, bringing us to that higher goal God has ordained. We are part of a story that God is working out, in and through us and all His creation. This view, according to Gunton, speaks against a deterministic notion of the cosmos such as grew out of the Modern period, in favor of an open view of where we are headed. For in a deterministic universe there is nothing new that was not already in the initial state; the end is no different from the beginning. The universe cannot be seen as "static" in this sense,[48] but "God the Spirit [is] conceived as the perfecting cause, the true source of the dynamic of the forward movement of the cosmos."[49] Thus there is an incompleteness to how the universe is developing that we should not expect to see embodied in the laws of nature.

It is important to note, however, that this incompleteness is not at all related to the "openness of God" movement, holding that God changes as the creation evolves.[50] There is no reason to think that God has to change in any sense in order for Him to be continually involved in the unfolding of the universe He has created according to His covenantal promises.[51] Openness in God gives creation too much power; openness or incompleteness in creation reflects God's power in His covenantal promises to bring about His ends according to His higher purpose.

Perhaps an analogy would help to illustrate the two extremes. Consider a windup toy truck. The first view, the deterministic universe, is like winding up the truck and letting it go. Then the way the spring motor works and the friction of the wheels on the table and so on completely determine the movement of the truck from the beginning on. In other words, the future of the movement of the toy truck in this case is built into the truck, the starting conditions, and its environment. The truck is simply a deterministic machine.

To illustrate the openness of God view, we need to add a couple of things: We need a connection between the truck and a "controller," and a mechanism for feedback from the "free will" of the truck. So first let the truck have a little cable attached to its top so that the controller can steer the truck by twisting the cable. Next let us also add to the toy truck a couple of bits of radioactive material. Such material decays randomly, and the controller will not know when it will decay. Finally let us suppose that the truck has a detector of some sort to tell the controller when each bit decays. Now we suppose that the controller turns right whenever one decays and left when the other decays. The fact that the controller chooses to follow the truck around wherever it "decides" to go means that the truck is affecting the controller, and they are "evolving" together. In the openness of God view, God's purposes are affected, and even perhaps substantially determined, by the free behavior of His creation.

We might, of course, be tempted to think of an intermediary view with the cable but no feedback as a metaphor for the way God actually works, because there are laws, and there is a mechanism for God to work "above" the laws. But this picture entirely misses the fact that even the laws themselves are continually sustained by God, that He is continually in relation with the whole of His creation in His sustaining activity. Thus it would be a poor metaphor indeed because it would tempt us to think in a dualistic fashion, with the independent laws built in and the controller only acting when he wishes through the cable. This illustrates that we should not think of God's actual relation to the world as something in between the mechanistic view and the openness of God view either, but rather it is something very much richer.

The point is that we do not only have a choice between the deterministic view and the openness of God view, but we have a genuine third choice. This choice is the view that the creation is open *with reference to itself*. In other words, while God may have predestined what will come to pass, all means for bringing about that destiny are not within the confines of creation alone, but they also reside in the sustaining and unfolding power God wields over His creation. God still is orchestrating the story through the Trinitarian mediation of His covenant faithfulness. This seems to be the view favored by Scripture; and it has consequences, as we shall see in later chapters.

Gunton goes on to remind us that the universe is a free creation of God, and therefore it is *contingent*. This word has two meanings, one, that the universe is dependent on God, and, two, that the universe could be otherwise from what it is; God could have created it differently. That is to say, it is not *necessary* in philosophical parlance that it had to be the way it is. While God has chosen to create the present world, in its radical dependence on Him, the creation was entirely according to His good pleasure, and it could have been otherwise. In this context, Gunton makes another important point. Contingency is not the same thing as freedom.[52] In other words, the fact that the universe is contingent does not imply that it has in itself an autonomous freedom of any sort. Contingency merely speaks of the freedom God has in creating, not the freedom of any created being. The created beings must be seen as having a freedom appropriate to their "creatureliness," but in keeping with their dependency on the creator who sustains them. This is true equally for bugs, electrons, and people; each has its own appropriate freedom. All these issues will return in the next chapter as we seek to express what our brief study in history and theology can teach us about the notion of scientific law.

Supernatural Laws and Natural Miracles

We close this chapter with an observation from C. S. Lewis. In his essay "Miracles," Lewis says of the pre-scientific age: "but there is one thing often said about our ancestors we must *not* say. We must not say 'They believed in miracles because they did not know the Laws of Nature.' This is nonsense."[53] For, as he points out, they noticed the Virgin Birth, the water changed to wine, and the walking on water as miracles precisely because they recognized the regularities of nature. If a man were completely ignorant of the laws of nature in a practical way, he would preclude the perception of the miraculous because he would not notice them. So Lewis here makes the same point we made earlier, that miracles can only be recognized by virtue of their contrast to the backdrop notion of the laws of nature, whether we know what these laws are in some precise mathematical sense or not. But Lewis goes on to consider the miracle with which we began the chapter:

> God creates the vine and teaches it to draw up water by its roots and, with the aid of the sun, to turn the water into a juice which will ferment and take on certain qualities. Thus every year, from Noah's time till ours, God turns water into wine. That, men fail to see. Either like the Pagans they refer the process to some finite spirit,

> Bacchus or Dionysus: or else, like the moderns, they attribute real and ultimate causality to the chemical and other material phenomena which are all that our senses can discover in it. But when Christ at Cana makes water into wine, the mask is off. The miracle has only half its effect if it only convinces us that Christ is God: it will have its full effect if whenever we see a vineyard or drink a glass of wine we remember that here works He who sat at the wedding party in Cana.[54]

Indeed Lewis's point is a good one. The laws of nature are in a certain sense little different from the miracles; both occur within the same familiar categories, and yet both are wonderful. If we take his lesson to heart, whenever we look at the world, we will see a miraculously upheld wonder[55] in all of creation; we will see Christ behind both the mundane and the miraculous, or in our common terminology, the natural and the supernatural.

With this thought in mind, let us go on in the next chapter to consider the nature of these "laws of nature" from the vantage point of the theology we have discussed.

Chapter Six

The Laws of Nature and the Gospel of Grace

So the law was put in charge to lead us to Christ that we might be justified by faith.

GALATIANS 3:24

IN THE PREVIOUS CHAPTER, we have learned that the laws of nature, those regularities that we observe on a daily basis, that we trust will continue in order that we can live a life with some predictability, these laws are related to God's faithful unfolding of his covenant promises, mediated through Christ, in the power of the Holy Spirit. This is a far cry from a mechanistic view of the world! By virtue of this radically different view, we can gain some insight into what the laws are and what characteristics they might have. While we are now almost in a position to return to the question of what a law of nature is, in the context of these doctrines, let us start with a few clarifying remarks.

First, biblically, the term *law* naturally brings to mind the word *torah*, the Old Testament word for law. W. J. Dumbrell argues that this word is not well represented in the modern notion of law as standing for legislative rules to which we are subject. He suggests that a more appropriate notion would be to think of *torah* as referring to "the complete covenant obligation."[1] The term refers to directions for life within the framework of the relationship with God that is presupposed. This tells us that the notion of law is wider than the mere legislation, but entails the response by the person, and the subsequent response by God. This is a good framework to have in mind when considering how to view scientific laws in relation to God's covenantal faithfulness to His people.

So what formulation of covenantal law can we compare with a scientific law that seems consistently "obeyed" by those subject to the law? We should certainly not think of simply the legislated form of the law. For example, "Thou shalt not murder" is an imperative to humans, but that imperative can be broken. Dumbrell's comments suggest, however, that we should include the whole covenant obligation, which can be spelled out more fully in the conditional structure of the covenant with its accompanying stipulations in the form of blessings and cursings. Our example, "Thou shalt not murder," along with the implications of breaking that command, can be written in the conditional form as "if you murder, your life will be forfeit." More generally, the conditional form of covenant law can be written in the form of blessings and cursings: "If you obey, you will be blessed; if you disobey, you will be cursed." This formulation of the law will be followed irrespective of how we respond because God is the one who carries out the consequences. In other words, the stating of a law of nature describes the regularities that will inevitably be carried out by God's decrees through Christ (see, e.g., Col. 1:15-18), just as His covenant promises describe how He will carry out His relationship with us. And just as His covenant promises are sure, so are His decrees in the so-called natural world: ". . . so is my word that goes out from my mouth: It will not return to me empty, but will accomplish what I desire and achieve the purpose for which I sent it" (Isa. 55:11).

In relating the Mosaic Covenant to covenantal treaties of the time, O. Palmer Robertson ascribes a similar precedent of covenant over law in the Old Testament economy:

> Essential to the Hittite treaty form was the recognition of the historical context in which legal stipulations functioned. The historical prologue of the documents set the current relation of conquering lord and conquered vassal in the light of past interchanges.
>
> Nothing could be more basic to a proper understanding of the Mosaic era. It is not law that is preeminent, but covenant. Whatever concept of law may be advanced, it must remain at all times subservient to the broader concept of the covenant.[2]

Later Robertson moves to the relation of the new covenant to the old:

> The Mosaic covenant was glorious. But the new covenant is more glorious. The Mosaic covenant never was intended to be the end of God's covenantal dealings with his people. Instead, at the very time of its institution, the Mosaic covenant was represented as being *progressively related to the totality of God's purposes*[3] [italics mine].

Finally, in Robertson's words, "The covenant of law consummates in Jesus Christ"[4] in the sense that in fulfilling the law, He consummates all of God's purposes in giving the law. We expect the same of the rule of creation that we know as natural law, that it also will be wrapped up in the "totality of God's purposes." Ultimately Christ will give everything back to the Father. This provides us a rich new perspective of natural law in its relation to the gospel of grace. For in the regularities of nature, we are reminded that God upholds them in His covenant faithfulness, just as He fulfills His covenant promises with respect to the gospel. In this sense, the regularities of nature, like their counterparts in the covenant obligations given to Israel, serve as a continual testimony of God's faithfulness to us while they serve as a backdrop for the unfolding of the fulfilling of the promises, and the covenant promises take precedence. Let these regularities therefore be an encouragement to us; whenever we experience them, through the eye of faith, let us be reminded of the faithful God whom we serve and in a very real sense is serving us through them.

What Is a Law of Nature?

This larger covenantal framework of the law given above forms the context from which we can answer the question: "What is a law of nature?" But first we need to make a few remarks. We want to discuss in what sense these laws can be said to be "real." Let's start with an example. It is our experience that if we drop a ball off our porch, it speeds up. And this same thing happens every time we do it; so we can even count on it. The ball behaves in this repeatable fashion every time, and in that sense the effect is a real phenomenon. It is not a product of our imagination, and it is also not simply a generalization of the way things behave. Rather there is a real constraint on the ball that it must behave that way. In other words, there is a law involved that must be obeyed. The law does not exist independently of the rest of the created universe, and certainly it is not independent of God, and hence it is not something that God Himself must obey. Rather it is part and parcel of the way God governs His creation, an inherent part of God's upholding of creation in His faithfulness. All who are "under the law" must "obey the law" and can be said to be "subject to the law."[5] In the example above, the ball is subject to the law of gravity as are we all. So there is real order in creation in the form of laws that have necessary consequences for the entities subject to them. Nevertheless, these laws need not be thought of as "built-in" to creation in any way other than that they are part of the continuing covenantal faithfulness of God upholding what He has created, through His sustenance in Christ.

We also wish to stress that there are two sides to this issue. When speaking of laws of nature, scientists may be referring to the actual regularities as described above, but just as likely, they may refer to our description of the law that we may formulate using language, or in the above example, using mathematics.[6] The fact of the matter is that we don't really know if our descriptions coincide with reality exactly, and all we have to work with is our descriptions and our experience, which means the descriptions often become the thing of conversation when speaking of law rather than the reality itself. In the above example, we might illustrate the first sense of law by saying that it is a law of nature that things accelerate when they fall, and then use the ball dropping off the porch as an example. This is a law of nature in a general sense and is undoubtedly true. In the other sense we might refer to the "law of gravity" as the account of the falling ball within the mathematical framework used to describe it, by which we really mean Einstein's theory of general relativity. But however accurate we find Einstein's theory to be as a description of the phenomena, we can never know if we have captured the reality precisely, and in view of the fact that God's purposes are not merely material, it would be surprising if we have. And of course our example of gravity lends itself to a mathematical description that is a special case in which our description has rather precise ramifications. There are also other observed regularities in nature that we cannot describe so precisely; there are biological regularities, psychological regularities, linguistic, logical, economic regularities, and so on. In all these cases we note that the regularities occur, which indicates operative laws, and it is generally our task in science to try to understand and describe them.

Now that we have seen the two sides of law, the reality of the consequences on their subjects as well as our descriptions of them, we can return to the question: "What is a law of nature?" Our answer: *A law of nature is God's sustaining of, or man's description of, that pattern of regularity that we observe in nature as God works out His purposes towards His own ends in His covenant faithfulness, through His Son, the eternal Word, by means of His Spirit.* So "law of nature" then can mean either the relations God upholds in creation that provide for creation's order and regularity, or it can mean our attempts to grasp part of that order in a verbal or mathematical description of it. This definition is couched within a Trinitarian and covenantal form and also brings together two sides of law—its "objective" orientation towards what is external to man as well as its status as a "subjective" product of man's observation and insight regarding the world.[7] Thus it reflects and bears the marks not only of the world but also of man's interpretive activities. These two sides of the law are often seen in antithetical terms, but this need not be the case when we note that both the objective and the subjective sides are features of creation and are together bound up in God's sovereign purposes for creation. Thus we see the importance of teleology[8] in relation to scientific law. In some contexts it might be important to know which side we are focusing on, the reality of the law or our description of it, but in many contexts it is not important.

Let us first say a few words about the objective side of law. We expect order or patterns of regularity, and we expect things to work in a certain way consistently, for a number of reasons as discussed in the previous chapter. For example, God had promised in so many words to Noah that the creation would go on as it was until the judgment day. One reading of this would be that the patterns of the physical world would not change drastically, so that we would have some assurance that at least insofar as nature is concerned, things will be more or less the same tomorrow as they are today. Thus we are guaranteed a backdrop of constancy within which to function in our God-given task of serving Him. In this way, we see the regularities of nature as both personal and riddled with grace. This view seems to be borne out in the passages in Jeremiah 31 and 33 quoted in chapter 4.

However, since we only really know our experience of and our description of laws of nature, for the most part we will presume in what follows that we have the subjective side in mind. In our experience, of course, we don't just call anything we see a law. The status of *law* is given to a description of a pattern of recurring events, rather than just individual events. The law then represents an inductive leap from the particulars to the general pattern. However, we should be perfectly clear that we make no assumptions that the law is universal in any sense other than as related to God's purposes. In other words, it does not govern apart from God, and it only governs its appropriate subjects. Our notion is thus very close to G. C. Berkouwer's (1903-1996) view of general revelation when he says it refers to the "universality of *God's* action *in created reality* [italics ours]"[9] in the sense that the law is expected to produce recurring phenomena, and when we formulate a descriptive law of nature, there is an *expectation of universality of experience* in the descriptive domain of that law. However, we must always allow that God's purposes could be not completely in keeping with the description. God is above the law and can always do otherwise.

We should point out that even our usage of the term "law" is not universal terminology; people use the term "law of nature" in many ways. Even among Christians there are various notions of the meaning of the term. For example, some believe that a law of nature refers to something *exactly* descriptive of what is going on. (It may be for the most part, but as we have said, we make no claims that we can know that.) Others use the term in a way that more closely parallels the word "law" with its legal connotations. Thus a law would refer to a *prescription* for how nature behaves, or a *governing* of nature. This latter definition forces the invention of a new category for created reality: law, to which creation is subject. Indeed, some speak of a threefold metaphysics,[10] wherein law is properly understood to be a creature of God, mediating between God and His creation. However, this conception runs the danger of depersonalizing the mediator. If law is thought of as a third metaphysical category of a triune ontology, something created rather than identified with the mediating function of the Word, it becomes an impersonal mediator.[11] However, as we have seen in chapter 4, the mediation of Christ and the immanent presence of the Spirit precludes the need of any further mediation.

Dangers also lurk in our thinking about laws of nature in the form of the two tendencies we met in the previous chapter. Most prevalent, by now (after having gone through the mechanistic period of science) the tendency to think of the law as independent is embedded in our cultural thinking. The danger here is thinking of law plus creation as somehow independent of God, so that creation is seen as a machine complete with its own built-in laws. This can lead to a deist habit of thought, which is certainly to be avoided. The antidote is to dwell on the continued sustenance of God in Christ as necessary for upholding His covenantal laws. On the other hand, if we dwell too much on God's activity and not enough on the reality of the law in creation, we run the risk of making everything an independent temporal act of God, which lends toward occasionalism. The antidote to this is to remember that subjects of the law really must obey!

Covenant Law—Characteristics

In this final section of the chapter we pose the question: From what we know about God's relation to His creation, what can we expect concerning the nature of scientific laws? Before addressing this in our context, we would like to point out a couple ways one can go astray in approaching this question. Over the course of history, there have been many attempts to either ascribe attributes of God to the world or limit God's ability to act in the world. For example, Newton thought that because God is infinite, the universe must be infinite to reflect this quality of the Creator. That is why he proposed that space must be described by Euclidean geometry, which itself describes an infinite space. However, there is a basic logical fallacy here; there is no reason that the universe God creates should bear His attributes. If it did, it would also have to be eternal and unchangeable, and so on. Instead we should only expect that the universe should be an expression of His creative freedom consistent with His character. Thus there is no reason to expect the universe to be infinite.

On the other hand, some have suggested that because God is sovereign and reigns over whatever happens, chance has no place in His creation.[12] While there is some truth in this in the sense that nothing happens apart from His will, why would we think that just because God knows (and therefore presumably orchestrates) all outcomes, something in creation cannot appear random to us? There is a big difference between God insuring the outcomes He wills and His building of these outcomes into the universe as laws of nature. God is at work in upholding the universe at all times and is not limited to a cause-and-effect development to effect His purposes; so why not expect surprises? We should not confuse God's knowledge with what He reveals to us. What appears as randomness to us need not be randomness to God. In other words, why think that something that looks random to us cannot be used by God in a more definitive manner? The Scriptures clearly teach us that He works in the apparently chaotic behavior of the weather (Ps. 107:29; Nahum 1:3-4; Luke 8:24); so why not affirm that He is also at work in such apparent randomness as found in quantum theory?

Indeed, some have suggested that it is in the very randomness that we find God's actions. This of course goes too far; while we must affirm that God certainly can and does act through the apparent nondeterministic behavior of quantum systems, we must be quick to say also that if limited to this, it would be a very restricted view of God's action indeed.[13] God acts through the regularities as well as through the apparent randomness of the laws as He upholds them in Christ by His powerful Word (see Heb. 1:3) however He sees fit. Therefore we shouldn't insist that the world is made in the image of God; nor should we insist that God must follow some patterns "built in" to the world. Instead, we should ascribe to God the freedom that He has in carrying out His purposes. This speaks against both the idea of a purely mechanistic universe and the idea that divine action is limited to apparent randomness.

So if nature should not be viewed as taking on God's attributes, and if neither our mechanistic notions of nature nor the apparent randomness in the universe should be used to limit God's activity, can we make positive statements as to the appropriate way to view the situation? We would like to suggest that the covenant-Trinitarian view of creation implies certain characteristics that we should expect to find in the laws of nature. In short, the laws should reflect creation's creatureliness, creation's contingency, the perspectival nature of laws, the incompleteness and irreducibility of creation, and the importance of teleology. We address each of these points in the remainder of the chapter.

First, God's creation is *creaturely*. By this we mean that the creation is not God, that it had a beginning, and that it is not self-sustaining but dependent on God. This is the flip side of expecting the universe to have the attributes that God Himself has. On the contrary, it should be distinctive in its appropriate creatureliness, with characteristics that do not tempt us to fall into pantheism.

Second, if we think back to the medieval debate between necessity and freedom (absolute and ordained powers) as outlined in the previous chapter, we realize that the creation, as continually dependent on God, must be a *contingent* creation; it is not necessary in the philosophical sense that it must be the way it is; nor is it random or arbitrary. God could have created the universe differently; the universe He did create is the one He chose out of all the possibilities, and it could have been otherwise. Therefore it is contingent, the contingency depending on God's purposes. Since creation is dependent on God moment by moment for its sustenance, there is therefore no room for absolutely autonomous attributes in creation in any sense, and hence no absolute freedom. We should thus not be tempted to think in dialectical terms between necessity and freedom. As Gunton has argued, God has His inner freedom, which is expressed in a properly subordinate and creaturely freedom for us as sustained by Christ in the Holy Spirit and being directed toward His purposes.[14] Absolute freedom is not a creaturely characteristic.

Because creation is contingent, there is no merely logical argument for figuring out how creation must behave. This flies in the face of Aristotelian physics. His typical approach was to reason logically about the supposed purpose of an object to deduce how it would behave. For example, out of the four elements—earth, fire, water, and air—a rock is supposed to be made up mostly of earth. Therefore when dropped, it would seek its "proper place" on the ground where earthy things belong. He argued that heavier things would fall to the earth faster than lighter things because of this idea.[15] But the contingency of creation tells us that this was an incorrect approach to physics. We just can't get around studying nature itself to see how it behaves; laws can only be determined by painstaking measurement.[16] There are constraints "out there" in creation that we all run into, but we must use empirical methods to discover them. This is not to say that the laws are illogical, but merely that one can easily err in adopting faulty premises if one relies too strongly on what appears to be clear according to hunches formed in advance. History teaches us this lesson only too well.

Third, the laws of nature are inherently *perspectival.* Each one of us as creatures can only see things from our own vantage point or perspective (the egocentric predicament we met in chapter 2 in conjunction with the discovery of worldviews). Thus there is a relative aspect to our judgments; all of our experience is perspectival, or relative to our own perspective. No creature has the absolute perspective that God possesses. Therefore all that we are, including our understanding of meaning and even our being, can only be relative to Him. As finite creatures, our views are necessarily perspectival and dependent on whatever is accessible to us as individuals in our learning process, a situation that results in a form of epistemological relativity. This should not be confused with relativism, however, since we do have an absolute Judge, and we also have His revelatory words in the Scriptures. However it does have ramifications for our own understanding and interpretation of things, including the Scriptures, and in particular also for our understanding of nature.

This notion was not understood until fairly recently in the history of science, only coming to fruition in Einstein's theory of relativity. In his theory, relativity of perspective implies that each person's measurement depends on his own frame of reference (with respect to motion) relative to that of others. However, this does not imply that there are no mutually agreed upon "facts" in creation (what we might consider "relative absolutes") and that we are imprisoned within our perspectives. On the contrary, in Einstein's theory, if we know the relative motion between two reference frames, we can interpolate between them and agree on how each other perceives things even though individually we are only perceiving from our own reference frame. And perhaps more substantial, we can agree upon the mathematical form of physical laws. For this reason, Einstein himself suggested that the theory should be considered a theory of invariances rather than one that focuses mainly on relativity. The important point here is that we should expect our laws to reflect this relativity, and it may impose some constraints on what can be construed as objective.[17] The theory of relativity has forced us to abandon the notion that space and time are individually absolute; we now take them as relative to the perspective of the observer. However, the laws of physics remain the same regardless of perspective, thus constituting constraints of creation upon all of us.

Next we turn to the notions of *incompleteness*[18] and of *teleology* that we met in the previous chapter, two intimately related concepts. In fact, the flow is from the second to the first. Because God is bringing His creation to the ultimate purposes for which He has created it, and these purposes are higher than any aspect of creation itself, we should expect to see incompleteness in creation that is expressed in some way in the laws of nature. As we have seen in the previous chapter, the mechanistic view of the world made the mistake of thinking that the world would evolve according to completely mechanistic laws. But if this were the case, the end would be built into the beginning; nothing new would appear that in principle could not already be anticipated from the state of the universe at any given time.

However, because God's purposes are higher than those that mechanistic laws can express, there is no reason at all to expect the attempts of mere humans to formulate laws of nature to arrive at the possibility of predicting the future completely. In keeping with this, if

God is working throughout history and in all details to bring about His eternal purposes, there is every reason to expect that the laws that we formulate would in some way reflect this. In the previous chapter we have put forward a picture in which all of God's workings are of a piece; we cannot really separate laws from miracles insofar as He is concerned, because they are unified under His purposes for His creation. Here we suggest that even the laws themselves should exhibit an incompleteness, because they are only part of the story. (Remember, we are talking here about our descriptions of God's ordinances.) In other words, because God is actively working out His purposes in creation over time, at any given moment in history there is more to the story than creation itself; the end is not built into the beginning. That is to say that the laws of nature as we perceive them cannot embody the whole story of creation because they do not embody the full purposes of God for His creation. The ultimate purpose is fully understood and determined by God alone, and the "laws" we discover through experimental observation should therefore not be expected to be complete. God's purposes are not merely physical; nor are they merely biological, psychological, and so on. His purposes subsume all of these "sub-realms." It should therefore be no surprise if the laws we formulate exhibit an incompleteness of some sort, in the sense that we cannot predict the future completely, based on laws that merely describe each of these sub-realms.

Perhaps an analogy of human creativity might be helpful. Donald Knuth is well known for creating a computer program for typesetting mathematics called TeX.[19] Knuth spent several years developing his program, a large part of which went into understanding how he could create fonts on the computer that would have some resemblance to the aesthetically pleasing appearance of those created by typesetters. He started out by trying to study the actual fonts of the typesetters in order to find some simple mathematical description of them. But after several failed attempts he realized he would not get what he wanted in that way. Then in his own words, "Finally a simple thought struck me. *Those letters were designed by people.* If I could understand what those people had in their minds when they were drawing the letters, then I could program a computer to carry out the same ideas. Instead of merely copying the form of the ideas, my goal was therefore to copy the intelligence underlying the form."[20] So he finally realized that there was more to the fonts than merely the fonts themselves. Part of the story was what the designers were trying to get at in creating the fonts, and these ideas could not be read off from just examining the fonts alone. So ultimately Knuth had to go talk to the people who designed the fonts to figure out the broader framework.

Our attempt to formulate physical laws is actually rather similar. We write down mathematical equations to describe what we see, but we are only actually capturing a part of the story. To understand the whole picture, we would have to go to the mind of the Creator. The analogy of typesetters' fonts helps us see that the purposes for which the creation is made, those that structure the creation, can lie outside of creation itself as ends or goals set by the Creator.

The relation between our descriptive laws of nature and the actual outworkings of God's purposes can be viewed as analogous to the "letter" of the Old Testament law and the "Spirit" of the law. For "he has made us competent as ministers of a new covenant—not of the letter but of the Spirit; for the letter kills, but the Spirit gives life" (2 Cor. 3:6). The Spirit of the law can never be fully encompassed by writing down rules, but can only be worked out in its fullness by the Spirit of God working in our hearts. So it is with the laws of nature that we write down. They are "rules" describing God's outworkings of His purposes. In this sense, like the Old Testament law, the laws of nature are only a shadow of the reality they describe.[21] The point again is that there is more to the design of creation than is embodied in it, and the Creator continues to interact immanently in the universe, upholding the laws of nature as He sees fit. So remember also that when we find incompleteness, we should not think that it is "the place" where God interacts with the universe. He acts throughout. We need not look to one particular place or another to see Him working. We merely need to ask the Holy Spirit to train our hearts to use the eye of faith to see Him working everywhere.

How would we expect incompleteness to appear? In fact we already seem to see incompleteness appearing at many levels. We see incompleteness in the surprising world of quantum physics with its dependence on probability, its uncertainty principle, and the deep mysteries of so-called entanglement.[22] Chaos theory, which apparently describes a broad array of phenomena in nature and human activity, with feedback, can be argued to include such incompleteness.[23] We also observe a behavioral incompleteness in animals, whether it is called will or given some other name.[24] In humans, we have incompleteness in our own will, and in societal laws there is incompleteness exhibited in many respects due to the complexity of the systems. We even see an incompleteness to the structure of mathematics in Gödel's theorem.[25] So let us repeat: The real crux of the issue is that the fulfillment of God's purposes is not fully "built in" to the present world; it resides in God alone through Christ alone and in the promises of God that Christ is fulfilling in this era of history. Historical development is therefore important. Christ is the fulfillment of the promises now, but they are not yet realized. The kingdom is here now and not yet here. Only in the consummation when all things are put under Christ's feet will the fulfillment of His purposes for the world be complete. The incompleteness is not autonomous freedom *from* God, but it is creaturely freedom *under* God, in keeping with His ordained plan. Likewise there is no need to have a determinism, or absolute predictability *within* creation, in order to respect a sovereign God *over* creation. He has many more avenues available to Him for governance than building things in beforehand.

One word of caution before we end the chapter: By speaking of incompleteness in creation, we would like to remind the reader that we in no way mean to imply that there is any incompleteness in God.[26] There is no reason to believe, according to Scripture, that God is in any way ignorant of the future or that He is not the one who actually brings about His own purposes in the unfolding of history. On the contrary, the Scriptures tell us that He establishes His own unchanging purposes: "Because God wanted to make the unchanging nature of his purpose very clear to the heirs of what was promised, he confirmed it with an oath" (Heb. 6:17). And He is steadfast in His purposes, for His Word, which guarantees His purposes, never changes: "Your word, O LORD, is eternal; it stands firm in the heavens" (Ps. 119:89). By contrast, we humans are ignorant of the future, and we do not expect our attempts at expressing the regularities we observe in terms of laws of nature to give us the whole story that God has in mind. In other words, incompleteness in creation from our vantage point in no way implies incompleteness in God from His vantage point.

Finally, let us ask about the question of meaning. If the meaning of creation is not found in creation alone, but in God and His purposes, then creation itself is meaning; its meaning is what God intends for it, including what is yet to come. Meaning is therefore derived from the purposes of God and not from the laws we discover. Hence we should guard against any reductionist view that tries to reduce the complexity of creation into its constituent parts. Because God does not have a reductionist end as His goal, we should not expect an "explanation" of the meaning of creation to be found in a reduction to one aspect or another of His creation. Thus, for example, we would not expect everything to be explainable in terms of a small set of physical laws. Indeed, if the meaning of creation is found in its purpose in the mind of God, then the focus for any theorizing about creation ought to include its teleology, that is, its ultimate goal—where it is headed and also the means to get there. Since the purpose is carried out in time, stages of development are decreed along the way, and only they accumulatively reveal their meaning. This incompleteness or open-endedness (from our perspective) of purpose or goal of creation therefore implies also an *open-endedness of meaning* that cannot be captured in any given instance of time. We can expect the fullness of meaning only in the completion of history when all of God's purposes come to pass. Only this view of history avoids the rationalist error of looking for the meaning of things within the creation alone. It cannot be found at any one time in history, but it too must be found in the consummation of all of history under Christ. Therefore in contrast to Enlightenment thinkers, we conclude that we should not expect our scientific theories or laws to tell the whole story; nor should we even expect that the story of physics can tell us the story of biology and so on, but all are pointing to a higher glory.

Finally let's summarize what we have learned in this section. First we learned that understanding the Trinitarian nature of God in His relation to His creation is important in order to avoid the idolatries of deism and pantheism. God is transcendent and yet immanently involved in His creation. This led to the doctrine of God's covenant with creation, whereby He continues to uphold it faithfully in keeping with His purposes. Thus we see that the regularities of nature and God's miraculous demonstrations of His power in creation are all part of one picture, a picture focusing on His purposes in carrying out the gospel of grace. We also learned that the covenant with creation and the Covenant of Grace are one covenant. Last but not least, we looked at God's *faithfulness* in carrying out His covenant promises to His own ends as expressed in the very laws of nature themselves. This implies the creation displays constancy and predictability in a general sense, such that we can count on God's continuing support for our everyday living. And it also serves to point us to the gospel of grace.

In the next section we move on to consider our place as humans in the practice of science, in focusing on who we are, how we know, and the "doing" of science as a Christian enterprise before our Covenant God. As we move on, may we daily give Him praise and glory for His continuing faithfulness to us even in the mundane things of life in so many ways!

Section Three

Investigating His Dominion

Love the Lord your God with all your heart and with all your soul and with all your mind and with all your strength. . . . Love your neighbor as yourself. There is no commandment greater than these.

MARK 12:30-31

GOD'S REIGN EXTENDS OVER the whole creation to which He has given being. As was emphasized in the previous section, He doesn't reign from afar, but is involved in every aspect of the administration of His domain. His rule is covenantal in its administration in that it is through His rule that He carries out His promises to redeem His people from sin and ultimately all of creation from its corruption. All creation is under His rule, and all of it benefits from His covenantal faithfulness. In return, His creatures are to respond to His purposes and His actions on their behalf according to their creaturely capacities. His prime command to His human creatures is simply that we respond to His rule by loving Him and loving our neighbor. And lest we be tempted to apply the love command only to narrowly defined areas of our lives, Mark 12 teaches us that the command covers all aspects of our lives. The primary purpose of the passage is not to delineate in some formal sense the separate "parts" of a person as if heart, soul, mind, and body exist in isolation from each other. Rather, the passage emphasizes that the command to love God is holistic—every aspect of our lives is impacted by this command as every aspect interacts with God, His human creatures, and the rest of His creation.[1] One way to paraphrase this passage in Mark would be to say that we are to respond to God by loving Him in all our being, in all our knowing, and in all our doing. Here again the idea is not to use these categories to separate the components from one another. We should not attempt to isolate knowing from being and doing, for example, so as to try to develop an abstract idea of what loving God in our "knowing" should be in itself. Rather being, knowing, and doing are integrally related to one another: Who we are impacts what we know and what we do. What we know impacts who we are and what we do. What we do impacts who we are and what we know.[2] We are knowing, being, doing creatures, and we are called not only to love in each facet but to love in all facets at the same time. Distortions of Christian teachings such as legalism, antinomianism, or doctrinalism[3] seem to be the result of a fragmentation of the knowing, being, and doing aspects of the Great Commandment. These distortions arise not as much from their "content" as from their tendencies to isolate knowing, being, and doing aspects of human existence from one another.

For Christians then "science and Christianity" issues boil down to one question: What does loving God and neighbor entail in the natural sciences, or how are we to love God in all our being, all our knowing, and all our doing in the natural sciences? Recent developments in our understanding of science as a human activity encourage new ways of seeking an answer to these basic questions. The philosopher Del Ratzsch describes the current discussion of how best to think about science:

> Science is a complicated, historically shifting interplay among nature, theories, data and a host of often unstated non-empirical principles that shape our thinking, evaluating, theorizing and even perceiving. . . . Science is done by humans and it cannot escape what is inescapably human. . . . But that does not mean that anything goes. At some point our science has to confront nature in some way, and despite some flexibility, nature will just not stand for some things. . . . Science still strives to be empirical, rational and objective, but it turns out that those characteristics have an irremovable human shading to them. Still it is rationally possible to maintain that there is a core of objective truth to our scientific theorizing, result-

> ing in part from the way we are made, the way nature is made and the way the two interact.[4]

Such descriptions of the natural sciences seem to offer new opportunities for exploring Christian obedience to the Great Commandment in the sciences. Christian "being, knowing, and doing" convictions about "the way we are made, the way nature is made, and the way the two interact" are directly relevant to the contemporary discussions of the nature and meaning of scientific work. The chapters in this third section of the book focus on a theological exploration of Christian "being, knowing, doing" as we seek to love God and neighbor in and through the natural sciences, both in the science we do as believers and in our participation in science in our culture.

Chapter Seven

New Creatures at Work in the King's Realm

Therefore, if anyone is in Christ he is a new creation; the old has gone, the new has come!

2 CORINTHIANS 5:17

IN C. S. LEWIS'S BOOK *The Magician's Nephew,* Digory and Polly are tricked into traveling to other worlds by Digory's Uncle Andrew, the magician of the book's title. They arrive in a world that is in the process of being created—of being sung into existence by Aslan the Prince of the Narnian universe. While the children are thrilled by the process of creation and its outcome, Uncle Andrew experiences fear and loathing intermixed with a greedy contemplation of the commercial possibilities of the new world. Aslan creates a variety of creatures that begin talking among themselves and conversing with Digory and Polly, who find themselves able to understand the animal language. Uncle Andrew, though standing nearby as well, doesn't understand the animals' speech at all. In fact he hears snarls and growls instead of the conversation, joking, and laughing. Even the animals' faces, which look pleasantly curious to the children, look fierce and angry to Uncle Andrew. The animals soon notice Uncle Andrew sneaking away from the group, and after a long discussion concerning what kind of creature he might be, they rush toward him to investigate. Uncle Andrew runs and then faints away in fear, sure he is about to be consumed by what seem to him to be vicious wild beasts. At this point, Lewis explains the discrepancy between Uncle Andrew's perspective and the children's perspective on the animals by commenting, "What you see and hear depends a good deal on where you are standing; it also depends on what sort of person you are."[1]

In the context of the story, the comment seems only mildly surprising, but what would you think if this explanation were given in the context of a scientific conference. Imagine that a scientist attending the conference has just questioned a presenter's interpretation of some experimental data. The presenter replies, "Well, sir, what you see of my data and hear of my explanation depends on where you are standing; it also depends on what sort of person you are." Maybe the statement, "what you see and hear depends a good deal on where you are standing," would work if it referred to being too far away from the speaker to hear the explanation intelligibly or too far from the projection screen to see the data clearly. But the "it also depends on what sort of person you are" would definitely be over the top. You can easily imagine the grumbling and catcalls that would erupt.

Think for a moment about why the consideration of "where you are standing" and "what sort of person you are" sounds so strange in the context of modern science. As was discussed previously, we have been taught that scientific methodology, properly executed, should eliminate the impact of subjective personal biases—that a scientist's personal characteristics, his self-understanding, his beliefs about the ultimate nature of reality and his status in that reality are not properly part of science. The basic idea is that if we clear our minds of personal convictions in order to approach the study of the world as generic reasoning, sensing beings, all will be well in our science. Thus if at the end of a scientific investigation someone claims that personal characteristics and convictions actually have a role to play—as in the hypothetical scientific meeting described above—there is much consternation, and serious offense is taken. The impression that science is properly to be kept separated from such personal value commitments is deeply embedded in our cultural instincts about science.

Where does our sense of what science is about, of what constitutes faithful "hearing and seeing" in science, come from? As believers, we should ask whether our instincts about science are in accord with the basic professions we as Christians make about the nature of humans and the nature of nature. We will approach these issues in this chapter by focusing on being issues, issues related to what in philosophy is referred to as ontology. In philosophy a study of ontology involves a formal inquiry into the "nature of what there is," or the nature of being, or what persons and things and universes really are. In the introduction to this section of the book we emphasized the interconnectedness of knowing, being, and doing in the Great Commandment. We pointed out that our love for God should be holistically expressed in what we do and how we do it, in what we know and the way we know it, in who we are and how we fit into the way the universe really is.

Although these three aspects of our response to God are thoroughly intertwined, there is a sense in which being issues do have a primary role. Human knowing and doing involve responses to who God is, and consequently to who we are as humans and what the rest of creation is as it exists under God's rule. Or put another way, knowing and doing are interactive modes of response to the nature of God and the actions of God that arise from His nature and will—actions such as His bringing creation into being and His actions to reconcile the cosmos to Himself in Christ.

If this is right, then it seems that our Christian ontological convictions need to be central to our knowing and doing in science, not added as an afterthought after the "real science" is already done. Some basic questions to consider: What kind of being do humans have? What is this place where we stand? How should Christian understanding of the historic fall into sin be factored into the science we do? In our science, how can we take seriously the impact of the new birth by which Christians are remade into true sons and daughters of the Ruler of the Universe? How should our science take seriously not only the re-creation of individuals in Christ, but also the constitution of a new people as the body of Christ in the world and as the bride of Christ at the conclusion of created history? How should our understanding of the ultimate destiny of all of creation impact our understanding of the science we do now?

Three brief points before we start pursuing these questions: First, engaging these questions will require substantial theological discussion that at times will seem far removed from science, but as we work through the theological issues, it should become clear that they are not really far removed and in fact are primary to faithful treatment of the scientific issues. Second, the approach we are taking is not science-exclusive in its application. It is relevant to virtually all areas of human endeavor. Third, as we engage these questions, we think it will become clear that most of us are instinctively Modernists in the way we frame the questions and judge the answers. So we will frequently point out Modern tendencies that we believe continue to tempt us down the wrong paths as we seek a faithfully Christian science.

Modern Science and the Domestication of Being in the Universe[2]

Historians of science now widely recognize that Christian convictions about the nature of nature, the nature of humans, and the nature of the Author of these natures helped birth modern experimental science.[3] Some examples of these crucial convictions: Nature is a creation of God and not part of God and thus can be studied without fear of invading God's "personal space." While nature is not God, it reflects the order and rationality of the mind of its Maker, and thus humans created in the image of their Maker can expect to find various aspects of creation to be comprehensible. Nature is real, not just an illusion, and further it is good and worthy of study. Nature is the free creation of a God who could have brought into being many different kinds of worlds with different characteristics. Empirical investigation is thus needed to find out how He did in fact choose to order this world in which we find ourselves. Armchair reasoning concerning how God must have done it can never substitute for getting one's hands dirty in investigating the creation itself.[4] These Christian convictions concerning the nature of the world in which humans "are standing," the sort of beings we are, and the kind of Creator who brought all things into being provided essential presuppositions, justifications, and motivations for the development of the experimental methodology that is the hallmark of modern science.[5]

Ironically, the success of scientific investigation, birthed as it was in a Christian context, has led to the common perception that science provides its own grounding and further that science somehow undercuts Christian convictions. There are many in modern science as well as in modern culture at large who would claim to adhere to a comprehensive "scientific worldview." This outlook, which claims to embrace only concepts and views that can pass scientific muster, has often been referred to as "scientism."[6] While most Christians will recognize and reject the obvious idolatry of such a scientific "religion," more subtle expressions of the cultural science of our day may impact the way we all think about science and what we now seem to "see and hear" in terms of science. And many of these instincts of our cultural science are alluring to us because they were originally rooted in Christian convictions, but now as we argue have become unhelpful and even dangerous distortions of those Christian convictions.

Several examples of these more subtle distortions will help set the stage for the being issues to be discussed in the succeeding sections of the chapter. First, Christian convictions about the comprehensibility of nature gave much needed hope that the systematic study of nature would increase human understanding. While this assumption is rooted in the reality of a transcendent Creator God, the success of that systematic study has led over time to inflated assessments of human abilities, such that for many "discovering" God, or determining which beliefs about God are to be "allowed" for "modern" people, are considered essentially scientific matters. While most Christians would reject this role for science, we often find ourselves looking hopefully for validation or fearing the ridicule of the science of the day in ways that belie this rejection.

Second, as modern science developed, confidence in the precision of the Creator's work led to the dominance of investigational modes in which understanding was sought primarily by examining smaller and smaller components of larger systems and phenomena. This has developed in our time into a situation in which scientific methods and expectations have often become unreflectively reductionistic. That is, we instinctively think that the only respectable way to get to the bottom of what something "is" is to dissect it into smaller and smaller components. Consequently we find it difficult to think in ways that take into account the constitutive aspects of context and interactive relations. We have a hard time giving due consideration to the idea that part of what something is may reside in its relationships to other things—in its context as much as in what it is "in itself."

Third, while the Christian de-deification or disenchantment of nature (Christian teaching opposing the idea that nature is haunted by fickle spirits of some kind) encouraged scientific endeavor, the success of science in providing comprehensive material-based explanations encourages a mind-set that assumes that creaturely being is only properly to be understood in material terms.

Fourth, the orderliness of the universe and thus the predictability of interactions among various components has led to assumptions in which mechanical process—tight systems of material and logical cause and effect—tend to dominate our conceptions of "being." We are most comfortable with mechanistic scientific concepts. Finally, we have come to assume that the ideal belief-forming "machinery," in science at least, is a sensory/logical unit that keeps subjective (i.e., non-mechanistic) humanness out.

The bottom line here is that the success of modern scientific investigation has had the long-term effect of domesticating many Christian teachings relevant to "being." Reducing the "wildness" of our convictions makes it all too easy for us to settle into a more comfortable, more manageable materialist, reductionist, and mechanical view of both the universe and of scientific investigation in it. This taming has multiple effects in that it often leads to the dethroning of God, the despiritualization of His creation, the depersonalization of humans, and the secularization of science.

We Christians have often inadvertently contributed to this domestication of "being" by agreeing, often with some embarrassment, to stand in the religious corner of the modern world—just happy not to be sent out of the room completely. Our religious convictions are tolerated in the larger modern world as long as we keep our "spirituality" or "superstitions" in the religious corner and out of the rest of life. The very separation of sacred and secular in this way is a potent domesticating move that tames the wonder of living in a world that is ruled by God from top to bottom. How can we best resist the domestication of "being" that seems to have accompanied the success of modern science?

Science and *HisStory*

The idea that we inhabit a contingent universe, a universe that exists in a dependent relation to God, has historically been a central feature of a Christian understanding of the nature of the universe, or to use the formal term, the ontology of creation. But how are we to picture this relationship in faithful ways—in ways that can actually guide our understanding of the meaning and purposes of human activities in this contingent universe, activities like science? It turns out that the metaphors that we adopt as we think about science and God's world can have a powerful influence on our domestication propensities.

Various metaphors have been used by Christians historically to try to get a better conceptual handle on the relation between God and His world: God as the Artist expressing Himself in the universe as a work of art, or God as the great Thinker of Ideas and the universe as the embodiment of these divine ideas, or God as the Engineer with the universe as His exquisitely designed machine. These ontological metaphors encourage quite different visions of the significance and meaning of human activity, such as science, in the universe. And since it seems that God has creationally embodied elements of His thoughts, artistry, and design in "stuff," such that it reflects in various ways His rationality, creativity, and orderliness, each of these metaphors has been used faithfully by Christians pursuing scientific study in various contexts in the past and present.[7] Here however we consider the overall context in which the study of nature occurs as well as the nature of the object of study. So the question is broader than just the nature of the stuff we study, but is also concerned with the relation between all the players in scientific endeavor as well as being concerned with the status of the endeavor itself: Who are we as humans doing science? Where are we standing as we do science? What is the activity of science "really"?

The all-encompassing ontological metaphor we will adopt to explore these issues is that of creational existence or "being" as story. We believe that this metaphor is a biblically warranted one, and yet we use "story" here with a bit of caution given our current Postmodern cultural context. Postmodern references to "story" or "narrative" often carry with them a relativist sense such that "story," as a subjective account of the meaning of events or experiences, fully eclipses the reality or significance of the actual historical events themselves. Of course we are not using story in this relativistic sense at all. Rather we want to encourage the idea that the whole of creation in time and space be seen as divine theater. Our idea here is not that creation is *a* theater, but that created being *is* theater.[8] Created reality is not simply the stage or an incredibly complex prop for a story that God is telling; created reality in a real sense *is* the story He is telling in time and space.

The Scriptures reveal an episodic structure for the story, which can be described in terms of creation, fall, redemption, and consummation. This structure does help us organize and make sense of elements of the story, but having said this, we must immediately point out that the story is a strange one told in a strange way, especially given our modern sensibilities related to time and sequence.

For example, although the story is played out in created time according to God's purposes, there is a sense in which the story is not strictly attached to created time per se. In the Scriptures this supratemporal "license" in telling the story makes for all kinds of interesting textures and currents as the story unfolds: intricate typologies, prophetic pronouncements that find fulfillment in temporally creative ways, episodes that refer forward or backward in historical time or in which historical time and God's "time" frame appear to be drastically different, leading to unexpected delays, misdirected human expectations, jarring "intrusions," and strange "now but not yet" realities. Examples in Scripture are numerous: Adam and Eve were to die upon eating the forbidden fruit; yet they died physically hundreds of years later and then died "in Christ" much later in created time. The Old Testament saints in Israel were saved not by the blood of goats and lambs but by the death of the Son of God on the cross—which had not yet happened in created time. The Lamb was slain before the foundation of the world,[9] and yet still had to die in history. Grace had already been expressed and applied at the beginning of time but had not yet come to fruition in time. God has already prepared the good works that we are to do, and yet we are to act them out in history.[10]

Paul constantly appeals to the fact that Christians are citizens of heaven now, even though our historical experience of that reality is not yet. Some have interpreted the harsh "in-history" judgments ordered by God (the Israelites clearing the Canaanites from the promised land, for example) as "intrusions" of the final Judgment at the end of time into historical time.[11] What is now, is partly tied up in what has been and what will be. The story is "pushed" by what has been as well as "pulled" by what will be. We humans must recognize that though God has graciously made us integral to His story, reality is His to form, the story is His to tell in His own way, in His own time—and all for His Glory.

Science in a Dynamic Christocentric Story

The story played out in created history is first and foremost the story of the preeminence of the Son. At the end of the story, it will be clear to all that God by the power of the Spirit has accomplished His purposes for His creation in and through the work of the Ruler/Redeemer Son. This story develops and moves toward a consummation or a bringing to fullness of that preeminence, and thus the creational pattern is dynamic; it is looking forward, becoming something it was not before, not simply returning to some original state. His rule unfolds and develops over created time in such a way that history is not just a time delay until King Jesus swoops in on the clouds of heaven. His preeminence is being increasingly demonstrated by the daily unfolding reality of His reign in history, a reality that is to be both witnessed to and participated in by His people.

However, the unfolding of Christ's reign in history is not just a matter of an obvious and "telegraphed" crescendo; it is also a matter of a more hidden gestation. Gestation in biology refers to the period of time a developing organism is carried in the uterus before its birth. The extensive development taking place doesn't become obvious to outside observers until birth. Likewise in Christ's rule, in addition to kingdom demonstration, there is also kingdom gestation—a quiet, more hidden aspect of the unfolding of Christ's preeminence in creation in preparation for the day it will burst forth in all its fullness.

Science for believers should be seen in terms of its role in both the gestation and demonstration of the reign of Christ.

The Story Metaphor—Resisting Materialism and Reductionism

Our Modernist-shaped instincts lead us to assume that science is and should be exclusively about the "seen," the material "stuff" of the universe. But the story is being played out—is being gestated and demonstrated—in both the seen and the unseen, and if science is a part of that story, it must be pursued with both the seen and unseen in view. In today's materially minded context, it takes conscious effort for us to consistently affirm this in word and in deed. Our tendency is to think of the seen almost entirely in its own terms when we are about our "secular" pursuits, while occasionally and often with some embarrassment we say, "Well, of course there is the unseen." Talk of the unseen is usually carefully restricted to "God-talk safe zones" such as church or Christian small groups. Francis Schaeffer, in his book *True Spirituality*, points out the basic unfaithfulness of this kind of "wimpy" supernaturalism:

> According to the biblical view, there are two parts to reality: the natural world—that which we see normally—and the supernatural part. When we use the word "supernatural," however, we must be careful. The supernatural is really no more unusual in the universe from the biblical viewpoint, than what we normally call the natural. The only reason we call it supernatural is that normally we cannot see it. That is all. From the biblical view—the Judeo-Christian view—reality has two halves, like two halves of an orange. You do not have the whole orange unless you have both parts. . . .
>
> I would suggest that this may be illustrated by two chairs. The men who sit in these chairs look at the universe in two different ways. We are all sitting in one or the other of these chairs at every single moment of our lives. The [Christian] sits in his chair and faces this total reality of the universe, the seen part and the normally unseen part, and consistently sees truth against this background. The unbeliever, however, is the man who sits in the other chair,

> intellectually. He sees only the natural part of the universe and interprets truth against that background. If indeed there is only the natural portion of the universe then to sit in the [Christian's] chair is to delude oneself. If, however, there are two halves of reality, then to sit in the naturalist's chair is to be extremely naïve and to misunderstand the universe completely.
>
> However to be a true Bible-believing Christian, we must understand that it is not enough simply to acknowledge that the universe has these two halves. The Christian life means living in these two halves of reality. . . . I would suggest that it is perfectly possible for a Christian to be so infiltrated by twentieth-century thinking that he lives most of his life as though the supernatural were not there. Indeed I would suggest that all of us do this to some extent. The supernatural does not touch the Christian only at the new birth and then at his death, or at the second coming of Christ, leaving the believer on his own in a naturalistic world in between. Nothing could be further from the biblical view. Being a biblical Christian means living in the supernatural now—not only theoretically but in practice.[12]

The story metaphor can also help us resist the dominance of reductionism—the idea that we are only making progress in understanding the universe when we break it down into smaller and smaller components isolated from the whole. Story-thinking forces the relational nature of created being and a rich conception of its contingency to the forefront of the discussion. As emphasized in various ways in chapters 4, 5, and 6, the contingency of the universe is based on a moment-by-moment dependency in past, present, and future tense. This dependency is not just interesting background information, but is held to be an integral element of what the universe really is. Created being has its existence and meaning only in relation to its Author and Sustainer and the story He intends to tell in and through it. This Author doesn't stand outside the story but actually enters into it in the incarnation of the Son and by the presence of His Spirit. Individual characters and settings have real existence and significance in themselves, but they cannot be isolated from the story itself without loss of meaning and significance and even a diminishment of their reality.

In the providence of God, the characters would not be the same without the story, and the story would not be the same without the specific characters. In view of this it makes no sense to contend that if we want to really get to know a character in the story, some feature of nature, we must first try to isolate the character entirely from the story. It makes no sense to contend that a true understanding of the story is advanced by focusing on isolated parts without at some point considering each part in the context of the whole or that if we want to understand the story better, we will consciously try not to pay attention to the Author's "notes" and His commentary concerning the structure of the story and His purposes in telling it.[13]

The bottom line here is that the story metaphor emphasizes that all aspects of the universe, all players and events, are embedded in a relational web held together only in its ultimate relation to God. All that is, including scientists, the objects of scientific study, and the process of study, exists to tell a holistic, comprehensive story of the preeminence of Christ the Son in created history, through which the perfections of God are revealed to His ultimate glory. Telling the truth about what things are, whether in science or other areas of study, can only ultimately be done in terms of their context in the story.

Science in His Gospel Story

The story is a gospel story from beginning to end. All aspects of the story—from creation to the Fall, to redemption, and then to consummation—all of it demonstrates that in Christ, God does for His creation what it could never do for itself. This comprehensive gospel is the glue that holds the episodes of the story together. Any human activity, including science, that is isolated from this kind of gospel ontology will eventually shrivel and become a grotesque and idolatrous parody of its function in the story. Consequently we need to carefully guard against ways of thinking about created being that lead to consideration of any of it in isolation from this gospel.[14]

We humans play a central role in this gospel story. God chose to bring into being persons in His image, reflecting Him in ways that no other created entities can. God deals with us as persons, gives us choices as persons, and holds us responsible as persons. No, the story is not essentially about us—it is about Christ—but demonstrating God's holiness, power, and grace in His dealings with image-bearing creatures dominates the story He is telling. God-to-human communication, reconciliation, and transformation are central to His purposes. Further, humans are commanded to be a central means through which much of the unfolding of the creational story takes place.[15] And it is not just humans as isolated individuals in view here, but a special human community, a community called into being by God Himself. It is the church as the body of Christ on earth that is the central means by which the kingdom of Christ advances, and it is the church that is the bride who will be a center of attention at the wedding feast of the Lamb at the consummation of history.[16] The church then, composed of redeemed human beings, must be central to our consideration of the unfolding of God's purposes in the universe. Science is a gift given to humans in our times and is thus a means by which God's holiness, power, and grace will be demonstrated. And for Christians, science can never be considered as an endeavor totally isolated from God's church.

Although the dealings of God with His human creations are the most prominent in the story, His work in humans doesn't exhaust His purposes. His purposes, in fact, involve the whole creation. He takes pleasure in and glorifies Himself in nonhuman being as well as in human being.[17] Consistent with this pleasure in and care for His nonhuman creations in history, the coming consummation of history will involve the reconciliation of all things, the summing up of the whole creation in Christ, who will then present it all to the Father.[18] In the sciences we need to be conscious of the fact that we are dealing with Someone else's stuff, stuff that He loves for itself, stuff that is part of the gospel story. We can do nothing less than love it ourselves and handle it with respect, humility, and care.

The recognition of the dominance of the gospel in the story can counteract the tendency for Christians to divide what is in essence a single story of grace expressed in the preeminence of Christ into two stories or at least two separated storylines: a "creation plot" and a separate "redemption plot." In this dualistic way of thinking, the "creation story," which focuses on the power of a Creator God who demonstrates His wisdom and benevolence in the miraculous origination and design of the cosmos, is often treated as if it were a self-contained story in some sense detachable from the other story of sin, rebellion, the costly atonement of the cross, and resurrection and new life in Christ. It turns out to be difficult to have such a "two stories" mind-set and not to end up privileging one over the other in ways that distort the meaning of the gospel. If one is operating consciously or unconsciously under a dualistic two-stories framework, the role and meaning of scientific endeavor will also vary according to which story is seen as privileged.

If the redemption story in narrow terms is privileged over the creation story, then science is too easily seen in narrow, pragmatic terms: an interesting diversion while we wait for the final stage of the redemption story; an apologetic tool useful mostly for its role in legitimating belief in God; an applied discipline, valid because it provides an outlet for showing love to one's neighbor by addressing human needs with technology. On the other hand, if the creation story is seen as the privileged one, then the redemption story is too easily subordinated in various ways. When the details of the "how" and "when" of the creation episode are taken as the central battleground of the Christian faith, the redemption story might become a sidelight. Christian interest in science might become almost entirely focused on a narrow set of origins issues rather than broadly on the impact that faith in Christ's redemptive rule might have on the investigation of God's world. For others who might appreciate the "creation story" in terms of the broad development and unfolding of the natural and cultural world over time, there is the danger that the redemption story may come to be seen simply as a "patch" for the story of creational development. For them, redemption might unconsciously come to be seen as taking care of the sin "difficulty" and then fading into the background as humans get to work on unfolding the in-built potentials of the universe to bring the creation story to its fruition—a process in which modern science would be seen as playing a prominent role.

But creation and redemption are not two relatively independent stories that merely intersect at certain points; nor is the one simply in service of the other. The creation with its history is not just a rich but ultimately dispensable backdrop for the redemption story; nor is it to be a substitute or a proxy for the redemption story. Neither one is ultimately reducible in terms of the other. They are inseparably unified in one story, and that one story culminates in the summing up of absolutely all things in Christ according to the good news of the gospel. Christian engagement in science then must reflect in multifaceted ways the unified Christocentric focus of the one grand story of the universe as it unfolds through the work of the Spirit under the reign of the triune God.

Science in a Creation-Fall-Redemption-Consummation Universe

We've already introduced creation, fall, redemption, and consummation as episodes that provide thematic as well as a temporal structure for all of history. Each of these episodes in a sense "attacks" central elements of Modern ways of thinking, and thus each has been a focus of contention in the Modern era. Various Modernist domesticating strategies have been attempted to make them more fit for consumption. But the clash with Modernism turns out to be deeper than a simple disagreement about supernatural events in the past, present, and future (although it includes this). The clash is fundamentally a disagreement about the nature of reality—about ontology. If, as we've been urging, created being is "theater," then creation, fall, redemption, and consummation are more than simple episodes or acts in a play. Each is actually a deep ontological statement about what the universe really is. In the following sections we want to explore these episodes and the ontology they imply as they relate to the conduct of a faithful science in our times. We want to recapture some of the wildness of created being that has been lost from the Modern domesticated version.

Science and Creation *Ex Nihilo*

Creation *ex nihilo*, or creation out of nothing, is an important statement of the historic Christian confession that God is the absolute originator and sustainer of all that exists in the universe. The doctrine of creation *ex nihilo* emphasizes that all that exists outside of God is absolutely dependent on Him for its origin and sustenance. As discussed in the second section of the book, created being is absolutely contingent on the will and purposes of God such that all other persons and things exist only in Him and have genuine meaning only in reference to Him: "You are worthy, our Lord and God, to receive glory and honor and power, for you created all things, and by your will they were created and have their being" (Rev. 4:11).

Second, creation *ex nihilo* emphasizes that created being is in *essence* distinct from God's being. Created being, even created human being, is not an extension of God's being. There is a "being" chasm between God and His creation that is only bridged by God's determination to relate Himself to His creation by His Son, the Word made flesh, and by His Spirit who bears witness to the Word.

This triune God who creates, sustains, and relates is I AM, the self-existent One. As one seventeenth-century catechism puts it, "God is a Spirit, in and of himself infinite in being, glory, blessedness and perfection; all-sufficient, eternal, unchangeable, incomprehensible, everywhere present, almighty, knowing all things, most wise, most holy, most just, most merciful and gracious, long-suffering and abundant in goodness and truth."[19] His being is not contingent on anyone or anything else. His attributes are not derivative in any sense from the characteristics of another being. He is the ultimate definition of the attributes He possesses. His thoughts alone are absolute; His perspective is the only absolutely true perspective.[20] Further, this ultimate, transcendent One is not an impersonal power or force; He is a multidimensional Personality who thinks, wills, plans, communicates, acts, and makes judgments as a whole, personal being. His knowledge is not just a matter of infinite information storage capacity, but is a connected whole knowledge held in His being in a personal way.[21] Thus He is a whole creative Personality, not simply some kind of one-dimensional technical overachiever. Since He is a personal being, His knowing, as is the case with His "doing," ultimately flows from His "being" who He is.

These understandings of creation and its triune Creator undercut a variety of the domesticating moves in science and theology in the Modern era. First, there is what could be called the "theistic move" that attempts to separate the consideration of a designing creator/originator of all things from the person and work of Jesus Christ. This move has often been fostered by Christians in the Modern context who see an advantage in moving the discussion of the existence of God from the theological/religious sphere into the realm of science and philosophy so that the issue becomes a matter of scientific/philosophical method and judgment. This move might end up in effect, if not in reality, denying a basic tenet of Christian orthodoxy, the Trinity, and thus marginalizing and distorting the gospel. The Christian God is the triune God—the creator, designer, sustainer, redeemer, and "completer," all in one package. It seems to us that any serious discussion of God that doesn't regularly refer to a triune and redeeming God ceases to be a discussion of the Christian God. In its extreme we might consider this move a "theistic heresy."

A second Modern move, related to the theistic move but with a somewhat different focus, is the "deistic move" that essentially divorces the creator role for a deity from any active sustainer role. From a Christian perspective this might be called the transcendence heresy. It is true that God is not a part of His creation, but this view denies God's interaction and care for His creation through Christ and by His Spirit. The deistic move thus ends up denying the Trinitarian doctrine of creation and the centrality of the gospel as well.

Third, in even more obvious ways, all attempts to tell a story of nature somehow creating itself, the "naturalistic move," is a denial of the Christian doctrine of creation in terms of the dependency of creation on its Creator.

Fourth, a more recent creation heresy envisions a God whose being is somehow tied up in the being of His creation such that His ultimate destiny is linked to an as-yet-to-be-determined destiny of His creation.[22] This "process move"[23] constitutes what could be called the "immanence heresy" in that it essentially denies the biblical God who is not only close to His creation, by His Word and Spirit, but also transcends His creation, really rules it, and will complete it in consummation.

Finally, the twentieth-century evangelical and fundamentalist fix-ation on the when and how of creation, while not a heresy, is often pursued with such single-mindedness that it is as if specific answers to these questions are somehow more central to Christian belief than the more settled Christian teachings concerning the who (the triune God), what (everything), and why (for His glory) of creation.

The Radical Nature of the Fall

The Christian doctrines of the Fall and of supernatural redemption are of central relevance for our ontological "who we are and where we're standing" discussion. These two doctrines have also been especially scandalous to Modernist thinking. These doctrines directly attack Modernism's conceptions of human individualism and human potential and its optimistic assessment of humanity's ability to develop and complete its own grand self-help programs. In the face of such a mind-set these doctrines seem shockingly out of step, and Christians have often sought to tame these doctrines in various ways so that they don't seem quite so offensive in the Modern world. But when we Christians participate in their domestication for Modern consumption, we dilute their ability to deliver the stinging "snap out of your self-sufficiency delusion" slap that we humans throughout history, and especially the Modernist-minded, really need.

The doctrines of the Fall and of redemption really are radical, and they exhibit a strongly connected "radicality." The degree to which one understands and feels the depth and desperation of the Fall is in direct proportion to the degree to which one understands the radically lavish provisions of redemptive grace of which human regeneration is the centerpiece. "Cheap grace," to use Dietrich Bonhoeffer's phrase,[24] can only flourish where the Fall has been thoroughly domesticated. And when grace has been devalued, a retreat of robust Christian faith into a sterile moral legalism or into a human-generated religious sentimentalism inevitably follows.

The Christian doctrine of the Fall is rooted in the actions of Adam and Eve, who, when presented with the choice to obey and trust God or to rebel and "go it alone," chose to disbelieve and reject God and to trust in themselves. This rebellion had broad, cosmic consequences. The scriptural account of the Fall in Genesis 3 does not tell the story of a "surgical" strike by Satan that can be turned back by a correspondingly narrow redemptive counterattack. As a result of the rebellion of Adam and Eve, creation history as a whole is declared to be a battleground between the "seed of the serpent" and the "seed of the woman." The propagation of the race is associated with pain, social relationships become disordered, work becomes "painful toil," "thorns and thistles" actively oppose human endeavor, the human body is itself corrupted and destined to decay, and a sense of despair and futility becomes a natural feature of human life.[25]

When Adam and Eve rejected God's commands, every facet of their humanness and of their lives in the world became corrupted by their willful rebellion. Their new sinful nature could not be isolated or quarantined to some particular human component or characteristic. Sin corrupted the whole human being. Even more radical is the fact that "in Adam," the natural state of all subsequent human beings would be corrupt and sinfully rebellious from conception. All humans after the Fall by nature oppose God at every turn.[26] Finally, through Adam's sin, all of created being became corrupted and unruly. In the Fall then all humans and the entire universe along with us fell under the sway of the kingdom of darkness—all humans in bondage to sin and all of creation "in bondage to decay."[27]

The Christian doctrine of the Fall has always generated questions and has been assailed in various ways in the Modern period. Questions concerning how exactly the sin nature was passed from generation to generation were raised early in church history. A common modification of the doctrine has been to try to limit the impact of the Fall to some particular aspect of human being—say, the will or a moral capacity, which might then be separable from human reason, for example. In the Modern era, the doctrine has often been decried as too pessimistic, too dark. Why would Christians want to indulge in such negativity about humans and human capacities? The doctrine has been declared to be fundamentally unfair. Shouldn't everyone be able to start life with a clean slate—not declared guilty before life begins? In modern individualistic, egalitarian terms, it is unthinkable that an innocent newborn, apart from Christ, is under judgment just because he is "in Adam." If we can't isolate a material sin "gene" that accounts for the particulate inheritance of sin, then the idea that the sin of Adam infected the human race must be bogus. And certainly the idea that creation itself is corrupted by Adam's fall is an incoherent concept from a materialist, reductionist perspective. After all, how could a hydrogen atom be impacted by the Fall? Would the proton or the electron be the corrupted component?

Scientists in Rebellion, Nature in Bondage: A Relational Thing

To come to terms with the Fall in the radical way it is presented in Scripture, one must appreciate the Bible's deep use of what we could call relationally defined ontology. That is, that being, whether human or nonhuman, is as essentially linked to story and relational context as it is to individuality and isolated physical operation. A more conventional expression of this relationally defined ontology comes from the central use of what is usually referred to as federal representation in the doctrines of redemption. Both Adam and Christ act as representative "heads" of the human race. All humans alike are under judgment "in Adam" as our federal head and upon Christian conversion, the perfect Christ becomes our federal representative before God; our sins are federally focused on him by relationship, and He dies for those sins in our place. We moderns find the federal motif challenging because we can't find a material or mechanical explanation to connect those federally represented to their federal head, and so we too easily retreat into taking these teachings as somehow symbolic. But federal representation something like what we've described seems to be clearly taught in Scripture as central to the story. Taking these relational descriptions as symbolic doesn't seem to work. The Scriptures teach that we actually participate in the Fall in Adam; we are "organically" related to Christ in salvation; we become spiritual children of Abraham and thus actually become the righteous children of the King.

> *For just as through the disobedience of the one man the many were made sinners, so also through the obedience of the one man the many will be made righteous. (Rom. 5:19)*

> *God made him who had no sin to be sin for us, so that in him we might become the righteousness of God. (2 Cor. 5:21)*

The reason we must be given new being in Christ is that without a new federally defined being, we are stuck in old being in Adam. The change in being occurs by a change in relation—a change in federal representation. The Scriptures do teach a radical fall in which after Adam's sin, all humans are by nature deserving of wrath. We are under condemnation not primarily because of what we know or don't know, not because of what we do or don't do, but because of who we are in fallen Adam. (Of course, being ultimately plays itself out in knowing and doing; so our condemnation can also be justified in terms of rebellion expressed in our knowing and doing.) So the fall of humans into sin effects a relational change between humans and God that brings all humans under the curse, justly under the judgment of God.

Now what about the effects of the Fall on nonhuman creation? The Fall is all-encompassing, not because created "stuff" becomes sinful, but because part of what it is, is tied up in who humans are as creational representatives. Originally created human being existed in a relational web that exuded the life and joy of unhindered relationship with God, a web of relation that extended to all of creation. Humans were given responsibility over it all—to be "gods" of creation, as it were. In the Fall the open and clean relationship between humans and God was severed, and the life and joy that flowed through all human relationships were cut off at their source. All relations in which humans are involved were impacted, bringing disorder, corruption, and fear to all creation in all its relations. In Scripture sin per se is limited to the human realm and is tied most specifically to the human mind/will.[28] A proper distinction can be made between sin that involves human pride and rebellion, and corruption, which is represented in Scripture as a result of sin and thus also subject to the judgment of God. Corruption is related to human sin and spread abroad in creation as a whole because of human sin. Again the Modern instinct is to judge the truth of this according to whether we can detect "corruption particles" that are passed from humans to the rest of creation. But this is to force the strong relational ontological sense in

Scripture into the Modern mechanistic/materialistic explanatory comfort zone.

So Adam was first and foremost the federal head of the human race, but he was also the representative of all creation. In Adam all creation fell—not into sin as did all of Adam's human lineage—but into corruption. Part of what creation is, is tied up in its relation to humans and thus in human relation to God. So in this sense, hydrogen atoms haven't become sinful, but they are subject to the corruption and evil that has infected all creation by relation to the sin of Adam. Fallenness then is a state of being in a relationship of judgment with God. At the Fall, the universe as a whole came under God's righteous judgment. And according to the Scriptures, the universe will only be made right again when we humans are made right. It will be perfected with us and is eagerly awaiting our glorification.[29]

So in this view the Fall really is a radical challenge to Modern ways of thinking in a number of ways. It teaches a basic human rebelliousness that grows out of an active enmity between humankind in Adam and the Lord of the universe. The universe itself is shot through with evil and corruption—destined only for destruction if left to itself, with no hope of self-generated healing. Against such a bleak background, it is clear that minor tweaking of creation will not do. Even a major reorganization of existing components will not be enough. Only re-creation in Christ—a new birth for humans and ultimately for all created beings—will do the job.

The Fall and its implications have become a major fork in the theological road and, as we argue, a major fork in the ontological road. Abraham Kuyper, the Dutch Reformed theologian introduced in chapter 3, referred to the Fall as the fork in the road in the Modern context. In Kuyper's terms, acknowledgment of the Fall separates the Modernist "normalists," who believe in a cosmos undisturbed by sin and evil, from the Christian "abnormalists," who recognize that a cosmos-wide "disturbance" has taken place and thus live in hope that "a regenerating power" from outside can indeed make it right again.[30] That regenerating power—expressed in God's intention and action to make all things new in Christ—is the topic of the next section, but before we go on, we want to mention several ways in which one's understanding of the Fall impacts scientific endeavor. First, given the basic issue of human rebellion against God, it should be clear that human science—unless it is constrained by God's grace—will tend to lead away from God, not toward Him. We Christians should not be in the least surprised when science is used by some in opposition to God and His commands. Expectations that "pure" science will inevitably lead toward the God of the Bible seem out of step with the reality of living in the fallen universe. Second, in science not only are the humans doing the scientific work subject to their sinful nature, but what we study, the universe itself, is in an "abnormal" corrupted state. Thus the work is going to be difficult and arduous. "Thorns and thistles"[31] will be an ever-present reality. In addition, while science properly involves making extrapolations beyond immediate data and making generalizations based on limited observations, the fact that we live in an abnormal rather than a normal universe ought to introduce a level of caution and humility into these activities. Finally, as science involves fallen creatures working in a fallen creation, triumphalism concerning our own attainments in science and in the vindication of elements of Christian faith by that science seems out of place. Rather, the better attitude would seem to be the simple giving of thanks and humble participation in these temporal expressions of God's favor as we see science working, coupled with looking forward to the full fruition of these gifts of grace in the age to come.

The Radical Nature of Redemption

If the Fall is as radical as Scripture indicates, then God's response must be correspondingly and gloriously radical. And it is. Perfect justice is dispensed, and lavish grace is expressed—and the focal point of both is Christ. While justice is eternally satisfied by Christ's work on the cross, it has temporal in-history consequences also. While grace is decisively expressed in Christ, it is expressed in temporal historical ways as well. The lavishness of God's grace expressed in Christ is seen both in His delaying comprehensive judgment of human sin and creational corruption for a time and in His promise to remake all things by the power of His might in the fullness of time in Christ. His promise is not just to repair the problem, to get creation back to time zero, but it is to remake or regenerate creation, to bring into being new heavens and a new earth populated by humans who are new creations in Christ. He is re-creating a total reality that supercedes the present reality in all respects; yet it will in some sense be relationally connected to the present reality as its completion or perfection.

We want to briefly focus on three aspects of the story most easily placed under the "redemption" episode. The three aspects are God's work in Christ to recreate new human individuals, His work in Christ to create a new people of God—the church, and finally His work in Christ to create new heavens and a new earth as the final and fitting realm of His eternal kingdom.

Old Self, New Self: Old Scientist, New Scientist?

The radical nature of God's re-creational activity through Christ is best illustrated by its application to humans. The Scriptures insist that in the (now) natural fallen state, a human exists as the "old self" dedicated to rebellion, evil intention, and evil behavior. The Scriptures further teach that the old self must die, and only then is the "new self" created, a new creature that as Christ's younger sibling, is now the object of the Father's special pleasure and care rather than a vessel for just wrath. This regeneration of human selves in the Son by the power of the Spirit transforms the human relation to the Father and thus transforms everything—nothing is left untouched. When God becomes your Father, every aspect of life is changed—even your science? Is this right though? If science is independent of "what kind of person" one is, then one's science will be the same before and after regeneration in Christ. Couldn't restoration to the Father just be the fixing of an individual sin problem, one problem in the area of an individual's spirituality? Is sin like one bad apple in the barrel that constitutes a human, and if the bad apple is taken care of before it spoils the whole barrel, might the other apples not even be impacted? Let's take a closer look at human regeneration to see if a piecemeal approach to human redemption does justice to its biblical description. If a piecemeal approach won't work, then what are the implications for human regeneration and science?

Who is the old self, and what are his characteristics? The Scriptures leave no doubt: The natural man hates God; he finds the things of God to be foolish; he is immoral, is full of selfish ambition, practices deceit, is blind, has a hardened heart, is enslaved to the basic principles of the world, is dead in trespasses and sin, is futile in thinking and darkened in understanding, is alienated from God, and is an enemy of God in his mind.[32] It is pretty clear that the old self is dedicated to hating God with all his heart, soul, mind, and strength and hating the neighbor as he hates God. Or put another way, in all its knowing, being, and doing the old self inevitably expresses hatred for God. As Paul argues from Old Testament themes:

> *There is no one righteous, not even one; there is no one who understands, no one who seeks God. All have turned away, they have together become worthless; there is no one who does good, not even one. Their throats are open graves; their tongues practice deceit. The poison of vipers is on their lips. Their mouths are full of cursing and bitterness. Their feet are swift to shed blood; ruin and misery mark their ways, and the way of peace they do not know. There is no fear of God before their eyes. (Rom. 3:10-18)*

Everything that the old self is, knows, and does is an expression in one way or another of his hatred for God and rebellion against His rule. The "web" of relationships that emanate from the old self are all poisoned in one way or another. If the old self is as despicable before God as the Scriptures describe it, then it comes as no surprise that the remedy is not simply reeducation or reformation. The initial remedy is death.

> *For we know that our old self was crucified with him so that the body of sin might be done away with, that we should no longer be slaves to sin—because anyone who has died has been freed from sin. (Rom. 6:6)*

While death is the inevitable end of the old self, for the people of God hope springs from death. The death of the old self is followed by the re-creation of a new self. Human "being" can be regenerated by the power of the Spirit. By regeneration, humans are re-created, become "new creatures" in Christ. Regeneration gives humans a new nature that can respond appropriately to God. This work does more than reset the "being" clock; it replaces the old corrupted and perishable mode of being with a new mode that is incorruptible and imperishable.

> *And he died for all, that those who live should no longer live for themselves but for him who died for them and was raised again. So from now on we regard no one from a worldly point of view. Though we once regarded Christ in this way, we do so no longer. Therefore, if anyone is in Christ, he is a new creation; the old has gone, the new has come! (2 Cor. 5:15-17)*

As new creations, redeemed humans are both established as new persons and are called to work at "being" new persons and to "image" God's redemptive acts with respect to their own lives, the lives of others, and the creation in general.

> *Do not lie to each other, since you have taken off your old self with its practices and have put on the new self, which is being renewed in knowledge in the image of its Creator. (Col. 3:9-10)*

Human re-creation involves more than simply restoring image-bearing. Regenerated human "being" expands and transforms image-bearing and image-bearing tasks in a variety of ways. New creatures in Christ reflect deity in new and better ways than before the Fall. The task of ruling and caring for creation[33] given before the Fall, growing out of human "being" as it was established at creation, is not simply restored; it is given in a new and better form based on human reconstitution as new creatures in Christ. The "unfolding" task now should not only explore and develop the potentials of creation, but in and through doing so, it bears witness to God's redeeming work in the "now," as well as pointing to the "not yet" of consummation. Our work now as transformed image-bearers includes the task of bearing witness to and participating in God's work to reconcile all things to Himself in Christ.

> *All this is from God, who reconciled us to himself through Christ and gave us the ministry of reconciliation: that God was reconciling the world to himself in Christ, not counting men's sins against them. And he has committed to us the message of reconciliation. We are therefore Christ's ambassadors, as though God were making his appeal through us. We implore you on Christ's behalf: Be reconciled to God. God made him who had no sin to be sin for us, so that in him we might become the righteousness of God. (2 Cor. 5:18-21)*

When humans are made new creatures in Christ, we are removed from an entire web of relationships—to God, to self, to others, to creation—that is estranged from God and under His curse, relationships that have the "stink of death" associated with them because they are rooted in rebellion against God. Reconciliation to God and the creaturely transformation that makes that reconciliation possible in turn transform the foundation and the trajectory of all relationships a human can experience.

> *To the pure, all things are pure, but to those who are corrupted and do not believe, nothing is pure. In fact, both their minds and consciences are corrupted. (Titus 1:15)*

New relationships are established to self, to others, and to the rest of creation. These new relationships center around the new aspect of image-bearing—that of restoration, of redemption, of bearing witness to the present and coming transformation of all things in Christ. The regeneration of a human sets in motion a transformation "wave"—a ripple effect of his transformation that emanates from him, which he both "rides" and participates in propagating. Regenerated humans become centers of redemption ourselves—not in the sense of generating redemption under our own power but in the sense of resonating[34] the redemption we have received through our restored relationship to God. We are to resonate our redemption into all our relationships within creation until the reverberations of His transforming power bring down the curtain on the present age. We are called based on who we are in Christ to transform, to redeem all that we touch by the power of the Spirit.

The faithful scientific work of believers then grows explicitly out of who we are in Christ. Our work in science is part of our obedience to God's command that we demonstrate our "new creature" status in God's world. If Christians are called to "full-time Christian scientific work," the calling involves an active and continuous exploration of how our redemption can and does play out in the establishment and conduct of the specialized kinds of relationships with creation that we are to establish and nurture as we engage in scientific endeavors. One's call to science is not just about "finding out stuff" about God's creation. The call is to a science that has an integrally transforming character as aspects of creation are brought into explicit relation to the Christian scientist himself and thus are connected through him to the transformation of all things that has come and will come in Christ. What a glorious scientific task in the kingdom!

A New People: The Church and Science

Having discussed the wonder of redemption in God's transformation of individual humans, calling each out of darkness into the light and calling each to know and to do according to his new nature, we now turn to the corporate human aspect of redemption. God's redemptive work in and through humans in history is carried out not only in terms of His personal relationship with individual humans, but is fundamentally rooted in a people He calls to be His own. When individuals come into a new relationship to God through regeneration, they are also brought into a new relationship with other believers—God's "called out ones," that is, His church. The Scriptures present God's work of redemption in individuals and His building of His church, the community of the saints, as inseparable in history.

> *As you come to him, the living stone—rejected by men but chosen by God and precious to him—you also, like living stones, are being*

> *built into a spiritual house to be a holy priesthood, offering spiritual sacrifices acceptable to God through Jesus Christ. . . . But you are a chosen people, a royal priesthood, a holy nation, a people belonging to God, that you may declare the praises of him who called you out of darkness into his wonderful light. Once you were not a people, but now you are the people of God. (1 Peter 2:4-5, 9-10)*

The church in this most comprehensive sense,[35] as the people of God, was established in the earliest phases of human creational history—as the seed of the woman in Genesis 3 through whom and for whom God's victory in Christ would come. And it is this church, existing in various institutional forms throughout history, that will constitute the great gathering of the saints at the end of time, a people that no one can number who will render the consummate worship due our Lord.[36] This people from all times and nations will, in unity, be presented as the spotless bride of the Lamb,[37] the supreme exemplar of the holiness, power, and grace of God exercised in history. The church then in this comprehensive sense is properly seen as the central focus of God's "gestation and demonstration" work in history, uniquely among created institutions embodying the "the fullness of Christ."[38] The church and God's work in history are inseparable, and His purposes in Christ can never be properly considered apart from His work in and through His church. A creational ontology that does not give central place to the church as a real, "in-the-world" spiritual and physical entity will inevitably be distorted. Christ's church has a continuity that transcends creational time and space and yet has distinctive local and temporal manifestations in time and space. His church has explicit structural aspects and duties—that is, it is an institution, and yet it also has dynamic and adaptive aspects; it is also properly considered as "organism."

First, consider the church as the people of God throughout history in terms of the dominant scriptural picture of the church as an organism, a living, growing, adaptive entity that quietly spreads throughout the world as the leaven of the kingdom. The Scriptures consistently use this organic terminology to describe the kingdom and thus the church in this comprehensive sense. Individual Christians are properly to see themselves as part of this growing, spreading throng of "called-out" ones—dispersing over the whole creation—to declare the rule of Christ in all ways, to all people, in all places, and to touch all things in order to leave no stone unturned in a corporate quest to be His transformed and transforming instruments. Each of us is His child, but even more gloriously, we are a redeemed people, working as a whole body all across His realm. Each believer has a customized set of gifts, a distinctive context, and thus a unique role to play in God's kingdom; yet each is to draw strength and encouragement and to seek significance primarily from the divinely constituted and sustained body of Christ. Our individual callings are to be seen in terms of His body, which corporately receives His equipping, His commands, and His commission to declare His rule and to praise the strength of His might across the whole universe.

The church throughout history has always existed in structured forms—that is, as an institution with its own particular tasks and callings in different times in history. While the calling of the church as a comprehensive, trans-historical organism is the same throughout created history, the calling of the church as institution is more specifically defined in different historical phases. The form and calling of the church as an institution in the patriarchal period differs significantly from that of the Mosaic/national period, which also differed substantially from the New Testament period instituted at Pentecost.[39] The New Testament institutional church is given specific responsibilities to oversee the sound teaching of the Word—with the proclamation of the gospel, the warning to flee the wrath that is to come by seeking grace in Jesus Christ, as central to this task.[40] Institutional faithfulness to the Word also includes the responsibilities to engage in ministries of mercy,[41] to rightly administer the New Testament sacraments,[42] and to guard the purity and effectiveness of the institution by exercising church discipline regarding sound doctrine and right behavior. The New Testament describes the work of the apostles to organize new local churches and to explain the designation of offices within the church and the duties and qualifications of those called to these governing offices. God provides the church as an institution with peculiar gifts of His Spirit, and the institution is also described in organism terms as a body in which each member exercises gifts in unity and for the good of the institution as a whole. Thus the institution is given specific responsibilities, and it is also given the gifts and the authority to faithfully carry out those responsibilities.

To expand those responsibilities beyond what is given or to claim authority beyond what is given would be unfaithful to the church's institutional calling—as would be abdicating those responsibilities or shrinking back from exercising the authority assigned to it. In the same way, members of the body who don't recognize the legitimate authority of the institution or refuse to participate explicitly in the institutional callings are being unfaithful to who they are in Christ. Institutional church authority has been and continues to be a thorn in the flesh of the Modernist mind-set because the ultimate source of its authority transcends the human and the natural. But the fact remains that the Scripture gives the church the task of representing in institutional form the authority of Christ in the context of its institutional calling. While the authority is from God Himself, the exercise of that authority is in and through human agency. Individuals are called by God to offices of service in the church, and the service that some of these officers render is to be the means through which Christ's authority can be expressed in concrete forms among His people. The responsibility of church officers to exercise this authority and the responsibility of members to submit is not without bounds; nor is the exercise of this authority isolated from sinful and creaturely limitations. The Scripture itself is the ultimate touchstone for judgments concerning sound doctrine and godly behavior. Those charged with exercising authority are themselves held accountable to the Word, and thus there are always to be checks and balances and feedback loops that officers are to heed to avoid "lording over" those they are called to serve. The officers are to strive to exercise Christ's authority and not simply their own.

This is all to say that in terms of "being," the authority of Christ does have concrete expression in the world in particular areas through His church. Human allegiance to God and thus to His people is not allowed to remain in an abstract or individualized form. Allegiance to Christ must ultimately be played out in a concrete time and space commitment to a particular institutional expression of His church—in its human, local, and historical context. Individuals are to unite with some institutional expression of Christ's church, and the uniting inevitably means placing oneself under its authority.

We want to draw out several implications of this discussion for science. These implications relate to the ontological "who we are" and "where we are standing" thrust of this chapter. First is the recognition that as believers doing our science in isolation from Christian community should be a foreign concept. Second is the recognition that doing our science in complete isolation from the authority of the New Testament institutional church is a denial of both "who we are" and "where we are standing" from a Christian perspective. The warfare image of church versus science that is deeply embedded in contemporary Western culture fosters reactionary positions both inside and outside the church. These positions distort and strain what should be the natural connections between the work of a Christian scientist and his conceptions of his responsibilities to the church. We will discuss both of these implications for a Christian scientist in the context of the church as an organism and as an institution.

The work of Christians in science should be consciously seen as work done in the context of an explicit commitment to extend the church as organism into all areas of life. Neither the scientist nor the community of believers should see science as a vocation best carried out in isolation from the people of God. Within the community there should be a sense of teamwork and explicit affirmations of the various callings of God's people, including callings in the sciences. For scientists there should be an interest in reporting back to fellow believers what is seen and heard of the kingdom in carrying out scientific callings. There should be a prominent concern with how the fruits of scientific work can be communicated to fellow believers in a way that encourages and stimulates the church in both its broad organism tasks and in its specifically focused institutional work.

The connection Christian scientists have to the church is not just in general organism terms but is also in institutional terms. This means that at various times scientific judgments might properly come under scrutiny in terms of the church's institutional responsibility to exercise Christ's authority in guarding sound doctrine. The idea that the church has real authority runs counter to Modernist perceptions of the church as ultimately a voluntary social and cultural institution with authority only in terms of the rules its members set up for themselves. In addition, in situations in which judgments related to science are made in a church context, it is particularly tempting for Christian scientists to take on the Modernist posture of the scientist as a courageous spokesperson for objective scientific truth over against the misconceptions and superstitions of outdated religious dogma. It is not easy to throw off the Modernist assumption that a Christian scientist's commitment to truth is able to be superimposed completely on his scientific commitments in the context of the scientific community. It's all too easy to see ourselves as Christian scientists standing outside of the church as the "objective" critics of church teaching. But our ultimate allegiance as scientists is not to our scientific disciplines as such but to Christ's church—not just in abstract terms but in concrete terms. It must be recognized that there may be times when that ultimate commitment will cost us in the scientific discipline or at least make us feel foolish among our scientific colleagues.

On the other hand, it is too easy for church assemblies and officers to feel threatened by the onslaught of cultural pressures and so to react harshly, without due consideration for the limits the Scriptures place on the church's stewardship of Christ's authority. The church is to guard sound doctrine, and this requires making interpretational judgments concerning Scripture. But in doing this, the church is to be gentle in correction, and, as with the exercise of Christian parental authority, the exercise of church authority should not provoke its scientific members to wrath by uninformed, overextended, or seemingly arbitrary judgments. It is the responsibility of church leaders to exercise informed discernment—to listen to people with the relevant expertise and to respect the science of the surrounding culture and not to unnecessarily contradict it. They should be as prepared to insist upon the scriptural legitimacy of a breadth of interpretations and views as they are to establish narrower limits based on Scripture when required.

There will always be tensions in the human administration of Christ's authority and in human submission to it. But a Christian understanding of "who we are" in Christ and "where we're standing" in His world has to mean that Christians in the sciences take the authority of the church in relevant areas seriously. It seems to us that Christians in the sciences should gently and winsomely seek to inform the church in our areas of expertise, but at the end of the day, unless we are convinced that the gospel itself is being compromised by church decisions, we should be willing to submit, even if a particular decision might be against our individual judgment or runs contrary to the consensus judgment of our scientific discipline. Patience and humility are essential virtues for all parties in these issues. May the God of grace have mercy on His people in these things.

So the practical reality of the church as organism and institution is a basic Christian ontological commitment that has significant implications for the scientific endeavors of Christians. There is a divinely originated and sustained church in history that new creatures in Christ are by nature imbedded in. This church both as organism and as institution plays a central role in the now-but-not-yet establishment of the King's rule in His realm. And the supremacy of Jesus Christ is the ontological glue that holds it all together, that provides the ultimate connection between God's purposes in the church and in the world.[43]

Redeemed Scientists and the Redemption of All Things

It is clear that although the re-creation of humans to form a people for God's own possession is the centerpiece of God's glorification of Himself in Christ, the rest of creation is in view as well, with Christ as the creator and re-creator of it all. Though the teachings about creational regeneration are less prominent in Scripture than are the details of human regeneration, clear parallels and explicit connections are to be found concerning the continuity of human and nonhuman regeneration in Christ.

> *Though outwardly we are wasting away, yet inwardly we are being renewed day by day. For our light and momentary troubles are*

achieving for us an eternal glory that far outweighs them all. So we fix our eyes not on what is seen, but on what is unseen. For what is seen is temporary, but what is unseen is eternal. Now we know that if the earthly tent we live in is destroyed, we have a building from God, an eternal house in heaven, not built by human hands. . . . For while we are in this tent, we groan and are burdened, because we do not wish to be unclothed but to be clothed with our heavenly dwelling, so that what is mortal may be swallowed up by life. Now it is God who has made us for this very purpose and has given us the Spirit as a deposit, guaranteeing what is to come. (2 Cor. 4:16b—5:1, 4-5)

I consider that our present sufferings are not worth comparing with the glory that will be revealed in us. The creation waits in eager expectation for the sons of God to be revealed. For the creation was subjected to frustration, not by its own choice, but by the will of the one who subjected it, in hope that the creation itself will be liberated from its bondage to decay and brought into the glorious freedom of the children of God.

We know that the whole creation has been groaning as in the pains of childbirth right up to the present time. Not only so, but we ourselves, who have the firstfruits of the Spirit, groan inwardly as we wait eagerly for our adoption as sons, the redemption of our bodies. For in this hope we were saved. But hope that is seen is no hope at all. Who hopes for what he already has? But if we hope for what we do not yet have, we wait for it patiently. (Rom. 8:18-25)

Just as in the case of humans, the nonhuman creation has been estranged from God and waits in eager expectation, "groaning" for its redemption. Also just as with humans, its corruption is a terminal case, and only the death of its "old" reality and rebirth as a new creation in Christ will do.

But the day of the Lord will come like a thief. The heavens will disappear with a roar; the elements will be destroyed by fire, and the earth and everything in it will be laid bare. Since everything will be destroyed in this way, what kind of people ought you to be? You ought to live holy and godly lives as you look forward to the day of God and speed its coming. That day will bring about the destruction of the heavens by fire, and the elements will melt in the heat. But in keeping with his promise we are looking forward to a new heaven and a new earth, the home of righteousness. (2 Peter 3:10-13)

So the entire creation, humans as well as the rest, is waiting in hope based on the gospel promises of God in Christ. The coming fulfillment of God's promises to us has already been demonstrated in Christ, the firstborn from the dead, the One who is already glorified in the presence of the Father. A deposit guaranteeing the reality of God's promises has already been made in us now by the regenerating presence of the Spirit in our bodies. Our lifestyle in the now and our hope in the not yet is connected to the coming re-creation of all things, the ultimate reconciliation of all things in Christ. And further, the re-creation of all things is impacted by the way we live out our lives as new creatures now in that expectation. Finally the rest of creation is looking to us to see what God will ultimately do for it and is groaning for our final redemption because its liberation will ultimately come in and through ours.

The universe "where we are standing" is thus linked with us in a common destiny in Christ. Our science, as a specialized way of relating ourselves to the universe, can be done with this in view. We are dealing with a reality that is on its way to liberation, and at some level we are demonstrating to it what the reign of Christ is like even as we are being used to bring the reign of Christ to its fullness in history. Our science is a part of this awesome task.

Science and Consummation: Science in Light of Eternity

We have been advocating an ontological approach to creation in which the story God unfolds in history is taken to be central to what creation is. We have also been advocating a kind of "relational realism" in which various relationships that materialists might characterize as merely mental or symbolic constructs have real being, e.g., federal representation and "new creatures in new relational webs." Having discussed three major related episodes in the story, we now come to the final episode, often referred to as Consummation, since it is the pinnacle, the fulfillment, or the completion of all that has come before. We have all been encouraged at various times to evaluate our day-to-day activities by asking: What is the value of activity X in light of eternity? The basic idea of course is that we should not be spending our time and energy on things that "won't last," that don't have eternal value. We cover three basic questions relevant to our understanding of what it means to do science in light of eternity: How is the present created order fulfilled in the consummation order? How should our recognition of consummational realities impact our actions in history, for example, the science we do? And finally, what is the ultimate end of the story that we are looking forward to?

For many, a prominent question that arises in considerations of Consummation concerns the continuity of "this world" with "the next." Does the Consummation involve bringing into glory a cleaned-up version of the present created order and thus at least some of the results of our work? Or is there a complete break between this messed-up present order and the new order to be established in glory such that none of our accomplishments, say, in science and technology, will make it to glory with us? This question is often framed practically for Christians as we make judgments concerning where to invest our lives and time. However, it seems to us that this focus tends to miss the whole point of consummational commitments in the "now" lives of believers. Each believer must face temporal prioritization issues, but we would do better to avoid framing them in "will it just burn?" or "am I just polishing the brass on a sinking ship?" terms. Ontological commitments concerning continuity and discontinuity in the Consummation are much more powerful than the "will it just burn?" question would recognize.

First then the Scriptures do teach a distinct discontinuity between this age and the next:

> *At that time his voice shook the earth, but now he has promised, "Once more I will shake not only the earth but also the heavens." The words "once more" indicate the removing of what can be shaken—that is, created things—so that what cannot be shaken may*

remain. Therefore, since we are receiving a kingdom that cannot be shaken, let us be thankful, and so worship God acceptably with reverence and awe, for our "God is a consuming fire." (Heb. 12:26-29)

But the day of the Lord will come like a thief. The heavens will disappear with a roar; the elements will be destroyed by fire, and the earth and everything in it will be laid bare. Since everything will be destroyed in this way, what kind of people ought you to be? You ought to live holy and godly lives as you look forward to the day of God and speed its coming. That day will bring about the destruction of the heavens by fire, and the elements will melt in the heat. But in keeping with his promise we are looking forward to a new heaven and a new earth, the home of righteousness. (2 Peter 3:10-13)

So apparently the present heavens and earth will pass away in spectacular fashion. But to what ends? How are we to look at this distinct discontinuity in the story? One function of discontinuity is to contrast the impermanent nature of the created order with the permanent nature of the kingdom of Christ. Certainly also there is the element of judgment, of the cleansing of God's works in history from sin, evil, and corruption. But imbedded within judgment and the passing of an age is great hope and encouragement for the people of God. The death of the old clears the way for the birth of the new, "the home of righteousness." So the judgment of all things is not entirely an end in itself in the story, and God doesn't just minimally preserve His kingdom in the midst of the final season of judgment. He demonstrates His righteousness, power, and grace by building and completing His kingdom work through judgment. Judgment of this present age is not an ending as much as it is part of its completion. In addition, discontinuity is a characteristic of Consummation because certain elements of the present age are no longer needed, given the full revelation of God's glory and the unhindered relationship with His people.

I did not see a temple in the city, because the Lord God Almighty and the Lamb are its temple. The city does not need the sun or the moon to shine on it, for the glory of God gives it light, and the Lamb is its lamp. The nations will walk by its light, and the kings of the

> *earth will bring their splendor into it. On no day will its gates ever be shut, for there will be no night there. The glory and honor of the nations will be brought into it. Nothing impure will ever enter it, nor will anyone who does what is shameful or deceitful, but only those whose names are written in the Lamb's book of life. (Rev. 21:22-27)*

So the break between this world and the next emphasizes the permanence of God's kingdom, the cleansing of judgment, and the removal of anything superfluous in the new heavens and the new earth.

But there are elements of continuity in Consummation as well, connections between the history of the originally created order and the recreated order:

> *For the Lord himself will come down from heaven, with a loud command, with the voice of the archangel and with the trumpet call of God, and the dead in Christ will rise first. After that, we who are still alive and are left will be caught up together with them in the clouds to meet the Lord in the air. And so we will be with the Lord forever. Therefore encourage each other with these words. (1 Thess. 4:16-18)*

God's people will be brought into the new order prepared for them and are thus the central element of continuity. Yet also notice from the Revelation 21 passage just quoted above: "and the kings of earth will bring their splendor into it," and "the glory and honor of the nations will be brought into it." What exactly the "splendor" and the "glory and honor" that will be brought "into it" refer to would be difficult to say, but the passage does further encourage the idea that discontinuity is actually in service of continuity. Discontinuity is preparative for that which will be continuous. It is part of the process by which what exists in the present order is brought to full fruition in Christ. Thus this age and the age to come are related to one another by a kind of developmental pathway: "The kingdom of the world has become the kingdom of our Lord and of his Christ, and he will reign for ever and ever" (Rev. 11:15).

But this development doesn't appear to be simply a continuous physical process, like a plant developing from a seed. This development seems to be focused on relational continuity—it is all about where things stand in relation to Christ. To focus on the continuity of "stuff" seems to be materialist in a certain sense and seems to miss the point. The continuity is not to be thought of in terms of things that are able to be transported across the discontinuity "chasm." Even humans who have already been re-created in the present order will be reconstituted as newly embodied individuals—with bodies that apparently are the same—only different.

> *But someone may ask, "How are the dead raised? With what kind of body will they come?" How foolish! What you sow does not come to life unless it dies. When you sow, you do not plant the body that will be, but just a seed, perhaps of wheat or of something else. But God gives it a body as he has determined, and to each kind of seed he gives its own body. All flesh is not the same: Men have one kind of flesh, animals have another, birds another and fish another. There are also heavenly bodies and there are earthly bodies; but the splendor of the heavenly bodies is one kind, and the splendor of the earthly bodies is another. The sun has one kind of splendor, the moon another and the stars another; and star differs from star in splendor.*
>
> *So will it be with the resurrection of the dead. The body that is sown is perishable, it is raised imperishable; it is sown in dishonor, it is raised in glory; it is sown in weakness, it is raised in power; it is sown a natural body, it is raised a spiritual body. If there is a natural body, there is also a spiritual body. So it is written: "The first man Adam became a living being"; the last Adam, a life-giving spirit. The spiritual did not come first, but the natural, and after that the spiritual. The first man was of the dust of the earth, the second man from heaven. As was the earthly man, so are those who are of the earth; and as is the man from heaven, so also are those who are of heaven. And just as we have borne the likeness of the earthly man, so shall we bear the likeness of the man from heaven. (1 Cor. 15:35-49)*

So it seems that our new bodies will be related to our current bodies by spiritual development—a development explicitly tied to our relation, our identification with Christ. They will be bodies fit to inhabit the new age of the Consummation of our relation to Christ.

All this encourages the idea that at Consummation humans and the rest of creation with us will be remade—will be transformed. The continuity between what is now and what will be at Consummation is based primarily on its constant relation to Christ—not necessarily on some kind of physical continuity. The physical in some sense will itself be reconstituted anew—it will be like what was before and yet will be different. Its continuity will be sustained by relation to Christ and by its role in demonstrating His preeminence.

For believers, then, "living in light of eternity" has nothing to do with discounting the present order or the stuff of which it is composed or avoiding specialized relationships to it such as that established in scientific work. We are to live in the sure hope of the coming Consummation of all things—the bringing to fullness of all things in Christ as they become related to Him in the highest and fullest way. Our relation to Him in the here and now and our relation to the people and the "stuff" around us are contributing to that fullness as the web of relations is itself even now transformed by the work of the Spirit. All that we touch in history is connected in a unique way to Christ the Redeemer/King and will be connected to Him in fullness when He gathers His people to Himself at the end of the age. The calling of God's children to science then is a calling that connects all that we handle to the Christ-centered transformational web that is filling the whole earth with His glory and will come to its full fruition in the Consummation. In science then there is no aspect of His world that cannot be related to Christ and thus no aspect that is excluded from the calling of those involved in the sciences. It is a matter of establishing the habit of being conscious that we are connecting all we do in science, whether basic or applied, to the demonstration of the preeminence of Christ, the ruling and healing King of all that is. Continuity and discontinuity then are primarily about the ultimate relation of all of creation to Christ as God's purposes in Him are written "large" at the end of created history.

Science as a Foundation for Glory or Glory as a Foundation for Science: Being Pulled into Glory

A basic Christian conviction is that the story and thus created history is linear and not circular. One of the implications of seeing reality in more of its story aspects is that it changes the way we might think about the dynamics in the story and how the story is driven. Typically in Modernist mode, we tend to think about history in more mechanical terms, being driven by forces and causes from behind, and we think about justifying what we do and how we think in terms of how they extend what is driving it from behind. Thinking in story mode though can open up considerations that may helpfully balance our dominant mechanistic instincts.

A written story of course is not driven by the paper or the ink on the pages of the book. It is driven by the plot according to the purposes of the author. For those reading the story, the meaning of the story and the pivotal points are sometimes obvious during the reading, but often are somewhat unclear until the end. In fact, often it becomes clear that an author had certain ends in view and that the story in terms of details and pacing is best understood more as being pulled by its conclusion than as being pushed by "forces" from behind. By God's grace, the Bible gives us a written commentary on the story being told in history, and that written commentary does give us some insight into the ultimate ends. We need to recognize that much of the story will not be sensible to us until Consummation, but we do have enough insight into this final event to orient our thinking to some degree to its pull on created reality.

In Modern terms we are constantly tempted to turn things the other way and to try to understand even the episodes of the story entirely in terms of their general temporal order, to try to construct a unified story primarily from "below." But the episodes of the story make the best sense in view of the ending—the Consummation. History might better be seen as suspended from and being pulled into the Consummation rather than being driven from below by forces and events that mechanistically interact to generate the next event. Seeing each episode from the view of the Consummation reorients some of the contentious issues often associated with each episode and unifies them in a way difficult to see from the bottom-up approach.

For example, from this perspective, to try to work out the whole trajectory of history as imbedded in some sense in the creation episode—as front loaded—doesn't make sense and tends toward the isolation of the creation and redemption episodes that we have warned against. The creation episode in Scripture clearly provides hooks to attach the ropes "let down" from the Consummation—the who (God in Christ), the what (all things), and the why (to glorify Himself by demonstrating the preeminence of Christ) are all there. To invest major foundational power in the specifics of how and when questions concerning the creation seems strange from a consummational pulling perspective. Likewise, the function of the Fall is to establish the fact of "abnormalism" in history and the absolute need for God to rescue the creation, in love to do for it what it cannot do for itself. The Fall itself does not provide the resources to explain or to solve the problem of evil in some foundational way. The problem of evil is ultimately solved in Consummation by the absolute triumph of Christ over it. Questions concerning evil, justice, and grace are best addressed looking forward from the Fall, through redemption, and they are finally and fully resolved in Consummation. In short the meaning and unity of history is found in its ultimate Consummation, not in inbuilt elements of its beginnings.

This is directly relevant to instincts we have as believers about science and our involvement in it. Through the Modern age the temptation has been to use the science of the day to establish or shore up firm foundations for Christian belief—and certainly there is a proper role for science in apologetics and in the encouragement of believers. But our primary task in science is to bear witness to the coming Consummation rather than to build the perfect apologetic building from below. Our science isn't to be primarily about shoring up the foundations, but about continuously connecting our personal stories—in all our being and knowing and doing—to the Cosmic Story being unfolded in Christ.

Finally the Scriptures teach that though the story of history is the story of the preeminence of Christ, the ultimate end of the story in terms of the Trinitarian economy is the returning of all things to the Father.

> *But Christ has indeed been raised from the dead, the firstfruits of those who have fallen asleep. For since death came through a man, the resurrection of the dead comes also through a man. For as in Adam all die, so in Christ all will be made alive. But each in his own turn: Christ, the firstfruits; then, when he comes, those who belong to him. Then the end will come, when he hands over the kingdom to God the Father after he has destroyed all dominion, authority and power. For he must reign until he has put all his enemies under his feet. The last enemy to be destroyed is death. For he "has put everything under his feet." Now when it says that "everything" has been put under him, it is clear that this does not include God himself, who put everything under Christ. When he has done this, then the Son himself will be made subject to him who put everything under him, so that God may be all in all. (1 Cor. 15:20-28)*

All of created reality was brought into being and unfolded in and through Christ, was redeemed in and through Christ, and is drawn back up into Christ to be presented to the Father.

Keeping Our Stories Straight

Much of the preceding discussion may seem pretty abstract and far away from real science in the laboratory trenches. And in a certain sense a contemplation of "being" issues will always have an abstract feel. Keep in mind that at the start of the chapter we pointed out that human knowing and doing are largely responses to being, and in the next two chapters those knowing and doing responses will be the focus. But before we close this chapter we want to say that we have found these "being" issues extremely relevant in day-to-day work in science—and also extremely challenging in terms of "keeping our stories straight" as we live and work in a culture that often narrates a story quite different from the one we've just looked at. We will end this chapter with some encouragement to keep working to tell our own Christian story and not become absorbed into the other stories, such as the Modern or Postmodern stories around us.

We often find it difficult in dealing with modern science to stay focused on the story we know is being played out in God's time and in His way. We find it so easy to slip into the Modern story instead in which science plays the lead role. The Modern story involves emancipation from darkness and superstition by the autonomous exercise of reason and human cleverness. It involves a triumphal building of the edifice of human knowledge from the bottom up, so that the knowledge we obtain is ours and ours alone. The Modern story idolizes individualism and limits its science to naturalistic explanation. It envisions a material universe that is ultimately a closed system of cause and effect in which freedom can only be found in apparent randomness. Analysis by reduction to underlying impersonal forces or by appealing to cold statistical probabilities are considered the only possible tools of explanation. By contrast in the terms of the Christian story, we should recognize that our science need not be bounded by naturalism. We are free to theorize in broader ways without the constraints of naturalistically understood closed systems. As discussed in chapter 6, we should not expect to find ultimate closure from within the created realm itself. We should not entirely be wedded to reductive analysis and should be more open to seeing non-reductive relations and interactions. Finally, we should strive to see our work as individuals as important and valid as we contribute our part of the story; yet we should find our ultimate human identity not in individualism, or in a scientific discipline, but as members of the community of Christ.

Who We Are as New Creatures in the Scientific Story

Finally we turn to a "being" issue that has been vexing to many in the sciences. The issue involves coming to terms with the relationship between regeneration, sanctification, and scientific practice—that is, coming to terms with the impact of our being "in Christ." What difference does the new birth and the process of sanctification make in the science we do? Even in asking the question many people become a little suspicious as to where this will lead—worried that somehow this has to mean that Christian scientists are by definition better at science than non-Christian scientists.

This question concerning the impact of being a Christian on the quality of science one does is really a species of the more common question people raise about why it is that one can't always distinguish Christians from non-Christians based on their behavior. Shouldn't all Christians be nicer, more honest, and so on, than all non-Christians? But in fact we all know some non-Christians who are easier to get along with than some of our Christian acquaintances. So if Christianity is so transforming, the question goes, then why do we know so many abrasive, hard-to-get-along-with, petty, selfish Christians? Christians have various ways of trying to deal with this: "Well, just try to imagine how George would be if he weren't a believer," for example—an argument that becoming a new creature leads to measurable moral progress. One just has to take into account the starting point. But this explanation isn't very satisfying and doesn't seem to take into account the extreme language the Bible uses to describe the difference between "old" creatures and "new" creatures in Christ. We don't pretend to be able to clear this kind of question up neatly, but several points can be made. In considering the difference being in Christ might make, our modern instincts often direct us down two different paths. On the one hand we are tempted to relegate the impact of our being in Christ to "subjective feelings" or the "merely psychological"—that is, the impact is not really real. On the other hand we are tempted to evaluate the impact of our being in Christ only in ways that would count in the Modern world. If all we allow to count is what is seen, then we are sitting in the naturalistic chair of "unfaith," in Francis Schaeffer's terms.

To try to work through some of this, it might help to picture the following scene: Two science-types in white lab coats are working side by side at a lab bench. They have been given the task of following the same experimental protocol, using the same materials at the same time in an effort to determine where some variance in results might be coming from. They both think about the regulation of the gene they are examining in terms of the same conceptual model. One of them is a believer, and the other is not. Does belief or unbelief, regenerate or unregenerate, make any difference here? The natural response is to say, well, no. If all goes well, their results will be the same, and just knowing that one was a believer and one was not wouldn't be enough for us to say whose results we would trust more. In fact it may be that the unbeliever has better "lab hands" than the believer. But if we think about this in terms of sacred/secular dualism, to say that there is no difference would seem to be to admit that science after all is a value-free, neutral endeavor in which new birth/no new birth makes no difference—so leave your religion at the door of science, please. To say that perhaps the Christian was humming a hymn while waiting for the centrifuge to stop spinning in one of the steps in the procedure would be a copout that displays the kind of sacred/secular distinctions Christians often retreat to when placed in a tough spot in the Modern world.

It seems to us that to accept the isolated "looks the same, is the same" assessment gives in too easily to a materialist/reductionist perspective of what is really going on in the universe. The story ontology we have suggested with its emphasis on a supratemporal, relational web of connections throws a different light on the lab situation above. First, events in the seen are always linked with and are embedded in demonstrations in the unseen. We remain largely unaware of these realities, but the Scriptures provide so many hints of such things[44] that we can be assured that no event in the seen world goes unnoticed or has no impact in the unseen. Christians are always on the clock as believers, whether in the lab or not, and the reality of a Christian's actions will always be different from a non-Christian's, even if in the seen they look the same.

Second, because as believers who have been grafted into Christ, we are connected to a web that literally transforms all that we touch. What we do in faith is pleasing to God and in fact consecrates the things connected to the redemptive web through us.[45] Our actions unfold further the growing light, spread the fragrance of Christ, declare the present rule of Christ, and hasten the coming triumph of Christ. All this is true, not primarily because of what these actions look like, but because of who we are in Christ in the doing of them. In contrast the Scriptures teach that actions of unbelievers constitute rebellion, increase the darkness, carry the stench of death, and hasten the coming judgment, not primarily because they look this way in the seen, but because of who unbelievers are without Christ. Actions in the seen that look the same may actually be part of radically different "full reality" programs.

In the scene from *The Magician's Nephew* discussed in the introduction to this chapter, C. S. Lewis goes on to describe the process by which Uncle Andrew came to a distorted perception and understanding of what was actually happening around him as Aslan was creating the Narnian world by singing it into existence:

> "Of course it can't really have been singing," he thought, "I must have imagined it. I've been letting my nerves get out of order. Who ever heard of a lion singing?" And the longer and the more beautifully the Lion sang, the harder Uncle Andrew tried to make himself believe that he could hear nothing but roaring. Now the trouble about trying to make yourself stupider than you really are is that you very often succeed. Uncle Andrew did. He soon did hear nothing but roaring in Aslan's song. Soon he couldn't have heard anything else even if he had wanted to.[46]

Thus we end this chapter with both a warning and a call. The warning is that unless we Christians encourage one another to continuously work through and rehearse the "being" truths of the faith, what we will see and hear will become distorted. If we steadfastly refuse to see and hear specifically as Christians, we may succeed in blinding ourselves, becoming unable to see as we should even if we wanted to. The call then is to consciously dedicate ourselves to the "being" truths revealed in the Word and to find ways to encourage one another to stay centered on those truths.

Chapter Eight

A Gracious Revealer and the Making of Scientific Knowledge

But he said to me, "My grace is sufficient for you, for my power is made perfect in weakness." Therefore I will boast all the more gladly about my weaknesses. . . . For when I am weak, then I am strong.

2 CORINTHIANS 12:9-10

ASK A FRIEND TO TELL YOU something that he knows, and it is very likely that your friend will be able to come up with some knowledge that he claims to know is true. Then ask your friend to defend or to justify his truth claim. Invariably he will appeal to some standard. For example, he might say, "I know that Mongolia is in central Asia because I have a Rand McNally map on my wall that shows this to be the case." Or, "I know that my birthday is February 10 because my parents told me about their trip to the hospital on that date, and '2/10/61' is written on my birth certificate." As with many knowledge claims, these two assertions are justified by direct appeals to the authority of a "reporter" believed reliable.

Now what if your friend claimed to know that taking cod liver oil twice a day leads to long life because his grandmother took cod liver oil all the time, and she lived to be ninety-seven. "Well," you might say, "I'm happy for her, but has the longevity-producing effects of cod liver oil been proven scientifically?" Consider what your expectations would be in asking for "scientific" proof. In our culture "scientific" knowledge is generally held in high regard, and "scientific" proof is considered a high standard for justifying truth claims. For most people, scientific knowledge is considered to be "knowledge approved by trained professionals who have used scientific methodology to obtain reliable information about how the world really works." And while there might be some level of awe for the "trained professionals" who can do complicated experiments, "scientific" usually carries with it the idea that this knowledge would be accepted by anybody who has the proper training and intelligence and does the same experiments. For knowledge to be scientific in this view, in principle, anyone who does the same experiments will obtain basically the same data and will come to the same conclusions unless personal bias interferes.

Now ask your friend to tell you what has been revealed to him lately, and you are likely to get a puzzled look. After considering for a minute, he might tell you about something he has recently learned that was previously unknown to him—hence a revelation. Or he might relate a story involving a series of apparently unrelated events and exclaim, "And suddenly I had the revelation that they were all connected—I could see how it all fit!" Possibly he might relate a story of a mystical experience that gave him unique personal knowledge. If your friend is a Christian, he might consider the guidance of the Holy Spirit in his life or the gaining of insight from Scripture as a kind of spiritual revealing. But it is very unlikely that "science" would come up in the context of "revelation" except by way of contrast.

Finally, ask your friend if he has "made" any knowledge recently, and you are likely to get a "now I know you're just kidding around" look. Whether your conversation is about science or about revelation, it is unlikely that your friend would talk about knowledge that was "made." Most people would say that obtaining scientific knowledge or revealed knowledge is more like discovery and description than construction. Knowledge is discovered—like the discovery of a new star or a new bacterial species—not made the way a painter "makes" a picture or a novelist "makes" a character. A character in a novel doesn't exist until he is constructed in the mind of the writer and fleshed out on the pages of the novel. But surely a star or a bacterial species exists before it is discovered. So why is this chapter given the strange title, "A Gracious *Revealer* and the *Making* of Scientific Knowledge"? We'll try to explain.

A Gracious Revealer and the Making of Scientific Knowledge

What We Know and When We Came to Know It

In this chapter we want to consider in general what loving God in our knowing might involve and more specifically what faithful knowing in the natural sciences might entail. The nature of knowledge is formally examined in a branch of philosophy known as epistemology. The study of knowledge explores the meaning and justification of various kinds of knowledge claims. Epistemology as a discipline often focuses on description. What does someone mean when she says she knows that DNA is the blueprint for life? What is the justification consciously or unconsciously behind her claim? How do molecular biologists attempt to establish the facts of DNA function? Frequently though there are also prescriptive elements in epistemological studies. Epistemological analysis might lead to recommendations: "His belief is unjustified, and you probably should reject it," or conversely, "Her belief is justified, and you are being irrational if you don't accept it."

In the Modern world, science has long been the dominant epistemological standard that all knowledge claims have to come to terms with in one way or another. In many ways the Modern world is distinguished from the pre-Modern by its scientific approach to knowing. As described in chapter 2, the application of an experimental scientific methodology generally following the pattern Francis Bacon recommended in the early seventeenth century proved to be a powerful engine for discovery and technological achievement during the succeeding centuries. Given such success, it is not surprising that discussions of truth and knowledge in the Western context were more and more carried out in terms of science. And as we've seen, a variety of beliefs concerning the knowing power of science became increasingly imbedded in Western culture: Scientific knowledge is understood to be the universal paradigm for human knowing and is primarily understood to be a matter of dispassionate intellectual assent to demonstrated facts. Scientific truths, thus conceived, transcend cultural differences and are global in their reach. The scientific facts, objectively discovered and articulated, will be the same for all honest, rational people in all times and places.

In contrast, Postmodern accounts of knowledge and truth arise from a variety of complaints about Modernist truth-seeking methods and the social costs of Modernism's truth assertions. In the Postmodern schema those who want to insist on "Truth" may simply be naive, but more likely they have some kind of oppressive intent. In Postmodern thinking, the sharp fact/value distinction[1] typical of Modern thought must be collapsed so that all can see that fact claims are in reality simply strong value claims. In fact, a Postmodernist would say that insistence on fact/value distinctions is a form of Modernist coercion. (Look at the previous sentence carefully, and you will see one of the more obvious challenges Postmodernists face in making strong statements of this sort.) Much of the Postmodern agenda then has to do with disabusing Modernist-minded people of an arrogant commitment to their own values as "Truth" by "deconstructing" their arguments, positions, and truth claims to expose the hidden social agendas, prejudices, and oppressive purposes. Such deconstruction liberates the weak and exploited from the epistemological imperialism of dominant groups who have controlled the epistemological agendas and definitions to maintain their own privileged status.

Some threads of Postmodernism are more militant and reactionary, and others are more pragmatic and positive.[2] The militants utilize an "in your face" deconstructionism—angrily striking back at controlling oppression and decrying and lamenting the inevitable victimization of persons by social forces beyond the control of the individual. The "kinder and gentler forms" of Postmodernism promote relativistic perspectives in the hope that if humans would be more laid back about pursuing the Truth, we would all get along better. And for the Postmodernist, getting along is a nobler goal than misguided attempts to penetrate absolute truth and to force others to see things your way. Each group should be free to construct a contextual reality that suits it best and furthers its values of community.[3] Postmodern instincts concerning truth and knowledge favor the local, the communal, the holistic, the different, the underdog, and the relative as opposed to the global, the individual, the reductionistic, the uniform, the dominant, and the absolute.

The Science Wars: Scientific Knowledge as a Contested Concept

Given that the natural sciences are paradigmatic of Modernist approaches to knowing and truth, it is no surprise that the status and claims of Modern science have become a target of Postmodern critique. A new appreciation for the sociological aspects of scientific endeavors[4] led ultimately to the prominent emergence of an area of study often referred to as "science studies"[5] or the sociology of scientific knowledge (SSK). In fact an often vitriolic debate dubbed the "Science Wars"[6] has broken out in the academy, which essentially pits Modernist conceptions of science against Postmodern "re-imaginings" of science.

SSK advocates emphasize the social aspects of doing and evaluating science and also point to what they see as the heavy social costs of strictly adhering to Modernist beliefs about the epistemological authority of science: e.g., the fouling of air and water, the development of weapons of mass destruction, and the intellectual and cultural imperialism of the West that has led to the marginalization of the two-thirds world. Rather than embracing a Modern creed that insists that truth is always better than fiction, proponents of the more extreme versions of SSK thinking suggest that truth is a fiction and that we need to consciously choose truths that preserve humanist values better than scientific Modernism has.

Working scientists haven't taken kindly to what they perceive as a radical program to devalue science by reducing the content of scientific knowledge to sociological convention.[7] The defenders of the traditional conception of Modern science emphasize the success of the scientific endeavor—the vast improvements in human understanding and quality of life achieved in modern times primarily through the power of science. They cast themselves in the role of defending the civilized rational approach to truth and knowledge against Postmodern barbarians howling outside the Modern gates who would return humankind to the darkness and superstition of the past. In the heat of the defense of Modern science, the "barbarian" class is expanded to include not only the "intellectual anarchists" from the "academic left" but also any group that seems to be questioning the absolute epistemological authority of Modern science: e.g., proponents of alternative medicine, New Age spiritualists, and "ideological zealots" on the "religious right."[8] In the view of the defenders of Modern science, these barbarians must be opposed because their way of thinking is ultimately wedded to an irrationalism that, if left unchecked, will destroy the foundations of Modern civilization.

Idolatry and Despair

Although there appears to be great contrast in the patterns of Modern and Postmodern thought, they lead to related forms of idolatry. Richard Middleton and Brian Walsh in their book *Truth Is Stranger Than It Used to Be* describe the situation in the following helpful terms:

> [T]o a very large degree the issues before us in developing a Christian perspective in a postmodern culture are at the intersection of order as given and order as task. If we only notice the given . . . then we will likely succumb to the temptation of an authoritarian and absolutistic realism. . . . If, however, we only attend to the reality-constructing activity of ordering our own world, then regardless of how much goodwill we have, and regardless of how much we want to avoid totalizing violence . . . it is likely that we will end up with competing tribes with nothing to appeal to beyond their own tribally defined "realities." Paradoxically the cultural-historical result [of Modernism and Postmodernism] will be the same. Tribal particularism is just as prone to totalizing violence as absolutistic realism.[9]

As Middleton and Walsh argue, the Modern scientific mind-set deftly transforms God's "given" into human "taken." The "taken" is then deified by asserting its objective status on the basis of autonomously exercised human truth-detecting capacities. The Postmodern mind-set tends to deify "order as task," essentially declaring God's impotence as the Truth-giver,[10] while worshiping human creative and constructive capacities as ultimate.

Idolatry always leads to death and despair, and the idolatries of Modernism and Postmodernism are no exceptions. The Modernist idolatry of autonomous human certainty leads to the death of human knowledge, as the Postmodern deconstruction of Modernist knowledge illustrates. The Postmodern idolatry of autonomous human subjectivity ultimately leads to the fragmentation of human communities into smaller and smaller self-interest groups constantly at war with one another. Both the Modern and the Postmodern forms of idolatry appear to lead in the end to battered and isolated human selves trapped in lives of "quiet desperation."

Obedience and Hope

How should Christians respond to these two knowledge idolatries of our day in ways that properly emphasize God-given order and also the God-given task to bring order? Consider the following description of Adam's work as described in Genesis 2. This is an interesting vignette for a number of reasons, but especially from the standpoint of "order as given" and "order as task" in scientific endeavors.

> *Now the* Lord *God had formed out of the ground all the beasts of the field and all the birds of the air. He brought them to the man to see what he would name them; and whatever the man called each living creature, that was its name. So the man gave names to all the livestock, the birds of the air and all the beasts of the field. (Gen. 2:19-20)*

In one sense God is the One who gives order here. He created the animals in their various forms. Yet He brought them to Adam to see what Adam would call them. It doesn't appear to be some kind of game—God having already given the right names to the animals and Adam trying to guess them. It would be strange indeed if Adam worked at his task by trying to re-create in his own mind what God was thinking when He created, rather than to look at the characteristics of the animals themselves to determine what seemed to him to be appropriate names. It would also seem incongruous if the first thing Adam did to begin his task was to try to forget or set aside his knowledge that God had brought these animals into existence and was the One who brought them to him. He wasn't saying to himself, "Let's see...if God didn't exist, and if He didn't act in the world, then what would I call this animal?" Lastly, one doesn't get the idea from the passage that Adam willy-nilly named the animals in terms of any random impulse that popped into his mind. Naming that was entirely arbitrary, having nothing to do with the actual animals brought to him would also be a strange response to the task God gave to Adam.[11] The receiving of order as divinely given and the constructing of order as a divinely appointed task seem to flow naturally together in Adam's work as it was obediently done. Echoing Middleton and Walsh then, we believe that to follow Adam's example Christians must develop perspectives on the sciences that take seriously God's call to obediently receive knowledge of the world as it is given and also to obediently find joy and hope in the God-given responsibility for "order as task."[12]

Deciding Whom to Please Epistemologically

Addressing the question of faithful ways of knowing for Christians is the major task of this chapter. To do this we will need to paint a general epistemological picture using broadly theological brush strokes, which will lead away from a narrow focus on knowing in science to Christian conceptions of knowing in general, though we will try to provide specific applications in the sciences. We will begin by returning for a moment to the "science wars" section above. Which side of the "science wars" is closer to the truth about science as a human endeavor: the Modernist vision of the objective human discovery of scientific truths or the Postmodern vision of creative construction of the scientific truths that suit us best? Most of us in Western culture would instinctively side with the Modernists. The radical implications of a strong SSK program seem too bizarre in view of daily life experiences. In daily life we know that some things you just can't get away with believing or disbelieving, no matter what the cultural context or social goals—and besides something like progress in real understanding seems to be happening in the sciences. Consider, for example, the improvements in health care practices and outcomes in the past 150 years—largely the result of scientific work. In fact most of those involved in SSK studies wouldn't push things quite so far as to reject any real scientific progress in understanding the world; they just want recognition that there are more sociological-cultural factors in science than we might realize. In the same vein, most defenders of generally Modernist perspectives in science wouldn't completely deny that some significant elements of science are socially impacted.

Even if one discounts the extremes, though, the fact remains that epistemology has gotten much more complicated in the Postmodern age, primarily because the old Modernist standards for knowledge have been called into question. While a Modernist-minded person will ultimately appeal to a universal standard of logical and empirical scientific method, a Postmodernist is more likely to take seriously a community consensus and to accept knowing as a more "local" phenomenon. So there are competing or at least different authorities to appeal to for knowledge claims, and the question of whose standards are to be used has become an essential preliminary to any epistemological discussion.[13] Rather than asking simply, "How does my knowledge claim measure up to some assumed universal scientific standard?" echoing the Modernist dissenters we met in chapter 3, we are faced with a more basic question: "Whom or what do I most trust and want to please in an epistemological sense and why?"[14]

Placing a decision concerning pleasing or trusting at the center of epistemological issues in science is particularly jarring to our Modernist sensibilities. We have always assumed that there is or should be some clearly defined rational and empirical method for handling these epistemological issues such that knowing and truth with regard to the facts of science are more about proper method than personal trusting or pleasing. But such mechanical, impersonal, or abstract notions of truth and knowledge seem to be foreign to scriptural discussions of truth and knowledge. In Scripture these categories are richly furnished with personal and relational elements such as trust, commitment, faithfulness, obedience, and love.[15] While Christians will readily admit that trust in a faithful Person who is the Way, the Truth, and the Life is at the heart of Christian belief, many will not have considered the relevance of such trust in approaching scientific knowing. We suggest that the most basic question in scientific issues is not, "Does a particular knowledge claim qualify as scientific knowledge?" (and thus in Modern terms qualify as "real" knowledge). The most basic question should be, "Whom am I ultimately trying to please in my scientific knowing?"[16] When this question is put in these terms, most Christians will likely give as an answer something like, "Well, I'm trying to please God in my scientific knowing . . . right?" But giving such an answer is the easy part. The hard part is trying to figure out what such "pleasing" should look like in our knowing in general and more particularly for our knowing in the sciences. How exactly should Christian obedience in scientific knowing play itself out in terms of submission to "order as given" and creative engagement in "order as task"?

Revelation: The Source of ALL Human Knowledge?

As a first step in addressing the "hard part," we want to focus on the Christian doctrine of the nature and role of God's revealing activity in the world. For many people, though, making a direct connection between revelation and scientific knowledge raises all kinds of questions. To claim that there is a sense in which Watson and Crick's discovery of the structure of DNA, for example, is a result of divine revelation and not ultimately derived from their own ingenuity, good fortune, and shrewd use of the work of others[17] does seem odd. In fact for many in Western culture, revelation of any kind from a source that transcends the material world is simply an incoherent concept. In this view modern people should have moved beyond taking such claims of supernatural communication seriously. Such a view is reflected, for example, in what Harvard biologist E. O. Wilson says in the closing chapter of his book *Consilience: The Unity of Knowledge*:

> The legacy of the Enlightenment is the belief that entirely on our own we can know and in knowing, understand and in understanding, choose wisely. That self-confidence has risen with the exponential growth of scientific knowledge, which is being woven into an increasingly full explanatory web of cause and effect. In the course of our enterprise we have learned a great deal about ourselves

> as a species. We now better understand where humanity came from, and what it is. *Homo sapiens* like the rest of life was self-assembled. So here we are, no one having guided us to this condition, no one looking over our shoulder, our future entirely up to us. Human autonomy having thus been recognized, we should now feel more disposed to reflect on where we wish to go.[18]

In direct contrast to Wilson's "entirely on our own, we can know" perspective, Colin Gunton's book *A Brief Theology of Revelation* describes a radical human inability to know anything "on our own":

> [W]e, being who and what we are, cannot know unless we are taught by that which is other than we, and that means by the Spirit of God. . . . Though nature is relatively passive under our enquiry . . . it remains true that knowledge of her comes as gift, and is therefore a species of revelation. . . . If there is revelation of the truth of the world, it is because the Spirit of truth enables it to take place. To put it another way, the creator Spirit brings it about that human rationality is able, within the limits set to it, to encompass the truth of creation. We therefore neither control nor create our knowledge, even though the concepts by which we express it are in part the free creations of our minds. Does it not then follow that all knowledge depends on disclosure or revelation?[19]

Gunton succinctly attacks both Modern and Postmodern pretenses concerning knowledge by claiming that we humans ultimately "neither control nor create our knowledge." He makes the radical claim that a proper doctrine of revelation holds that it is God alone who creates and controls not just "religious" knowledge but all human knowledge.

Of course, Wilson's autonomous vision of human knowledge, which leaves no room at all for revelation from a transcendent source, would be rejected by Christians, but what about Gunton's statements? Is his position an overreaction to Modern declarations of epistemological autonomy? Would a more moderate perspective that allows for a mix of autonomy and dependency be more advisable, reserving the term "revelation" for the specialized communication that leads to specific knowledge about God? In his book *I Believe in Revelation,* Leon Morris articulates a commonly assumed "middle" point of view: "Revelation . . . does [not] refer to the kind of knowledge that we might obtain by diligent research. It is knowledge that comes from outside ourselves and beyond our own ability to discover."[20] While the view Morris articulates might seem to establish a moderate balanced view, it seems to us that any strict distinction between knowledge obtained "by diligent research" and "knowledge that comes from outside ourselves" leaves humans firmly embedded in the Modernist knowledge quagmire. When knowing is broken into fundamentally different categories, human knowers, as whole beings, will inevitably experience some serious epistemological dissonance. Once knowing is fragmented, the resulting dissonance seems to be ultimately resolvable only in the complete conquest of one type of knowing by the other, or in a strongly dualistic isolation of one type of knowing from the other.[21] Christians have experienced these fragmenting pressures throughout the Modern period most acutely in the forced choice pose of many of the questions concerning Christian belief: science *or* Christianity, reason *or* revelation, scientific demonstration *or* faith. Morris's distinction between revealed knowledge and "self-service" knowledge seems to perpetuate these fragmenting tensions.

If human knowledge is indeed created and controlled by one Being, there will be essential unity in its nature and its revelation. The personal Being who reveals is also the One who created the persons to whom His revelation is addressed. Human recipients of revelation are specifically constituted as whole persons who are to receive revelation as whole persons. Revelation, though multifaceted, is not fractured into isolated bits to be fed to single aspects of human being in isolation from others. Humans are not simply data processing machines receiving and storing impersonal "files" of revealed knowledge. The unity of revealed knowledge is rooted in the unity of the Revealer and in His constitution of humans as whole persons fit to appropriate and participate in His revelation according to His purposes. To create radically different categories of knowledge ultimately does violence to the integrity of the Revealer, to the unity of the purpose for revelation, to that which is revealed, and to the persons who are called to respond to revelation.

The emphasis here is consistent with, but distinct from, more traditional discussions of the doctrine of general revelation. General revelation is usually taken to refer to a kind of knowledge concerning God's power and righteous requirements that is available to all humans from creation, and history thus leaves all humans without excuse before God. Psalm 19, Romans 1 and 2, and Acts 14 are the usual scriptural references given in support of this doctrine. Our present discussion, though, is broader than the traditional concerns of the doctrine of general revelation, and these passages, though relevant, don't directly address the expanded use of the term "revelation" that we are advocating.

There is an interesting passage in Isaiah 28, though, that does seem to assume such an expanded understanding of revelation. It is a wisdom poem placed in the context of a series of woes and judgments being declared against Israel. Although the specific point of the poem in this context is unclear, as a wisdom poem it speaks of God's revelation to farmers in very direct terms:

> *Listen and hear my voice; pay attention and hear what I say. When a farmer plows for planting, does he plow continually? Does he keep on breaking up and harrowing the soil? When he has leveled the surface, does he not sow caraway and scatter cummin? Does he not plant wheat in its place, barley in its plot, and spelt in its field? His God instructs him and teaches him the right way. Caraway is not threshed with a sledge, nor is a cartwheel rolled over cummin; caraway is beaten out with a rod, and cummin with a stick. Grain must be ground to make bread; so one does not go on threshing it forever. Though he drives the wheels of his threshing cart over it, his horses do not grind it. All this also comes from the LORD Almighty, wonderful in counsel and magnificent in wisdom. (vv. 28:23-29)*

The knowledge the farmer has of the appropriate methods for planting, harvesting, and processing his crops, which on one level we might say is a result of study or trial and error, is represented as a result of God's teaching and instruction—His revealing activity.[22] It may not be such a stretch after all to say that God revealed the structure of DNA to Watson and Crick!

OK, OK, So It's All Revelation. Now What?

Revelation, as we are using the term, involves the entirety of God's disclosure of His holiness, power, and grace in the preeminence of Jesus Christ. It is a broad and rich concept involving the entire "fabric" of disclosure—the God who reveals, the purposes for His revelation, the forms it takes, the objects of His disclosure, and human responses to revelation. Each of these elements is relevant to our conception of human knowledge in general and to our conception of knowing in science in particular. Even while we attempt to make some useful distinctions between the various elements of the whole revelational fabric, keep in mind that these distinctions should ultimately enrich the unity of revelation and the human knowledge that depends upon it.

The God Who Knows and Purposes

Who is this disclosing God, and why is revelation to humans given? The Bible teaches that this disclosing Being is the all-knowing and all powerful Ruler of the universe. God is omniscient; He knows all things in all their relations. Further, God didn't make His own knowledge; nor is there a fundamental knowledge that exists outside of God that He somehow got to know. God's knowledge comes along with His being God. Unlike human knowledge, God's knowledge is not created; it just is. He is a knowing God who defines a category of knowing that He has all to Himself: "'For my thoughts are not your thoughts, neither are your ways my ways,' declares the LORD. 'As the heavens are higher than the earth, so are my ways higher than your ways and my thoughts than your thoughts'" (Isa. 55:8-9).

He is a knowing God who also purposes, who plans according to the counsel of His own will. He has purposed to reveal His glory by acting in created history to demonstrate His holiness, power, and grace. He is doing this by summing up all things in Christ—ultimately to show that from Him and through Him and to Him are all things.[23]

Not only does He know and purpose, but He is omnipotent—He can bring about all that He purposes in creation through His power exerted by His Word.

These elements of the doctrine of God clarify several important issues from the outset in the discussion of revelation and human knowledge. Human knowledge is radically contingent on God and His purposes, as is every other aspect of the created world. God, being who He is, is under no *a priori* obligation to provide humans with His thoughts or to provide humans with certain knowledge of the facts in some abstract formal sense. God is not somehow selfishly keeping His thoughts to Himself. It is just that being God and entirely dominating the category of God's knowledge are of a piece. But in His grace, according to His purposes, He has taken upon Himself certain obligations with regard to humans that have distinct knowing implications. As we've pointed out in previous chapters, His obligations to humans are those according to His covenant promises: He has committed Himself to demonstrating His faithfulness or, to put it another way, to showing His truth to His people in Christ. Consequently humans are called, not to think God's thoughts *per se*, but to think the true or the faithful thoughts He gives humans to think in the furtherance of His purposes in demonstrating His faithfulness in Christ. God Himself is ultimately the maker of scientific knowledge. Human minds are brought into being by Him and held by Him in an appropriate relation to the world according to His purposes. Human knowledge is made as we submit to the order He has constructed in the universe and as we engage in God-given order-as-task activities. He creates human knowledge through His revealing activity, which is in service of, is sufficient for, and is unified by His purposes to sum up everything in Christ.[24]

In summary, God alone is the True One; He is the supremely Trustworthy One. The truth for humans can never be abstracted from the personal faithfulness of God, expressed in His sure purposes in Christ, and remain fully true. True human knowledge gained about the world through careful scientific investigation is rooted in God's revealing faithfulness as He enables faithful human responses to His revelation.

The God Who Creates, Enters into Creation, and Redeems

Revelation relies on aspects of God's character, His purposes, and His power that reside outside created history. The doctrine of revelation is thus rooted in the doctrine of a transcendent God. As we have been emphasizing in previous chapters, this transcendent God is also the immanent God who constructs and enters into history as the Creator/Redeemer.

God's action in history is radically Christocentric from beginning to end. Christ is, after all, the Alpha and the Omega as well as the Mediator of creation and redemption. The Creator and Finisher of all that is, then, is not distant from what He has made. In the Incarnation He actually enters physically into the fabric of what He created, bringing redemption to it all. Christ is the focal point of all aspects of creation and of every moment of its history. There is nothing good in created reality that is good on its own. All that is good is good only "in Christ,"[25] and nothing that is ruined by sin will be redeemed except "in Christ."[26] Nothing known by humans will be known except it be known in Christ "in whom are hidden all the treasures of wisdom and knowledge."[27] Creation, incarnation, and redemption accomplished in and through Christ reveal in unmistakable terms the holiness, power, and grace of the Father. Revelation then in an ultimate sense is the revealing of God in Christ, the incarnate Creator/Redeemer. Jesus Christ is the Creator, the Word become flesh, the King, the Elder Brother, the Reconciler, the Judge, and the Bridegroom to come. Jesus Christ is the revelation of God.

Creation and Revelation

Having said that revelation is ultimately in and through Christ, it can next be said that revelation in Christ is intertwined with the creation brought into being through Christ. All created elements are forms of revelation. Thus the doctrine of creation is intimately connected to the doctrine of revelation and has important implications for our consideration of revelation.

Firstly, the doctrine of creation establishes a proper form of revelational absolutism. The Christian doctrine of creation is widely recognized as an important contributor to the scientific revolution in the past, and the doctrine is essential in our times to blunt the force of Postmodern absolute relativism. The main point here is that created reality exists apart from any human conception or lack of conception of it. Created reality has an objective existence in and through Christ, and it exists in certain ways regardless of human ideas about it. Created reality is not just "all in our heads." It is really there, and it has objective revelational force, whether we humans in our sin catch on or not.

Secondly, neither the doctrine of creation nor the intertwined doctrine of revelation are primarily about isolated events that exist only in a static past tense. The doctrine of creation in its broad sense encompasses both the origin of the universe and its subsequent history. Creation is not static, and revelation, in the broad sense that we are using it here, is unfolding as well.[28] God's purposes in creation, though determined before He laid the foundations of the universe, progressively unfold in a historical sense. He is upholding, and He is bringing forth anew all through created time. His creation is developing, His mercies are new every morning, and His purposes are coming closer to fruition with each passing day. Thus the woven fabric of the revelation of His holiness, power, and grace continues to be produced in the "loom" of created history. Yes, revelation in a final sense is once and for all in Jesus Christ, but the historical process through which His preeminence in creation is increasingly demonstrated is integral to the fulfillment of God's purposes in Him.

So the outlines of a revelational approach in the sciences begin to emerge. A revelational approach to science requires that the purposes of God in Christ must always be the ultimate perspective from which to view investigation of His universe. Scientific knowledge as human knowledge is a part of creation and is contingent on God's revealing activity. Science does deal with objective elements of creation, and yet human knowledge of that creation will always be creaturely and thus relative in some sense. Furthermore, His revealing activity is according to His purposes as He unfolds them. While we know the ultimate ends of His purposes, He alone knows the specific in-history means

He will use and the paths that human knowledge must take to accomplish His purposes in Christ. On a moment by moment basis, Christians called to the sciences are to respond to God's revealing work by both submitting to revelation as it is given and by unfolding revelation further as they focus on their specific scientific tasks.

The Created Forms of Revelation

Having pointed out three general concepts imbedded in the relationship between the doctrine of revelation and the doctrine of creation, we now turn to a discussion of the basic forms that revelation takes. Each form exhibits in different ways the objective, mediated, and dynamic characteristics just discussed. In keeping with our emphasis on the unity of revelation and the unity of "revealees," we are consciously resisting a fairly common notion that science is narrowly focused on "general revelation" and, properly done, should go "as far as it can" on general revelation alone. Rather, everything that we do should be done in view of everything we know. The different forms of revelation are threads woven into the one whole fabric in such a way that our task is always to take all forms seriously and to handle them all faithfully at the same time. We will start the discussion with revelation in the form of words, the Scriptures, and then move to a wordless form: the universe as a whole.

God's Revelation in the Scriptures

The first form to be discussed is the one that most Christians immediately think of when the term "revelation" is used—the Christian Scriptures. This is also the revelational form that has generated the most controversy in the Modern age. At a basic level, this conflict over the Scriptures has been generated by opposing commitments regarding naturalism and supernaturalism. Of course if one holds to naturalism, any sense in which the Christian Scriptures can be a form of revelation that transcends nature is ruled out. However, a major part of the Modern discussion has been among those who are essentially supernaturalists but who differ on the relationship between supernatural revelation and the Scriptures. The various positions in this debate and the arguments behind them are of great interest and importance, but they are beyond the scope of this book. We will therefore simply describe the position we hold concerning the inspired nature of Scripture and then explain how the characteristics of "objectivity," "mediated," and "dynamic" hold for it and how we see this form of revelation in relation to science.

The position we affirm, historically often referred to as "verbal plenary" inspiration, has often been misunderstood and misrepresented by friend and foe alike. Simply stated, this position holds that the individual words as well as the grammatical, textual, and literary contexts of the words in Scripture are the ones God intended them to be, and as such they tell the truth as God intends it to be told. The basic sense is that God has spoken in Scripture, and "He ain't lyin'." This is where the first characteristic of revelational forms comes in—the words of Scripture and their contexts (with the standard qualification "in the original manuscripts") exist as objective revelation. God has brought into being an objective revelation that exists in the form of human language. Real words were put on real "paper" at some point in real history. They are a specific class of the created objects that we are called to respond to in faithful ways.

Along with this static element of inscripturated words, there are two major dynamic aspects of this form of revelation as well, although neither is indicative of some kind of fundamental evolution of the form itself. First, there is a developmental aspect—an unfolding over time—of the story the Scriptures tell of God's interaction with His people. As a reader moves through the Old Testament to the New Testament, there is clear movement as God further unfolds His plans in history and makes a fuller picture of His purposes known to His people. For example, the book of Hebrews points to what is now "better" and "clearer" through Christ in the New Testament period, while also insisting on an underlying unity and continuity with God's revelation and way of working among His people in the Old Testament.

Second, there is a dynamic element as well in the fact that Scripture is a form of revelation that speaks anew to each generation. There is not something magical here; nor is this to be taken to mean that the words of Scripture are ultimately plastic—open to being molded to fit our times. Rather God has graciously provided revelation in human language, in words that are by their very nature somewhat elastic or stretchable, and this elasticity, by God's grace, enables each generation to faithfully strive to fit its times and issues to Scripture.[29] What a wonder it is to be able to read David's psalms for example and through words to be able to fellowship with David concerning the goodness and mercy of God, although separated from David by a great expanse of time and cultural space. Even more amazing, consider that we are able to fellowship with God Himself through human language even though distinct from Him as creature must be from Creator. Thanks be to God that His written Word is dynamic in these senses, giving it both immanent and transcendent character. And thank God we have a Teacher to help us appropriate this revelation . . . but that is getting ahead of the story.

Lastly then several prominent mediation issues commonly arise in discussion of the scriptural form of revelation. The first is at the level of inspiration, the inspired production of words and text through human agents, and a second is in the understanding of the words—the way the words function as revelation. So how did God inspire the Scripture? A common misconception is that the inerrancy and verbal inspiration positions must include a magical bypass of human creaturely capacities. Many people, both friends and foes of inspiration and inerrancy alike, have in mind some kind of mechanical dictation process in which the writer is essentially in a trance, and an involuntary twitching of the arm produces an inspired manuscript. Verbal plenary inspiration emphatically does not imply such a mechanical mediation process. God didn't unmake the writers as humans in a historical context. The writers wrote according to the breadth of their own experience: They did research, gathered documents, addressed issues of their own day, and made use of common cultural concepts of their own time. The verbal inspiration doctrine explicitly teaches that God fully authored the writing of His scriptural revelation by fully mediating it through whole human beings—yet keeping them and thus Himself from lying. The doctrine doesn't preclude the possibility of God giving the writers the privileged information that prophecy concerning future events might require (although it is worth noting that prophecies were often mediated through dreams, visions, and poetic expression). The doctrine just insists that God could and did use ordinary means as well to accomplish His work of graciously producing a revelation in word form.[30] Certainly there is strangeness and mystery in this contention, but these claims are no more or less mysterious than other often-repeated claims in Scripture that God does and will accomplish His purposes even through the mediation of frail, sinful people.[31]

A second mediating issue related to scriptural revelation has to do with the status and function of the words themselves. There are several pitfalls to be avoided if the actual words of Scripture are to be taken seriously as revelation. In the classic liberal approach of the nineteenth century, any claim to divine authorship for the words of Scripture was to be rejected outright. The words of Scripture were held to be generally authentic expressions of the religious experiences of the human authors or of the people-group to which the authors belonged.

The neo-orthodox movement of the early twentieth century rightly recognized that this liberal approach essentially replaced the historic understanding of revelation—God speaking to humans about Himself—with an understanding of revelation as "humans speaking to humans about God." In the liberal view, the status of scriptural words was essentially the same as the status of the words in any human conversation and thus can be spiritually helpful but need not be taken seriously as God's words. Neo-orthodox theologians sought to reestablish the category of revelation in its original sense but within a framework that largely accepted the presuppositions of Modern historical-critical "scientific" approaches to Scripture. To do this, a distinction was made between the words themselves and transcendent revelation that could come through the words. So even though neo-orthodoxy developed as a reaction to liberal theology, by distinguishing between revelation and the words of Scripture, it too diminished the importance of taking the actual words of Scripture seriously.[32] In contrast, we believe that the words are indeed the words of God, such that the words have the objective status of revelation as well as the function of mediating revelation.

While the rejection of verbal inspiration undercuts the concept of scriptural revelation in various ways, supporting mistaken views of verbal inspiration can also cause significant damage to the concept. Inerrancy and verbal plenary inspiration are sometimes seen as legitimating an almost magical quality to the individual words, such that their grammatical, textual, and theological context are not necessarily recognized as full partners with the revealed words. While most evangelicals who hold to biblical authority would not engage in "biblical fortune telling" (the "open and point method" for seeking God's will in the Bible), it is fairly common to hear that our confidence in Scripture should be strengthened by the fact that one can find modern scientific notions taught in the Scriptures in various places.[33] Yet both the open-and-point method and any notion of biblical encoding of modern scientific notions make the same mistake of confusing "inspired" with "magical." Holding that the Scriptures are inspired entails taking the actual words seriously *and* respecting the normal form and function of words in human language as they were written in Scripture.

Finally, as to mediating issues, some forms of Postmodern thinking raise questions of a different sort concerning the words of Scripture. A basic concern from a Postmodern perspective is that words often turn out to be quite flexible carriers of meanings. Even a cursory examination of the history of almost any word in a modern language will show that relationships between words and meanings can be quite unstable over time. Even in contemporary usage, many words have imprecise meanings. In addition, there appears to be no mechanical process by which thoughts and intended meanings are converted into words in the mind of a speaker or writer, nor by which words are connected to meanings in the mind of a hearer or reader. Thus, from this perspective, talk of inspired words involved in the mediation of revelation seems pretty silly on several counts. These Postmodern emphases do begin to uncover many strange and wonderful aspects of language and communication that we usually take for granted. But if we've come this far in trusting the Creator of brains and tongues and language, are we really ready to countenance the idea that He can't communicate what He desires after all. Words, in fact, do communicate, although not in the "hard" mechanical way we might assume with a Modernist mind-set. God has graciously chosen to reveal Himself to us in human forms of communication, subtle though they may be in various aspects. The strangeness of human word-meaning issues isn't a frustrating surprise to Him. In fact, it can be argued that His inscripturated Word is vastly enriched and made transhistorically user-friendly by these features.[34]

So the words of Scripture are divinely inspired in a holistic creaturely mediated way so that the product is in this sense 100 percent human and 100 percent divine. God's revelation in Scripture comes in and through the words, and thus the words are integral to His revealing purposes in Scripture. We are distorting revelation if we too easily look past the words to try to establish the "real" meaning "behind" them. Yet these words also come to us in a holistically mediated way—in grammatical, textual, and theological contexts that are further embedded in the cultural and historical contexts of both the writer and the reader. We don't need to profess naïveté or ignorance about these wonderfully complex aspects of scriptural revelation in order to defend the truth of the Scriptures. The Christian God is not somehow held hostage to creaturely characteristics. In fact, He uses them to demonstrate "the surpassing riches of His grace in Christ Jesus." There is a sense in which we risk insulting Him if we make scriptural revelation out to be a more simple affair than it appears to be. Our responsibility is clear: "Do your best to present yourself to God as one approved, a workman who does not need to be ashamed and who correctly handles the word of truth" (2 Tim. 2:15). He has made His promises to us; He has sent us the Spirit teacher; the real question is whether we will trust Him and believe what He says He has done for us.

Although God has brought into being other forms of revelation (which we will review shortly), and all forms in one sense have equal authority in composing the revelation of God in Christ, there is an appropriate priority given to scriptural revelation. This priority is rooted not in the fact that Scripture is uniquely revelational, but in the fact that it is a revelation in words. This makes it "special" in several ways. First, words, although somewhat "elastic" as previously discussed, are not plastic in an unlimited way. Consider the difference between trying to understand what an author is saying in prose and what a composer is "saying" in a piece of music. The written piece is potentially much more definite because it is "wordy." Second, words can entail self-interpretive commentary as well as commentary concerning the other forms of revelation. So while it is true that no form of revelation is completely self-interpreting, scriptural revelation goes further in this respect than the other forms. Third, because it is composed of words, Scripture can clearly distinguish between "is" and "ought." The words of scriptural revelation communicate specific imperatives concerning how our lives ought to be lived before our God. Due to the Fall and our human creatureliness, oughtness is difficult to discern with any specificity from the other forms of revelation. Thus it is proper that the non-scriptural forms of revelation be viewed through the "spectacles" of scriptural revelation as the Reformer John Calvin described it.[35] So while Scripture is not a standalone revelational form in a strict sense (the other forms are to be utilized in various ways to aid in interpreting Scripture), it can and should take the revelational lead, so to speak, in informing us about revelation in general and pointing us in appropriate interpretive directions both for itself as well as for other forms of revelation.

In conclusion then it seems to us that much contemporary thinking about the relationship between Scripture and science has been distorted by various Modern or Postmodern instincts. Whether one submits the Scriptures to "objective" scientific analysis, or whether one attempts to vindicate scriptural authority by finding Modern scientific concepts taught in its pages, Modernist epistemology is setting the agenda. In addition, to operate as if science and Scripture have no relevance for one another at all is to adopt the fact/value framework of Modernism and to deny the ethical nature of all knowledge. And if we too easily read into the words of Scripture our scientific meanings for them, rather than respecting their own meanings as given, we are dancing to a Postmodern tune.

Scripture does have much to say that is relevant for the sciences, and in seeking to understand what it is saying, we must submit to the objective nature and the contextual integrity of the actual words of Scripture. On the other hand, Scripture is not a substitute for the exploration of other forms of revelation, which also need to be taken seriously in their own objective existence and contextual integrity. John Calvin's spectacles metaphor is a sound one, but those who are committed to the full authority of Scripture must make sure that they don't spend all their time polishing and admiring the spectacles while just holding them in their hands. The spectacles are to be actually worn so they can do their proper work of directing attention beyond themselves to the other forms of His revelation that come into our view through them, and ultimately direct attention to the Creator and Redeemer of it all.

God's Revelation in the Universe

Not only are the words of Scripture, individually and as a whole, components of revelation, but the details of the universe, individually and as a whole, are components of revelation. God's revelation in the universe, like scriptural revelation, has objective, mediated, and dynamic elements to it as well. As we've already pointed out, there is something in the universe rather than nothing because of God's gracious intention to demonstrate His holiness, power, and grace in and through Christ. A real, though contingent, creation exists objectively and persists temporally only in Christ, and that creation does reveal its Creator.

> *The heavens declare the glory of God; the skies proclaim the work of his hands. Day after day they pour forth speech; night after night they display knowledge. There is no speech or language where their voice is not heard. Their voice goes out into all the earth, their words to the ends of the world. (Ps. 19:1-4)*

Revelation in the universe is, of course, mediated through the stuff of which the universe is composed. This revelation is both in and through the stuff in a way analogous to the revelation that comes in and through the words of Scripture. The mediating stuff is not incidental to what is revealed, but it is integral to God's revelatory purposes in the universe. Thus we are not to treat a created feature of the universe as if its value lies only in its ability to function as some kind of symbolic revelational unit. Neither are we to treat any detail of the created universe as if it were devoid of revelational significance. The universe itself and its revelational content cannot be separated any more than the words of Scripture and their revelational content can be separated.

The revelation of the universe also has a dynamic element. Not only are the components of the universe a form of revelation, but the events that occur in created time and space are revelatory as well. History, the providential unfolding of God's purposes in space and time, is thus a part of the revelation of the universe. Natural history is revelational, as stars are born and die, mountain ranges rise and wear down, and year follows year in sequence. Human history—the rise and fall of nations and cultures, the development of technologies and art styles, even the rise and fall of interpretive frameworks in science—is revelational. An individual human life lived out one moment at a time, as one grows and develops, takes on new challenges, endures new defeats, and wins new victories, is revelational. History—whether natural, cultural, or personal—reflects the God who is unfolding it in His providence to demonstrate the preeminence of Christ. To thoughtlessly abstract our thinking about God's purposes in Christ from historical process would be to disrespect the way He has chosen to work out His purposes. History is not something God is anxious to just "get out of the way." The specific events of history—whether natural, cultural, or personal—and the sequence in which they occur play an integral role in the unfolding of His purposes in Christ.

At the end of time it will be clearly seen that all things and historical events in the universe explicitly demonstrate the preeminence of Christ in one way or another. As a result no one will be able to deny the reality of His absolute rule. This is the root of the revelational integrity of the universe, and it is the root of our responsibility to look carefully at all aspects of the created universe and to take seriously what we see. We dare not denigrate or look past the way things are in creation or the way things have occurred in creation, either by refusing to look at data we don't like or by mishandling the data we do see. A science that intentionally ignores aspects of the universe as it exists or engages the creation in a selectively manipulative way shows a rebellious disrespect for the One who chose to bring it all into being and to unfold it in the way He desires.

God's Revelation in Humans

Although human beings are part of the revelation of the universe as a whole, we are also set apart from the rest of creation within the revelational fabric. Of all that was produced across the universe, of all the creatures on the earth, only humans are made in the image and likeness of God. "So God created man in his own image, in the image of God he created him; male and female he created them."[36] Although there has been much discussion through the ages as to what exactly it is in humans that constitutes the image, we believe that there is much to recommend the view that it is the human as a whole being that images God. The whole complex of created humanness, including physical form, is God-imaging, and thus the whole human being is a distinctive, objective form of revelation.

There is another reason that humans occupy a special place in the revelation story. Humans are a form of revelation, and yet we are also the ones called to receive that revelation. Image-bearing humanness and human activity are themselves to be revelatory—to humans. We are a central means by which God demonstrates the preeminence of Christ, and as humans we are major constituents of the audience before whom this demonstration is to be made.

> *When I consider your heavens, the work of your fingers, the moon and the stars, which you have set in place, what is man that you are mindful of him, the son of man that you care for him? You made him a little lower than the heavenly beings and crowned him with glory and honor. You made him ruler over the works of your hands; you put everything under his feet: all flocks and herds, and the beasts of the field, the birds of the air, and the fish of the sea, all that swim the paths of the seas. O LORD, our Lord, how majestic is your name in all the earth! (Ps. 8:3-9)*

These uniquely human aspects of revelation highlight two ironies related to Modern attitudes toward science. In many ways Modern scientific methodology reflects an attempt to get the humanness out of science or at least to quarantine it to some limited part of the process so that it doesn't harm the supposed purity of science.[37] This would seem to be a strange attitude for Christians just unreflectively to go along with. For Christians, it would seem that the humanness of science per se cannot be seen as a regrettable intrusion, something to be gotten out of the way so that we can see the "real" revelation. Secondly, it is ironic that many Christians would readily speak of the natural sciences as studying "general revelation" but would be more hesitant to speak about the social sciences and the arts in such terms. It seems one could even make a biblical case that studying psychology or art is more centrally revelatory than astronomy or biology.

God's Revelation Is Objectively Revelatory

We have argued so far that the purposes of God and His power to accomplish them in Christ are central to the discussion of revelation. And the discussion so far has focused on one sense of the term "revelation"—on the stuff of revelation— and we have suggested that all created elements are objective forms of revelation in this sense. We want to close this section by emphasizing that not only do these forms objectively exist as the stuff of revelation, but the Scriptures teach that the stuff is objectively revelatory. The gracious Revealer brings revelatory stuff into being, and He declares that what He has brought into being is also revelatory in the sense that it clearly and faithfully reflects the God who reveals Himself through them regardless of whether humans accurately or fully recognize what is being revealed. Revelation should not be narrowed to a magical moment in which something "becomes" revelation for a human subject. Revelation does demand a human response—but as Romans 1 teaches, the reality of its revealing function is not dependent on its proper appropriation by humans.

> *The wrath of God is being revealed from heaven against all the godlessness and wickedness of men who suppress the truth by their wickedness, since what may be known about God is plain to them, because God has made it plain to them. For since the creation of the*

world God's invisible qualities—his eternal power and divine nature—have been clearly seen, being understood from what has been made, so that men are without excuse. For although they knew God, they neither glorified him as God nor gave thanks to him, but their thinking became futile and their foolish hearts were darkened. Although they claimed to be wise, they became fools and exchanged the glory of the immortal God for images made to look like mortal man and birds and animals and reptiles. Therefore God gave them over in the sinful desires of their hearts to sexual impurity for the degrading of their bodies with one another. They exchanged the truth of God for a lie, and worshiped and served created things rather than the Creator—who is forever praised. Amen. (Rom. 1:18-25)

This familiar passage teaches that though the revelation is clear, human responses to it differ. The problem associated with human misappropriation is not a clouded or garbled revelation, but a problem of the heart leading to willful rejection of the truth being revealed. Created reality is faithfully revelatory—it doesn't cease to be revelatory because humans persist in distorting and rejecting it. The subjective issue of how a person will respond to revelation is separable from the reality that it is objectively revelational.

The Spirit Who Teaches and Guides

Having discussed who it is that reveals and the various forms His revelation takes, we haven't even come close to exhausting the richness of what is implied in the term "revelation." We now want to shift to the aspect of revelation as the means by which God makes or constitutes human knowledge, and this requires that we focus more directly on the work of the Holy Spirit. As has already been discussed in chapter 4, in historical Trinitarian doctrine, the Spirit is the immanent enabler of the work of the Father that is mediated in and through the Son. In the Scriptures, the Spirit's enabling role is connected with revelation in a variety of ways. He is called the Spirit of revelation, and revelation is said to come by the Spirit;[38] He is the Spirit of knowledge and truth[39] and the teacher Spirit.[40]

Most Christians are comfortable with this description of the

Spirit's enabling and applying of truth and knowledge within the context of "saving faith," or "spiritual truth," or in the inspiration of Scripture. But expanding the Spirit's enabling work to "scientific truth" may cause some consternation. First, there is no Scripture passage that directly says, "and the Spirit will lead you into all scientific truth." Second, "habits of the mind" involving the Modernist distinction between "religious truth" and "scientific truth" are pretty deeply rooted. In either case it is instructive to ask the following question: "If there is true human knowledge about the creation, and the Spirit does not enable it, where does it come from?" This question ultimately leads back to the problem of knowledge in Modern and Postmodern thinking. Who ultimately creates and controls human knowledge? Using the Trinitarian formulation, we are arguing that all true human knowledge results from revelation by God the Father, in and through the mediating work of the Son, by means of the enabling work of the Holy Spirit. God is the gracious revealer who is also ultimately the maker of all scientific knowledge.

If the Spirit is our teacher and all of created reality is His classroom, what of the students, the "revealees"? What kind of students are human beings, and what does this imply about human reception of revelation and the status of human knowledge? A major student feature impacting human knowing in the Spirit's classroom is the reality of sin. By the Fall, all aspects of human being were corrupted and perverted. The result is that human knowing is truncated, human knowing capacities don't work as they should, and human knowledge is sought and utilized in rebellion against God. Without God's gracious intervention, humans would necessarily and always distort what is revealed beyond recognition. But God's gracious intervention does come in and through Christ and is applied by the Spirit so that human knowing is sufficient for the fulfillment of God's purposes.

A second feature impacting human knowing is the fact of human "creatureliness." As has already been discussed, the fact that we are creatures made of created stuff indicates that all revelation will be mediated through our created stuff in one way or another. Because of this, human reception of revelation will always require the creaturely response of human reflection in human consciousness, interpretation, and formulation. Thus the field of human knowledge is not populated by "brute" facts as such, but only by humanly appropriated facts, and human appropriation always involves human interpretation of some sort. How could it be any other way unless there is a human-free way to appropriate revelation—but in God's providence, there doesn't seem to be. We remain creatures even as God reveals His truth to us. Philosopher of science Del Ratzsch describes this feature of human knowing in terms of science:

> Science is done by humans and it cannot escape what is inescapably human. Our science is limited to humanly available concepts, humanly available reasoning, humanly shaped notions of understanding and explanation and humanly structured pictures of what the world must be like. How could it be otherwise? Science seems to have a serious and incurable case of the humans.[41]

There is an interpretive task to be prosecuted in all human knowing, and as Christians we need not deny this. We are simply to strive by the Spirit's power to interpret faithfully. We must work to make faithful human knowledge; yet God is the one who ultimately gives it. Our recognition of the reality of this interpretive task is both humbling and liberating. We should always be mindful that the authority of God and the objective nature of His revelation are distinct from the authority of human interpretation and the human elements of our appropriation of that revelation. This kind of epistemological humility is liberating in that it graciously lifts from us a burden we were never meant to bear. The knowing we are called to is nothing more, but also nothing less, than true creaturely knowing in service to the True One. Sometimes a faithful creaturely response to God's teaching will be to make definitive truth claims and to stand by them. At other times a faithful response might be: "I don't claim to know that, but I do claim to know the One who does know."

Epistemological Piety and Science

We opened this section of the book by discussing God's command to love Him with all our heart, soul, mind, and strength and to love our neighbor as ourselves. Or as we paraphrased it, the command is to love God in all our knowing, all our being, and all our doing. In one sense, this chapter considering what loving God in our knowing might entail has been an extension of Blaise Pascal's thought presented in chapter 3. In another sense it has been an exposition of a particular vision of what Nicholas Wolterstorff has called "epistemological piety."[42] We close this chapter by first connecting traditional conceptions of Christian piety with epistemological piety and then by connecting epistemological piety in general to particular characteristics of Christian knowing in the sciences.

Christian piety sometimes gets a bad name from the various human distortions of it. The term may conjure up a vision of a standoffish otherworldliness or a prim air of self-righteousness or maybe a legalistic obsession with a list of shallow do's and don'ts. These distortions of piety are ironic in that their self-focused and self-serving characteristics epitomize what could be called anti-piety. Anti-piety focuses on a narrow self-centeredness while a biblical piety focuses on the finished work of Christ and proper human responses to what God has done in Christ. By the Spirit we are to accept who we were in Adam and take seriously who we are "in Christ." We are to die to self in terms of justifying our own goodness, and we are to rely entirely on Christ's righteousness. Both legalism (I'll determine the standards, thank you . . . and, by the way, I'll set them so that they seem pretty demanding but are actually within my reach. Then I will have proof of my righteousness) and antinomianism (Christ has done it all; so it ultimately doesn't matter what I do) are in essence rebellious denials of the gospel. The meaning of our piety is not ultimately found in actions themselves or in the status of an accomplished deed as to its essential righteousness. The meaning of piety resides in its ability to point beyond the human doer to the unfolding purposes of God as He demonstrates the preeminence of Christ, the obedient and righteous ruler of all things. In this context to focus on whether or not one of my particular actions is "truly" righteous in itself seems incongruous. Sanctification, as the process of growth in piety, is the Spirit's work to make Christ's righteousness increasingly real in our experience and in the experience of others as they experience us.

A major theme in Paul's epistles is that human righteousness in Christ is both a gift and a task:

> *For we are God's workmanship, created in Christ Jesus to do good works, which God prepared in advance for us to do. (Eph. 2:10)*

> *Work out your salvation with fear and trembling, for it is God who works in you to will and to act according to his good purpose. (Phil. 2:12-13)*

Biblical piety then involves commitment to what Francis Schaeffer called "active passivity,"[43] a moment by moment resting on the finished work of Christ and a seeking by the power of the Spirit to "live into" the good works God has already prepared for us to do in Him. God is the One who builds righteousness into us in the furtherance of His purposes in Christ, and yet we are called to actively participate in the work being done in us. Paul constantly asks of his readers: "Is what you are doing consistent with who you are in Christ? Are your responses to Christ's work fitting for one who has been made a child of the living God?"

> *For you were once darkness, but now you are light in the Lord. Live as children of light (for the fruit of the light consists in all goodness, righteousness and truth) and find out what pleases the Lord. (Eph. 5:8-10)*

These themes and the tone for piety they set are almost directly transferable to our consideration of knowledge, truth, and revelation in the light of the Great Commandment. How are we to begin to know in ways that are pleasing to God—to approach knowledge as both gift and task? The first step is to acknowledge who we are as fallen creatures "in Adam," that we have fallen and are naturally in rebellion in our knowing. We must die to self epistemologically (renounce knowing autonomously) and learn what it means to be knowers who are consciously depending for our knowledge on God's revealing work through Christ by the power of the Spirit. Further, we need to resist the temptation to become epistemological legalists by giving knowing a narrow technical definition that seems to place truth entirely within human grasp. We also need to resist the temptation to become epistemological antinomians, to renounce our knowing tasks by adopting a Postmodernist "eat, drink, and be merry" epistemology. As is the case with piety, the meaning of our knowledge is not ultimately found in the making of truth claims or in the establishment of the status of those claims in terms of formally certain truths. The meaning of our knowledge resides in its ability to point beyond the human knower to the unfolding purposes of God as He demonstrates the preeminence of Christ, the obedient and righteous ruler of all things. In this context an inordinate focus on whether one of our particular knowledge claims can be proven to be certain in itself seems out of place. We are to "live into" the knowledge He has already prepared for us to know. God is the One who constructs knowledge in us in the furtherance of His purposes in Christ, and yet we are to be active as well. We should cultivate the art of active passivity in our knowing, taking both the gift and the task seriously in the confidence that God, by His Spirit, is able to bring about His human knowing purposes in and through us even as we strive to be His faithfully knowing servants.

Epistemological piety then is simply one expression of the comprehensive piety the Spirit works in those who are both made new in Christ and are also called to be new creatures in Christ. Mary's faithful response to God's declaration of His specific work to be accomplished in and through her is a striking example of this kind of active passivity:[44] "I am the Lord's servant. . . . May it be to me as you have said" (Luke 1:38). We are to be the epistemological clay in the hands of the all-knowing Potter, content to be of whatever knowing use in the household that the Master of the house might decree.

What then might be some of the specific marks of this kind of epistemological piety in relation to the natural sciences? How are we to go about pleasing Him by living into the scientific knowledge He intends? The first mark is a conscious personal commitment to teachability or to a conceptual malleability in scientific endeavors under the tutelage of the Spirit. Engaging in scientific study entails that we sit at the feet of the Spirit-teacher. We are to approach the details of creation with the attentiveness that befits a good student as these details are basic tools the Spirit uses to construct our scientific knowledge.

Second, epistemological piety in the sciences would require that all the forms of revelation must be taken seriously in any scientific endeavor. Our scientific knowing is to be continuously clothed by and woven into the revelational fabric as a whole. As Cornelius Van Til insisted, "All human knowledge is simultaneously knowledge of self, world and God. Knowledge in one area cannot be adequate without knowledge of the other two."[45] Among other things this would indicate that we make appropriate use of the spectacles of the Scriptures in our science. The fear that proper attention to Scripture would distort one's science is ironically misplaced from this perspective. Likewise taking all forms of revelation seriously requires that we relentlessly seek out and carefully examine "constraints of creation," that is, to proactively seek out and submit to "order as given." There should be no tendency to shrink back in fear from what is there to see in creation; nor should there be a tendency to distort what there is to see according to our own self-focused knowledge agendas. To ignore order given in the world or to avoid attempting to describe and make sense of that order is to succumb to a rebellious antinomianism. To stubbornly bend what we see to fit our own self-focused knowledge agendas is to succumb to legalism. Taking all forms of revelation seriously also implies intentional and respectful interaction with the scientific views of fellow scientists, believing and nonbelieving alike. In scientific matters we are to be "quick to listen, slow to speak, and slow to become angry," not just out of commitment to some abstract humility, but in the realization—and even expectation—that God is working in and through others in bringing about His knowing purposes in the world in general and in bringing about His knowing purposes in us personally.

Third, Christians ought to be bold in developing and trying out creative ideas about how the world might work or new ways of thinking about even "settled" scientific questions. This is simply to take seriously the constructive "order as task" element of a call to scientific work. One reading of the parable of the talents in Matthew 25 might be that the unfaithful servant only took "order as given" seriously and refused to take the risks of "order as task." In playing it safe he failed to serve the Master and was judged harshly for it. Epistemological piety in science encourages trying out new ideas and taking intellectual risks, even while remembering that though we are indeed free in Christ, we are not to use our freedom as an occasion for sin. In our creative risk-taking we are not to use our epistemological freedom to distort the revelational fabric, to drop the spectacles of Scripture, or to ignore inconvenient creational features.

Finally, epistemological piety requires that we doggedly pursue a Christocentric focus in everything we do in science. Pursuing a supposedly neutral objectivity or settling for a watered-down theism simply will not do. If the story of creation is about Christ from beginning to end, how could we do anything less than engage in a science that in all its knowing strives "to discern and unfold the implications of His preeminence in all things"?[46]

✳ ✳ ✳

In C. S. Lewis's book *The Magician's Nephew,* Aslan, the Lord of the Narnian world, has just finished his work of creating that world by singing it into existence. He now stops to commission his creation for its work under his rule:

> "Narnia, Narnia, Narnia, awake. Love. Think. Speak. Be walking trees. Be talking beasts. Be divine waters. . . . Creatures, I give you yourselves," said the strong, happy voice of Aslan. "I give you forever this land of Narnia. I give you the woods, the fruits, the rivers. I give you the stars and I give you myself."
>
> "Hail, Aslan. We hear and obey. We are awake. We love. We think. We speak. We know."
>
> "But please, we don't know very much yet," said a nosey and snorty kind of voice.[47]

We humans in this world have received a similar commission, and though we too might not know very much yet, we have been given Him who knows all and brings all to pass, and He has given us His creation, His Spirit, and ourselves. What more could we knowing creatures want?

Chapter Nine

"Well Done, Good and Faithful Scientific Servant"

So you also when you have done everything you were told to do, should say, We are unworthy servants; we have only done our duty.

LUKE 17:10

DEAR GOD, it's me—Your servant in science. I wanted to thank You that my latest paper was accepted by such a prestigious journal. We put a lot of work into it, and it was nice to see our work recognized. The work in the lab seems to be going well in general. You've brought me a couple of good grad students, and that new post doc seems to be pretty sharp too. With this paper I should be in good shape for a promotion next year. The extra money will sure come in handy for the kids' school expenses. I'm really thankful for your tangible blessings in all this.

Lord, You got me through grad school, and by Your grace I've been doing well in research—for which I'm grateful. But . . . when it gets down to it, I'm just not feeling easy about this whole direction for me. I'm not sure how exactly I ended up with this particular research focus. I have learned a lot, but sometimes I have to ask myself, "Who really cares?" If no one ever found out about what I'm researching, the world would still go on. Lord, You've given me a good marriage, blessed me with kids, a good church, but . . . Lord, I don't want to sound ungrateful . . . but what I really want is to do something significant for the kingdom of God. I mean, the time is going by. The years fly now, and it doesn't seem like I'm doing much of eternal significance. Oh, I have taught my share of Sunday school classes. And there was that short-term mission trip the year before last. And, yes, there was the meeting in Chicago where I was able to share my faith with several folks in my field. They were kind of surprised that a good scientist could be a believer. And there was a lab tech several years ago that I invited to church, and he wrote to me recently saying that he had become a believer, and he thanked me for my kindness to him and the several conversations that we had had that were instrumental in his coming to You. . . . Maybe I ought to quit the research game and join a student ministry. I seem to have a good rapport with college students. Or maybe . . . as we just heard at the missions conference at church last month about the great need for missionaries in third-world areas, and last week a representative from a relief agency made a presentation, my heart just went out to those needy people. Maybe I should explore the missions direction.

But . . . well, I am pretty good at the research. Maybe my next grant ought to be directed at some applied project, something that will help people more directly. But that would require starting from scratch in a new area, would take quite a bit of time to ramp up. Maybe I ought to just work harder at my present research. There are some promising results that could lead to a significant advance in understanding this area, and then maybe I'd command more of an audience for my witnessing.

Lord, I just want to do something significant for the kingdom. I long to hear You say at the end, "Well done, good and faithful servant." Please direct me to something that really counts.

* * *

How many of us have engaged in similar soul-searching over the significance of the tasks that take up the majority of our waking hours? God has been good to us, and we want to do something to show our gratefulness, and we've wondered about our callings before God. Have we missed something? Does what we're doing really count "for the kingdom"? Christians working in the sciences often wonder about such things. What is it about my scientific work that makes it count, that makes it a legitimate Christian calling? Or is science just an interesting thing I do while Christian activities in my life are played out in other avenues? In this chapter we turn to a consideration of Christian "doing" in the sciences. What might loving God in our scientific doing look like? How is it related to the being and knowing discussions of the last two chapters? Is it simply being a conscientious worker—a kind and fair laboratory director? Is it related to how many mistakes one makes in the lab? Is it witnessing at the lab bench or discussing spiritual things over coffee at scientific conferences? Is it developing arguments from science to defend the faith, encourage the church, and convince the world of God's existence? Is it just showing that people who are good at science can be Christians—that there is nothing about modern scientific skills that works against heartfelt religion? Or is it just a way to earn a living? Labor well done is in general a noble thing, and besides if one gives faithfully to the church, it does move the kingdom ahead. Will God welcome a believer who spends a lifetime in the sciences into the kingdom saying, "Well done, good and faithful servant—who happened to be a scientist"? Or will He say, "Well done, good and faithful scientific servant"?

Faith and Faithfulness

Well, what are the actions of a good and faithful servant? At the root of faithful Christian service to God is simply believing God. And believing God is different from merely believing in God. We are told in James (2:19) that even the demons believe in God, but they ultimately don't believe God, and believing God on a moment-by-moment basis is at the root of redeemed human doing. As Dietrich Bonhoeffer puts it in his book *The Cost of Discipleship*: "Only he who believes is obedient; only he who is obedient believes."[1] Of course there is a specific biblical word that refers to a commitment to believing God—faith. But how is faith related to doing science? In the Modern context religious belief and faith are often contrasted with scientific evidence, analysis, and proof. In the specific context of science, faith is often thought of as something one wants to keep out of science. To do good objective science one must put subjective "faith" on the shelf. But for Christians faith is not something that pollutes or opposes scientific investigation. Christian faith basically involves believing what God says. The philosopher Arthur Holmes describes it this way,

> Faith is . . . an openness and wholehearted response to God's self-revelation. It does not preclude thinking either about what we believe or about what we are unsure of, nor does it make it unnecessary to search for truth or to examine evidence or arguments. Faith does not cancel out created human activities; rather it motivates, purges, and guides them. It devotes "all my being's ransomed powers" . . . to God.[2]

If believing God is the primary identifier of His faithful servants, then a faithful scientific servant would be one who demonstrates his faith or his trust in God in and through the "doing" of his scientific work. In what follows we will explore the ways that faith or believing God might operate in the doing of science. More specifically, we will briefly explore the following: Faith provides strong motivation for scientific engagement, both in view of what God has done for us and in view of what He says He is doing in and through us. Faith provides the foundation upon which work in science is ultimately based. Faith drives us to engage in science as part of a lifestyle of worship that includes attentiveness, submission, and stewardship. Finally, faith provides the confidence to pursue our scientific work in creativity and freedom, in full assurance that all faithful work will ultimately be meaningful and productive in the kingdom.

Motivations: What God Has Done For Us

Faith, that is, believing God, provides powerful motivation for scientific study in view of what God has done for us and in view of what God is doing through us. God says that He has Himself paid for our sins and transformed us from enemies who hated Him to beloved children. God has done for us what we could not do for ourselves. He has forgiven us and empowered us by His Spirit, through whom we are guaranteed an eternal inheritance. If we really believe what He says He has done for us, how could we not take broad interest in what He has brought into being in the universe, simply out of gratefulness and the fitting desire to know and love the One who has lavishly provided for us. If it is true that He has removed our sins from us as far as the east is from the west, how could we not be interested in responding to Him "from the east to the west" of His works? When God becomes our Father, our new relationship with Him changes the nature of our relationships to everything else in the universe. In view of this, how could we not explore the various dimensions of these new relationships? Responding to God by paying attention to His work across the breadth of His supernatural universe seems only fitting for those who have received His favor.

Motivations: What God Is Doing in and Through Us

When God saves us, we are not just let loose in the world with grateful hearts and best wishes from God. God doesn't give us a pep talk and then send us off, hoping that we will do our best for Him. Rather He has promised to work in and through us to accomplish His grand purposes, through His power at work in us. "Work out your salvation with fear and trembling, for it is God who works in you to will and to act according to his good purpose" (Phil. 2:12-13).

> *His divine power has given us everything we need for life and godliness through our knowledge of him who called us by his own glory and goodness. Through these he has given us his very great and precious promises, so that through them you may participate in the divine nature and escape the corruption in the world caused by evil desires.*
>
> *For this very reason, make every effort to add to your faith goodness; and to goodness, knowledge; and to knowledge, self-control; and to self-control, perseverance; and to perseverance, godliness; and to godliness, brotherly kindness; and to brotherly kindness, love. For if you possess these qualities in increasing measure, they will keep you from being ineffective and unproductive in your knowledge of our Lord Jesus Christ. But if anyone does not have them, he is nearsighted and blind, and has forgotten that he has been cleansed from his past sins. Therefore, my brothers, be all the more eager to make your calling and election sure. For if you do these things, you will never fall, and you will receive a rich welcome into the eternal kingdom of our Lord and Savior Jesus Christ. (2 Peter 1:3-11)*

What greater motivation can there be than to be called to "live into" the lives of purpose and grace that God has already laid out. Those called to the sciences have these "very great and precious promises" for motivation—God is working in and through our scientific efforts.

One of the roles we are called to "live into" as loved children is that of priestly service:

> *[Y]ou also, like living stones, are being built into a spiritual house to be a holy priesthood, offering spiritual sacrifices acceptable to God through Jesus Christ. . . . [Y]ou are a chosen people, a royal priesthood, a holy nation, a people belonging to God, that you may declare the praises of him who called you out of darkness into his wonderful light. (1 Peter 2:5, 9)*

God himself is in the lab with us. He sees what is really going on. He sees how we are responding to His creation. He knows the entire context of our doing and knows whether we are offering "spiritual sacrifices" and "declaring His praises" through our science or whether we are up to something else. For Christians, science is to have a distinctive element of doxology and of deliberate praise-giving, an awareness of the priestly duty to further uncover the wonder of His works and to consciously "wave" them in His presence as an offering of praise, to call attention to the Author of it all. He is personally watching, and He takes pleasure in what He is doing in and through us. Christian scientists are to be scientific priests, personally bringing pleasure and praise to the Maker of it all.

Not only is God an audience for what we are doing scientifically, but others are always watching as well. Our priestly service has a bidirectional character.

> *Therefore, if anyone is in Christ, he is a new creation; the old has gone, the new has come! All this is from God, who reconciled us to himself through Christ and gave us the ministry of reconciliation: that God was reconciling the world to himself in Christ, not counting men's sins against them. And he has committed to us the mes-*

sage of reconciliation. We are therefore Christ's ambassadors, as though God were making his appeal through us. We implore you on Christ's behalf: Be reconciled to God. God made him who had no sin to be sin for us, so that in him we might become the righteousness of God. (2 Cor. 5:17-21)

The way we handle His creation as well as the way we handle disagreements with others about His creation is seen by others. If we are indeed children of the Creator/Redeemer God, we will be interested in His works in creation in themselves, and we will be interested in handling them before others with care and humility. We are to do our scientific work "as though God were making his appeal through us," exhibiting "brotherly kindness . . . and . . . love" so that our "knowledge of our Lord Jesus Christ" is not "ineffective and unproductive" in "the ministry of reconciliation" God has given us.

Not only are other people watching, but the Scriptures indicate that in some sense the rest of creation is watching how we respond in belief to God's actions as well. Redeemed image-bearers are the first-fruits of Christ's redemptive work from among the created things. There is the sense that we humans are the demonstration to the rest of creation as to what God will ultimately do for it, and the rest of creation is waiting for us to be revealed fully as recreated children. Even now we are demonstrating to the rest of creation what it is like to be "in Christ." The way we treat the rest of creation matters in this demonstration and matters in terms of the reconciling of all things. Human regeneration is linked in this sense to creational regeneration,[3] humans, being shown the way by our Elder Brother, are a vanguard of the new creation, and we should understand that our science is a reflection of this in some way.

He chose to give us birth through the word of truth, that we might be a kind of first fruits of all he created. (James 1:18)

The creation waits in eager expectation for the sons of God to be revealed. For the creation was subjected to frustration, not by its own choice, but by the will of the one who subjected it, in hope that

> *the creation itself will be liberated from its bondage to decay and brought into the glorious freedom of the children of God. We know that the whole creation has been groaning as in the pains of childbirth right up to the present time. Not only so, but we ourselves, who have the firstfruits of the Spirit, groan inwardly as we wait eagerly for our adoption as sons, the redemption of our bodies. (Rom. 8:19-23)*

We should be motivated in part by a sense of solidarity with the rest of God's creatures but also by a special sense of responsibility to lead the way, to demonstrate to the rest of creation what redemption looks like and acts like. Does this involve some kind of strange nature mysticism? No, but it attempts to believe what God says about our role. How is a "demonstration" made to non-personal creatures and inanimate stuff? Do we need to know this in order to take seriously the implications of Romans 8? No—we need only to believe what He says in this passage.

Not only are our actions being observed in the "seen" world of humans and nature, but there are many indications in Scripture that our activities are being monitored by other beings in the unseen. We are being used, being presented by God as a demonstration of His holiness, power, and grace to those in the heavenly realms. The premise of the book of Job involves just such a scenario: "Then the LORD said to Satan, 'Have you considered my servant Job? There is no one on earth like him; he is blameless and upright, a man who fears God and shuns evil'" (Job 1:8).

In Ephesians Paul refers to this to encourage the church that its behavior and development in the "seen" has demonstration value in the "unseen": "His intent was that now, through the church, the manifold wisdom of God should be made known to the rulers and authorities in the heavenly realms" (Eph. 3:10). And in 2 Corinthians, Paul motivates his readers by arguing that the things that occur in the unseen as a result of the things that occur in the seen actually exhibit the more stable reality:

> *[W]e do not lose heart. Though outwardly we are wasting away, yet inwardly we are being renewed day by day. For our light and momentary troubles are achieving for us an eternal glory that far outweighs them all. So we fix our eyes not on what is seen, but on what is unseen. For what is seen is temporary, but what is unseen is eternal. (2 Cor. 4:16-18)*

Who can say exactly what significance a particular day of work in the lab or a series of experiments might have in the "unseen"? We don't need to know this specifically; we just need to be aware that faithfulness in our scientific work is an issue of record in the heavenlies now. We need to be motivated by the spooky fact that we are not alone in the "seen," but that the significance of what a Christian scientist does in the lab or in the field is seen and does reverberate through the heavenlies in some fashion.

Finally, not only are our actions being watched by others, reverberating now in the unseen, but they will resound through eternity as part of the story of God's righteousness, power, and grace demonstrated in creation and re-creation. A major theme of the book of Revelation is that the deeds of humans on the earth have eternal consequences, consequences that will be reviewed in eternity to the glory of God. The story of the preeminence of Christ in creation and re-creation as it is told to His glory in eternity will include the historical process by which it was unfolded. A record of human doings will be reviewed in eternity. Faithful action on our part now is part of a timeless record of praise to the Author of faith and righteousness. What we do in faith matters in the "not yet" as well as the "now." What will be demonstrated in and through us in eternity is tied up in part in what is unfolding in and through us now—even in the science we do.

Foundations: Finding Firm Footing

As we've been arguing in the previous chapters, believing what God says about His triune nature, His covenant promises, His giving being to us and His universe, and His revealing purposes in created history all provide essential foundations for various aspects of scientific study. The kind of God He is and the kind of universe He brings into being and sustains makes the study of His universe productive and meaningful. The sovereign God of the universe in His tri-unity is both the transcendent ruler of all that is as well as the immanent actor in all that comes to pass. He is the external point of reference for all truth in the universe as well as the immanent revealer and constructor of truth within the universe. His actions with regard to creation are those of a covenant-keeping faithful lover. He has set His love on His people and His creation in such a way as to demonstrate through it the riches of His love in Christ. In our science then we can expect regularity and novelty, the expected and the unexpected without boredom and without fear. We can approach the world as it is, taking as a given our appropriate contact with it, thus avoiding the Modernist preoccupation with developing "in the world" guarantees of the mind-world connection that has ultimately led to Postmodern skepticism. The mind-world connection in God's universe though is not "hard-wired," and thus we are given the privilege of responding to God as persons rather than as machines. Further, cause-and-effect relations in the universe are held together by the faithfulness of a personal Being, such that we need never fear that our careful study will reveal a universe of self-contained determinism. There is freedom in our study, and yet there are constraints. There is regularity in the world; yet there is novelty and incompleteness—and both the freedoms and the constraints as well as the regularities and incompleteness are all in service of God's ultimate purposes in Christ, which by faith we are participating in no matter how prominent or obscure the particular focus of our scientific study.

Actions: Obedience to His Commands

While particular formulations of the interdependency of faith and action (works) have been debated down through the centuries, the idea that believing what God says and active obedience to His commands go hand in hand has been basic to Christian conviction. And believing obedience in Christ is always rooted in the authority of Christ and the obedience that that authority commands. There are several overriding "Great" command statements that especially stand out in Scripture. At the conclusion of Christ's ministry, having completed His earthly work, he gave the Great Commission:

> *All authority in heaven and on earth has been given to me. Therefore go and make disciples of all nations, baptizing them in the name of the Father and of the Son and of the Holy Spirit, and teaching them to obey everything I have commanded you. And surely I am with you always, to the very end of the age. (Matt. 28:18-20).*

In a kind of parallel passage, having completed His creative work, God gave what has been referred to as the "Creation Mandate" or the "Cultural Mandate": "God blessed them and said to them, 'Be fruitful and increase in number; fill the earth and subdue it. Rule over the fish of the sea and the birds of the air and over every living creature that moves on the ground'" (Gen. 1:28).

In the Gospels, Jesus sums up all of God's commands in the Great Commandment: "Love the Lord your God with all your heart and with all your soul and with all your mind and with all your strength. . . . Love your neighbor as yourself. There is no commandment greater than these" (Mark 12:30-31).

The Great Command in one sense simply describes the breadth of obedience—an entire lifestyle of worship that is to be the proper response to the authority of Christ. All that we know and are and do is to be pressed into service to love God and neighbor. This command makes it clear that thinking is a kind of doing, which along with other actions are to be involved in a lifestyle of obedient worship. Thoughtful understanding and analysis are loving actions—part of "bringing every thought captive to Christ." The breadth of action involved in scientific knowing and doing work enables a full range of expression of the elements of this lifestyle of worship. Analytical thinking and careful theoretical consideration and construction are every bit as "action-esque" as developing a vaccine or cataloguing species diversity in a rainforest. This is one reason why attempts to isolate scientific activity from "religion" should be so dissonant for Christians. Worship is a holistic activity, requiring that we bring all we are and know to all we do mentally and physically on a moment-by-moment basis.

The lifestyle of worship described in Mark 12 can be helpfully re-described in a variety of ways. The purpose statement of our own college, Covenant College, refers to this kind of activity as "discerning and unfolding implications of His preeminence in all things."[4] In the next sections of this chapter we want to examine some aspects of this discerning and unfolding activity—that is, doing—in the sciences. These activities can be fruitfully discussed as actions involved in attentiveness, submission, and stewardship.

Actions: Attentiveness

Surely one of the characteristics of those who love God will be attentiveness to what He has done and what He is doing. Attentiveness or simply paying close attention is one of the primary marks of genuine human love. All of the movements, likes, dislikes, interests, and activities of the beloved are given careful attention by the lover. For lovers of God, this attentiveness to God will include attention to His universe, and science is, in a certain sense, a form of specialized attentiveness to God's universe. For a Christian, this attentiveness does not have as its primary goal a dispassionate analysis of the isolated facts. Imagine the results of a courtship that involved the "scientific" study of the intended spouse in this dispassionate sense. Knowledge of the beloved and love in its richest senses are a far cry from the picture that comes to mind with the phrase "objective analysis." This is not to say that the attentiveness of love is sloppy as to details or haphazard in the conclusions drawn. It simply means that careful study doesn't entail coldness of the heart or a mind-set of neutral detachment. We humans are creatures living in a created world, and getting to know that world as we are supposed to know it doesn't require an uncreaturely transcendence. What it does ultimately require is the creaturely transcendence that comes by faith—believing the One who is transcendent. So good science from this perspective doesn't require becoming or pretending to become unhuman or uncreaturely. In fact true attentiveness of this sort involves self-consciously living fully as a human creature in God's world.

This scientific attentiveness toward God's world will include both broad theory construction as well as minute, detailed description. On the one hand, we should seek out the broadly explanatory themes, the general regularities seen in creation, the unifying themes and laws of nature. Not to notice the big picture, not to seek coherence of the details, would certainly be disrespectful to the One who faithfully upholds in regular patterns. On the other hand, God is also a God of specifics, of particulars. Individual organisms and individual stars exist, not just generalized categories. Individual events take place, not just broad regularities. Descriptive aspects of study as well as theoretical and explanatory aspects of science are part of the attentiveness due the works of our Creator. The details of nature are to be objects of our careful attention. Given who our beloved is, we Christians ought to be the ones most careful about getting it right in the details, about accurately representing the world in our thinking and in scientific papers, presentations, and discussions. We are not to consciously distort or ignore data to make the world fit our ideas or to score rhetorical points against opposing arguments. This is not just a matter of the rules of science, not just a matter of scientific integrity, but a matter of love and respect for the Maker and Redeemer of it all.

Attentiveness in science should also always have an eye for the effects of the Fall. To be oblivious to the "abnormal" state of creation would be strange for lovers of the One who created and whose creation has been corrupted by rebellion and evil. The whole creation is subject to futility in the present age, and proper attentiveness will uncover various ways that this subjection to futility might be exhibited concretely. Paying attention to the brokenness of creation should bring a sense of sadness and loss over the corruption of an originally good creation. It should also drive us to place our hope in and take comfort in the promises of God to make it all right again. This should lead naturally to a predisposition for the application of scientific knowledge to appropriately address the effects of sin and evil in creation in order that our science might bear witness to God's work to make it right again.

Living fully in God's world in science also involves attentiveness to the process of scientific study and the human, social, and cultural aspects of science. Attentiveness would call us to think about humans thinking about and doing science. In other words we need to be attentive to humans as humans give attention to the world. Attention is to be given to the broader cultural elements of science as it is done in real places at real times in history. Being self-consciously attuned to these elements of scientific endeavor, in both our own work as well as the work of others in the past and present, need not be seen as undercutting the legitimacy of science or the validity of scientific achievements. It should enhance our appreciation of the richness and wonder of human understanding of the world, while also maintaining humility concerning the contingent nature of our scientific pronouncements and our ultimate dependency on the favor of God in scientific work.

Awareness of and involvement in the broader scientific culture of our day is part of Christian calling in science as well. This involvement is not to be seen as a necessary evil or only in reactionary terms. We are to do more than just play the role of scientific cultural critic. We are to work productively for the "good" of the science of our day as a positive response to the favor of God concretely expressed in His world. Such involvement might bear risk in terms of the temptation to compromise our first loyalty to God and His church—but it is an essential part of the call to be *in* the scientific world and yet not *of* the scientific world. Part of obedience to the "in the world" command is to stay abreast of scientific developments, especially when we are going to be critical of contemporary understandings. We don't have to agree with all consensus conclusions in the scientific world, but we ought to know them well and what they are based upon. At best, speaking out when we are obviously behind in our scientific homework is embarrassing to our Christian brothers and sisters, and at worst it brings the Christian faith and Christ's gospel into disrepute.

Finally, there should be some sense of a corporate attentiveness to God's world. Christians should corporately work to see to it that as many aspects of God's world are given proper attention by His people as possible. We should take seriously the idea that there are corporate responsibilities in helping individuals discern particular callings within the community of Christ, and there are responsibilities for the individual to consider his or her calling in the context of the needs of the church as a whole. Christians ought to be encouraging one another to follow callings across the spectrum of the sciences, so that coverage of God's world is maximized and so that Christians have expert commentary available from fellow believers across the whole spectrum of God's works. No area of the study of God's world should be overlooked by His people.

Actions: Submission

While attentiveness is a mark of loving relationships in general, the relationship between the God of the universe and humans living at His pleasure in His universe under His rule indicates that submissive humility would be a major theme of this love relationship as well. In many ways scientific experimentation at its root is a submissive activity. The ideal of scientific investigation is often described in terms of systematically and meticulously testing human ideas about how things might work against what is really there. The quality of experimental design is judged by how clearly an experiment will test the human idea behind it or, to put it in another way, how directly the experiment will show whether or not the human idea is "in submission" to the way things actually work. Ideally, creation would have the final say in judging the legitimacy of our ideas about how it might work.

For Christians this submissive aspect of science is expanded and personalized in a variety of ways. As discussed in chapter 8, submission to the revelation of Scripture helps a believer frame questions in seeking a proper way to submit one's thoughts to the "judgment" of creation. This is part of the Scripture's spectacles role previously discussed. Further the submission of one's speculations about how things might be to the way God has constituted His world is a very personal issue for believers. One is not simply going through some rational exercise or just seeking entertainment by trying to solve intricate puzzles according to the rules of the science "game." For believers, science is a process of personally significant and proactive submission based on our positive desire to submit our thoughts to the way things actually are as God has personally constituted them.

With this in view, our rationality, so vaunted in Modern thought as an autonomous entity that humans ought to serve on its own merits, is actually to be seen as a gift He gives in part so that our submission to Him might have some consistency. Reason is a tool for obedience, not an end in itself to be served for its own sake. From this perspective, to make our rationality, graciously given as a gift to be used in His service, into some kind of abstract standard outside the context of godly submission is the height of Modernist hubris. This inversion of submission is the hallmark of the Modern age, requiring that God and His self-revelation conform to human-approved modes of thought. A Modern mind will ask: "Can we any longer accept the doctrine of the virgin birth, since we are now independent-thinking scientific people?" Or "The Resurrection can't be what the Scriptures represent it to be, can it? We know that no one, once dead, lives again." We are not saying that questions concerning settled beliefs ought never to be raised in view of new discoveries, but the spirit and context of such questioning is what is at issue. In the early seventeenth century, Francis Bacon, the "father of modern science," decried even in his day the use of human reason in such a way as to "treat God no better than a suspect witness" in a legal proceeding.[5]

This understanding of the role of reason is not meant to suppress the asking of difficult questions. Christians are free in Christ to ask probing questions even when those questions might make some uncomfortable. To ask a variety of questions concerning how God might accomplish some of His purposes in creation is good and proper—even required for attentive worshipers. But these questions are always in the context of our acknowledgment that we know so much less than He does and that we are not in a position to require our own sense of rational satisfaction from Him. It is one thing to ask how we might best understand His works. It is quite another to seriously ask whether our comprehensive explanations leave room for God to act, or whether given the laws of physics God might actually be able to accomplish certain things. We are not in a position to demand explanations. We seek the understanding that comes from

His revelation through His Word and His world so we might know how better to please Him by submitting our wills and our thoughts to Him and His ways. Faithful questioners ought to be the first to profess their trust in God whether their questions are ultimately answered "satisfactorily" in human terms or not.

Another way in which submission and humility can be exercised is in the context of teaching and writing about science. Although it is proper that in an educational context the focus would be on things well understood, that emphasis can give students an inflated view of the level and extent of human understanding about the universe. In our experience, even college students seem genuinely surprised at how easily they can ask questions about things that aren't understood well at all. They often seem somewhat disconcerted about being on the edge of human knowledge. We need always to have before us the fact that the reality hiding behind our comfortable terms and descriptions is often wonderfully untamed and awe-inspiring. It is proper to emphasize what we don't know as well as what we do. This is not part of a "God of the gaps"[6] mentality, as if the glory of God depends on human ignorance. It is simply a recognition that although many of God's works might seem amenable at some level to human description and manipulation, submission and even just basic honesty require that when we have no idea, we ought to say so. In so doing we must always keep in mind that humans having a pretty good idea about how things work doesn't diminish God's might. The wonder is that we can grasp at all by His grace some measure of the strangeness and wildness of His universe. This measure of grasping though should never be used to tame Him or His world. A faithfully submissive scientific servant will look for and point to God's wildness in His works as well as to His gracious and revealing accommodation to human capacities.

Submission as a category of faithful action, of course, does not only involve vertical aspects of human submission to God; it also involves various horizontal aspects of humility and submission to humans. Scriptural instructions concerning the dynamics of this horizontal submission are centered on three major themes: selfless humility as a general response to God's grace, unity within the body of Christ, and the centrality of the gospel.

First then, a believer's work in the sciences should be easily recognized by those around us as the work of humble and unselfish servants of our Lord.

> *Do nothing out of selfish ambition or vain conceit, but in humility consider others better than yourselves. Each of you should look not only to your own interests, but also to the interests of others. (Phil. 2:3-4)*

> *Therefore, as God's chosen people, holy and dearly loved, clothe yourselves with compassion, kindness, humility, gentleness and patience. (Col. 3:12)*

Generosity with time, resources, and encouragement ought to be basic characteristics of our relationships with those working with us in the sciences. Even in the often fierce competition in research, it is clear that Christian scientists ought to be looking out for the interests of others, even of those in competing research groups. Christians in science should avoid temptations to establish their own credentials by being harshly critical of the work of others. Looking out for the interest of others would require taking care of the business of the discipline, contributing appropriate time and effort to meetings, professional organizations, refereeing research reports, and helping students and junior colleagues in their development. Personally, we should be committed to the extra effort that clear communication with colleagues requires. We should be examples of handling criticism well, not defensive in the face of peer review processes. Because of our standing in Christ, we should feel less pressure to promote ourselves—knowing that as we are faithful to our callings, God will ultimately direct our paths. Basically even within the rough and tumble world of active research, Christians should demonstrate their submission to God by putting themselves at the service of their colleagues and their disciplines.

The New Testament epistles also have much to say regarding disagreements among believers in general that are applicable to disagreements among believers about scientific issues. Many of the passages related to the handling of disagreements center around the unity of believers that is achieved in part by mutual submission to one another.

> *As a prisoner for the Lord, then, I urge you to live a life worthy of the calling you have received. Be completely humble and gentle; be patient, bearing with one another in love. Make every effort to keep the unity of the Spirit through the bond of peace. There is one body and one Spirit—just as you were called to one hope when you were called—one Lord, one faith, one baptism; one God and Father of all, who is over all and through all and in all. But to each one of us grace has been given as Christ apportioned it. (Eph. 4:1-7)*

A major rationale given for unity is the recognition that God has equipped different Christians with different gifts and that it is only by submitting to one another and not insisting on the superiority of our own gifts and concerns that the effectiveness of the church will be maximized. By submitting to one another in disagreements, we are submitting to the God who brings his people together and equips them in various ways to accomplish his purposes. We should rather be seen as being wrong, losing an argument, than to push a disagreement to the point where it leads to a divisive spirit among God's people.

The apostle Paul instructs Timothy and Titus extensively concerning how to handle controversial issues and the divisions they cause. On the one hand Paul tells Timothy to tirelessly oppose those who would damage the gospel by false teaching, and he uses some of his harshest language to describe those who seek to bind the consciences of God's people by insisting on their own additions to the gospel.

> *The Spirit clearly says that in later times some will abandon the faith and follow deceiving spirits and things taught by demons. Such teachings come through hypocritical liars, whose consciences have been seared as with a hot iron. They forbid people to marry and order them to abstain from certain foods, which God created to be received with thanksgiving by those who believe and who know the truth. For everything God created is good, and nothing is to be rejected if it is received with thanksgiving, because it is consecrated*

by the word of God and prayer. If you point these things out to the brothers, you will be a good minister of Christ Jesus, brought up in the truths of the faith and of the good teaching that you have followed. (1 Tim. 4:1-6)

When the gospel is being distorted, Paul instructs Timothy to say so in no uncertain terms and assures him that by raising the issues, he is doing his job as a "good minister of Christ." On the other hand, Paul harshly condemns those who divide God's people over issues that have no direct impact on the meaning of the gospel.

But avoid foolish controversies and genealogies and arguments and quarrels about the law, because these are unprofitable and useless. Warn a divisive person once, and then warn him a second time. After that, have nothing to do with him. You may be sure that such a man is warped and sinful; he is self-condemned. (Titus 3:9-11)

So being unwilling to "let it go" when it comes to minor issues is grounds for expulsion from the church as a "warped" and "self-condemned" person. Perhaps even worse are those who distort the gospel by elevating minor issues to gospel prominence and who do this for their own advantage.

If anyone teaches false doctrines and does not agree to the sound instruction of our Lord Jesus Christ and to godly teaching, he is conceited and understands nothing. He has an unhealthy interest in controversies and quarrels about words that result in envy, strife, malicious talk, evil suspicions and constant friction between men of corrupt mind, who have been robbed of the truth and who think that godliness is a means to financial gain. (1 Tim. 6:3-5)

Paul sums up his teaching concerning these things in 2 Timothy 2:23-25:

Don't have anything to do with foolish and stupid arguments, because you know they produce quarrels. And the Lord's servant must not quarrel; instead, he must be kind to everyone, able to teach,

> *not resentful. Those who oppose him he must gently instruct, in the hope that God will grant them repentance leading them to a knowledge of the truth, and that they will come to their senses and escape from the trap of the devil, who has taken them captive to do his will.*

The bottom line seems to be that if we persist in trying to raise the profile of disagreements in which the gospel is not at stake, in such a way that the unity of God's people is fractured, we are sinning against God and against His people and should be disciplined by the church. And even if we are convinced that central gospel-related issues are at stake, Paul insists that we must still be "kind to every one . . . not resentful" and that we must "gently instruct, in the hope that God will...[lead] them to a knowledge of the truth." These instructions need not squelch discussion and disagreement concerning scientific issues in the church. Iron can sharpen iron in vigorous debate. Paul's counsel has more bearing on the status or profile that these disagreements are given in the life of the church and on the spirit in which the disagreements are handled. We must take our unity with fellow believers seriously in the discussion of scientific issues, and the church must be willing to discipline persistently divisive members. May God grant that more of the controversies over scientific issues in the church would be occasioned by such discernment as Paul urges on Timothy and Titus, and may that discernment be exercised in humility, submission, and gentleness.

So God's faithful scientific servant will seek to be submissive in all aspects of the work of science—in his methods, in his interactions with those in his discipline, and in his interactions with fellow believers. Faithful submission is a rich and complex part of "doing" obedience—certainly not a passive process. Submission to God, to His Word, to His world, and to others is essential to obedience. This concept is reminiscent of the discussion of knowledge in chapter 8, that human knowledge is both a thing given and a task to be accomplished. And this brings our discussion from faith in action through submission to faith in action through stewardship. Taking seriously our submission to the Ruler of the universe as He unfolds His purposes also requires that we take seriously our role in that unfolding.

Actions: Stewardship

Faithful doing in the sciences will not only involve the attentiveness of a lover and the submission of a humble servant, but it also requires the entrepreneurial boldness of a loyal steward. A steward is commissioned and empowered to make good use of resources that are ultimately the property of another. We have previously pointed out that Christian knowing and doing are interactive modes of response to being. In keeping with this notion we now turn to a discussion of what we are to do in stewardly response to the gifts of being and to the gifts of knowing that flow from being. What are some of the stewardly actions in the sciences that would arise from the "doing" aspects of the Great Commandment, and how might gifts and resources related to the sciences be used to demonstrate love for God and love for neighbor?

In very general terms stewardship will involve believing what God says about the gifts He gives and the ways He intends for them to be used, and then boldly applying oneself to the wise and fruitful use of those gifts. The primary gift is the gift of Himself in Christ, Emmanuel; then there are the various gifts that come through Christ by His Spirit: that of being a new creature in Christ as a unique individual, the gifts of human capacities, and the gift of being in the world, not just generically, but in specific historical settings. All of these gifts provide each of us with the resources and the challenges of specific existential, social, ecclesiastical, and cultural contexts—all of which are to be areas of focus for our stewardly doing.

The Stewardly Scientific Self

Our first focus will be on a kind of stewardship before God that is personal and individually focused, on aspects of scientific stewardship that arise from the gift of being constituted by God as unique individuals. These personal responses may have public aspects, but for the most part our concern here is on stewardly doing related to the "private" or the "unseen," which He does see even if no one else ever does.

The first such gift is the empowered "new self."[7] Because of who we become in Christ, all subsequent experiences of God's world are "funneled" through our new being and are thus transformed in transit by the "new self" power that comes from God. This is simply a matter of believing what God says He has done for us in Christ. One stewardly response to this "new self" power is to consciously broaden the top of the funnel, to actively "inhale" the full breadth of the world that He opens uniquely before us as individuals. As experiences and thoughts transit our new beings, they are literally and on a moment-by-moment basis transformed by being transferred from a web of death into a web of life in Christ. This is a "plundering of the Egyptians" as things of the world under Satan's sway are liberated and find their true worth in the praise of their Maker and Lord.

Here is an excerpt from a letter one of us wrote to a former student to encourage this kind of stewardly mind-set as she first experienced the wonder and frustration of scientific research in a laboratory setting.

> Dear ____________
>
> . . . God has created an incredible world and by His grace has put some extremely intelligent people in it. I'm still constantly amazed at the clever people I've run into in science. The shamc is that many of these movers and shakers are doing their thing for their own glory rather than for our Lord's—and that's where you and I come in. By God's grace I believe we are used to sustain a redemption "wave" that begins at our regeneration and spreads in ever-widening circles around us as we are faithful to God. The things you are learning, the clever techniques you are working out, need to be redeemed—literally "rescued from loss" by your appropriating them for the glory of God. Let God hear a constant stream of thankfulness and new offerings for His glory rising from a new source at (the research institution at which the student was working). Let Him know often that one of His redeemed is there on post, inhaling the fruits of common grace and exhaling confessional praise to the Author of all that is "good and lovely and pure and excellent."

For those called to the sciences, this way of thinking introduces a powerful existential element to our scientific stewardship. Each Christian in science is uniquely gifted and uniquely placed. No two of us have exactly the same perspective, the same interests and skills, or the same mix of educational preparation, past and present projects, and co-workers. The glory is that we are called to be stewards of what we have been given—not of what someone else has or what we wish we had. To personalize this: Only you can bring glory to your God in your science in this unique way. Those obscure details of your experiments or the arcane features of your specialized area or the quirky mix of people in your research group—these all form your personal domain of transforming responsibility. No one else will do because in God's providence no one else is specifically situated where you are. Moment by moment you can be His unique stewardly instrument, just by being who you are in Christ at the time and place of His choosing.

While this kind of "existential transformationalism" is on one level simply a matter of being—a wordless and "natural" outcome of the reality of our new being in Christ—stewardly responsibilities require that it not be left at this more passive level. As humans we have been given the gift of consciousness, of being able to watch ourselves live and react even as we are doing it. Finding joy in the study of God's world is a common experience in the sciences—both the quiet, constant "baseline" enjoyment of many of the day-to-day activities in science and also the more intense "stabs of joy" that C. S. Lewis describes in his book *Surprised by Joy.*[8] How are we to be good stewards of these joys? Recognizing and raising our consciousness of the science version of the "When I run, I feel His pleasure" sentiments popularized in the 1981 movie *Chariots of Fire* is one way. Certainly, as C. S. Lewis points out, this kind of joy cannot be sought after in direct pursuit, but when it comes at those unexpected and surprising times, it ought to be consciously recognized, received thankfully as a gracious gift, and reveled in as a foretaste of joy to come.

While a response of grateful contemplation of the things in science we're privy to, a kind of running the "fingers of the mind" fondly over the works of God, is proper stewardly activity, it should in turn often move us toward the constructive capturing of these things in human expressions. Mary, the mother of Jesus, who responded to God's work in her life by pondering these things in her heart but also gave voice to them in the Magnificat, is a good example of the progression we have in mind here. Science does provide God's children with many different opportunities and many different forms for doxological contemplation, and we ought to take advantage of them as they arise. Creation does have a quality of "visual poetry," and who better but scientists who understand aspects of it well to give voice to some of the wordless poems we find ourselves surrounded by. Not only is creation a stimulation for praise for the existence of things in the world, but scientific work also provides the raw materials for constant reflection on gospel themes as it illustrates the reality of a fallen world and uncovers human inability while also revealing God's provision, goodness, and faithfulness. Consciously looking for these opportunities and communicating our experiences in them is not usually associated with doing science, but it just seems that these activities should naturally come with the science territory for believers.

The more typical form of expression in science, the peer-reviewed scientific report, is a primary stewardly activity that is not only a specialized personal response to living and working as a scientist in God's world, but it also introduces some of the social/cultural elements of good stewardship that we want to address next. Capturing our experiences in the lab or in the field in words, figures, charts, graphs, or equations is a specialized form of human contemplation that is not only good scientific practice but is godly stewardship for a believer. Certainly a Christian who consistently resisted systematic recording, reporting, and peer examination of his experiences in God's world would be a poor scientific steward. In the kingdom, it is not exactly "publish or perish," but keeping one's insights entirely to oneself would seem a selfish response to who we are and what we've been given in Christ.

The Stewardly Scientific Neighbor

The scientific stewardship discussion thus far has emphasized that each individual Christian scientist is a unique vehicle and is used by God in uniquely personal ways. But certainly a stewardship that ended rather than began with a focus on the narrowly vertical dimension of the self before God might lead to a grotesque form of self-absorption. So we now turn to a discussion of stewardship in terms of its horizontal dimensions—how science is to be stewarded for the good of "the neighbor." We've already discussed this in terms of submission and humility, but we now want to extend that discussion into how a Christian can work for the positive scientific benefit of those around us—in order to be a good scientific neighbor.

Science operates in a community context, and many of the values of that community with regard to what constitutes good scientific practice have to do with stewardship of the work and the resources of the community. Science is very much a cooperative venture in which each individual depends to a great extent on others in the field to do their work well. The mentoring and training of new initiates into the community have to do with the development of skills and ways of thinking that will allow newcomers to make good use of what has come before so that they can make their own contributions to the work of the discipline. This training takes considerable time and resources, but most scientists consider training new initiates a natural part of their commitment to science in order to ensure that their areas of study are properly stewarded in the future. Initiates are also taught to avoid a variety of science-impeding practices: use of methods not appropriate for the questions at hand, improper use or omission of needed experimental controls, posing poorly defined questions, making unsupported generalizations, proceeding without becoming well versed in previous work, poor record-keeping, poor written explanations, and incomplete descriptions of experimental methods. These all muddy the scientific waters and thus waste the resources and efforts of the science community. On the positive side new initiates are taught to value a variety of science-enhancing practices: clear definition of experimental problems, keeping up with one's specialized literature, careful systematic work in the lab, and the full reporting of experimental procedures to enable others to easily repeat and check one's work. A primary goal of each community is to develop a series of connected explanations that account for the way the aspect of the universe it focuses on seems to work. Good explanations are valued not only because in a technical sense they attempt to tell the truth about the world, but also because they contribute to the communal project in positive and enriching ways. Thus explanations valued by the community are as clean and simple as possible; they engage and connect a lot of data and demonstrate predictive power. Good explanations contribute to satisfyingly coherent pictures of the way things work, and they stimulate other work by suggesting productive avenues for further research. This is not to take away from the truth-seeking elements of science by reducing scientific product and practice to social convention, but it does highlight that for believers the responsibility to be a steward of science before God at some level involves being a good neighbor in terms of the accepted practices of our communities.

In considering the broader implications of scientific stewardship in service of the neighbor, a Christian is always to have an eye for practical application, especially for applications that soften or counteract the effects of the Fall in God's world. For believers there should always be an eye for application that will be useful for the neighbor, always a sensitivity to use the power of knowledge for the good of the neighbor. Within this general concern, it seems proper that particular attention be paid to addressing those effects of the Fall that impact humans and particularly to those that disproportionately impact the poor and the oppressed. This is not a matter of spurning basic research or of devaluing work applied to environmental stewardship. As we've discussed previously, Christians more than anyone have incentive to pursue basic research and to treat nonhuman aspects of creation with care and respect—it is all God's stuff, and in the vertical dimension it all deserves to be explored and examined and cared for. This is just to say that as we go about our work, Christians ought always to be considering the question of explicit redemptive application of science in a fallen world. Further, the concern for the poor and the oppressed is not to distort science by making it into a program for social and economic advancement. This is just to recognize the specific biblical emphasis on issues of justice and care for the poor as well as to respond to the general biblical principle that generosity is the proper response of those to whom much grace has been shown and many gifts given.

Finally, in considering the stewardly use of science for the good of one's neighbor, the issue of the use of science in apologetics naturally arises. From a believer's perspective, what could be more loving to one's neighbor than to encourage and help the neighbor to accept the blessings of the gospel? And there is the often-quoted passage from 1 Peter 3:15: "Always be prepared to give an answer to everyone who asks you to give the reason for the hope you have."

It is only natural for believers working in the sciences to see the wonder and kindness of their God as well as the brokenness wrought by the Fall displayed in their areas of study. Seeing such things will naturally incline them to share such impressions and convictions with their non-Christian neighbors. But, as the long history of science-informed apologetics demonstrates, there are dangers inherent in such projects, especially when they become formalized and institutionalized programs for "defending the faith." When such programs come into play, it is so easy to forget that the "reason" referred to for our hope in 1 Peter 3:15 is most succinctly expressed as "Jesus."

Science-based apologetics has the potential to distort both science and theology in a variety of ways. First, the use of scientific evidence in apologetics may inadvertently cede to science the ultimate truth authority. It can be a tacit admission that science defines the ultimate reality and that our own faith will live or die by the latest scientific arguments. Overemphasis on science-based apologetics might also tend to distort what Christians value about science. We may only notice and highlight what seems to have "God-argument" value and pass over those aspects of the world that seem to have less debate-winning potential. In terms of distorting our theology, an overemphasis on design-based apologetics, for example, may consciously or unconsciously lead to a situation in which the central features of the gospel—sin and redemption in Christ—take a distant second place to the issue of whether or not a designer god is required to explain certain features of the universe. In many cases the design discussion generates so much heat that the gospel message is never even on the table. In fact, the gospel often doesn't seem relevant to apologetic discussions—a strange situation indeed from a Christian theological perspective.

An apologetics debate context also tends to give Christians a courtroom lawyer mentality in which admitting the validity of anything raised by the "other side" comes to be seen as weakening "our case." This instills a polarizing oppositional mind-set in all science discussions with non-Christians such that we find it hard to admit that "they" are right about anything. In fact, we convince ourselves that "they" are so easily shown to be wrong that short weekend conferences are all that is needed to give people with no scientific expertise all the necessary tools to debunk the fruits of countless lifetimes of work by "them." In these ways, the proper and central offense of the gospel message, inherent in its proclamation, too easily devolves into the offensiveness of an argumentative messenger. We would do well to be reminded of the larger context of the "always be ready" passage in 1 Peter:

> *Finally, all of you live in harmony with one another; be sympathetic, love as brothers, be compassionate and humble. Do not repay evil with evil or insult with insult, but with blessing, because to this you were called so that you may inherit a blessing. . . . Who is going to harm you if you are eager to do good? But even if you should suffer for what is right, you are blessed. Do not fear what they fear; do not be frightened. But in your hearts set apart Christ as Lord. Always be prepared to give an answer to everyone who asks you to give the reason for the hope that you have. But do this with gentleness and respect, keeping a clear conscience, so that those who speak maliciously against your good behavior in Christ may be ashamed of their slander. (1 Peter 3:8-9, 13-16)*

Better to be seen as losing a debate than to provide an opportunity for unbelievers to justly condemn us as mean-spirited and our tactics as ill-informed misrepresentations. We don't fear what they fear—a failure to look good in our self-sufficiency. When we give good reasons but lack gentleness and respect, we lose the tool that is sure to silence their "slander"—their own shame in attacking those whose winsome behavior is clear to all.

While there are significant dangers in wielding science-derived apologetic tools, to ignore apologetic impacts in the sciences would show lack of good stewardship as well. To put science on the shelf in discussing our faith in the context of our whole lives would not be a faithful response to what God is doing in the sciences. It would be strange if believing scientists censored themselves in public from noting the joy and encouragement in belief they experience in their science and if they never invited unbelievers to check it out. It is ironic indeed that we are tempted to establish our credentials in science by insisting that our faith has nothing to do with our science, so that we can be effective witnesses for Christ! For believers, Christianity has much to do with our science, and we should just be open about this as well as being transparent concerning our struggles to come to grips with the implications of our faith for our science. In addition, recognizing that science is an authority in our culture and that it does command an audience, we should consider how that authority can be utilized in good and proper ways to encourage unbelievers to consider the claims of Christ. But it ought always to be focused in one way or another on the claims of Jesus Christ, the Ruler of the universe—not simply on the generic necessity of an unnatural force to explain the existence of certain features of the universe.

So to see science primarily as a tool to be used to bludgeon people into the kingdom or to see nothing in science that enriches our hope in Christ would both be failures in stewardship. A faithful scientific servant will not shy away from discussing the Godward direction and interpretation of his work and the sense that the things he handles enrich his faith, but neither will he be quarrelsome and arrogant, always spoiling for a good fight with an atheist. We need to rediscover the art of rhetoric, which in its original sense did not refer to manipulative and overblown argumentation, but referred to the systematic removal of obstacles to clear understanding and communication. Our apologetics should be more about presenting a winsome and accurate explanation of Christian understanding, always with a gospel theme and respect for the neighbor, than about no-holds-barred verbal warfare.

The Stewardly Scientific Church Member

A Christian scientist also has special responsibilities in stewarding the connections between the cultural institution of science and the church. These responsibilities are to be carried out with bi-directional communication in mind—relating science to the church as well as the church to science.

Let's first consider the direction of relating science to the church. As we previously mentioned in chapter 7, there is a sense in which a Christian scientist is a caretaker of particular gifts in the church, and thus the work of Christians in science is done in the context of a commitment to extend the church as organism into all areas of life. A Christian scientist should encourage fellow believers to see science as a vocation best carried out in the context of and with the support of Christian community. As scientists experience the wonder, wisdom, power, care, and wildness of God in scientific work, they should readily relate these experiences to brothers and sisters in Christ to encourage and stimulate growth among the faithful. They should seek avenues to bear testimony of the specific ways in which following their callings in science as believers lead to science-specific experiences of joy and opportunities for praise. Their interactions with the church over time should include informing and teaching as well as encouraging. They should be willing conduits through which new developments in science are communicated and to some extent digested by science laypeople. The various fruits of scientific work should thus be communicated to fellow believers in a way that encourages and stimulates the church in both its broad "organism" tasks and in its specifically focused institutional work. In this way, scientists should be willing to be a means through which some measure of the Reformation motto *Ecclesia reformata semper reformanda,* "the church reformed and always being reformed," should be occurring as the church faithfully attempts to respond to the science of the day.

Christian scientists are also to be ambassadors in the other direction as well—in stewarding a relationship between the church and the institution of science. Here, of course, the first requirement is that Christian scientists not succumb to the pressure to leave their Christianity "at the door" when entering the world of science. It is not a matter of belligerently "wearing your Christianity on your sleeve" or of forcing explicit Christian references into situations where they don't fit. It is a matter of bringing all we know as believers to all we do in a transparent way—so that Christian conviction will be seen as a natural part of the way a Christian does science.

A second aspect of this "church to science" stewardship is the self-conscious "mining" of one's particular Christian tradition for distinctive insights and emphases that will enrich the Christian conception of science as a whole and ultimately will enrich science in general. And we need not fear that emphasizing differing Christian perspectives will somehow damage science or pollute it in some way. As Charles Thaxton and Nancy Pearcey argue in their book *The Soul of Science,* contrary to Modernist revision of the history of science:

> [T]he progress of science was a far cry from the simple "emancipation" from religion [as many modernists might characterize it]. On the contrary, science has been shaped largely by debates *among Christians* over which philosophy of nature gives the best way to conceptualize the kind of world God created and the nature of His relationship to it.[9]

As Pearcey and Thaxton go on to show, for most of the history of science these "debates" among Christian perspectives enriched, enlivened, and encouraged science and provided a variety of productive metaphors for making sense of the objects of scientific study. Pearcey and Thaxton also make the important point that, for the most part, the rich variety of Christian perspectives that gave rise to these scientific debates were all held by believers who were unified concerning central matters of doctrine and faith:

> [W]hile orthodox Christians have held certain fundamental theological convictions in common, they have often differed on how to express and apply their theology in areas such as science. Christians begin with Scripture and creation—God's Word and God's world. But the way we relate the two is through the intermediary of philosophy—a philosophy of nature and God's relationship to it, an abstract conception informed by Scripture but not uniquely determined by Scripture. Christians who share theological orthodoxy may embrace different philosophies of nature.[10]

Christian reflection on science, as is the case with Christian reflection on a variety of other issues, will exhibit some striking differences in perspective. All Christian traditions that share theological orthodoxy will nonetheless be able to trace their distinctive threads of thought and perspective within that umbrella of orthodoxy. Christian scientists should bring elements of their own specific Christian traditions to bear on the particular aspects of attentiveness, submission, and stewardship we have discussed and in so doing will enrich their science, their tradition, and thus bring pleasure to God. We are responsible to be good stewards of what has been passed along to us as well as to consider what inheritance we will leave to others. There should be a strong family resemblance among Christian perspectives in the sciences, but certainly there need not be, will not be, and even should not be lockstep uniformity if the children are to faithfully explore the fullness of the scientific tasks that their Father calls them to.

Confidence in Our Doing

So, in looking back over the chapter, what have we claimed that a faithful scientific servant will be about in his scientific work? God's servant in science will be firm in faith, will believe what God says, will be highly motivated by what God has done, will be obedient to the commands of God, and will act out that obedience in science-related attentiveness, submission, and stewardship. And looking back to the previous chapters, His faithful servant will strive to know in terms of what God reveals and in science will strive to be a new creature living faithfully within the story God is telling in history. Well, who is up to such a thing? Certainly none of us can handle such a high calling; so what are we to do?

In the parable of the talents recorded in Matthew 25, three servants are given resources to use while the master is away. The first two put the resources they were given to work and present the master with the increase upon his return and are blessed with the master's commendation and reward. The third servant says that he has done nothing but buried his resources in the ground because he was fearful of the master and therefore would not take risks. His lack of confidence that he could accomplish the tasks set before him by his master led him not even to try, and he was harshly judged by his master. Fear of failure is never a good reason to opt out of the "doing" assignments God gives us. But God is even merciful in terms of our fears. He doesn't say, "Here is your task. Now just get busy in spite of your fear. You're just going to have to deal with your fear yourself and get over it." No, in His grace, He himself provides the perfect antidote to our fear:

> *This is love: not that we loved God, but that he loved us and sent his Son as an atoning sacrifice for our sins. Dear friends, since God so loved us, we also ought to love one another. No one has ever seen God; but if we love one another, God lives in us and his love is made complete in us.*
>
> *We know that we live in him and he in us, because he has given us of his Spirit. And we have seen and testify that the Father has sent his Son to be the Savior of the world. If anyone acknowledges that Jesus is the Son of God, God lives in him and he in God. And so we know and rely on the love God has for us.*
>
> *God is love. Whoever lives in love lives in God, and God in him. In this way, love is made complete among us so that we will have confidence on the day of judgment, because in this world we are like him. There is no fear in love. But perfect love drives out fear, because fear has to do with punishment. The one who fears is not made perfect in love. (1 John 4:10-18.)*

Astonishingly God tells us that we can have confidence because as we live in Him and He in us, "in this world we are like him." It is this expression of God's perfect love that drives out fear.

What are the impacts of this brief gospel sermon in 1 John? In a broad sense, exploring the implications of this Gospel is the work of a lifetime. But one impact in terms of our focus here is that in science as, in fact, in all of life, we are free to "play" boldly to "win" . . . rather than being enslaved to fear so that we "play" fearfully and timidly lest we lose. Anyone who has participated in competitive sports knows the difference between the joy of playing all-out to win in contrast to the fearful agony of playing merely to "not lose."

Basketball seems to illustrate this so often. A top-notch team is scheduled to play a mediocre team that they are predicted to beat easily. In the first half the favored players just can't seem to hit their stride. Their play is tentative and sloppy. At the half they are clinging to a small lead in spite of their poor play. During the halftime break, the coach of the favored team angrily berates the players, tells them of the awful publicity they will get if they fail and the tournament berths they will forfeit. In fact he tells them that their scholarships are at risk. They will have an extra thirty sprints to endure in the next practice if they continue to mess up. As the team leaves the locker room to play the final half, they have a "you better not embarrass me by losing" ringing in their ears. Obviously this is a recipe for disaster, and often an upset win by a weaker team is the result. A team playing only to keep from losing is tentative, lacks a productive "edginess," always feels a little off-balance and awkward, and is dispirited by always seeming to be in the wrong place at the wrong time, making the wrong choices. On the other hand, when a weak team is up against a much better team, the weaker team sometimes plays in an inspired fashion, throwing themselves into the competition, taking risks, doing things they never thought possible—having fun and somctimes even winning the game. There is a huge difference between playing to win because you have nothing to lose and playing only to keep from losing.

The wonder of the grace of God is that we are free to play boldly to win because in Christ we have absolutely nothing to lose. God has perfected His love for us by accepting the sacrifice of His Son in our place and giving us His Spirit that we may be in Him and He in us, "so we can know and rely on the love God has for us"—no matter what!

With this in mind, let's return to the praying scientist with whom we opened the chapter. It certainly could be that God would call him away from his scientific service, but it wouldn't be because his work in the sciences is somehow not kingdom work. "Doing" in the kingdom simply involves faithful work wherever the King of the realm might call us to serve. If we believe what He says, then in the sciences He has provided everything that we could want or desire in Christ, and if we believe this truth, it will truly set us free. Our work in the world, our science, can thus be attacked with confidence and joy, never holding back in the fear of failure or of what others will think. We can take risks, explore new ideas and new ways of seeing things, and have a blast doing so . . . because perfect love casts out fear. The confidence of faith will spill over into a style of science that engages all we are and know and do in service of the One who rules it all . . . and who loves us truly. If our praying scientist is called to serve the kingdom in the sciences, and by God's grace he serves as a true and secure child of the King, he can have every confidence that he will be welcomed into the rest prepared for God's people with the pronouncement that is his greatest desire to hear: "Well done, good and faithful scientific servant. Come and share your Master's happiness."

Chapter Ten

The Kingdom of Christ and the Culture of Science

> *I have given them your word and the world has hated them, for they are not of the world any more than I am of the world. My prayer is not that you take them out of the world but that you protect them from the evil one. They are not of the world, even as I am not of it. Sanctify them by the truth; your word is truth. As you sent me into the world, I have sent them into the world.*
>
> John 17:14-18

In John 17 Jesus prays for His disciples as He prepares to go to the Father, leaving them behind. The world in which He is leaving them is a dangerous place because of the very real power of Satan, "the god of this world." Jesus's followers, however, have believed, obeyed, and become partakers of the truth of the Father revealed fully in the Son. Thus in a fundamental way they are not "of the world," though they have work to do in the world.

Christians have always struggled with the tension of being in the world but not of the world. This tension is in part a result of what has been referred to as the "Christ and culture problem." But what exactly is culture in this sense, and what is the "problem" that causes tension? In his classic book entitled *Christ and Culture*, H. Richard Niebuhr defines culture as:

> . . . the "artificial secondary environment" which man superimposes on the natural. It comprises language, habits, ideas, beliefs, customs, social organization, inherited artifacts, technical processes and values. This "social heritage," this "reality *sui generis*," . . . to which

> Christians like other men are inevitably subject, is what we mean when we speak of culture. . . . Culture is the work of men's minds and hands.[1]

Thus culture, on this account, refers to the entire arena of human activity, which certainly includes science. The "problem" arises from the fact that not only are individual humans fallen and in rebellion against God, but the cultural structures, practices, and ways of thinking these humans develop in producing the "artificial secondary environment" will also reflect human rebellion in various ways. In fact, the frequent biblical warnings about the "world" are most often referring to the powerful and dangerous influence that fallen human culture can have on God's people.

> *Do not love the world or anything in the world. If anyone loves the world, the love of the Father is not in him. For everything in the world—the cravings of sinful man, the lust of his eyes and the boasting of what he has and does—comes not from the Father but from the world. (1 John 2:15-16)*

Our cultural context inevitably grips us. Its hold often steers us away from obedient submission to God's ways and dependence on His provision for us. In contrast, though, the Scriptures also speak of God's love and care for His "world." It is clear that He also takes pleasure in all He has made and glorifies Himself in creaturely capacities and attainments: "The LORD is gracious and compassionate, slow to anger and rich in love. The LORD is good to all; he has compassion on all he has made" (Ps. 145:8).

Furthermore, even as we inhabit the cultural "secondary environment," we are encouraged to notice and to take thought of the "true . . . noble . . . right . . . pure . . . lovely . . . admirable . . . excellent . . . [and] praiseworthy" (Phil. 4:8) elements to be found in it, even though in this world all that is good develops right alongside much that is rebellious and twisted. In science, for example, the good of advances in vaccination technology comes along with the capacity to produce ever more effective biological weapons; the wonder of the cosmos presented in a PBS special might be found right alongside a case being made for atheistic naturalism in the same program. Human culture exhibits much that is wonderful and much that reflects God's goodness to His world and His people, but it also exhibits much that reflects human sinfulness and rebellion. The order of this world and various aspects of human culture are to be valued and appreciated, but they are also to be resisted and disavowed insofar as they attempt to claim the primary allegiance of human hearts, a claim that is only rightly made by God Himself.

These conflicting realities comprise the Christ and culture problem that we are called to navigate as we follow our Lord, and living in a kind of dynamic tension is inherent in our calling to be in the world but not of it. In this chapter we will focus on this Christ and culture problem as it relates to Christian involvement in contemporary science. We will develop some theological resources for understanding and grappling with the problem, and then we will suggest how we might work faithfully to be in the scientific world but not of it.

The Culture of Science

Years ago one of us gave his father Carl Sagan's book *Cosmos* as a birthday present. The book is based on the TV series of the same name, in which Sagan utters his much-quoted credo: "The cosmos is all that is or ever was or ever will be."[2] Sagan was a Cornell University astronomer and a dedicated popularizer of science who wanted to convey to the general public a sense of the power of science and something of the wonder he experienced in contemplating scientific discovery. During his career, he became a kind of spokesperson/apologist for modern science, and in this role he was often outspoken in his criticism of much that characterizes conservative Christian belief. Within the evangelical subculture, he became the embodiment of all that was evil, threatening, and arrogant in modern science. How could a book written by such an author be a suitable gift to give a Christian parent? Well, the *Cosmos* book and TV series were for the most part a wonderful and wonder-producing tribute to various aspects of our universe, written by one who obviously loved it and treated it with wonder and respect. For a believer, the book provides a wonderful occasion to revel in the works of the Author and Sustainer of "all that is or ever was or ever will be." Christians are able to do this even though the material was conceived and written by one who was consciously supporting a Modernist agenda antagonistic to historical Christian conviction and to God Himself. The same kind of spiritual irony is also a part of the daily lives of Christians more directly involved in scientific work in our culture. There is much that we find joy in as believers, but there is also much that is offensive to the God who rules the universe that is the object of scientific work.

An especially enjoyable aspect of science for us is the wide variety of people one gets to meet and work with. One of us remembers in graduate school starting to keep a list of all the different nationalities of the people he worked closely with and giving it up when the count quickly went past twenty. These colleagues displayed a wide array of cultural backgrounds, personal histories, and religious convictions and yet worked relatively easily together on common scientific tasks in a mutually productive and enriching way.

Not only are there diverse cultural backgrounds in most research groups, but the personal motivations for doing science are quite varied and add interest and "texture" to the scientific work. Probably the most common motivating factor is an intense fascination with the way certain aspects of the world work, and this is often coupled with an intense desire to prove oneself superior or at least worthy in a competitive intellectual "game" involving those aspects. For some individuals, science is primarily an interesting diversion—something entertaining to do at the public expense. For others it provides a path to fame or at least a way to demonstrate intellectual superiority over "the masses." To a few, science seems to offer a pathway to fortune. Many are driven in part by a desire to be helpful in some way, to advance the group project or provide useful practical information that could help combat disease or enable technological achievements. Here again, the common project of science seemed to be able to harness quite varied personal motivations for the accomplishment of the common task.

Further, the scientific culture into which we were inducted as graduate students highly valued hard work, persistence, openness, and honesty. As part of this culture we also experienced kindness and consideration in innumerable ways—from the simple sharing of reagents among lab bench mates when we ran unexpectedly short, to the concerted efforts of an established mentor to promote her students' success. People were commonly generous with their time and expertise—going out of their way to help us as new members of the community in mastering new concepts or techniques, troubleshooting experiments, or taking time to read and comment on written work. The sharing of results and materials among colleagues and many other kinds of cooperation were universally expected and commonly practiced.

Thus we find much that is good and right in the halls of modern science. We have met and worked with an incredible variety of clever, interesting, highly motivated non-Christian people who were obviously competent in their work and often brought joy to us as believers and found joy in their own tasks as well. The modern vision of science as a great reconciler that brings out the best in humans by providing challenging tasks in a common neutral space seems to be substantially realized in our experience.

And yet . . . and yet various tensions were embedded in the common work we did. Some were just a result of the normal sin and selfishness that infects all humans, Christian and non-Christian alike: the temptation to be petty, to backstab, to talk down the work of others, to overextend or exaggerate the importance of one's work, to let scientific competition and disagreement spill over into personal animosity. But some of the tensions with our non-Christian colleagues resulted from the fact that there was a great distance between our own broader convictions as believers and their basic convictions. It was widely assumed among our colleagues that science had in some way invalidated traditional religious belief, and some consciously saw their science as confirmation of a materialist understanding of the universe that left no room for a consideration of a God or His claims upon them. Our own Christian convictions were variously considered to be quaint, dangerous, "okay for us," bizarre, or "whatever."

Although there would occasionally be flashes of genuine animosity concerning our "religious" beliefs, in general, as long as these convictions didn't appear to interfere with our scientific productivity, there was no explicit condemnation of them. In interacting with the scientific culture, we cycle constantly between feeling "at home" in that culture, enjoying its challenges, accomplishments, and cooperation, and feeling that at some basic level we as Christians are about something quite different in the science we strive to do as believers.

Thus in science one finds a mix of the noble and the base that seems to characterize all human activity in a fallen world, but this in a strikingly cooperative culture. In each lab, in each discipline, a widely varied group of people with a wide variety of worldviews, lifestyles, and motivations are able to gather around "the science," find productive work to do together, and develop a strikingly unified picture of the way the world works. In short, we found much evidence of God's favor and much good to praise Him for in blessing this human endeavor we call science, whether done by Christians or not. At the same time there was a consistent sense of a dark edge in that same scientific culture, of something deeply oppositional to Christian conviction, especially Christian conviction not kept safely "in its place." Explicit Christian convictions were not welcome in the halls of science and sometimes generated surprising hostility.

Evangelicals and Twentieth-Century Science: A Short Cultural Story

It often seems that among evangelicals, the converse is true as well: Contemporary science is not always welcome in the evangelical subculture. Most evangelicals have feelings ranging from mild unease to shrill combativeness whenever public conversation turns to scientific topics. When the kids ask to watch a PBS science special, we have mixed feelings—gratified that they are interested in God's world, but worried that the program will focus on evolution or that it will intermix explicit footage of mating behaviors in the animal world with discussions of analogies to human sexuality. We scan each issue of *National Geographic* as it arrives in the mail, hoping that the articles include travelogue descriptions of the Great Wall of China or pictorials of spiders in Ecuador rather than articles dealing with human origins or the latest fossil finds of proposed transitional species in evolution. We engage in discussions in the context of Christian education as to whether to adopt "secular" science texts or whether to choose one of the few "Christian" science texts available—often with the conviction that the secular texts are better in some sense but dangerous in other senses. Popular apologetics conferences often include speakers who debunk the latest conclusions in evolutionary biology while at the same time marshalling the latest discoveries in other scientific disciplines as arguments for the existence of the Christian God.

Most evangelicals assume that science should be an ally of Christianity, but that somehow it isn't living up to its obligation in our contemporary context. The fact that science in modern culture isn't generally perceived to be an obvious Christian ally is evidence enough for many evangelicals that a well-organized secularist conspiracy exists within the sciences. Thus when considering the science establishment, many evangelicals experience quick flashes of anger and resentment. This mind-set leads them to easily take offense and often to read events and statements in mainstream science in the worst light possible. The sense of this mind-set is more one of betrayal than simple opposition. What is this all about? Why is there a kind of schizophrenia at work with vociferous attacks leveled at the science of the day by evangelicals, even while they profess a deep love for science and its "legitimate" discoveries? How did this kind of love-hate relationship with the cultural science arise?

These quickly triggered hostilities interspersed with profuse professions of love are reminiscent of the kind of tensions found in family interactions where deeply personal wounds in the past tend to color all subsequent interaction and are always lurking just below the surface. This "dysfunctional family" scenario with regard to science and evangelicals grows out of a broad and complex story of changes in conceptions of science, Christianity, and education in America during the nineteenth century.[3]

Evangelicals in the United States in the early nineteenth century had a strong sense of connection, even alliance, with the science and learning of the day:

> In post revolutionary America . . . it was a widely shared article of faith that science, common sense, morality and true religion were firmly allied. . . . All the major protestant parties agreed that the common sensically based scientific understanding of God's revelation in nature confirmed his revelation in Scripture. They disagreed sharply, however, on how much weight to give to reason and to scripture when there was apparent conflict. Nevertheless, everyone it seemed . . . was in the same debate. Moreover, all were convinced that in a fair controversy universal truth would eventually flourish. . . . Objective science was the best friend of faith.[4]

And further:

> By the end of the 18th century, American Protestants of all sorts had adopted [a] two tiered worldview, founded on empiricist epistemology, with the laws of nature below, supporting supernatural belief above. . . . Generally, evangelical American scientists assumed the total objectivity of their enterprise, but then related it to their Christianity by noting the harmonies of scientific truth and truth in the higher realms of religion and morality.[5]

It was widely assumed by Christian and non-Christian alike that science was a totally objective enterprise that was best done without reference to religious belief. One should do the day-to-day work of science as if having no Christian convictions. There was nothing impious about this. It was just a matter of doing good science. Such a "secularization" of science was not something to be feared by Christians, but rather to be encouraged because science thus objectively done would inevitably get at the truth, and the objective science "below" would inevitably support Christian religious claims "above" since Christianity was in fact the true religion. This kind of independent confirmation of Christianity by science would ultimately clinch the case for Christianity among unbelievers. After the science was done without reference to one's faith, then there were various avenues to relate it to one's faith—noting the exquisite design of various organisms, for example. This confidence in the objectivity of science led to Christian support of an explicitly secularized understanding of proper scientific methodology.[6]

Ironically, the idea that serious scientific work was to be done without reference to one's deeper convictions led to the eventual marginalization of Christian convictions, not only in science but in serious academic work in general, as other academic disciplines sought to emulate scientific methodology. Attempts to bring in Christian convictions at the end of the research process, which seemed natural for many scientists at the beginning of the nineteenth century, were often seen as superfluous and "unscientific" as the nineteenth century closed. And after Darwin, the Christian "trump card" of divine design for connecting "objective" biology to Christian conviction rang increasingly hollow in the minds of many biologists.

For those assuming an inevitable and obvious congruity between science and Christianity, the sense of being "turned out," or more accurately of gradually becoming obsolete in the scientific and broader academic culture, was especially galling given the dominance of Christianity in higher education during most of the nineteenth century. The rather rapid realignment of the intellectual world in the United States during this period contributed to an extended conflict between conservative Christians and various permutations of theological and cultural "liberals" in the early decades of the twentieth century. These poisoned waters provided much of the animosity that characterized the creation-evolution warfare that emerged soon after Darwin and continues to our day.

Of course the story is much more complex and much more interesting than that just given, but we think Mark Noll is correct in arguing that a major feature of the evangelicals-and-science story is the serious trauma that lurks behind the various stances evangelicals have tried out in the twentieth century with regard to science. Noll argues that "contemporary evangelical thought is best understood as a set of intellectual assumptions arising from the nineteenth century synthesis of American and Protestant values and then filtered through the trauma of fundamentalist-modernist strife."[7]

One of these basic nineteenth-century assumptions was the total objectivity of science, and one of the basic elements of the trauma was the increasing realization that the theologically liberal Modernists were able to play the science card to support their theological positions in ways that reminded the theological conservatives of the former support they felt from science. And for many conservative Christians there has subsequently always been the secret hope that the "science cavalry" would eventually come to their aid to overcome the distinct disadvantage many evangelicals felt was theirs in the culture wars of the late twentieth century.

The personal and collective evangelical experiences with science that we have just described illustrate the kinds of Christ and culture tensions Christians encounter in dealing with Modern science. How should we respond to these tensions? Should Christians establish separate institutions for doing science in an attempt to separate ourselves from the "ungodly" science? Or should we simply attempt to be members in good standing of the American Society for Virology or the American Physical Society, for example? Are we to work for the advancement of the cultural science—to be strong supporters of public science funding, for example, or should we seek to cut funding because we find some of the pronouncements made by those receiving those funds to be anti-Christian? What basic principles and motivations should guide our involvement in contemporary science, and how should we understand the fact that the cultural science seems to work so well?

Abraham Kuyper: Common Grace and Antithesis

To begin to approach these questions, we first refer to a foundational theological account of God's kingdom and His rule in human affairs as it relates to human cultural history. Abraham Kuyper (1837-1920) extensively developed the concepts of common grace and antithesis (briefly discussed in chapter 3) as basic features of such an account. His approach starts with the recognition that humanity is fractured into two opposing battle arrays—one side opposing God at every turn, and the other composed of those who have been regenerated by the Holy Spirit, working in service of the true King. He refers to this situation as the "antithesis." In order for any cooperative cultural activity to take place, God must graciously act to temper in some measure the full impact of this antithesis. It is by His common grace that He restrains sin, promotes cooperation among regenerate and unregenerate alike, and propels positive development of the good potentials of His creation through a variety of human institutions and human spheres of activity. Common grace and antithesis taken together provide a framework for appreciating the good and the true that may emerge from human cultural activities while still recognizing the seriousness of sin and the comprehensive and humanly ineradicable clash between God and the forces of Satan that takes place within those same human cultural activities.[8]

Kuyper's insights here are extremely helpful, and our discussion in this chapter follows the basic contours of his common grace/antithesis framework for understanding and responding to cultural activity in a fallen world. However, we have recast Kuyper's basic insights by using terms such as favor, judgment, "constraints of creation," and battle rather than the common grace and antithesis terminology. This shift in terminology serves several purposes. Significant controversy has been generated over the years in certain quarters over the use of the term "grace" in the "common grace" formulation, and introducing new terms allows us to side-step that controversy to a certain degree. Also, the difficulty people have in getting comfortable with the term "antithesis" seems to be a barrier to some in gaining an appreciation of Kuyper's work in this area, and more user-friendly terms may help. Finally we believe that in some ways the focus on common grace and antithesis can harden into habits of mind that may point away from the centrality of the gospel in Christ rather than toward it. We hope that the nuances of the terminology we adopt will be helpful in keeping the discussion more firmly pointed in gospel directions. So the terms we have adopted are related to common grace and antithesis concepts in our use but are not directly super-imposable on them.[9]

The basic account of God's rule in human affairs and His kingdom as it relates to human cultural history using such terminology goes something like this: The arm of God, as it extends timelessly through history, is the arm of justice—His just rule will be demonstrated, evil will be vanquished in battle, His holiness will be vindicated. Not one wrong in history will remain unaddressed by His justice. His justice is not arbitrary, piecemeal, or tentative—it is fairly administered, it is comprehensive, and it is absolutely sure. But history is also the arena of His favor. God's outstretched arm brings favor and love, restoration and healing, a preservation of the good and a restraint of evil in history. His favor is not given in a stingy fashion as if spending favor in the temporal realm is somehow a bad investment. Nor does He sprinkle on just enough favor to keep things going as He effects a strategic withdrawal from a broken world to prepare for an exclusively heavenly triumph. Rather His mercy and goodness, which are inextricably linked to His justice in His character, gloriously flourish in the midst of just judgment, even while the battle between God and those who oppose Him is raging.

If we want to be able to address some of the specific questions we have posed concerning our response to Christ and culture tensions in science, we need first to explore in some detail the dynamics of battle, favor, and judgment as God prosecutes His purposes in history. So we will digress a bit and then get back to the science-specific issues.

The Creation—a Battlefield Under the Judgment of God

Because sin and evil have altered everything, the whole universe is under God's judgment in a comprehensive way. God could have wiped everything clean at the point of the Fall, and the epic battle of good versus evil in created time would never have taken place. But as recorded in Genesis 3, God acted graciously, making vows of deliverance as well as of judgment, and the battle was joined in the creaturely realm. Speaking to Satan, God said, "And I will put enmity between you and the woman, and between your offspring and hers; he will crush your head, and you will strike his heel" (Gen. 3:15).

This vow of judgment, this joining of battle, is to be a source of fear and awe, but it is also to be a source of hope and joy for humans and for the rest of creation as well:

> *Worship the* L*ORD in the splendor of his holiness; tremble before him, all the earth. Say among the nations, "The* L*ORD reigns." The world is firmly established, it cannot be moved; he will judge the peoples with equity. Let the heavens rejoice, let the earth be glad; let the sea resound, and all that is in it; let the fields be jubilant, and everything in them. Then all the trees of the forest will sing for joy; they will sing before the* L*ORD, for he comes, he comes to judge the earth. He will judge the world in righteousness and the peoples in his truth. (Ps. 96:9-13)*

The vows of judgment and deliverance lead to a relentless battle in history against an intractable foe. This foe is often an under-appreciated figure in a modern world that thinks it has outgrown belief in such beings as Satan. Yet the Scriptures give Satan a central place in the drama that unfolds in created time. Satan's career as a sinner and "accuser" ("accuser" is one translation of the word usually rendered "Satan") began before the beginning of human history: "He who does what is sinful is of the devil, because the devil has been sinning from the beginning" (1 John 3:8a).

When the world was created and peopled by Adam and Eve, Satan saw a chance to play his accuser role and in Eve's presence accused God of being a pretender to the throne of the universe. Adam and Eve allied themselves with Satan in accusing God and bringing about the Fall with its release of sin and evil into creation. Because Satan is the powerful being who orchestrated the Fall, spoiling a good creation, using his power of deception to enlist the human race on his side, the Scriptures refer to him as the "god of this age": "The god of this age has blinded the minds of unbelievers, so that they cannot see the light of the gospel of the glory of Christ, who is the image of God" (2 Cor. 4:4).

He is a powerful foe and the enemy of every thing that is right (Acts 13:10). He sows bad seed among the good seed in God's field (Matt. 13:24-29). He is like a lion seeking victims (1 Peter 5:8) and is a schemer who seeks to gain a foothold in the lives of humans to entrap them in bondage to sin (Eph. 4:27; 6:11; 1 Tim. 3:7). Satan is a potent force behind evil and sin in the world, driven by hatred and empowered for a time to lead a fallen humanity in relentless rebellion against God and thus into the darkness.

It is important to note that it is God who chose to engage in the battle for creation, and it is He who sets the terms for the fight. Judgment on this present age is ultimately a result of God's decision to set His favor on a universe and its people in spite of the sin and evil that infected it. God establishes the kingdom of light in the darkened world, and therefore a battle is joined:

> *[Give] thanks to the Father, who has qualified you to share in the inheritance of the saints in the kingdom of light. For he has rescued us from the dominion of darkness and brought us into the kingdom of the Son he loves. (Col. 1:12-13)*

This kingdom of light that opposes the kingdom of darkness is the kingdom of Jesus Christ, who was declared the victor even from the beginning and who is appointed to carry out the battle in created time, that God might be "just and the one who justifies" in Christ:

> *The reason the Son of God appeared was to destroy the devil's work. (1 John 3:8b)*

> *Since the children have flesh and blood, he too shared in their humanity so that by his death he might destroy him who holds the power of death—that is, the devil. (Heb. 2:14)*

The devil will be destroyed, and though he has been given power for a time, his days are numbered.

Unexpected Twists and Turns in the Path to Victory

The pace of the battle is not necessarily even throughout history, though the victory is already assured, and the final campaign unfolds progressively in time. A pivotal moment in that campaign that has quickened the pace of the battle was the actual bodily coming of the King, an event distinctively marking the beginning of the end for Satan in created time. But even the bodily presence of the King did not end the struggle. The authority of the incarnate King in His creation was itself exerted in an unfolding pattern. It is noteworthy that at the beginning of His ministry, at the point of His temptation, Jesus did not explicitly dispute Satan's authority on the earth:

> *Again, the devil took him to a very high mountain and showed him all the kingdoms of the world and their splendor. "All this I will give you," he said, "if you will bow down and worship me." Jesus said to him, "Away from me, Satan! For it is written: 'Worship the Lord your God, and serve him only.'" (Matt. 4:8-10)*

And as His ministry developed and grew, Jesus often paused to rejoice, to praise the Father for the unfolding of His plan to progressively bring about total victory in and through Himself as the Christ. Early in His ministry, after Jesus had already demonstrated His own authority over demons and thus over Satan, He then sent out the seventy-two with instructions to preach and minister "in his name." The result, as Luke records it was:

> *The seventy-two returned with joy and said, "Lord, even the demons submit to us in your name." He replied, "I saw Satan fall like lightning from heaven. I have given you authority to trample on snakes and scorpions and to overcome all the power of the enemy; nothing will harm you. However, do not rejoice that the spirits submit to you, but rejoice that your names are written in heaven."*
>
> *At that time Jesus, full of joy through the Holy Spirit, said, "I praise you, Father, Lord of heaven and earth, because you have hidden these things from the wise and learned, and revealed them to little children. Yes, Father, for this was your good pleasure. All things have been committed to me by my Father. No one knows who the Son is except the Father, and no one knows who the Father is except the Son and those to whom the Son chooses to reveal him." Then*

he turned to his disciples and said privately, "Blessed are the eyes that see what you see. For I tell you that many prophets and kings wanted to see what you see but did not see it, and to hear what you hear but did not hear it." (Luke 10:17-24)

In this passage Jesus rejoices that the tide of battle has definitively turned, in that demons now quail before the name of Jesus uttered by His disciples. Satan's power is drastically weakened. Jesus exalts in His Father's plan to win the battle through the weak and lowly in the world's eyes. He cautions the disciples against focusing on their own power in the battle and instructs them to rejoice foremost in the overall trajectory of God's ultimate plans for them. He then reminds them of the privilege they have of witnessing God's specific work in their own historical setting—a privilege of which others only dreamed: the power of Satan in the world broken by the incarnation of the heavenly King, the reign of death ended by the resurrection of the promised Messiah, the Spirit fully poured out to consolidate and extend the kingdom in the world, Christ's church established as an "in-history" institution over which the "gates of hell" would never prevail.

We Christians living in the twenty-first century need to remind ourselves often that we do live in the midst of a real battle and that the "god of this age" is yet to be finally vanquished. Real forces of evil and opposition to God are arrayed against Him and against His true children in all areas of life, certainly including science. It really is a dangerous world, and we are still susceptible to the deception of the god of this age as he opposes the kingdom, even in and through the sciences.

We also need to remember that the progress of the kingdom is difficult to specifically identify with particular human movements and human successes. Events will unfold that may seem at first to be significant setbacks, but in time may be seen as a movement forward for the kingdom. And there may be events and movements that we are tempted to directly identify with the advance of the kingdom, which in time show themselves to be utter defeats. It is especially when we have engineered strategies that seem to "work" that we must be mindful of the devil's deception, our dependency on grace, and the consistent themes that God glories in using the weak and despised to do His work. Thus our hope is never to be settled on "the strength of the horse," and triumphalism in any human movement, including our science, is totally out of place.

Yet we also need to remember that by God's grace we live in post-incarnation times. The King has openly and bodily declared His rule over the whole creation, and His Spirit is powerfully present with us in the battle. The apostle John reminds us that "the one who is in you is greater than the one who is in the world" (1 John 4:4). Thus we are fully equipped to participate in the battle, and we need not fear in the midst of the battle and the judgment that the battle entails.

The Creation—a Field of God's Favor Given Through the Son

History is not only the story of judgment and battle; it is also the story of God's favor, a favor focused in a unique way on God's redeemed people but also spread abroad widely in God's creation. We are not only to bear up under God's just judgment in the world, but we are to bear witness to and consciously find joy in His favor in history as we point toward the coming order of consummated justice through which the consummation of God's favor will also come. Creation is not only a place where evil is opposed by definitive judgment in battle. It turns out that judgment and battle are directly related to favor. Satan's evil designs are opposed by the tangible demonstration of God's favor in His realm. One could even say that favor is central to God's plan for the total destruction of evil and death, a favor that is ultimately bought with a price dear to God Himself. Rather than all of creation sharing in his fate as Satan surely wished, God entirely confounds Satan's intentions by superimposing unmerited favor upon perfect justice. Thus creation, including all areas of human activity, is an arena of favor as well as judgment.

The Psalms speak often and eloquently of the multiplicity of favor God showers on His world. We here quote extensively from Psalms 65, 104, and 145 because they convey so poignantly the joy and pleasure of God in showing favor to His creation.

You care for the land and water it;
you enrich it abundantly.
The streams of God are filled with water
to provide the people with grain,
for so you have ordained it.
You drench its furrows and level its ridges;
you soften it with showers and bless its crops.
You crown the year with your bounty,
and your carts overflow with abundance.
The grasslands of the desert overflow;
the hills are clothed with gladness.
The meadows are covered with flocks
and the valleys are mantled with grain;
they shout for joy and sing. (Ps. 65:9-13)

He makes springs pour water into the ravines;
it flows between the mountains.
They give water to all the beasts of the field;
the wild donkeys quench their thirst.
The birds of the air nest by the waters;
they sing among the branches.
He waters the mountains from his upper chambers;
the earth is satisfied by the fruit of his work.
He makes grass grow for the cattle,
and plants for man to cultivate—
bringing forth food from the earth:
wine that gladdens the heart of man,
oil to make his face shine,
and bread that sustains his heart.
The trees of the LORD are well watered,
the cedars of Lebanon that he planted.
There the birds make their nests;
the stork has its home in the pine trees.
The high mountains belong to the wild goats;
the crags are a refuge for the coneys.
The moon marks off the seasons,
and the sun knows when to go down.
You bring darkness, it becomes night,

and all the beasts of the forest prowl.
The lions roar for their prey
and seek their food from God.
The sun rises, and they steal away;
they return and lie down in their dens.
Then man goes out to his work,
to his labor until evening.
How many are your works, O LORD*!*
In wisdom you made them all;
the earth is full of your creatures.
There is the sea, vast and spacious,
teeming with creatures beyond number—
living things both large and small.
There the ships go to and fro,
and the leviathan, which you formed to frolic there.
These all look to you
to give them their food at the proper time.
When you give it to them, they gather it up;
when you open your hand,
they are satisfied with good things.
When you hide your face, they are terrified;
when you take away their breath,
they die and return to the dust.
When you send your Spirit, they are created,
and you renew the face of the earth.
May the glory of the LORD *endure forever;*
may the LORD *rejoice in his works—*
he who looks at the earth, and it trembles,
who touches the mountains, and they smoke.
I will sing to the LORD *all my life;*
I will sing praise to my God as long as I live.
May my meditation be pleasing to him,
as I rejoice in the LORD.
But may sinners vanish from the earth
and the wicked be no more.
Praise the LORD*, O my soul.*
Praise the LORD. *(Ps. 104:10-35)*

The L*ORD* *is gracious and compassionate,*
slow to anger and rich in love.
The L*ORD* *is good to all;*
he has compassion on all he has made.
All you have made will praise you, O L*ORD;*
your saints will extol you.
They will tell of the glory of your kingdom
and speak of your might,
so that all men may know of your mighty acts
and the glorious splendor of your kingdom.
Your kingdom is an everlasting kingdom,
and your dominion endures through all generations.
The L*ORD* *is faithful to all his promises*
and loving toward all he has made.
The L*ORD* *upholds all those who fall*
and lifts up all who are bowed down.
The eyes of all look to you,
and you give them their food at the proper time.
You open your hand and satisfy the desires of every living thing.
The L*ORD* *is righteous in all his ways*
and loving toward all he has made. (Ps. 145:8-17)

These wonderful psalms speak of a God who is good to all, whose favor is bountifully and generously spread throughout creation. His favor takes many different forms and comes to His world and His creatures in many different ways and to many different degrees. God loves His universe and personally cares for it. God takes pleasure in His care of both His human and nonhuman creations, and He enjoys the accomplishments of His creatures as they positively respond to His favor. As John Murray puts it simply in an excellent article entitled "Common Grace," "Creation is the recipient of divine bounty."[10]

A Complex Relation Between Judgment and Favor

But what about the sin, evil, and rebellion that infect creation as a whole? How is it possible that a righteous God could take pleasure in any aspect of a corrupted creation or in the attainments of rebellious human beings? Maybe God's favor and pleasure are only expressed toward an untainted nature and not toward sinful humans? No, Scripture does not allow a romanticized separation of nature from humans in this way. God also gives generously to His human creatures, providing for their sustenance, joy, and well-being (Ps. 65:9-13; Ps. 104:14-15). He takes pleasure in their activities as each goes out in the morning "to his work, to his labor until evening" (Ps. 104:23), and His enjoyment of the humanly manufactured ships parallels His enjoyment of "leviathan" at play in the seas (Ps. 104:24-26).

Is God's basic attribute of righteousness somehow a counterweight to the favor He shows in His broken and sin-sick creation? Hardly. Look at the constant refrain in the passages from the Psalms above: "The Lord is gracious . . . slow to anger . . . rich in love . . . good to all . . . has compassion on all he has made . . . is faithful to his promises . . . is loving toward all he has made . . . satisf[ies] the desires of every living thing." The passage from Psalm 145 quoted above definitively makes the link in the Hebrew parallelism of verse 17: "The LORD is righteous in all his ways and loving toward all he has made." So is His righteousness a counterweight to His favor? Absolutely not. His lovingkindness toward all that He has made and His utter righteousness are of a piece and are united in His actions toward His creation.

Is His favor only expressed to humans that are part of the people of God? No, His favor is spread widely among all humanity. In the New Testament, Paul picks up on these same themes in his preaching to pagan Gentiles, making the reality of God's favor to unbelievers the centerpiece of his argument:

> *In the past, he let all nations go their own way. Yet he has not left himself without testimony: He has shown kindness by giving you rain from heaven and crops in their seasons; he provides you with plenty of food and fills your hearts with joy. (Acts 14:16-17)*

> *The God who made the world and everything in it is the Lord of heaven and earth and does not live in temples built by hands. And he is not served by human hands, as if he needed anything, because he himself gives all men life and breath and everything else. From*

> *one man he made every nation of men, that they should inhabit the whole earth; and he determined the times set for them and the exact places where they should live. God did this so that men would seek him and perhaps reach out for him and find him, though he is not far from each one of us. "For in him we live and move and have our being." As some of your own poets have said, "We are his offspring." (Acts 17:24-28)*

Finally, is judgment forgotten when the Scriptures speak so freely of God's seemingly indiscriminate favor? Not at all. In Psalm 104 just quoted above, judgment clearly is a present reality situated in the midst of God's glorying in His creation. Verse 35 of Psalm 104 reads, "But may sinners vanish from the earth and the wicked be no more."

And does Paul just leave the pagans feeling warm and fuzzy about a God who shows them His favor? Note that his sermon in Acts 17 concludes with a stark warning:

> *Therefore since we are God's offspring, we should not think that the divine being is like gold or silver or stone—an image made by man's design and skill. In the past God overlooked such ignorance, but now he commands all people everywhere to repent. (Acts 17:29-30)*

So we have come full circle. Favor presumed upon becomes a form of judgment. When it is shown to fallen humans, Christians and non-Christians alike, favor always calls for repentance because we know we have not deserved it and have not responded to it as we should. Favor received without repentance and thankfulness will testify against us in judgment.

In summary then, even in a fallen universe, God loves what He has made and shows favor to it all in various ways and takes pleasure in it as He cares for it and enables its unfolding. He restrains to various degrees the evil and the chaos unleashed in the natural world after the Fall. It is His hand of favor that dampens and restrains the extent of evil that humans would do if given over wholly to their rebellion against God. In His kindness He ordains and sustains human authority, which is to varying degrees a restraint on human sin and a promotion of what is good and right. He graciously delays pouring out the wrath that sinful humans justly deserve. He gives positive gifts to His creatures and guides in their exercise of them. Human achievement in technology, in the arts, and, yes, in all the sciences are all entirely a result of His favor. All human cooperation that leads to the common good is a gift from His hand; all positive cultural development is ultimately due to His favor.

His favor, expressed in all these ways and more, does not rest on merit found in the objects themselves, but in the righteous love of God expressed fully in the work of Christ, the Creator and Redeemer. His favor is not somehow narrowly focused only on what good somehow survives the ravages of sin and evil. This favor is not ultimately rooted in what has been, in what was good at creation and has somehow survived to merit God's favor. Favor is so lavishly expressed by God because it is ultimately looking forward—demonstrating and picturing in various ways the good that will be fully realized in the coming consummation. Thus this unmerited favor toward His creation is expressed in real time and space, has real historical significance and consequence, but is at the same time in its essence mysteriously connected to the "not yet" of the coming consummation of all favor and judgment in Jesus Christ.

Kingdom Responses in the Culture of Science: Stewards of Favor and Judgment

So what does all this discussion of battle, favor, and judgment mean for Christians responding to the cultural science of our day? Let us return to the science-specific questions posed earlier in the chapter to explore this further: How should Christians come to terms with the tensions of being in the world but not of the world in regard to the cultural institution we refer to as "science"? How should we respond when the science of the day seems to support Christian conviction? How should we respond when the science of the day is put to use to justify rejection of the gospel? Should we be attempting to take science back, to reinstate a cultural science of the past that was widely seen as Christian-friendly, or should we just passively let the science of our culture go its own way? And how should we understand the fact that the cultural science seems to work so well? We can now approach these questions through the favor and judgment motifs we have developed.

Stewarding God's Favor in the Cultural Science

Stewardship of God's favor in the cultural science requires that we imitate God's disposition of favor and that we seek to be agents of His favor as well. A basic pathway for imitation is to simply show kindness and magnanimity even to those who use their connection to institutional science to actively oppose the Christian faith.

> *But I tell you: Love your enemies and pray for those who persecute you, that you may be sons of your Father in heaven. He causes his sun to rise on the evil and the good, and sends rain on the righteous and the unrighteous. (Matt. 5:44-45)*

> *But love your enemies, do good to them, and lend to them without expecting to get anything back. Then your reward will be great, and you will be sons of the Most High, because he is kind to the ungrateful and wicked. Be merciful, just as your Father is merciful. (Luke 6:35-36)*

Enemies of the faith are at work in the cultural science. The sense of battle here is a reality, not just a construction of Christian paranoia. But as obedient imitators of our Lord, we must cultivate attitudes and actions of goodwill toward the enemies of Christ.

We ought also to find joy in the favor God shows to sinful humans working in His world even as He does. We should not let our understanding of and involvement in the battle rob us of our joy in His favor or of the wonder and pleasure we find as His favor is lavished on His creation—both in the nonhuman world around us and in the attainment of humans in it. Real favor is to be found in the institutional expression of science—and we should not be bashful about pursuing it and exalting in it. So enjoy, marvel, watch that PBS science special, renew that *National Geographic* subscription—respond to developments in the sciences with the enthusiasm we naturally feel as the marvels of God's world are further unfolded through cooperative scientific effort. We live in amazing times in the sciences, and we need not dwell in fear and apprehension of unfolding wonders or keep a tight leash on our admiration for scientific achievement because we fear it will somehow aid "the enemy." Praise be to God for the marvelous favor He shows in the science of our times.

We are not only to be appreciative passive observers, but we are to be active agents of His favor in the sciences. The Old Testament experience of God's people in exile provides a poignant example of the call to be agents of favor even while recognizing that the powers that be do not necessarily have the concerns of God's people in mind. The Jewish exiles had been carried away from their promised land as judgment for their unfaithfulness. Their great desire was to return to the land and thus to experience the favor of God again after the season of judgment. But through the prophet Jeremiah God told them not just to pine away for the future favor of the return to the promised land. They were not to hold back from cultural involvement in their homesickness for their own country, but were to work intentionally and comprehensively for the good of the city of their captivity. They were to pray for the prosperity of their captors, to be conscious agents of God's favor even while in exile:

> *This is what the LORD Almighty, the God of Israel, says to all those I carried into exile from Jerusalem to Babylon: "Build houses and settle down; plant gardens and eat what they produce. Marry and have sons and daughters; find wives for your sons and give your daughters in marriage, so that they too may have sons and daughters. Increase in number there; do not decrease. Also, seek the peace and prosperity of the city to which I have carried you into exile. Pray to the LORD for it, because if it prospers, you too will prosper. (Jer. 29:4-7)*

So we would be shirking our "agents of favor" calling in science if we just concentrate on getting home to our Lord, letting the sciences go their own way without our attention and support. Not to seek productive interaction with the science of our day, not to support scientific endeavor, not to seek areas in which we can agree with science would be a rejection of His command that we be agents of His favor.

Stewarding God's Judgment in the Cultural Science

Now what about judgment? Is there a parallel between our responses to the institutional science with regard to God's favor and our responses with regard to God's judgment? Are we to be imitators and agents of God's judgment on modern science? While we are explicitly commanded to imitate and be agents of God's favor in His world in various ways, the New Testament people of God are never instructed to imitate God's wrath against sinners or to be direct agents of God's temporal judgment on unbelievers. Rather:

> *If it is possible, as far as it depends on you, live at peace with everyone. Do not take revenge, my friends, but leave room for God's wrath, for it is written: "It is mine to avenge; I will repay," says the Lord. On the contrary: "If your enemy is hungry, feed him; if he is thirsty, give him something to drink. In doing this, you will heap burning coals on his head." (Rom. 12:18-20)*

Yet His judgment is often exercised in the world, and His final judgment is inescapable. It seems to us that we are called to exercise a kind of stewardship with regard to His present and coming judgment. How might we be good stewards of judgment as we are in the world but not of the world of science?

First of all, being good stewards of God's judgment requires that we recognize our own sinfulness and the judgment it deserves. We are fallen, sinful, and under judgment just like everyone else. Yet, gloriously, graciously—for the people of God—that judgment ultimately falls on Christ. We always need to be aware of our own sin, our tendency to be arrogant, and our propensity to think that we can use our status in Christ to lord it over unbelievers. We are always tempted to be like the unmerciful servant of the parable recorded in Matthew 18. The servant's master forgave him a huge debt, but the servant immediately went out to try to collect small debts from his fellow servants. To forget the grace we have been shown and to act as if it is our own character, righteousness, or intellectual capacity that distinguishes us from expressions of unbelief in the cultural science is essentially a denial of the gospel. Being stewards of God's judgment in science begins with our own repentance.

Not only are we to take heed for ourselves as to whether we will incur God's righteous judgment, but we also cannot neglect to remind those around us that the God who provides all that they may enjoy and accomplish in science requires a certain response to His favor. We must cooperate, find joy in, seek peace and productivity in our common scientific work with unbelievers, but we would be remiss if we enjoyed these things together with them but never connected the favor they enjoy with the call to repent and believe the One who is the source of all favor. In simply being able to engage in scientific work, unbelievers are experiencing a measure of the goodness of Christ, but unless they repent and believe, it is only piling up wrath for them. In effect we need to find ways to regularly say, "Congratulations, this is a great study—a wonderfully clever set of experiments—that uncovers some of the marvels of our world. Now I urge you to flee the wrath that will come. If you continue to presume on the favor of God in an unbelieving way, His wrath will surely come." This kind of response would tend to decrease one's popularity, but if we participate in God's favor together with our scientific colleagues but never warn them, what will we say to them when it is too late, and we remained silent?

Finally, being a steward of God's judgment in the sciences may at times call for us to adopt a more public prophetic voice that will sound shrill and will bring us grief. We are speaking here, of course, not about prophecy in terms of foretelling specific future events, but in the sense that God's prophets were called to speak hard truths that called their audiences to account before God. Those working in the sciences must not only be willing to opt out of the cultural practice when necessary, but also to speak prophetically against it at times. We must consistently assert our belief in the rule and purposes of God in His created universe over against a universe that by chance creates itself and thus lacks purpose and value. We must defend the special status of humans—the special rights and responsibilities that we humans have as image-bearers before God—to respond to His gracious rule in belief. We must promote justice in science and its uses, and we must speak out against the use of scientific knowledge to carelessly exploit and degrade the creation. Bearing the reproach of Christ and the offense of Christ before a watching world—yes, even in the sciences—is a part of stewarding God's judgment. We are instructed not to be surprised when we suffer for Christ, but we are further instructed to make sure our suffering is for the right reasons. We need to be sure that the offense we might cause in the name of our Christian convictions is actually the offense of Christ and not just offensiveness brought about by other motivations. This prophetic role needs to be exercised wisely and sparingly as we ought to take great care when claiming to speak for God. Even so, we should not shy away from speaking as His children even when it might be unpopular.

Of course, Christians will often disagree about the timing and substance of public critiques of the science of our day. This need not be a problem if we remain open to sharpening and being sharpened by our brothers and sisters all the while remembering that we are ultimately not to sit in judgment over the servants of another. In our disagreements with fellow believers we need to constantly remind ourselves that the most prominent apologetic for the faith given in Scripture is the way Christians show love to one another.

So the tensions we Christians experience in our considerations of science are best seen in the context of the larger picture of Christ-and-culture dynamics. Science is a cultural enterprise that reflects God's favor and yet calls for His judgment at the same time. Keeping in mind the interplay of favor and judgment as God moves His creation toward consummation should help us avoid the heady attraction of an overly aggressive Christian triumphalism on the one hand and the dispirited complaints of Christian defeatism and withdrawal on the other. Christians have always struggled to live faithfully in the times God has placed them, and our struggles to be faithful in the cultural science of our day is just part of our continuity and solidarity with fellow believers of the past and future. Like them, our only real need is to trust Him completely and to act upon that trust in faithfully approaching the scientific work He gives us to do.

Chapter Eleven

Looking to the Future

Therefore, prepare your minds for action; be self-controlled; set your hope fully on the grace to be given you when Jesus Christ is revealed.

1 PETER 1:13

A MAJOR OBSTACLE TO THE development of positive forward-looking evangelical perspectives on science is the ongoing impact of the "trauma" we discussed in chapter 10. This trauma was precipitated by a shift in the alignment of the cultural science relative to historic Christian belief. While in the eighteenth and nineteenth centuries scientific investigation was considered to be supportive of Christian faith, in the twentieth century science was largely considered to support a skeptical stance toward historic expressions of Christian faith. Christians struggled to develop coherent responses to this apparent realignment, but in many respects it seems to us that the issues have been distorted by reactionary impulses on both the Christian "side" and the science "side." The dynamics of the discussion of science and Christian faith issues in the culture in general as well as in the evangelical and scientific subcultures have continuously reinforced the offenses of the past, leading to hardened defensiveness and stalemated debate. If the twenty-first century is to see more productive treatment of these issues in the culture in general and among Christians with differing perspectives, a fresh start is badly needed. In attempting a fresh start, we would do well to consider the sound analysis and advice that Abraham Kuyper gave believers more than a century ago but that unfortunately went largely unheeded in the twentieth century:

> Formerly we [Christians] showed them [those taking a naturalistic position] the door, and now this sinful assault upon their liberty is

> by God's righteous judgment avenged by their turning us out into the street, and so it becomes the question, if the courage, the perseverance, the energy, which enabled them to win their suit at last, will be found now in a still higher degree, with Christian scholars. May God grant it! You cannot, nay, you may not even think of it, deprive him, whose consciousness differs from yours, of freedom of thought, of speech and of the press. That they from their standpoint pull down everything that is holy in your estimation, is unavoidable. Instead of seeking relief for your scientific conscience in downhearted complaints, or in mystic feeling, or in unconfessional work, the energy and thoroughness of our antagonists must be felt by every Christian scholar as a sharp incentive himself to go back to his own principles in his thinking, to renew all scientific investigation on the lines of these principles and to glut the press with the burden of his cogent studies.[1]

Kuyper first acknowledges that the cultural science has taken on a tenor decidedly in contrast with Christian conviction. In so doing though, he points out the injustice of attempts to exclude atheists in the past from participation in the cultural science.[2] There was a time when virtually all those in the sciences were more or less forced to pass off their work as a kind of natural theology and to explicitly square their work with Scripture or risk being branded as atheists and excluded from the cultural science. Kuyper points to the current relationship with the cultural science as, in a certain sense, a just judgment for Christian heavy-handedness in the past. What then is to be our response as believers to finding ourselves on the outside of the cultural science, looking in and recognizing that we are placed there in part as a result of God's judgment?

Kuyper then enumerates several possible responses Christians might have to the trauma of being "turned out" of the cultural science. A normal reaction would be to attempt to censor or restrict the opposing view—to try to recapture the cultural authority in order to put down the opposing view or to try to use other cultural authorities (e.g., political channels) to impose their own views. He rejects these strategies as ungodly assaults on God-given liberties of thought and expression.

Kuyper also cautions against resorting to "downhearted complaints." We Christians are tempted just to whine about how some in the science establishment are unfair to Christian viewpoints and how they use the power of their positions in the culture to unfairly keep Christian perspectives out. "They have all the microphones; they have the courts on their side. It's just not fair." We are tempted to explain all our problems in terms of some powerful naturalist conspiracy arrayed against us. Kuyper says, in effect, Well, of course those who come at the science from a naturalistic perspective will oppose you. What do you expect? The science one does is impacted in a variety of ways by the convictions one has. But don't use up all your energy just whining!

According to Kuyper, a strategic retreat is not an option either. We must not treat our Christian convictions in the area of science as entirely an issue of private mystical spirituality that only hovers ethereally over the hardheaded science we do. It is all too easy to buy into a Modernist picture, maintaining that the scientific work of Christians does not and should not differ from that of the non-Christian because the confession of Christ as Lord does not intersect at all with the science. Kuyper thus rejects the "unconfessional" option.

Rather, Kuyper encourages Christians to go back to our own basic principles and based on them to engage in vigorous scientific work. Our task as Christians in science then is not primarily negative—just to find ways to tear the other side down or to try to recapture some lost golden age of Christian dominance in science, but to faithfully do our own scientific work—to do it well, to "own" our convictions, and to fully participate in the cultural tasks we have been given. Referring back to a metaphor introduced in chapter 1, we are to grow vigorous scientific branches from the Christian theological tree. The branches are to receive their essential sustenance from the roots and trunk of the tree, but we are also to prune and care for the scientific branches so that they bear their fitting scientific fruit for the kingdom in their proper historical season.

Kuyper goes on to insist that an objective for Christians in the wider scientific culture is not to retake science, but to work to establish within the sciences what he calls the "liberty of science":

> . . . first by guaranteeing the full power of every leading life-system to reap a scientific harvest from its own principle;—and secondly, by refusing the scientific name to whatsoever investigator dare not unroll the colors of his own banner, and does not show emblazoned on his escutcheon in letters of gold the very principle for which he lives, and from which his conclusions derive their power.[3]

We should insist that all participants in science have a right, even an obligation, to work out their science in the context of their deeper convictions. But with such freedom also comes the responsibility to declare openly what some of these principles are. Among other things, this will require that Christians explicate the relevant components of a Christian "life-system" that may become part of the banner Christians raise above their scientific work. Then, again referring back to a metaphor from chapter 1, our task is to contribute our particular stream of science to the larger river of the cultural science, seeking to help the river flow in its proper channel but exercising due caution lest we find ourselves so completely under the power of its currents that we are in the end diverted from the true destination of our science as believers.

We think that Kuyper's analysis and advice is right on the mark. A fresh start in science-and-Christianity discussions is possible if we take seriously our responsibility to develop a science arising from our own first principles as Christians and our responsibility to help establish the "liberty of science" principles along the lines Kuyper suggests. This book has been written in the hope that such a fresh start might be made soon. Thus we will conclude with a brief overview of where we've been and then highlight several specific challenges that we believe must be successfully met if a more productive treatment of these issues is to come in the twenty-first century.

In the first section of the book we attempted to locate a faithful Christian approach to science in the midst of the general cultural shift from Modernism to Postmodernism. We showed that developments in a variety of areas both inside and outside science indicate that a simple picture of science providing its own foundation and sustaining power doesn't work. We provided a number of historical examples to show that being supportive of modern science and yet being critical of various aspects of it, and in particular of its all-subsuming knowledge claims, has had a long history in the evangelical tradition.

With this background, the remaining sections of the book are essentially an extended critique of many of the dominant Modernist instincts that often shape the way Christians think about science. This critique is coupled with positive suggestions as to how these instincts can be reined in, redirected, and refined by taking seriously a theology of science rooted in the Reformed Christian tradition.

In the second section we showed how a variety of unnecessary conundrums that seem to pit science against a Christian understanding of God's power and action in the world can be avoided by putting historic Trinitarian theology to work in our scientific thinking. A robust Trinitarian theology provides rich theological resources for conceiving of God's relation to the world and the actions that arise from that relation in ways that legitimate human scientific endeavor and yet avoid the idolatry of calling God and His actions to account according to Modern scientific conceptual frameworks. God's immanent and transcendent relation to the world and His work in creation, whether we perceive it as "miracle" or as "natural law," are seamlessly unified because of who God is in His triune being as He works out His purposes in history. We can understand our science then as one avenue of many through which we are able to see and respond to God's faithfulness as the rule and kind intention of the Father for His creation is mediated through the Son and brought to fruition by the Spirit in history.

In the third section we examined how doing science from a Christian perspective naturally flows from the Great Commandment to love God and neighbor, or as we put it, to love God with all our being, knowing, and doing. We explored a "relational ontology" that considered who humans are and what creation is in terms of their relation to God and how those relationships are impacted by the major episodes in redemptive history: creation, fall, redemption, and consummation. Such a gospel-based relational ontology reorients our conception of the meaning of our scientific work and its significance in history. Then we discussed the features and context of an "epistemological piety" that should be the true motivation of human knowing. "In Christ" we are to know by faithfully responding to God's revelation in His Word and world, responses that include both submission to "order as given" and creative stewardship in handling "order as task." Pleasing God in our knowing should be our prime concern, rather than narrowly pursuing the satisfaction of humanly formulated knowing criteria. Then finally, we discussed "doing" aspects of Christian vocation in the sciences. Being good stewards of our scientific gifts requires that we "do" as confident, attentive, and submissive servants who are committed to the gracious authority of His Word, His church, and His world. In seeking out ways to "do" as good neighbors in the scientific culture of our times, we are to be good stewards of God's favor and His judgment. We are to rejoice in the fruits of our common labors with our non-Christian colleagues, but also we are not to neglect our obligation, in love, to warn them of the wrath of God that will judge unbelief. And we are to take on more public and prophetic roles in science when situations arise that call out for such actions.

Where to From Here?

While the account of a Christian theology of science that we have given in the book provides a general framework for approaching science-and-Christianity issues in the church and in the culture, there are many specific contemporary challenges we have not directly addressed. In particular, we see four specific challenges that need attention soon if a fresh start in science-and-Christianity discussions is to be made. We present these to direct our own future work as well as to encourage others to take up these challenges.

First, we Christians need to find a way to handle our "in-house" disagreements concerning science-and-Christianity relations in a productive, mutually edifying manner. In the twentieth century, the rhetoric of discussions of these issues was often at its most vicious in disagreements among Christians. We need to work out a way to recognize the importance of developing specific well-thought-out positions on these matters without expecting or trying to enforce monolithic agreement among all Christians. We Christians have a long way to go in figuring out how to take the important questions and different answers with regard to science and Christianity seriously while being good stewards of our own specific Christian traditions and at the same time obeying the commands of our Lord regarding the unity of God's people.

A second challenge is that of developing a Christian theological account of the basis for doing common scientific work with people of all faiths. If the Modernist vision of science cannot be sustained—that it is a common and objective enterprise, the results of which all rational humans should be able to agree on when it is properly done—how are we to understand the commonness of the enterprise and the basis on which it would proceed? As the Postmodern turn proceeds apace, this will be a question increasingly asked in our culture at large. We believe that Christians can do a good service as well as provide a rationale for Christians to be engaged by working on a solution to this challenge.

Third, we need to accept the challenge of establishing some "quiet space" for developing more careful and subtle analysis of evolutionary concepts. The discussions of evolutionary theory both inside and outside the evangelical subculture are overheated and overly politicized. Both "sides" in evolution controversies seem to find it advantageous to treat evolution as a single unit, to be entirely rejected or embraced, either as a symbol of orthodoxy or as a symbol of being serious about science. The symbolic status of "evolution" obscures a clear understanding of the complex and multilevel issues involved. Modern evolutionary theory is a complex of many theories. The individual theories differ widely in the claims they make and in the kinds of supportive evidence they appeal to. Each theory needs to be presented and evaluated individually rather than always pressing for an all-inclusive up-or-down "vote" as if evolution is some kind of omnibus bill in a legislature. We just have to do much better in being informed, in communicating our perspectives, and in making more subtle judgments in this area than has been the case in the twentieth century.

Finally there is the challenge of developing new ways of approaching scientific issues in the political process as Christians. The twentieth century exhibited many episodes of such forays by well-meaning Christians that were arguably counterproductive. We must find better ways to respond to the realities of the internal politics of the institution of science. We need to develop some foundational principles for determining how Christian perspectives on science in the culture should be played out in the political process and what strategies are wise and proper for Christians to utilize.

God has indeed placed us in a strategic and exciting time in science. Not only are new discoveries about God's world and universe being made at an increasingly rapid pace, but in our times there is increasing interest in trying to better understand the connections between science and deeper, more basic reservoirs of human convictions and assumptions. In such a time as this, it is especially important that we follow Peter's scriptural directives to prepare our minds for action, to be disciplined and self-controlled in our knowing and doing, and always to keep the gospel at the forefront of our way of being in the world: "Therefore, prepare your minds for action; be self-controlled; set your hope fully on the grace to be given you when Jesus Christ is revealed" (1 Peter 1:13).

What a privilege to live in such a time as this! May God deliver His people from the idols of our age and engulf us in His glorious gospel of grace in all our knowing, being, and doing.

Notes

1: The Need for a Theology of Science

1. Of course there is an immense literature dealing with these historical topics. An extremely valuable overview can be found in John Hedley Brooke, *Science and Religion, Some Historical Perspectives* (Cambridge: Cambridge University Press, 1991).
2. See, e.g., Gene Edward Veith, *Postmodern Times: A Christian Guide to Contemporary Thought and Culture* (Wheaton, Ill.: Crossway Books, 1994); Stanley Grenz, *A Primer on Postmodernism* (Grand Rapids, Mich.: Eerdmans Publishing, 1996) and references therein.
3. There is some disagreement over how exactly to refer to these "deeper convictions"; they could be variously referred to as "philosophical," "metaphysical," "religious," or "theological." Although some helpful insights might be gained by trying to make these distinctions, for our purposes it doesn't really matter what term one uses. The basic point is that each of us has some underlying basic convictions that can properly be considered "religious" in the sense that they have to do with one's disposition toward or against God and His rule and the redemption He brings on the one hand, or what one adopts as eternal and therefore stands in the place of God on the other hand. Our choice of the word *theological* here is based on the affirmation that religious commitments lie at the root of all belief systems. We are thus using the word *theology* in a non-standard way, in *analogy* to Christian theology, as related to the "doctrines" that flow out of whatever one's heart's basic religious commitments are, i.e., the platitudes of one's worldview. Thus for example a "materialist theology" might uphold the eternality of the material world as a basic commitment, whereas the Christian embraces the truth of Scripture and of the gospel. The issue here is that all of us have foundational religious commitments of some kind, and our expressed beliefs or "doctrines" flow out of them, whether consciously or unconsciously. We expect that it will be clear from the context whenever this more general sense of "theology" is meant in the discussion that follows.
4. The direct meaning of the word *theology* is "a study of God." However, since God is not the object of our direct study, but rather, what we know about Him comes from what He has revealed to us in His Word, in the context of Christianity, we take the word *theology* to mean the interpretation and systematization of what He has revealed to us in Scripture. Thus in its wider meaning, theology can refer to whatever the Scriptures teach about a particular subject, such as a theology of the Covenant, a theology of baptism, or a theology of end times. It is in this latter sense that we use the term when we speak of a theology of science. As a cautionary note, however, we would also like to point out that when some speak of a theology of nature, they have an entirely different meaning in mind, closer to the notion of natural theology: learning our theological principles concerning nature as much from the study of nature itself as from the Scriptures. (This was illustrated metaphorically in the Modernist suggestion that the branch of theology should be grafted into the tree of science.) We consider this an inappropriate use of the term. A theology of nature should rather refer to what can be learned about nature from studying the Scriptures. Hence a theology of science would include a theology of nature, properly conceived, along with theological principles concerning the cultural activity of science as well.
5. Abraham Kuyper, *Lectures on Calvinism* (Grand Rapids, Mich.: Eerdmans Publishing, 1931), 19. See also chapter 3.

2: Modern Science in a Postmodern World

1. This term is apparently due to Jürgen Habermas. See, e.g., Stanley Grenz, *A Primer on Postmodernism* (Grand Rapids, Mich.: Eerdmans Publishing, 1996), 3.

2. For example, Immanuel Kant, in his famous essay "What Is Enlightenment?" (reprinted in *Modernism to Postmodernism: An Anthology,* ed. Lawrence Cahoone [Oxford: Blackwell Publishers, 1996]), defines the term to mean "Man's emergence from his self-incurred immaturity." Recent scholarship, however, has shed "light" on the "darkness" or "immaturity," so to speak, leaving the question whether "Enlightenment" is a suitable name for the period following. In view of the present Postmodern critique of Enlightenment thought, we may also question whether the thought of the time was suitably "enlightened." We can justify the use of the name, however, as self-reflective, in that the men formulating their opinions at the time at least thought that they were bringing enlightenment, and/or at least those who directly followed judged it so; thus the term can be preserved with some validity.
3. See chs. 4 and 5 for more details.
4. Strictly speaking, a mechanical philosophy is one that seeks to describe the universe entirely in terms of motion and local forces, excluding action at a distance. We often use the term somewhat more loosely, however, to mean a philosophy that ascribes the regularities of the universe to the notion that the universe works like a big machine or "mechanism" that operates according to definite "built-in" laws. Note that the idea of a mechanical philosophy was not entirely new. Ancient Greek natural philosophers such as Archimedes had already espoused such a view, and the translation of his writings into Latin in 1543 undoubtedly contributed to a revival of the view. (Nancy R. Pearcey and Charles B. Thaxton, *The Soul of Science: Christian Faith and Natural Philosophy* [Wheaton Ill.: Crossway Books, 1994], 69.) By 1605 Kepler apparently began to espouse a mechanistic philosophy and also several contemporaries of Descartes, notably Pierre Gassendi, made important contributions in this direction. (Margaret J. Osler, *Divine Will and the Mechanical Philosophy: Gassendi and Descartes on Contingency and Necessity in the Created World* [Cambridge: Cambridge University Press, 1994], 15ff.; John Hedley Brooke, *Science and Religion: Some Historical Perspectives* [Cambridge: Cambridge University Press, 1991], 120.)
5. Rene Descartes, *Descartes: Meditations on First Philosophy: With Selections from the Objections and Replies*, ed. John Cottingham (Cambridge: Cambridge University Press, 1996), 12.
6. Ibid., 14-15.
7. As Etienne Gilson reminds us in *Reason and Revelation in the Middle Ages*, the rationalism of Descartes's approach itself was not necessarily so new. For example, Roger Bacon, in the thirteenth century, pointed to mathematical demonstration and experimental investigation as two neglected methods of that period, believing that "in mathematics we are able to arrive at the full truth without error" (Gilson, 28-29), and Averroes pushed a purely rationalistic philosophy based on Aristotelianism in the twelfth century in order to support his Islamic faith. This radical move seems to be the reverse of the medieval attitude toward the relation of reason to faith, as indicated by Anselm's famous dictum: "For I do not seek to understand that I may believe, but I believe in order to understand." We will return to this reversal in the next chapter. (Etienne Henry Gilson, *Reason and Revelation in the Middle Ages* [New York: Charles Scribner's Sons, 1938], 24, 28-29, 40.)
8. Descartes, *Meditations*, 16. Descartes's words are, "Archimedes used to demand just one firm and immovable point in order to shift the entire earth; so I too can hope for great things if I manage to find just one thing, however slight, that is certain and unshakeable." Descartes is referring to Archimedes's famous quote relating to the principle of lever and fulcrum: "Give me somewhere [outside the earth] to stand, and I will move the earth." (*The Oxford Dictionary of Quotes*, 3rd ed. [Oxford: Oxford University Press, 1980], 8.)
9. The original reference to Descartes's *cogito ergo sum* is in his *Discourse on Method*, as quoted in John Cottingham's introduction to Descartes's *Meditations*. Descartes, *Meditations*, xxix. It is also repeated in the answer to the fifth objection to his philosophy. Descartes, *Meditations*, 68.

10. *Apologetics* comes from the Greek root *apologeia,* meaning "defense." Apologetics then refers to the defense of the faith.
11. Descartes, *Meditations,* xxxvii.
12. Francois-Marie Arouet de Voltaire, "On Bacon and Newton," in *The Portable Enlightenment Reader*, ed. Isaac Kramnick (New York: Penguin Books, 1995), 53-54.
13. Francis Bacon, *Novum Organum*—Part II "Reason and Nature," reprinted as "The New Science," in Kramnick, ed., *Enlightenment Reader*, 39-40.
14. I. Bernard Cohen, *Revolution in Science* (Cambridge, Mass.: Belknap Press, 1985), 148; also James T. Cushing, *Philosophical Concepts in Physics: The Historical Relation Between Philosophy and Scientific Theories* (Cambridge, Mass.: Cambridge University Press, 1998), 22.
15. Bacon, *Novum Organum*, in Kramnick, ed., *Enlightenment Reader*, 41.
16. Cushing, *Philosophical Concepts in Physics,* 24.
17. Inductive conclusions are those built up from many examples suggesting a general pattern. This method of proceeding is in contrast to deduction, in which the conclusions follow from the rules of logic.
18. Descartes, *Meditations*, 24ff., 44ff.
19. Brooke, *Science and Religion,* 56.
20. Ibid., 22.
21. Ibid., 57.
22. Thomas F. Torrance, *Theological Science* (Edinburgh: T&T Clark, 1996), 69.
23. This encyclopedia was first published by Robert Chambers in 1859 and is unrelated to Ephraim Chambers's eighteenth-century *Cyclopedia.* Robert and Ephraim just coincidentally shared the same last name. It is perhaps equally ironic that Robert Chambers also turned out to be the anonymous author of *Vestiges of the Natural History of Creation* (1844), published by his own printing company, in which he sought to show that all species had developed by natural laws without direct intervention of a creator. The work sold widely but was criticized by most scientists and denounced by a political opponent as a "blasphemous, materialist book." See Richard Milner, *The Encyclopedia of Evolution: Humanity's Search for Its Origin* (New York: Facts on File Publishers, 1990), 77-79.
24. *Chambers's Encyclopedia,* Vol. 12 (London: George Newnes Ltd., 1950), 12.
25. Marquis de Condorcet, "*Sketch for an Historical Picture of the Progress of the Human Mind,*" in *Modernism to Postmodernism: An Anthology,* ed. Lawrence Cahoone (Oxford: Blackwell Publishers, 1996), 81.
26. Without Newton's laws of forces and the law of gravity that explains the existence of orbits in terms of forces, the Copernican and Ptolemaic theories would only be two relative systems among others. With Newton's force law, the Copernican view as modified by Kepler becomes immensely simpler. Any other theory would require additional ad hoc forces to maintain the relative motions of all the planets.
27. The medieval view held that the heavens and the earth were metaphysically quite distinct and hence governed by different "laws." During this period, Christians had largely adopted the neo-Platonic dualism, in typically believing that the heavens were the realm of perfection and hence were quite literally "not of this world." Brooke, *Science and Religion*, 84-85.
28. Galileo's argument was essentially that if Jupiter had moons like the earth did, isn't it a mini solar system? Could our solar system be only one of many? Should they not have a common explanation? This would go some distance in demoting the heavens, but not as far as did Newton's unifying law of gravitation, which included not only the planets but the stars such as our sun as well and also provided an "explanation" for the behavior of planets.
29. Colin E. Gunton, *The Triune Creator: A Historical and Systematic Study* (Edinburgh: Edinburgh University Press, 1998), 129.
30. Brooke, *Science and Religion,* 118.
31. Ibid., 140.
32. One of Laplace's most famous contributions to science is an evolutionary model of

the development of the solar system, known as the nebular hypothesis. This model is clearly based on his commitment to a naturalistic explanation of all things. See Roger Hahn, "Laplace and the Mechanistic Universe," in *God & Nature: Historical Essays on the Encounter Between Christianity and Science*, ed. David C. Lindberg and Ronald L. Numbers (Berkeley: University of California Press, 1986), 270.

33. Ibid., 272.
34. As quoted in ibid., 268.
35. In a question from Napolean Bonaparte as to where God was in his theories, Laplace is reported to have answered, "I have no need of that hypothesis." See ibid., 256.
36. See Martin J. S. Rudwick, "The Shape and Meaning of Earth History," in ibid., 310ff.
37. See for example Lindberg and Numbers, eds., *God & Nature*, 2-3.
38. Quoted in Brooke, *Science and Religion,* 34.
39. Ibid., 35.
40. Thomas S. Kuhn, *The Structure of Scientific Revolutions*, 2nd ed. (Chicago: University of Chicago Press, 1970), 151.
41. Roger S. Jones, *Physics as Metaphor* (New York and Scarborough, Ontario: New American Library, 1982).
42. Bruce Gregory, *Inventing Reality: Physics as Language* (New York: John Wiley & Sons, 1990).
43. The term was originally coined in Gilbert Ryle, *The Concept of Mind* (Chicago: University of Chicago Press, 1949, repr. 1984).
44. See, e.g., John Locke, *An Essay Concerning Human Understanding* (London: Oxford University Press, 1969), 102.
45. See, e.g., David Hume, *Treatise on Human Nature* (Oxford: Clarendon Press, 1973), 187ff.
46. Hume was not questioning whether there actually is a cause-and-effect relationship. He assumed there was. Rather he was questioning whether we can know such things by reason. This is related to a meta-level question: How do we know what we know?
47. Thomas Reid, "The Philosophy of Common Sense," in Kramnick, ed., *Enlightenment Reader*, 214.
48. Frederick Copleston, *A History of Philosophy*, 5th ed. (Garden City, N.Y.: Image Books, 1993), Vol. 5, Part II, 175-76.
49. Thomas Reid, "Essays on the Intellectual Powers of Man," IV, iii [375b] (1785), as quoted in Nick Wolterstorff, *Thomas Reid and the Story of Epistemology (*Cambridge, U.K.: Cambridge University Press, 2001), 29.
50. Thomas Reid, *An Inquiry into the Human Mind*, ed. Timothy Duggan (Chicago: University of Chicago Press, 1970), 19.
51. Thomas Reid, *Thomas Reid's Inquiry and Essays*, ed. Keith Lehrer and Ronald E. Beanblossom (Indianapolis: Bobbs-Merrill, 1975), 98-99.
52. Whether justified or not (and there is a controversy on this point), Kant criticized Reid for not understanding Hume's real problem: "The question was not whether the concept of cause was right, useful, and even indispensable for our knowledge of nature, for this Hume had never doubted; but whether that concept could be thought by reason *a priori*, and consequently whether it possessed an inner truth, independent of all experience, implying a perhaps more extended use not restricted merely to objects of experience. This was Hume's problem." (Immanuel Kant, *Prologomena to Any Future Metaphysics* [Indianapolis: Bobbs-Merrill, 1950], 6-7.)
53. From the opening paragraph of Immanuel Kant, "An Answer to the Question: *What Is Enlightenment?*" reprinted in Cahoone, ed., *Modernism to Postmodernism*, 51.
54. Ironically, one of Kant's motivating goals was to "rescue" Newtonian physics from skepticism, but as we shall see, some of his categories of the mind as motivated by Newtonian physics turned out to be chosen inappropriately. In other words, certain aspects of Newtonian physics needed amending. So to "rescue" them by declaring them universal categories in our minds was not a very good idea.
55. Indeed, Kant himself referred to his contribution in analogy to the revolution of Copernicus, because rather than taking nature as primary, he takes the categories as

primary in order to deduce limits on nature, rather than vice versa. See Roger Scruton, *Kant: A Very Short Introduction* (Oxford: Oxford University Press, 2001), 39. See also Immanuel Kant, *Critique of Pure Reason,* trans. Norman Kemp Smith (New York: St. Martin's Press, 1965), 25.

56. Quoted in Edward Craig, ed., *Routledge Encyclopedia of Philosophy* s.v. (Cambridge, U.K.: Cambridge University, 1998). "Kant, Immanuel" from *The Conflict of the Faculties* (1798): (7: 69-70).
57. However, one might rather consider this an "anti-Copernican" revolution in the sense that it takes man, a relative creature, and puts him at the center.
58. Ironically, the most significant remaining holdout to the acknowledgment of worldviews is public education. The official position of the government is that education can be done from a "neutral" standpoint, not realizing that the exclusion of religion in the public square plays the role of a religion in its own right, effectively baptizing secularism as the official religion of the state.
59. As a consequence of his own wrestlings with the evangelical tradition and its notion of spirituality, Francis Schaeffer ended up in Switzerland where he founded L'Abri, an organization that ministered to many questioning intellectuals of the 1960s. Through his L'Abri conferences held in the 1960s and 1970s at Covenant College, and through the publication of his lectures at these and other public meetings, he helped to make the European notion of worldview commonplace among evangelicals in the United States. See, e.g., Francis Schaeffer, *The Complete Works of Francis A. Schaeffer: A Christian Worldview,* 5 vols. (Wheaton, Ill.: Crossway Books, 1982).
60. Here we have in mind such mainstream developments as from the philosophy of Johann Gottlieb Fichte (1762-1814) and Georg Wilhelm Friedrich Hegel (1770-1831), as well as reactions such as the Romantic movement.
61. For a somewhat more extensive treatment of this subject, see Grenz, *A Primer on Postmodernism,* 83-121.
62. The German term *Gefühl* does not quite connote the idea of sensation as the English rendition "feeling" suggests. Hence when rendering the term in English, usually a more descriptive phrase is used, such as "feeling of dependency." See, e.g., Stanley J. Grenz and Roger E. Olson, *20th Century Theology: God and the World in a Transitional Age* (Downers Grove, Ill.: InterVarsity Press, 1992), 44.
63. Ibid.
64. Ibid., 45.
65. See, e.g., Grenz, *A Primer on Postmodernism,* 98-99, and Alister E. McGrath, ed., *The Blackwell Encyclopedia of Modern Christian Thought* (Oxford: Blackwell Publishers, 1993), 591.
66. See, e.g., Dan McCartney and Charles Clayton, *Let the Reader Understand: A Guide to Interpreting and Applying the Bible* (Phillipsburg, N.J.: Presbyterian and Reformed Publishing, 2002).
67. Grenz, *A Primer on Postmodernism,* 99.
68. Ibid., 88-91.
69. Ibid., 92.
70. See ibid., 88.
71. Ibid., 99.
72. Torrance, *Theological Science*, 92.
73. The fundamental feature that differed was the parallel postulate. In Euclidean geometry, every point off a straight line has one and only one line through it parallel to the first. In Riemannian geometry there are no such lines, and in Lobachevsky's geometry, there are infinitely many. For an overview of this chapter of mathematics and its effects, see Morris Kline, *Mathematics, the Loss of Certainty* (New York: Oxford University Press, 1980). For a quick but more extensive introduction to the subject than given here, see Pearcey and Thaxton, *Soul of Science,* ch. 6-7.
74. However, within relativity theory, the measurements of one observer can be predicted through calculation by an observer in another reference frame, as long as he knows the relative motion between the two frames. The important thing is that there are

invariants in the theory that allow observers to do this, notably the distance in spacetime between two spacetime events. In general, all the laws of physics are the same in every reference frame. For as Arnold Sommerfeld said on the occasion of Einstein's seventieth birthday, "not the *relativizing* of the perceptions of length and duration are the chief point for him, but the *independence of natural laws,* particularly those of electrodynamics and optics, *of the standpoint of the observer.*" Sommerfeld goes on to say of Einstein's original paper on relativity that "the essay has, of course, absolutely nothing whatsoever to do with ethical relativism, with the 'Beyond Good and Evil' [a reference to Nietzsche]." Sommerfeld, "*Zum Siebzigsten Geburtstag Albert Einsteins,*" trans. and repr. in Paul Arthur Schilpp, ed., *Albert Einstein: Philosopher-Scientist* (New York: MJF Books, 2001), 99.

75. The difference between the two twins is that the one who made the trip experienced acceleration that the one who remained here did not.
76. See, e.g., Karl Popper, *Conjectures and Refutations: The Growth of Scientific Knowledge* (New York and Evanston: Harper and Row, 1965), 228ff.
77. See, e.g., I. Bernard Cohen, *Revolution in Science,* 23.
78. For a fuller discussion of these historical developments, see Del Ratzsch, *Science & Its Limits: The Natural Sciences in Christian Perspective*, 2nd ed. (Downers Grove, Ill.: InterVarsity Press, 2000). For a more technical discussion, see Frederick Suppe, ed., *The Structure of Scientific Theories*, 2nd ed. (Urbana, Ill.: University of Illinois Press, 1979).
79. See the essay by William R. Shea in Lindberg and Numbers, eds., *God & Nature,* 114.
80. For example, Galileo used the tides as support for his argument that the sun was at the center of the solar system. However, his explanation for the tides was completely wrong.
81. Brooke, *Science and Religion*, 39-40. Also see Pearcey and Thaxton, *Soul of Science,* and Francis A. Yates, *Giordano Bruno and the Hermetic Tradition* (New York: Random House Vintage Books, 1964).
82. See, e.g., Edward Grant, "Science and Theology in the Middle Ages," in Lindberg and Numbers, *God & Nature*, and Edward Grant, *The Foundations of Modern Science in the Middle Ages* (Cambridge: Cambridge University Press, 1996).
83. Pearcey and Thaxton, *Soul of Science*, 64.
84. Brooke, *Science and Religion*, 39.
85. Ibid., 26.
86. Ibid., 37.
87. Ibid.
88. Descartes, *Meditations,* John Cottingham, ed., xxxviii.
89. Again, we refer you to John Hedley Brooke's excellent study on this subject, *Science and Religion*, and also to the collection of essays, *God & Nature*, edited by David Lindberg and Ronald Numbers. Other more recent volumes could also be mentioned, such as Osler, *Divine Will and the Mechanical Philosophy*, and Kenneth J. Howell, *God's Two Books: Copernican Cosmology and Biblical Interpretation in Early Modern Science* (Notre Dame, Ind.: University of Notre Dame Press, 2002).
90. Brooke, *Science and Religion*, 145.

3: A Christian Science?

1. Philip Schaff, *History of the Christian Church,* Vol. 5 (Grand Rapids, Mich.: Eerdmans Publishing, 1907), 589-90.
2. Frederick Copleston, *A History of Philosophy*, 5th ed., Vol. 4 (Garden City, N.Y.: Image Books, 1993), 161.
3. Blaise Pascal, *Pensées* (London: Penguin Books, Ltd., 1976), 300, n887.
4. A flick of the finger away from the thumb.
5. Blaise Pascal, *Pensées*, W. F. Trotter, trans., (1660), http://www.ccel.org/ccel/pascal/pensees.html (accessed May 28, 2005), n77.
6. Pascal, *Pensées*, 52, n84.

7. Ibid., 85, n183.
8. Ibid., 84, n188.
9. Ibid., 64-65, n131.
10. Ibid., 83, n173.
11. Ibid., n170.
12. Ibid., 58, n110.
13. For information on the life and thought of Hamann, see the following: Isaiah Berlin, *Three Critics of the Enlightenment, Vico, Hamann, Herder*, ed. Henry Hardy (Princeton: Princeton University Press, 2000); W. M. Alexander, *Johann Georg Hamann, Philosophy and Faith* (The Hague: Martinus Nijhoff Publ., 1966).
14. Berlin, *Three Critics of the Enlightenment*, 280.
15. David Hume, *Treatise on Human Nature* (Oxford: Clarendon Press, 1973), 187.
16. As quoted in Berlin, *Three Critics of the Enlightenment*, 280.
17. Ibid., 281.
18. Ibid., 283.
19. Hamann to Jacobi, as quoted in Alexander, *Johann Georg Hamann, Philosophy and Faith*, 131.
20. Ibid., 134.
21. Hamann, *Briefwechsel*, Vol. 5, p. 272.3, as quoted in Berlin, *Three Critics of the Enlightenment*, 285.
22. Hamann, *Briefwechsel*, Vol. 7, p. 165.13, as quoted in ibid., 287.
23. Hamann, *Saemtliche Werke*, Vol. 3, p. 284, as quoted in ibid.
24. Hamann, *Briefwechsel*, Vol. 5, p. 265.37, as quoted in ibid.
25. Hamann, *Briefwechsel*, Vol. 5, p. 264.36, as quoted in ibid.
26. Simon Critchley, *Continental Philosophy: A Very Short Introduction* (Oxford: Oxford University Press, 2001), 20.
27. Ibid.
28. Hamann, *Briefwechsel*, Vol. 6, p. 350.17, as quoted in Berlin, *Three Critics of the Enlightenment*, 287.
29. Alexander, *Johann Georg Hamann, Philosophy and Faith*, 129.
30. Hamann to Jacobi, 27-30 Apr. 1785, as quoted in ibid., 75.
31. Hamann to Jacobi, 22-23 Apr. 1787, as quoted in ibid.
32. Ibid., 128.
33. Hamann, *Saemtliche Werke*, Vol. 1, p. 24, as quoted in ibid.
34. Hamann to Jacobi, 18 Feb. 1786, as quoted in ibid., 75.
35. See, e.g., Theodore Dwight Bozeman, *Protestants in an Age of Science: The Baconian Ideal and Antebellum American Religious Thought* (Chapel Hill, N.C.: University of North Carolina Press, 1977).
36. George M. Marsden, *Understanding Fundamentalism and Evangelicalism* (Grand Rapids, Mich.: Eerdmans Publishing, 1991), 128.
37. Charles Hodge, *What Is Darwinism?*, ed. Mark A. Noll and David N. Livingstone (Grand Rapids, Mich.: Baker Books, 1994), 14.
38. Charles Hodge, *Systematic Theology*, Vol. 1 (Peabody, Mass.: Hendrickson Publishers, 1999), 4.
39. Ibid., 4.
40. Ibid., 9-10.
41. Ibid., 10.
42. Ibid., 17.
43. Ibid., 18-19.
44. Hodge, *What Is Darwinism?*, 53-54.
45. Ibid., 54.
46. Perhaps not surprisingly, the next generation of Princeton theologians took the argument a step further. If the Bible can stand up to scientific scrutiny, we can put it to the test. Quoting A. A. Hodge and B. B. Warfield, "The writers of this article are sincerely convinced of the perfect soundness of the great Catholic doctrine of Biblical

Inspiration, i.e., that the Scriptures not only contain, but ARE, THE WORD OF GOD, and hence that all their elements and affirmations are absolutely errorless, and binding the faith and obedience of men. Nevertheless we admit that the question between ourselves and the advocates of [modern criticism] is one of fact, to be decided only by an exhaustive and impartial examination of all of the sources of evidence, i.e., the claims and the phenomena of the Scriptures themselves." See A. A. Hodge and B. B. Warfield, in *Inspiration*, 237, as quoted in Mark A. Noll, *Between Faith and Criticism*, 2nd ed. (Grand Rapids, Mich.: Baker Book House, 1991), 18. This made for an extremely interesting episode during which scientific methodology in the European setting was analyzing biblical texts in ways corrosive of biblical authority, while Hodge, Warfield, and others applied the same scientific methodology to champion scriptural authority. They endeavored to show that the conclusions of the biblical critics were a mix of bias, overextended reasoning, and methodological errors. That is, they basically argued that the critics of traditional biblical authority were by and large engaged in inferior science.

47. For example, Hodge devotes substantial space to then current scientific theories and a discussion of the fossil record and the antiquity of man in his *Systematic Theology*. See, e.g., Vol. 2, ch. 1, pp. 1-41.
48. Hodge, *What Is Darwinism?*, 21.
49. Marsden, *Understanding Fundamentalism and Evangelicalism*, 135.
50. Mark Noll and David Livingstone provide some speculation about particular events that may have encouraged Hodge to do so, in their introduction to the reprinted version of the book. Hodge, *What Is Darwinism?*, 23.
51. Ibid., 66.
52. Ibid. Spencer espoused a popular liberal philosophy of the time that embraced evolution in all areas, not only in biology. He is responsible for coining the phrase "survival of the fittest," a phrase that Darwin also adopted. Ibid., 69, 80.
53. Ibid., 137. While Hodge in this passage is defending his right as a theologian to speak to the claims of science where they touch his area of expertise, because reasoning is important in portraying truth claims, it is perhaps not surprising that one of the foremost critics of evolutionary theory today is Phillip Johnson, himself a lawyer. Johnson also sees scientists overstepping the bounds of their authority, often through faulty reasoning, which Johnson, using his training in reasoning, seeks to expose. See, e.g., Phillip Johnson, *Darwin on Trial (*Downers Grove, Ill.: InterVarsity Press, 1991).
54. What is noteworthy here is that Hodge seems to believe that "intuitions" and "laws of belief" will lead to universal agreement. At that time, this belief may be quite understandable, but as we have seen, the rise of the understanding of the role of worldviews has brought this idea into question.
55. Hodge, *What Is Darwinism?*, 156-57.
56. Combining this with the fact that Hodge's complaint is not so directly biblical, but rather a combination of philosophical and scientific reasonings, leads one to think that he might allow for a consistently held theistic evolution, which is not Darwinism per se, as within the bounds of orthodoxy. In fact the next generation at Princeton appears to have done just that. Both Charles Hodge's son, A. A. Hodge, and B. B. Warfield allowed for theistic evolution as a viable interpretation of Genesis, within the bounds of orthodoxy. See, e.g., David Livingstone, *Darwin's Forgotten Defenders* (Grand Rapids, Mich.: Eerdmans Publishing, 1987), and Benjamin B. Warfield, *Evolution, Science, and Scripture*, ed. Mark A. Noll and David Livingstone (Grand Rapids, Mich.: Baker Books, 2000).
57. L. Praansma, *Let Christ Be King: Reflections on the Life and Times of Abraham Kuyper* (Jordan Station, Ontario: Paideia Press, 1985), 125-26.
58. Ibid., 42.
59. Ibid., 45.
60. R. D. Henderson, "How Abraham Kuyper Became a Kuyperian," *Christian Scholar's Review*, 22:1 (1992): 31.
61. Ibid., 33-34.

62. The German technical term *Weltanschauung* was rendered in English as "life system" in Kuyper's *Lectures on Calvinism*. The more usual translation nowadays for this term is "worldview."
63. Note, the term "Modern science" is being used technically here as that science associated with Modernism as growing out of the Enlightenment worldview, rather than as the merely generic term that refers to whatever is scientifically current.
64. These annual lectures on theology began in 1883 to honor Levi P. Stone, a former director and trustee of Princeton Seminary.
65. Calvinism was the dominant Christian tradition in Kuyper's home country, and indeed, according to Cornelius Plantinga, Calvinism in various forms also dominated American higher education through most of the nineteenth century. He refers to E. Digby Baltzell, *Puritan Boston and Quaker Philadelphia* (Boston: Beacon, 1979), 248. By the 1860s, of the two hundred colleges in America, about two-thirds were in the Calvinistic tradition. Cornelius Plantinga, Jr., *Engaging God's World (*Grand Rapids, Mich.: Eerdmans Publishing, 2002), ix. Princeton is a prime example; the Reformed theology in which Presbyterianism finds its roots derives directly from Calvinism, through John Knox who spent years of refuge with John Calvin in Geneva before returning to his native Scotland to aid in founding the Presbyterian church.
66. Abraham Kuyper, *Lectures on Calvinism* (Grand Rapids, Mich.: Eerdmans Publishing, 1931), 11.
67. The word *antithesis* as used by Kuyper refers to two sides set over against each other. In particular it refers to the forces of good stemming from God as over against the forces of darkness.
68. In "Sphere Sovereignty," the inaugural address for the Free University of Amsterdam, reprinted in Abraham Kuyper, *A Centennial Reader* (Grand Rapids, Mich.: Eerdmans Publishing, 1998), 488.
69. Kuyper, *Lectures on Calvinism*, 21.
70. By use of the word *science* here, Kuyper means to include all academic inquiry, including the so-called human sciences that we call "humanities."
71. Abraham Kuyper, *Principles of Sacred Theology* (Grand Rapids, Mich.: Baker Book House, 1980), 123.
72. For an interesting recent treatment of this subject, see Roy Clouser, *Knowing with the Heart: Religious Experience & Belief in God* (Downers Grove, Ill.: InterVarsity Press, 1999).
73. Kuyper, *Lectures on Calvinism*, 131-32.
74. Kuyper, *Principles of Sacred Theology*, 131-32.
75. Ibid., 175.
76. Ibid., 92.
77. Kuyper, *Lectures on Calvinism*, 132.
78. Kuyper, *Principles of Sacred Theology*, 106-7.
79. Ibid., 117.
80. Ibid., 117-18.
81. Ibid., 154.
82. Kuyper, *Lectures on Calvinism*, 133.
83. Kuyper, *Principles of Sacred Theology*, 224.
84. Ibid., 118-19.
85. Ibid., 159-60.
86. While we may be used to thinking of grace as particular for redemption, there is a history of the notion that there is a kind of grace or favor that God grants in restraining His judgment for a period of time while He works out His purposes before Christ returns to set up His kingdom. Common grace, according to Kuyper, cannot be saving grace. At its limit, it only "restores the original condition of Paradise and, without re-creating, reduces the Fall and its results to a minimum."
87. S. U. Zuidema, *Communication and Confrontation* (Toronto: Wedge Publishing, 1972), 65.

88. Ibid.
89. Kuyper, *Lectures on Calvinism*, 139.
90. Zuidema, *Communication and Confrontation*, 57-58.
91. As we have stated in chapter 1, Kuyper suggests that any robust worldview will have coherent answers to the three fundamental relations of human life: man's relation to God, man's relation to man, and man's relation to the world (*Lectures,* 19), for which each of the great life systems of the world has answers. This entails, of course, what counts as God (e.g., for a materialist it is the eternal material). These relations will be elaborated on in future chapters from the point of view of Christianity, as well as a fourth relation: God's relation to the world.
92. German Idealists also were looking for such an "organic unity," and some might think that Kuyper is merely "Christianizing" this notion, but this appears to be far from the case. For Kuyper the case for the organic unity of all knowledge rests on the Calvinistic principle of the sovereignty of God, and on the fact that He is the origin of all that is revealed. Kuyper also criticizes the German Idealists strongly concerning their starting points, recognizing appropriately that their formulations of organic unity would end with a form of pantheism. He describes the Idealist position as a kind of bottom-up approach. Kuyper develops his idea of organic unity most completely in *Principles of Sacred Theology,* First Division.
93. Ibid., 83.
94. R. D. Henderson, *Illuminating Law: The Construction of Herman Dooyeweerd's Philosophy, 1918-1928* (Amsterdam: Vrije Universiteit, 1994), 15-16.
95. Ibid., 27.
96. Dooyeweerd's magnum opus, *A New Critique of Theoretical Thought,* sought to address the impossibility of impartiality or complete objectivity in theoretical analysis, in contrast to the claims of Enlightenment philosophy. Herman Dooyeweerd, *A New Critique of Theoretical Thought,* trans. David H. Freeman and William S. Young (Phillipsburg, N.J.: Presbyterian and Reformed Publishing, 1969).
97. Herman Dooyeweerd, *Roots of Western Culture: Pagan, Secular, and Christian Options*, trans. John Kraay (Toronto: Wedge Publishing, 1979), 5.
98. Ibid., 9.
99. Ibid., 6; Dooyeweerd typically refers to Proverbs 4:23 in this context: "Keep your heart with all vigilance, for from it flow the springs of life" (ESV). See, e.g., ibid., 34.
100. Ibid., 9.
101. Ibid., 12.
102. Dooyeweerd's term "ground motive" is a quite literal translation of the Dutch *grond-motief*. However, the direct translation does not communicate well to the Anglo-American reader, although a more suitable term has proved difficult to find. Our alternate term, "basic driving force," emphasizes that this is a force under the surface of the clearly rational that affects and motivates us, and through general commonality of deep convictions of the individual people in a common culture, it affects all of society. Other terms such as "foundational motive," "foundational motivation," "basic motives of the heart," or "fundamental driving force" may help the English speaker understand better what is meant.
103. Dooyeweerd, *Roots of Western Culture,* 12.
104. "A ground motive can never be ascertained through the personal conceptions and beliefs of an individual. The spirit establishes community and governs its individuals even when they are not fully conscious of that spirit or when they do not give an account of it." Ibid., 9.
105. E.g., see the references on quantum theory in the previous chapter.
106. Dooyeweerd, *Roots of Western Culture,* 15-16.
107. Many Christians who work from the Scholastic ground motive see nothing wrong with explaining creation by taking it to depend on one or another of its component aspects, so long as that aspect everything else depends on is said to depend, in turn, on God. Thus they allow theories that take all creation to depend on matter, or form/matter, or sense perceptions, etc., so long as God is the ultimate cause of *those* explainers. This,

however, is at odds with the biblical teaching that all knowledge is impacted by knowing God (e.g., 1 Cor. 1:5; Eph. 5; Col. 2:1-3). Since the content of such theories is the same whether God is tacked onto the end of them or not, their explanatory power is being regarded as neutral with respect to belief in God in precisely the way Scripture denies. In view of this, Dooyeweerd developed a critique to show that any attempt to take any aspect of creation as independent of all others results in an incoherent theory. Thus creation is to be viewed as fundamentally irreducible in terms of its various aspects. For an "American friendly" exposition of these ideas, see Roy Clouser, *The Myth of Religious Neutrality: An Essay on the Hidden Role of Belief in Theories,* rev. ed. (Notre Dame, Ind.: University of Notre Dame Press, 2005).

108. One might think of the issue as concerning the relation between fixity and change, which relates more toward the idea of universals and particulars that so stumped Parmenides. For he concluded that, since everything was one (he was a monist), everything must have always existed, and he therefore convinced himself that there can be no change. See, e.g., W. T. Jones, *The Classical Mind: A History of Western Philosophy,* Vol. 1, 2nd ed. (New York: Harcourt, Brace & World, 1969), 21.
109. This is known as the problem of universals and particulars, or the problem of "the one and the many."
110. Dooyeweerd, *Roots of Western Culture,* 8.
111. Ibid., 13.
112. Ibid.
113. In his recent publication *Sovereignty and Responsibility* (Bonn: Verlag für Kultur und Wissenschaft, 2002), our colleague at Covenant College, Henry Krabbendam, takes this notion a step further. He argues that there is just one dialectic, and the dialectic always represents "warfare" between the universal (the "one") and the particulars (the "many") and that the dialectic does not merely become operational when one of the poles "happens to be" absolutized. Rather it is an essential component of fallen human thinking that emerged already as a (counter-)cultural force in Paradise at the occasion of man's rebellion against God, and has victimized all of unregenerate mankind since. According to Krabbendam, the Modernism-Postmodernism dilemma is just one of the more recent manifestations of the dialectic. Modernism with its emphasis upon "universality" and Postmodernism with its commitment to "particularity" are pitted against each other in a "warfare" that engulfs all of life, including the sciences. Krabbendam holds that the totality of life is dialectical by definition *unless and until humans renounce their rebellion against God.* Once renounced, life turns fully non-dialectical in principle by virtue of regeneration, and purposefully non-dialectical in practice in the process of sanctification. So, he says, this has vast implications for scholarship, whether in the arena of the sciences or otherwise (private communication). For Krabbendam's own explanation, see *Sovereignty and Responsibility,* 87ff. While Krabbendam's framework of analysis comports well with the thrust of the present work, short of adopting his terminology, which we think may be confusing in our context, we wish to commend his work to you for your own investigation. Also, his framework supports the idea that antithesis always "trumps" common grace. (We will return to this in chapter 10.) In addition, the careful reader will see a number of instances of "the one and many" problem, or the problem of universals and particulars, surfacing in the pages of the present volume, even though we do not always refer to it as such.
114. Dooyeweerd, *Roots of Western Culture*, 14.
115. Proverbs 4:23 KJV.
116. Dooyeweerd, *Roots of Western Culture*, 38.
117. Chapters 7 and 10 return to these themes.

Section 2 Jesus Christ, the Lord of Creation

1. As we begin this section, we would like to make the readers aware of a recently published work that anticipates the present work in several respects from the point of view of a more general framework. See James S. Spiegel, *The Benefits of Providence: A New*

Look at Divine Sovereignty (Wheaton, Ill.: Crossway Books, 2005), particularly note ch. 4.

4: In the Name of the Father, Son, and Holy Ghost

1. Colin E. Gunton, *The Triune Creator: A Historical and Systematic Study* (Edinburgh: Edinburgh University Press, 1998), 52.
2. The Forms provide the essence for unifying the particulars and, according to Aristotle, are also the cause of all other things. Frederick Copleston, *A History of Philosophy*, 5th ed., Vol. 1 (Garden City, N.Y.: Image Books, 1993), 202.
3. Gordon Clark, *Thales to Dewey: A History of Philosophy* (Boston: Houghton Mifflin Company, 1957), 94.
4. Here we follow Roy Clouser: Whatever is considered "just there" in a given system of thought and not dependent on anything else functions as "the divine" in that system. Roy Clouser, *The Myth of Religious Neutrality: An Essay on the Hidden Role of Belief in Theories*, rev. ed. (Notre Dame, Ind.: University of Notre Dame Press, 2005), ch. 2. See also Roy Clouser, *Knowing with the Heart: Religious Experience & Belief in God* (Downers Grove, Ill.: InterVarsity Press, 1999), 21.
5. Gunton, *The Triune Creator*, 34.
6. Gunton points to Origen in particular as being influential on this point. Ibid., 57.
7. Ibid., 54.
8. The Arian heresy, a heresy condemned at the Council of Nicea (325) and again later at the Council of Constantinople (381), held that the Son of God was a created being rather than co-equal with the Father. See, e.g., Alan Richardson and John Bowden, eds., *The New Dictionary of Christian Theology* (London: SCM Press, 1983), 40.
9. Gunton, *The Triune Creator*, 66.
10. Basil discusses this in his *Hexaemeron*, a study of the six days of creation as a defense against the Arian heresy.
11. Gunton, *The Triune Creator*, 71.
12. Ibid., 72.
13. Gunton suggests that this inability to accept that God could do anything that takes time should be understood as residual Manichaeism in Augustine's thought. Ibid., 77.
14. See, for example, John Calvin, *Institutes of the Christian Religion*, book II, trans. Henry Beveridge (Grand Rapids, Mich.: Eerdmans Publishing, 1972), section 20, and also his commentary on Colossians 1.
15. The plainest meaning of the word *logos* is simply speech. See, e.g., Henry George Liddell and Robert Scott, *An Intermediate Greek-English Lexicon Founded upon the Seventh Edition of Liddell and Scott's Greek-English Lexicon* (Oxford: Clarendon Press, 1889), 476-77.
16. Meredith Kline, *Images of the Spirit* (Eugene, Ore.: Wipf and Stock Publishers, 1998), 19-20.
17. O. Palmer Robertson, *The Christ of the Covenants* (Phillipsburg, N.J.: Presbyterian and Reformed Publishing, 1980), 4.
18. Because Elihu acts here as an accuser of Job, whom God has already proclaimed as righteous, one might think there is no reason to consider Elihu's words as true. However, he is only reflecting other more direct passages that make this association, e.g., Genesis 2:7 where God "breathed into [Adam's] nostrils the breath of life, and the man became a living being."
19. Calvin, *Institutes*, I.xiii, 14.
20. Compare this to the Nicene Creed: "And we believe in the Holy Spirit, the Lord and giver of life, who proceeds from the Father and the Son; who with the Father and the Son together is worshiped and glorified; who spoke by the prophets...."
21. Herman Bavinck, *In the Beginning: Foundations of Creation Theology*, trans. John Vriend, ed. John Bolt (Grand Rapids, Mich.: Baker Books, 1999), 23.
22. Kline, *Images of the Spirit*, 16.
23. Ibid., 17, n.11. Kline also adds, "Because the Angel was the Son, he enjoyed a name

more excellent [*sic*] far than the other angels associated with the theophanic Glory (Heb. 1:4ff.). Significantly, the comparison of Jesus, the image of God's glory, with angels leads to the topic of man as image of God, which also involves comparison with the angels (cf. Heb. 2:6ff.)." (His stating of "the Son's identity with the Spirit" seems inappropriate in this passage.)

24. Ibid., 20.
25. Colin E. Gunton, *The Promise of Trinitarian Theology*, 2nd ed. (Edinburgh: T&T Clark, 1997), 12.
26. Ibid., 13.
27. See, e.g., Rousas John Rushdoony, *The One and the Many* (Fairfax, Va.: Thoburn Press, 1978).
28. According to Stanley Grenz and Roger Olson, the idea of panentheism stems from Hegel's philosophy of the nineteenth century: "Hegel's view of the relationship between God and the world set the pattern for many later varieties of a theological alternative commonly called 'panentheism.' Subsumed under this label is any view that represents God and the world as inseparable yet distinct realities." Stanley J. Grenz and Roger E. Olson, *20th Century Theology: God and the World in a Transitional Age* (Downers Grove, Ill.: InterVarsity Press, 1992), 38-39. In the twentieth century, it is often associated with the process philosophy of Alfred North Whitehead (see, e.g., Grenz and Olson, *20th Century Theology*, 135-44).
29. See, e.g., Clark H. Pinnock, *Most Moved Mover: A Theology of God's Openness* (Grand Rapids, Mich.: Baker Academic, 2001).
30. See chapter 3 for a discussion of dialectic.
31. Bavinck, *In the Beginning*, 23.
32. Cornelius Van Til, *The Defense of the Faith* (Philadelphia: Presbyterian and Reformed Publishing, 1972), 25. "Subordinationism" here means the subordination of one person of the Trinity to another, rather than maintaining an equality.
33. Ibid., 27.
34. Gunton, *The Promise of Trinitarian Theology*, 144.
35. In the medieval period, people tended to think that God had to have the qualities He has by definition, or that His qualities were "necessary" in this sense. Thus God is sometimes referred to as a necessary being.

5: Supernatural Laws and Natural Miracles

1. William J. Courtenay, *Capacity and Volition: A History of the Distinction of Absolute and Ordained Powers* (Bergamo, Italy: Pierluigi Lubrina Editore, 1990), 11.
2. Ibid., 29-30.
3. Ibid., 30.
4. Cardinal Desiderius became the reluctant Pope Victor III in 1086.
5. This is not a mere "How many angels can dance on the head of a pin" question as medieval thought is so often caricaturized. Jerome's question was raised in relation to the year A.D. 410 when Rome was sacked by the invading Goths, and many were victims of rape. While Augustine sent a message of consolation to Rome, Jerome had sent a previous letter in praise of the "grandeur of virginity," which many years later sparked the controversy. Francis Oakley, *Omnipotence, Covenant, & Order: An Excursion in the History of Ideas from Abelard to Leibniz* (Ithaca, N.Y.: Cornell University Press, 1984), 41-42. (The actual phrase, "How many angels can dance on the point of a very fine needle, without jostling one another?" is found as a jest concerning medieval philosophy in Isaac D'Israeli's *Curiosities of Literature*, 1791.)
6. This was a serious question at the time, also because of the neo-Platonic notion that God was a necessary God—that is, a God who by definition had to have the characteristics He had. This could imply that all His actions are necessary actions, therefore imposing a kind of philosophical determinism. In other words, God would be limited in His actions by His nature. In contrast to Augustine, Anselm, and Aquinas, note that the Cappadocian fathers such as Basil, as well as Reformers such as Luther and Calvin, tended to distinguish between God's nature and God's energies or actions. God's

nature is unchanging, but His actions did not follow as necessary from His being. We only know God through this free expression of His actions. For a discussion, see Roy Clouser, *The Myth of Religious Neutrality: An Essay on the Hidden Role of Belief in Theories,* rev. ed. (Notre Dame, Ind.: University of Notre Dame Press, 2005), ch. 10.

7. A part of Damian's motivation had to do with contemporary dialecticians "whose literal view of scripture or to authoritative statements such as Jerome's led to gross misinterpretations and, in this case, to limitations on the range of divine power." So he was really worried about heresy. However, Courtenay states that the targets of Damian's arguments are not known for sure, although there are some suspects, whose identities are not important for our story. See Courtenay, *Capacity and Volition*, 27.
8. Ibid., 31.
9. Ibid., 34.
10. Ibid.
11. Ibid., 35.
12. Thus they avoided the philosophical determinism that could seem to follow from the concept of a necessary God. Ibid., 45.
13. Oakley, *Omnipotence, Covenant, & Order*, 50.
14. Courtenay, *Capacity and Volition*, 19.
15. The condemnations included some propositions that could be attributed to Aquinas. David C. Lindberg, *The Beginnings of Western Science: The European Scientific Tradition in Philosophical, Religious, and Institutional Context, 600 B.C. to A.D. 1450* (Chicago: University of Chicago Press, 1992), 265; Edward Grant, *The Foundations of Modern Science in the Middle Ages* (Cambridge: Cambridge University Press, 1996), 62.
16. Grant, *Foundations of Modern Science in the Middle Ages*, 57.
17. Lindberg, *Beginnings of Western Science,* 265.
18. Ibid.
19. Oakley, *Omnipotence, Covenant, & Order*, 56.
20. Ibid., 52.
21. Ibid., 56.
22. Ibid.
23. Ibid., 74.
24. Ibid., 75.
25. Quotation marks are for emphasis of a caricature.
26. Robert Boyle, *A Free Inquiry into the Vulgarly Received Notion of Nature* in *The Works of the Honourable Robert Boyle*, ed. Thomas Birch, new ed., 6 vols. (London, 1972), 5:197; *On the Excellency and Grounds of the Corpuscular or Mechanical Philosophy* in *Works,* ed. Birch, 4:68 [endnote in original].
27. *Christian Virtuoso* in *Works*, ed. Birch, 5:521 [endnote in original].
28. *Free Inquiry* in *Works*, ed. Birch, 5:216, 223 [endnote in original].
29. *Some Considerations* in *Works*, ed. Birch, 5:170 [endnote in original].
30. *Of the High Veneration Man's Intellect Owes to God*, in *Works*, ed. Birch, 5:149 [endnote in original]. This whole passage including endnotes appears in Oakley, *Omnipotence, Covenant, & Order*, 75.
31. A Whig interpretation of history is one that reads back onto a previous time the attitudes of one's own time and then judges the previous perspective accordingly.
32. John Hedley Brooke, *Science and Religion: Some Historical Perspectives* (Cambridge: Cambridge University Press, 1991), 14.
33. In other words, there will always be an explanation for the creation and operation of the universe, put forward on purely naturalistic assumptions, that seems plausible to those committed to naturalism. This is the nature of the antithesis; the worldview that rejects God will always have a way of reconciling its view to its experience that is at least believable to people who hold that worldview, even if it is false.
34. Oakley, *Omnipotence, Covenant, & Order*, 70.

35. This episode was purported to be a put-up job by the Royal Society itself, to further its cause.
36. While the received view of the theory of quantum mechanics emphasizes the statistical nature of the predictions, and it is true that no materialistic determinism without some other serious drawback can accommodate the theory, this does not preclude God's providence behind the scenes in any way. In other words, the theory of quantum mechanics does not present an argument that the universe is essentially random at its foundation, as some have claimed. It only tells us something concerning our knowledge of the universe.
37. In other words, we are talking about a "God's-eye view" here, with an emphasis on His purposes and not merely on what we, as finite and sinful humans, perceive every day.
38. Jonathan Edwards is often given as an example of an occasionalist. To give an idea of his claims, see Jonathan Edwards, *The Works of Jonathan Edwards (*Peabody, Mass.: Hendrickson Publishers, 2000), Vol. 1, ch. 3, 223. Here he makes some amazing statements about how the moon at an early time, for example, could not be its own cause at a later time. Through this and similar arguments he concludes that "God's *preserving* of created things is perfectly equivalent to a *continued creation*, or to his creating those things out of nothing at *each moment* of their existence."
39. In a recent theological study of miracles, C. John Collins classifies many "Amsterdam School" theologians, including Abraham Kuyper and G. C. Berkouwer, as occasionalists, whereas those of the "Old Princeton School" are classified as supernaturalists. C. John Collins, *The God of Miracles: An Exegetical Examination of God's Action in the World* (Wheaton, Ill.: Crossway Books, 2000), 21. Collins also includes a similar discussion in his more recent and excellent work: C. John Collins, *Science & Faith, Friends or Foes* (Wheaton, Ill.: Crossway Books, 2003). According to our formulation, in view of the dialectical nature of the problem, such strict classifications do not seem very appropriate.
40. According to Henry Krabbendam, we should at this point realize that if we persist in making a strict separation, we are engaging in apostate thought. As we have said, for Krabbendam all thought is either dialectical or non-dialectical, and the only way to achieve the latter is by faith and repentance, and then to humbly embrace from the regenerate heart what cannot be exhaustively understood with rational analysis. This is not to be viewed as a sacrifice of the intellect however; it is a humble acceptance of our creaturely limitation (private communication).
41. In an interesting comment along these lines, C. John Collins, who considers himself a supernaturalist, acknowledges this tension: "[N]othing in these definitions requires an 'autonomy' from God for either natural properties or for nature; if any of the theories we are examining asserts an autonomy for nature, that assertion does not arise by necessity from the word itself. In view of the discussion of concurrence in chapter 3, Christians who are supernaturalists would probably do well to avoid the use of the word *autonomy*." See Collins, *The God of Miracles*, 62.
42. For example, in a passage with which we have quite some sympathy, Abraham Kuyper expresses his view of laws of nature as follows: "What now does the Calvinist mean by his faith in the ordinances of God? Nothing less than the firmly rooted conviction that all life has first been in the *thoughts* of God, before it came to be realized in *Creation*. Hence all created life necessarily bears in itself a law for its existence, instituted by God Himself. There is no life outside us in Nature, without such divine ordinances—ordinances which are called the laws of Nature—a term which we are willing to accept, provided we understand thereby, not laws originating *from* Nature, but laws imposed *upon* Nature. So, there are ordinances of God for the firmament above, and ordinances for the earth below, by means of which this world is maintained, and as the Psalmist says, These ordinances are the servants of God. Consequently there are ordinances of God for our bodies, for the blood that courses through our arteries and veins, and for our lungs as the organs of respiration. And even so are there ordinances of God, in logic, to regulate our thoughts; ordinances of God for our imagination, in

the domain of aesthetics; and so, also, strict ordinances of God for the whole of human life in the *domain of morals*." Abraham Kuyper, *Lectures on Calvinism* (Grand Rapids, Mich.: Eerdmans Publishing, 1931), 70.

43. This idea that God is fully operative, and the creation is fully operative is often called concurrence or *concursus*.
44. Blaise Pascal, *Pensées* (London: Penguin Books, 1976), 90-91.
45. R. Hoykaas, *Robert Boyle: A Study in Science and Christian Belief* (Lanham, New York, Oxford: University Press of America, 1997), 104.
46. In Henry Krabbendam's words, "In my apologetics I refuse to acknowledge a 'metaphysical' tension in any context. Further, there is only epistemological tension if the mind operates as ultimate. Both poles of so-called tension-filled relationships fit very snugly in the regenerate heart. The mind has single occupancy only, which results in warfare. The heart has double occupancy which spells harmony" (private communication).
47. Colin E. Gunton, *The Promise of Trinitarian Theology*, 2nd ed. (Edinburgh: T&T Clark, 1997), 146. *Eschatological* and *eschatology* derive their meanings from the Greek word *eschatos,* meaning "last." Thus eschatology means the study of end times, or concerning end times.
48. Gunton puts it this way: "Determinism and reversibility both imply an essentially static universe, not in the sense that there is no movement, but that all that happens is decided in advance (determinism) and that any process can in theory be taken back the way it came. There is thus in principle no novelty. As in some forms of the ancient doctrine of creation, the end is not different from the beginning." Gunton, *The Promise of Trinitarian Theology*, 147.
49. Ibid., 153.
50. See, e.g., Clark H. Pinnock, *Most Moved Mover: A Theology of God's Openness* (Grand Rapids, Mich.: Baker Academic, 2001).
51. Indeed, the idea of change implies being subject to time, and from the Scriptures there is no reason to think that God is subject to time, which is typically taken to be a part of created reality.
52. Gunton, *The Promise of Trinitarian Theology*, 148-49.
53. C. S. Lewis, "Miracles," in *God in the Dock: Essays on Theology and Ethics* (Grand Rapids, Mich.: Eerdmans Publishing, 1970), 26.
54. Ibid., 29.
55. It is interesting to note that Hebrew uses the concept of "wonder" to refer to what we often call supernatural. The Hebrew concept of wonder is that which is too difficult to understand or beyond human understanding. There is no Hebrew word for our notion of "supernatural," per se.

6: The Laws of Nature and the Gospel of Grace

1. W. J. Dumbrell, *Covenant & Creation: A Theology of the Old Testament Covenants* (Grand Rapids, Mich.: Baker Book House, 1984), 91.
2. O. Palmer Robertson, *The Christ of the Covenants* (Phillipsburg, N.J.: Presbyterian and Reformed Publishing, 1980), 170-71.
3. Ibid., 198.
4. Ibid.
5. Dooyeweerd speaks of creation having a "law-side" and a "subject-side."
6. Philosophers tend to use "law" for the former sense, i.e., the reality, and something like "law statement" or "statement of the law" for the description.
7. In chapter 8, we refer to these two sides as "order as given" and "order as task," following J. Richard Middleton and Brian J. Walsh, *Truth Is Stranger Than It Used to Be* (Downers Grove, Ill.: InterVarsity Press, 1995), 163.
8. The word *telos* is Greek for purpose; thus teleology in this context refers to the character of nature in that it is being directed toward an end or purpose by God, which He alone fully comprehends.

9. G. C. Berkouwer, *General Revelation* (Grand Rapids, Mich.: Eerdmans Publishing, 1975), 286.
10. Metaphysics is a branch of philosophy that deals with the ultimate nature of things. Thus it deals with foundational issues, usually thought to be beyond the realm of science.
11. For the curious about Dutch Reformed views on this subject, according to M. D. Stafleu, this latter view is very close to that of Vollenhoven, the Dutch mathematician who started the Cosmonomic School of Philosophy along with Herman Dooyeweerd. Vollenhoven places the law between God and whatever is subject to the law. Dooyeweerd, on the other hand, speaks of the law as created in a different sense—creation has a law-side and a subject-side as we noted previously. (M. D. Stafleu, "The Idea of Natural Law," *Philosophia Reformata* 64 (1999): 88, 93-94.) Thus for Dooyeweerd the law is in creation almost as an Aristotelian purpose, except that it is under the direction of God, while for Vollenhoven, the law is the go-between, much more similar to neo-Platonic thought. In our formulation, the ordinances of God, which are reflected in our notion of law, are neither "in the mind of God" as the idealist would say, nor are they part of creation proper, but they represent the mediating activity of the covenantal God. God is transcendent but also immanent through Christ and the Spirit, and this immanent presence removes the need for further impersonal mediation.
12. See, for example, R. C. Sproul, *Not a Chance* (Grand Rapids, Mich.: Baker Books, 1994).
13. We quite agree with John Polkinghorne's assessment of this suggestion. Within a discussion of various views on God's workings in the universe, he says: "The idea of such a hole-and-corner deity, fiddling around at the rickety roots of the cosmos [only], has not commended itself to many." John Polkinghorne, *Science and Creation: The Search for Understanding* (Boston: Shambhala Publications, 1989), 58.
14. See the end of chapter 4.
15. This and many other of Aristotle's "logically derived" principles of physics turned out to be incorrect.
16. To be fair, Aristotle did perform experiments, but unfortunately he studied falling bodies by dropping them in viscous liquids. They of course reach terminal velocity, and heavier ones fall faster. However, he did not discover the principle of friction, and one can only wonder whether his logical predispositions precluded his investigations from going in the right direction.
17. In fact, some things that we formerly thought could be determined true or false simply have no fact of the matter. For example, when two events occur at different places in space, there is no fact of the matter as to whether they occur at the same time or not. They may appear to be simultaneous events to one observer, whereas to another they occur at different times. The fact of the matter has more to do with how light propagates to the different observers so that they can record when the events happened according to their own perception.
18. We would have preferred the term "openness" here, but that term has already been used in the "openness of God" theology, which is very different from our intent here. See, e.g., Clark H. Pinnock, *Most Moved Mover: A Theology of God's Openness* (Grand Rapids, Mich.: Baker, 2001). Therefore we have chosen the term "incompleteness" for the present work. Using this term is not so bad though, since incompleteness has been used in conjunction with quantum theory for a long time, as well as in conjunction with arithmetic in the context of Gödel's theorem.
19. TeX is widely used by mathematicians and physicists for publishing both papers and books. While Knuth was working on a series of books about computer algorithms, he became dissatisfied with the computer programs that were replacing traditional typesetting because, as he thought, they did not make beautiful mathematics books, or beautiful books at all for that matter. He thus spent some seven years to create a program to use to publish his own books. He has made this program freely available so that many publishing houses have now adopted it. (Indeed, because of the ease with which it can typeset high-quality books, it is sometimes used behind the scenes by pub-

lishers for books not necessarily containing mathematics.) See Donald Knuth, *The TeXbook* (Menlo Park, Calif.: Addison Wesley Publishing, 1991).

20. Donald Knuth, *Digital Typography* (Stanford: CSLI Publications, 1999), 8.
21. See, e.g., Colossians 2:17: "These [rules] are a shadow of the things that were to come; the reality, however, is found in Christ," and Hebrews 10:1: "The law is only a shadow of the good things that are coming—not the realities themselves."
22. Particle pairs that are coupled initially but fly off in opposite directions seem somehow to "know" what state each other is in, even though the state is not pre-determined until a measurement is made, and the particles are so far apart by then that, even at light speed which is the fastest speed possible, messages could not be sent between them. See, for example, Nick Herbert, *Quantum Reality* (Garden City, N.Y.: Anchor Press/Doubleday, 1985).
23. Chaos theory is a branch of physics for which small effects at one stage, through a deterministic evolution of a system, can drastically affect the outcome at a later stage. Often people caricaturize this theory by saying something like, "If a butterfly flaps its wings in China, it can cause a hurricane in Cuba." While strictly deterministic, the results are certainly unpredictable using only limited computational ability. For example, we cannot predict the weather more than a few days in advance, even with the world's most powerful computers. If any other "open" phenomena feed back into the evolution of a chaotic system at any stage, the outcome becomes unpredictable in principle. For a popular review of the subject, see James Gleick, *Chaos* (New York: Penguin Books, 1987).
24. The notion of instinct has long been used as a name for what was perceived to be some kind of built-in mechanism for the behavior of animals, as motivated by the mechanistic view. Nowadays researchers find that the actual situation is more complex and that even simple animals are involved in some level of "decision making."
25. Gödel's theorem tells us that any system of mathematics rich enough to contain integer arithmetic also includes true statements that are not provable by the system. This implies that we can always add new axioms to the system to encompass the true statements, thereby making the system "larger." Thus the number system exhibits an incompleteness as an axiomatic system very much like quantum systems are incomplete in physical reality. (Another of Gödel's theorems tells us that it is impossible to prove that such a system is consistent.) See, e.g., Gregory J. Chaitin, *The Unknowable* (Singapore: Springer, 1999).
26. This is in contrast to the "openness of God" movement mentioned in the previous two chapters. See particularly chapter 5.

Section 3 Investigating His Dominion

1. The summary of the law related in Matthew 22:37-40, Luke 10:27, and Mark 12:30-33 bring together teachings from Deuteronomy 6:5 and Leviticus 19:18. Luke 10:27 and Mark 12:30 give the fourfold rendition of human avenues through which love for God is to be expressed, while Deuteronomy 6:5, Matthew 22:37, and Mark 12:33 give a threefold rendition. The point is obviously to cover all the bases, not to make some technical distinction between isolated compartments of human being.
2. Numerous scriptural passages make these connections. Some examples: Matthew 7:15-20; Matthew 13:18-23; Matthew 15:16-20; John 10:25; Romans 1:18-32; Philippians 2:14-16.
3. These "isms" can be thought about in the following very general terms. Legalism: reduction of Christian obedience to a list of "do's and don'ts"; it's all about doing. Antinomianism: once a person has being "in Christ," the specifics of knowing and doing are unimportant; it's all about being. Doctrinalism: obedience is essentially about assenting to the correct doctrinal formulations, or in other words, it's all about knowing.
4. Del Ratzsch, *The Battle of Beginnings* (Downers Grove, Ill.: InterVarsity Press, 1996), 128, 129-30, 134-35.

Notes

7: New Creatures at Work in the King's Realm

1. C. S. Lewis, *The Magician's Nephew* (New York: Collier Books, 1970), 125.
2. William Placher's book *The Domestication of Transcendence* (Louisville, Ky.: Westminster John Knox Press, 1996) has had a seminal influence on ideas discussed in this section of the chapter. His concept of the "domesticating" effects that Modernism has had on Christian concepts over the last four hundred years is a powerful one. In the book he contrasts some of the ways Aquinas, Luther, and Calvin spoke of God and His actions with Modern ways of speaking about God and His grace and finds that the Modern forms inevitably tame the God of Christianity to suit Modern sensibilities. He argues that this domestication has created a variety of false problems that have dominated Modern theology regarding the knowledge of God, the meaning and exercise of His grace, and the breadth and forms of His action in the world.
3. For an excellent discussion of this shift and for numerous references see chapters 1 and 2 in Nancy R. Pearcey and Charles B. Thaxton, *The Soul of Science* (Wheaton, Ill.: Crossway Books, 1994).
4. Ibid., 21-37.
5. John Hedley Brooke, *Science and Religion: Some Historical Perspectives* (Cambridge: Cambridge University Press, 1991), 19-26.
6. See, for example, the discussion of scientific naturalism in Howard J. Van Till, Davis A. Young, and Clarence Menninga, *Science Held Hostage* (Downers Grove, Ill.: InterVarsity Press, 1988), 127-58.
7. These three metaphors are helpfully discussed in the context of early modern science in Pearcey and Thaxton, *Soul of Science*, 59-120.
8. John Calvin's reference to creation as "the theater of His Glory" forms the title of Susan E. Schreiner's excellent book, *The Theater of His Glory: Nature and the Natural Order in the Thought of John Calvin* (Grand Rapids, Mich.: Baker Books, 1991).
9. Revelation 13:8.
10. See for example Ephesians 2:10 and Philippians 2:12-13.
11. Meredith Kline, *The Structure of Biblical Authority* (Grand Rapids, Mich.: Eerdmans Publishing, 1972), 154-71.
12. Francis A. Schaeffer, *True Spirituality* (Wheaton, Ill.: Tyndale House, 2001), 56-57.
13. This essential "commentary" is of course the Scriptures.
14. See Ephesians 1 and 2 for Paul's extended discussion of the all-encompassing reach of the gospel in Christ.
15. For example, see Genesis 1:28; Matthew 28:19-20; 2 Corinthians 5:19-21.
16. For example, Ephesians 1:22-23; Matthew 16:18; Revelation 19:7.
17. For example, Psalm 65:5-13; 104:13-24; 145:9, 15, 16; Matthew 6:26-32.
18. Colossians 1:15-20; 1 Corinthians 15:14.
19. *The Westminster Standards* (Philadelphia, Atlanta: Great Commission Publications), The Larger Catechism, Question 7.
20. See, for example, Isaiah 55:8-9.
21. See, for example, Jeremiah 29:11-14.
22. See, for example, John Haught, *God After Darwin* (Boulder, Colo.: Westview Press, 2000), and David Ray Griffin, *Religion and Scientific Naturalism: Overcoming the Conflicts* (Albany, N.Y.: State University of New York Press, 2000).
23. The process philosophy of Alfred North Whitehead figures prominently in this line of thinking.
24. Dietrich Bonhoeffer, *The Cost of Discipleship* (New York: Collier Books, 1963), 45.
25. Genesis 3:14-24.
26. Romans 3:10-18.
27. Romans 8:20-21.
28. James 1:13-14.
29. Romans 8:18-23.

30. Abraham Kuyper, *Lectures on Calvinism* (Grand Rapids, Mich.: Eerdmans Publishing, 1931), 131-32.
31. Genesis 3:17-19.
32. See Galatians 5:19; John 12:39-40; Galatians 4:3-9; Ephesians 2:1-5; Ephesians 4:17-19; Colossians 1:21-22.
33. Genesis 1:28.
34. A system, such as a child's swing or a guitar string, that is driven by a frequency equal to its natural vibrating frequency will absorb energy, resulting in an increased amplitude of vibration. Therefore, we should tune our own natural inclinations to those redemption calls for, and thus transmit the energy of the Master into our efforts for Him and His kingdom.
35. See also Ephesians 5:22-33.
36. Revelation 7:9.
37. Revelation 19:7.
38. Ephesians 1:23.
39. Louis Berkhof, *Manual of Christian Doctrine* (Grand Rapids, Mich.: Eerdmans Publishing, 1978), 283-84.
40. John 8:31-32, 47; 14:23; 1 John 4:1-3; 2 John 9.
41. Matthew 18:18; 1 Corinthians 5:1-5, 13; 14:33, 40; Revelation 2:14-15, 20.
42. Matthew 28:19; Mark 16:16; Acts 2:42; 1 Corinthians 11:23-30.
43. Colossians 1:15-20.
44. A partial listing of such references: 2 Kings 6:15-17; Job 1 and 2; Psalm 34:7; Matthew 6:16-18, 19-21; 18:10; Luke 12:8; John 14:16-17; 2 Corinthians 4:18; Ephesians 5:10-18; 1 Timothy 5:21.
45. For example, 1 Corinthians 7:14 refers to a "sanctification" of spouse and children by reason of relationship with a believing spouse/parent. In 1 Timothy 4:4-5 everything is declared "good" if it is received with thanksgiving, because it is consecrated by word and prayer. In Titus 1:15-16, we are told that to the pure all is pure, but to the corrupt all is corrupt.
46. Lewis, *The Magician's Nephew*, 126.

8: A Gracious Revealer and the Making of Scientific Knowledge

1. Modernists would typically distinguish fact, that which can be established by objective dispassionate analysis, from value, which is dependent on a variety of subjective human sociological and psychological features. The facts are absolute while values are relative. It is interesting to note that although this strict distinction is typical of late Modern thought, earlier in the Modern period many considered ethics to be a scientific discipline in which scientific methodology could ultimately establish moral standards as matters of fact in the same way that properties of physical entities could be established.
2. Michel Foucault would be an example of the "militant" wing, while Richard Rorty would exemplify the pragmatic group. Nancey Murphy in her book *Anglo-American Postmodernity* (Boulder, Colo.: Westview Press, 1997) refers to similar groupings of Postmoderns as Continental and Anglo-American respectively.
3. Richard Rorty, "Solidarity or Objectivity," in John Rajchman and Cornel West, eds., *Post-Analytic Philosophy* (New York: Columbia University Press, 1985).
4. Thomas Kuhn, *The Structure of Scientific Revolutions* (Chicago: University of Chicago Press, 1962).
5. David J. Hesse, *Science Studies* (New York and London: New York University Press, 1997).
6. For examples see Andrew Ross, ed., *Science Wars* (Durham and London: Duke University Press, 1996), and more recently, Keith Parsons, ed., *The Science Wars: Debating Scientific Knowledge and Technology* (New York: Prometheus Books, 2003).
7. There are some interesting parallels between Postmodern strategies to deconstruct

Modern science in the twentieth century and Modernist strategies to "deconstruct" historic Christian beliefs in the eighteenth and nineteenth centuries.

8. Paul R. Gross, Norman Leavitt, and Martin W. Lewis, eds., *The Flight from Science and Reason* (New York: New York Academy of the Sciences, 1996); Paul R. Gross and Norman Leavitt, *Higher Superstition* (Baltimore: Johns Hopkins University Press, 1998).
9. J. Richard Middleton and Brian J. Walsh, *Truth Is Stranger Than It Used to Be* (Downers Grove, Ill.: InterVarsity Press, 1995), 163.
10. In the sense that given human characteristics, even God Himself is unable to communicate truths to human beings.
11. It is interesting to note in this context that taxonomists (taxonomy is a branch of biology that concerns itself with the proper classification of living creatures) over the centuries have regularly had discussions about whether classification systems were or should attempt to be "real"(directly reflecting evolutionary relationships or patterns in the mind of God at creation), or whether they were "merely" useful constructs of the human mind.
12. Even in developing these perspectives, we find ourselves involved in "gift" and "task" responsibilities. We must attempt to utilize the rich biblical and theological resources God has given as well as to creatively apply those resources to the task of developing faithful perspectives.
13. Alasdair MacIntyre, *Whose Justice, Which Rationality?* (Notre Dame, Ind.: University of Notre Dame Press, 1988).
14. We are indebted to William C. Davis, a member of the philosophy department at Covenant College for this terminology, having heard his exposition on this topic in the Covenant College freshman course entitled "The Christian Mind."
15. In Davis's lectures, he directs students toward passages such as the following to make this point: Truth—Psalm 19:9; 85:10-11; John 1:17; 4:24; 8:32; 14:6; 1 John 3:18-19; 2 Corinthians 4:2; 6:7, 7:14. Knowledge—Genesis 4:1; 8:11; Exodus 31:3; Psalm 119:66; Isaiah 33:6; Amos 3:2; 1 John 2:3; 3:4, 18-19; 4:7.
16. The designation of a claim as "scientific knowledge" is an important question, but is not primary in this way of thinking. The designation as "scientific knowledge" turns out to be more of an issue concerning the ground rules for a particular cultural form of science than of recognizing some kind of absolute eternal category. In any case, it is widely recognized that cleanly distinguishing scientific from nonscientific elements (the demarcation problem) is extremely difficult, if not impossible.
17. James D. Watson, *The Double Helix*, ed. Gunther S. Stent (New York, London: W. W. Norton Company, 1980).
18. Edward O. Wilson, *Consilience: The Unity of Knowledge* (New York: Random House, 1999), 325.
19. Colin E. Gunton, *A Brief Theology of Revelation* (Edinburgh: T&T Clark, 1995), 34-35.
20. Leon Morris, *I Believe in Revelation* (Grand Rapids, Mich.: Eerdmans Publishing, 1976), 10.
21. In Modern Western intellectual history, autonomous human knowledge exemplified by scientific knowledge came to be increasingly privileged over revealed knowledge until genuine revelation from a source outside human experience was rejected by many as pre-Modern superstition. This in our view is a major part of the story of the development of liberal theology, which found itself continuously accommodating to Modern scientific knowledge in its understanding of "revelation" until, as Karl Barth found, there was nothing "preachable" left in Christianity. This led to Barth's development of what generally came to be known as "neo-orthodox" theology as a repudiation of liberal theology. An initial move in the development of Barth's theology was to "rescue" revelation, but this came at the expense of unified human knowledge. Barth's overall theological strategy can be seen as an illustration of the dualistic result of accepting two essentially different "ways of knowing" as givens. See Stanley J. Grenz and Roger E. Olson, *20th Century Theology: God and the World in a*

Transitional Age (Downers Grove, Ill.: InterVarsity Press, 1992), 15-77, for a succinct description of the theological history leading up to and including Barth.

22. We first became aware of this passage in the context of revelation in Albert M. Wolters, *Creation Regained* (Grand Rapids, Mich.: Eerdmans Publishing, 1985), 28.
23. 2 Timothy 1:9; Ephesians 3:11; Colossians 1:15-23.
24. The use of the word *sufficiency* here might bring to mind doctrinal discussions of sufficiency. Historically the doctrine of sufficiency is related to the Reformers' motto *sola scriptura.* The doctrine basically states that Christians don't need to worry that there is some knowledge or instruction outside Scripture that is necessary for salvation. The related doctrine of perspicuity holds that although there may be parts of Scripture that are difficult to understand or about which there is much disagreement, one doesn't need an advanced theological degree to understand the basic gospel message. Both of these doctrines are often misunderstood. Sufficiency is sometimes taken to mean that all that is worth knowing is to be found in the Scriptures, and perspicuity is taken to mean that the "plain sense" of the words of Scripture will always be clear and will always constitute the best interpretation. These doctrines have more to do with the trustworthiness and omnipotence of God—He is able to accomplish the revelational purposes He has for Scripture—than with establishing epistemological limits or giving specific hermeneutical direction.
25. Genesis 1:31a; John 1:1-3; Ephesians 2:10.
26. Ephesians 1:10; 1 Corinthians 1:30; Romans 8:19-23.
27. Colossians 2:3.
28. This sense of "unfolding" is not calling into question the "closing" of the biblical canon. The Christian church has long affirmed that revelation of the inspired scriptural variety has ceased.
29. Vern S. Poythress, *Symphonic Theology* (Phillipsburg, N.J.: Presbyterian and Reformed Publishing, 1987), ch. 6.
30. Archibald A. Hodge and Benjamin B. Warfield, *Inspiration* (Grand Rapids, Mich.: Baker Books, repr. 1979) and Benjamin B. Warfield, *The Inspiration and Authority of the Bible*, ed. Samuel G. Craig (Philadelphia: Presbyterian and Reformed Publishing, repr. 1967) are classic statements of this basic position.
31. See, for example, Ephesians 2:10 and Philippians 2:12-13.
32. Grenz and Olson, *20th Century Theology,* 51-112.
33. As an example, I remember being impressed as a teenager by the idea that Proverbs 8:27 taught that the earth is a sphere . . . not flat. A Christian friend showed me the New American Standard Version rendering of the second part of this verse: "he inscribed a circle on the face of the deep." He argued that if people had just turned to the Scriptures for their geography, it would have saved a lot of trouble. In the context, both of the author's culture and of the verse in the text, the phrase refers to the circle of the horizon from a sailor's perspective and is not intending to give a modern geography lesson.
34. See Poythress, *Symphonic Theology*, especially ch. 6 and 7.
35. John Calvin, *Institutes of the Christian Religion*, I. iv. 1.
36. Genesis 1:27.
37. Del Ratzsch, *The Battle of Beginnings* (Downers Grove, Ill.: InterVarsity Press, 1996), ch. 8.
38. Ephesians 1:17; Luke 2:26; 1 Corinthians 2:10.
39. Exodus 31:3; Isaiah 11:2; 1 Corinthians 12:8.
40. Psalm 143:10; Luke 12:12; John 14:26.
41. Ratzsch, *The Battle of Beginnings*, 129.
42. Wolterstorff uses this term in his book *Thomas Reid and the Story of Epistemology* (Cambridge, U.K.: Cambridge University Press, 2001).
43. Francis A. Schaeffer, *True Spirituality* (Wheaton, Ill.: Tyndale House Publishers, 2001), 77.
44. Ibid.

45. John M. Frame, *Cornelius Van Til, An Analysis of His Thought* (Phillipsburg, N.J.: Presbyterian and Reformed Publishing, 1995), 122
46. Covenant College Purpose Statement, http://www.covenant.edu/welcome/purpose_statement.php (accessed 12/28/05).
47. C. S. Lewis, *The Magician's Nephew* (New York: Collier Books, Macmillan Publishing Company, 1970), 116-18.

9: "Well Done, Good and Faithful Scientific Servant"

1. Dietrich Bonhoeffer, *The Cost of Discipleship* (New York: Collier Books, Macmillan Publishing Company, 1963), 69.
2. Arthur Holmes, *The Idea of a Christian College* (Grand Rapids, Mich.: Eerdmans Publishing, 1987), 18.
3. The Greek word for regeneration, *palingenesis*, occurs only twice in Scripture. In Matthew 19:28, it refers to the making of all things new at the consummation, and in Titus 3:5 it refers to a Christian's rebirth in Christ.
4. Covenant College Purpose Statement, http://www.covenant.edu/undergrad/campus_facts/faith.php
5. Francis Bacon, *Advancement of Learning and Novum Organum* (New York: Willey Book Company, 1944), 298.
6. "God of the gaps" is a phrase with negative connotations to refer to the use of God as an explanation to bridge the "gaps" in human explanation. When this is done, God's "role" in the universe seems to shrink as human understanding grows.
7. See the section "Old Self, New Self" in chapter 7.
8. C. S. Lewis, *Surprised by Joy* (New York: Harcourt, Brace, 1956), 18, 238.
9. Nancy R. Pearcey and Charles B. Thaxton, *The Soul of Science* (Wheaton, Ill.: Crossway Books, 1994), xii.
10. Ibid.

10: The Kingdom of Christ and the Culture of Science

1. H. Richard Niebuhr, *Christ and Culture* (New York: Harper and Row, 1951), 32-33.
2. Carl Sagan, *Cosmos* (New York: Random House, 1980), 4.
3. See George M. Marsden, *The Soul of the American University* (Oxford: Oxford University Press, 1994) for an especially comprehensive and compelling account of this story.
4. Ibid., 91-92.
5. George M. Marsden, *Understanding Fundamentalism and Evangelicalism* (Grand Rapids, Mich.: Eerdmans Publishing, 1991), 131, 133.
6. The reader is invited to recall the various themes of chapter 3 related to this discussion.
7. Mark A. Noll, *Scandal of the Evangelical Mind* (Grand Rapids, Mich.: Eerdmans Publishing, 1994), 211.
8. See, e.g., Abraham Kuyper, *Lectures on Calvinism* (Grand Rapids, Mich.: Eerdmans Publishing, 1931), 132, 139.
9. The particularities of the common grace controversies among Dutch Reformed Christians and the details of our concerns about the particular directions some believers take the common grace/antithesis concepts are beyond the scope of the present work, but an example or two of how those discussions tend to point away from the gospel rather than toward it might be helpful. The common grace controversy (basically concerning the question of whether God shows something like real grace to the unregenerate) ends up focusing attention on some likely humanly inscrutable elements of God's providence and purposes, while bypassing the very "scrutable" issues that all people benefit from God's goodness and are responsible to respond to it in repentance and faith. Also even as proper distinctions should be made between common grace and special "saving" grace, doing so makes it tempting to divide God's purposes into two distinct programs for creation, one redemptive and one nonredemptive, and this doesn't seem right. Favor is less controversially seen as a single category, a con-

tinuum of God's good provision for His creation, favor that is unmerited but that requires an appropriate response from humans who observe and experience it.

10. John Murray, *Collected Writings of John Murray*, Vol. 2 (Carlisle, Pa.: The Banner of Truth Trust, 1977), 103.

11: Looking to the Future

1. Abraham Kuyper, *Lectures on Calvinism* (Grand Rapids, Mich.: Eerdmans Publishing, 1994), 139.
2. See, for example, John Brooke, *Science and Religion* (Cambridge: Cambridge University Press, 1991), 192-225.
3. Kuyper, *Lectures on Calvinism,* 141.

Works Cited

Alexander, W. M. *Johann Georg Hamann, Philosophy and Faith*. The Hague: Martinus Nijhoff Publishing, 1966.

Bacon, Francis. "The New Science." In *The Portable Enlightenment Reader*, edited by Isaac Kramnick. New York: Penguin Books, 1995.

_____. *Advancement of Learning and Novum Organum*. New York: Willey Book Company, 1944.

Bavinck, Herman. *In the Beginning: Foundations of Creation Theology*, translated by John Vriend, edited by John Bolt. Grand Rapids, Mich.: Baker Books, 1999.

Berkhof, Louis. *Manual of Christian Doctrine*. Grand Rapids, Mich.: Eerdmans Publishing, 1978.

Berkouwer, G. C. *General Revelation*. Grand Rapids, Mich.: Eerdmans Publishing, 1975.

Berlin, Isaiah. *Three Critics of the Enlightenment—Vico, Hamann, Herder*, edited by Henry Hardy. Princeton: Princeton University Press, 2000.

Birch, Thomas, ed. *The Works of the Honourable Robert Boyle*. New ed., 6 vols. London: Lubrecht & Cramer Ltd., 1966.

Bonhoeffer, Dietrich. *The Cost of Discipleship*. New York: Collier Books, Macmillan Publishing Company, 1963.

Bozeman, Theodore Dwight. *Protestants in an Age of Science: The Baconian Ideal and Antebellum American Religious Thought*. Chapel Hill, N.C.: University of North Carolina Press, 1977.

Brooke, John Hedley. *Science and Religion: Some Historical Perspectives*. Cambridge: Cambridge University Press, 1991.

Calvin, John. *Institutes of the Christian Religion*, translated by Henry Beveridge. Grand Rapids, Mich.: Eerdmans Publishing, 1972.

Chaitin, Gregory J. *The Unknowable*. Singapore: Springer, 1999.

Chambers's Encyclopedia, Vol. 12. London: George Newnes Ltd., 1950.

Clark, Gordon. *Thales to Dewey: A History of Philosophy*. Boston: Houghton Mifflin Company, 1957.

Clouser, Roy. *Knowing with the Heart: Religious Experience & Belief in God*. Downers Grove, Ill.: InterVarsity Press, 1999.

_____. *The Myth of Religious Neutrality: An Essay on the Hidden Role of Belief in Theories*. Rev. ed. Notre Dame, Ind.: University of Notre Dame Press, 2005.

Cohen, I. Bernard. *Revolution in Science*. Cambridge, Mass.: Belknap Press, 1985.

Collins, C. John. *Science & Faith, Friends or Foes?* Wheaton, Ill.: Crossway Books, 2003.

_____. *The God of Miracles: An Exegetical Examination of God's Action in the World*. Wheaton, Ill.: Crossway Books, 2000.

Condorcet, Marquis de. "From *Sketch for an Historical Picture of the Progress of the Human Mind*." Reprinted in *Modernism to Postmodernism: An Anthology*, edited by Lawrence Cahoone. Oxford: Blackwell Publishers, 1996.

Copleston, Frederick. *A History of Philosophy*. 5th ed., 9 vols. Garden City, N.Y.: Image Books, 1993.

Courtenay, William J. *Capacity and Volition: A History of the Distinction of Absolute and Ordained Powers*. Bergamo, Italy: Pierluigi Lubrina Editore, 1990.

Covenant College Purpose Statement, http://www.covenant.edu/welcome/purpose_statement.php (accessed on 12/28/05).

Craig, Edward, ed. *Routledge Encyclopedia of Philosophy* s.v. "Kant, Immanuel." From *The Conflict of the Faculties* (1798): (7: 69-70). London and New York: Routledge, 1998.

Critchley, Simon. *Continental Philosophy: A Very Short Introduction*. Oxford: Oxford University Press, 2001.

Cushing, James T. *Philosophical Concepts in Physics: The Historical Relation Between Philosophy and Scientific Theories*. Cambridge: Cambridge University Press, 1998.

D'Israeli, Isaac. *Curiosities of Literature*. London: J. Murray, 1791.

Descartes, Rene. *Descartes: Meditations on First Philosophy: With Selections from the Objections and Replies*, edited by John Cottingham. Cambridge: Cambridge University Press, 1996.

Dooyeweerd, Herman. *A New Critique of Theoretical Thought,* translated by David H. Freeman and William S. Young. 4 vols. Presbyterian and Reformed Publishing, 1969.

_____. *Roots of Western Culture: Pagan, Secular, and Christian Options*, translated by John Kraay. Toronto: Wedge Publishing Foundation, 1979.

Dumbrell, W. J. *Covenant & Creation: A Theology of the Old Testament Covenants*. Grand Rapids, Mich.: Baker Book House, 1984.

Edwards, Jonathan. *The Works of Jonathan Edwards*. Peabody, Mass.: Hendrickson Publishers, 2000.

Frame, John M. *Cornelius Van Til, An Analysis of His Thought*. Phillipsburg, N.J.: Presbyterian and Reformed Publishing, 1995.

Gilson, Etienne Henry. *Reason and Revelation in the Middle Ages*. New York: Charles Scribner's Sons, 1938.

Gleick, James. *Chaos*. New York: Penguin Books, 1987.

Grant, Edward. *The Foundations of Modern Science in the Middle Ages*. Cambridge: Cambridge University Press, 1996.

_____. "Science and Theology in the Middle Ages." In *God & Nature: Historical Essays on the Encounter Between Christianity and Science*, edited by David C. Lindberg and Ronald L. Numbers. Berkeley: University of California Press, 1986.

Gregory, Bruce. *Inventing Reality: Physics as Language*. New York: John Wiley & Sons, 1990.

Grenz, Stanley J. *A Primer on Postmodernism*. Grand Rapids, Mich.: Eerdmans Publishing, 1996.

_____ and Roger E. Olson. *20th Century Theology: God and the World in a Transitional Age*. Downers Grove, Ill.: InterVarsity Press, 1992.

Griffin, David Ray. *Religion and Scientific Naturalism: Overcoming the Conflicts*. Albany, N.Y.: State University of New York Press, 2000.

Gross, Paul R. and Norman Leavitt. *Higher Superstition*. Baltimore: Johns Hopkins University Press, 1998.

Gross, Paul R., Norman Leavitt, and Martin W. Lewis, eds. *The Flight from Science and Reason*. New York: New York Academy of the Sciences, 1996.

Gunton, Colin E. *A Brief Theology of Revelation*. Edinburgh: T&T Clark, 1995.

_____. *The Triune Creator: A Historical and Systematic Study*. Edinburgh: Edinburgh University Press, 1998.

_____. *The Promise of Trinitarian Theology*. 2nd ed. Edinburgh: T&T Clark, 1997.

Hahn, Roger. "Laplace and the Mechanistic Universe." In *God & Nature: Historical Essays on the Encounter Between Christianity and Science*, edited by David C. Lindberg and Ronald L. Numbers. Berkeley: University of California Press, 1986.

Haught, John. *God After Darwin*. Boulder, Colo.: Westview Press, 2000.

Henderson, R. D. "How Abraham Kuyper Became a Kuyperian." *Christian Scholar's Review* 22, no. 1 (1992): 30-35.

_____. *Illuminating Law: The Construction of Herman Dooyeweerd's Philosophy, 1918-1928*. Amsterdam: Vrije Universiteit, 1994.

Herbert, Nick. *Quantum Reality*. Garden City, N.Y.: Anchor Press/Doubleday, 1985.

Hesse, David J. *Science Studies*. New York and London: New York University Press, 1997.

Hodge, Archibald A. and Benjamin B. Warfield. *Inspiration*. Grand Rapids, Mich.: Baker Books, 1979.

Hodge, Charles. *What Is Darwinism?* edited by Mark A. Noll and David N. Livingstone. Grand Rapids, Mich.: Baker Books, 1994.

_____. *Systematic Theology*. 3 vols. Peabody, Mass.: Hendrickson Publishers, 1999.

Holmes, Arthur. *The Idea of a Christian College*. Grand Rapids, Mich.: Eerdmans Publishing, 1987.

Howell, Kenneth J. *God's Two Books: Copernican Cosmology and Biblical Interpretation in Early Modern Science*. Notre Dame, Ind.: University of Notre Dame Press, 2002.

Hoykaas, R. *Robert Boyle: A Study in Science and Christian Belief*. Lanham, New York, Oxford: University Press of America, 1997.

Hume, David. *Treatise on Human Nature*. Oxford: Clarendon Press, 1973.

Johnson, Phillip. *Darwin on Trial*. Downers Grove, Ill.: InterVarsity Press, 1991.

Jones, Roger S. *Physics as Metaphor*. New York and Scarborough, Ontario: New American Library, 1982.

Jones, W. T. *A History of Western Philosophy*. 2nd ed., 4 vols. New York: Harcourt, Brace & World, 1969.

Kant, Immanuel. *Critique of Pure Reason*, translated by Norman Kemp Smith. New York: St. Martin's Press, 1965.

_____. *Prologomena to Any Future Metaphysics*. Indianapolis: Bobbs-Merrill Company, 1950.

_____. "What Is Enlightenment?" Reprinted in *Modernism to Postmodernism: An Anthology*, edited by Lawrence Cahoone. Oxford: Blackwell Publishers, 1996.

Kline, Meredith. *Images of the Spirit*. Eugene, Ore.: Wipf and Stock Publishers, 1998.

_____. *The Structure of Biblical Authority*. Grand Rapids, Mich.: Eerdmans Publishing, 1972.

Kline, Morris. *Mathematics, the Loss of Certainty*. New York: Oxford University Press, 1980.

Knuth, Donald. *Digital Typography*. Stanford, Calif.: CSLI Publications, 1999.

_____. *The TeXbook*. Menlo Park, Calif.: Addison Wesley Publishing Company, 1991.

Krabbendam, Henry. *Sovereignty and Responsibility*. Bonn, Germany: Verlag für Kultur und Wissenschaft, 2002.

Kuhn, Thomas S. *The Structure of Scientific Revolutions*. 2nd ed. Chicago: University of Chicago Press, 1970.

Kuyper, Abraham. *A Centennial Reader*. Grand Rapids, Mich.: Eerdmans Publishing, 1998.

_____. *Lectures on Calvinism*. Grand Rapids, Mich.: Eerdmans Publishing, 1931.

_____. *Principles of Sacred Theology*. Grand Rapids, Mich.: Baker Book House, 1980.

Lewis, C. S. *The Magician's Nephew*. New York: Collier Books, 1970.

_____. "Miracles." In *God in the Dock: Essays on Theology and Ethics*. Grand Rapids, Mich.: Eerdmans Publishing, 1970.

_____. *Surprised by Joy*. New York: Harcourt, Brace, 1956.

Liddell, Henry George and Robert Scott. *An Intermediate Greek-English Lexicon Founded upon the Seventh Edition of Liddell and Scott's Greek-English Lexicon*. Oxford: Clarendon Press, 1889.

Lindberg, David C. *The Beginnings of Western Science: The European Scientific Tradition in Philosophical, Religious, and Institutional Context, 600 B.C. to A.D. 1450*. Chicago: University of Chicago Press, 1992.

Lindberg, David C. and Ronald L. Numbers, eds. *God & Nature: Historical Essays on the Encounter Between Christianity and Science*. Berkeley: University of California Press, 1986.

Lindberg, David C. "Medieval Science and Religion." In *The History of Science and*

Religion in the Western Tradition, edited by Gary B. Ferngren. New York: Garland Publishing, 2000.

Livingstone, David. *Darwin's Forgotten Defenders*. Grand Rapids, Mich.: Eerdmans Publishing, 1987.

Locke, John. *An Essay Concerning Human Understanding*. London: Oxford University Press, 1969.

MacIntyre, Alasdair. *Whose Justice, Which Rationality?* Notre Dame, Ind.: University of Notre Dame Press, 1988.

Marsden, George M. *The Soul of the American University*. Oxford: Oxford University Press, 1994.

_____. *Understanding Fundamentalism and Evangelicalism*. Grand Rapids, Mich.: Eerdmans Publishing, 1991.

McCartney, Dan and Charles Clayton. *Let the Reader Understand: A Guide to Interpreting and Applying the Bible*. Phillipsburg, N.J.: Presbyterian and Reformed Publishing, 2002.

McGrath, Alister E., ed. *The Blackwell Encyclopedia of Modern Christian Thought*. Oxford: Blackwell Publishers, 1993.

Middleton, J. Richard and Brian J. Walsh. *Truth Is Stranger Than It Used to Be*. Downers Grove, Ill.: InterVarsity Press, 1995.

Milner, Richard. *The Encyclopedia of Evolution: Humanity's Search for Its Origin*. New York: Facts on File Publishers, 1990.

Morris, Leon. *I Believe in Revelation*. Grand Rapids, Mich.: Eerdmans Publishing, 1976.

Murphy, Nancey. *Anglo-American Postmodernity*. Boulder, Colo.: Westview Press, 1997.

Murray, John. *Collected Writings of John Murray*. 4 vols. Carlisle, Pa.: Banner of Truth Trust, 1977.

Niebuhr, H. Richard. *Christ and Culture*. New York: Harper and Row, 1951.

Noll, Mark A. *Scandal of the Evangelical Mind*. Grand Rapids, Mich.: Eerdmans Publishing, 1994.

_____. *Between Faith and Criticism*. 2nd ed. Grand Rapids, Mich.: Baker Book House, 1991.

Oakley, Francis. *Omnipotence, Covenant, & Order: An Excursion in the History of Ideas from Abelard to Leibniz*. Ithaca, N.Y.: Cornell University Press, 1984.

Osler, Margaret J. *Divine Will and the Mechanical Philosophy: Gassendi and Descartes on Contingency and Necessity in the Created World*. Cambridge: Cambridge University Press, 1994.

The Oxford Dictionary of Quotes. 3rd ed. Oxford: Oxford University Press, 1980.

Parsons, Keith, ed. *The Science Wars: Debating Scientific Knowledge and Technology*. New York: Prometheus Books, 2003.

Pascal, Blaise. *Pensées*. London: Penguin Books, Ltd., 1976.

_____. *Pensées*, translated by W. F. Trotter, 1660. http://www.ccel.org/ccel/pascal/pensees.html (accessed May 28, 2005).

Pearcey, Nancy R. and Charles B. Thaxton. *The Soul of Science: Christian Faith and Natural Philosophy*. Wheaton Ill.: Crossway Books, 1994.

Pinnock, Clark H. *Most Moved Mover: A Theology of God's Openness*. Grand Rapids, Mich.: Baker Books, 2001.

Placher, William. *The Domestication of Transcendence*. Louisville, Ky.: Westminster John Knox Press, 1996.

Plantinga, Cornelius, Jr. *Engaging God's World*. Grand Rapids, Mich.: Eerdmans Publishing, 2002.

Polkinghorne, John. *Science and Creation: The Search for Understanding*. Boston: Shambhala Publications, 1989.

Popper, Karl. *Conjectures and Refutations: The Growth of Scientific Knowledge.* New York and Evanston: Harper and Row, 1965.

Poythress, Vern S. *Symphonic Theology.* Phillipsburg, N.J.: Presbyterian and Reformed Publishing, 1987.

Praansma, L. *Let Christ Be King: Reflections on the Life and Times of Abraham Kuyper.* Jordan Station, Ontario: Paideia Press, 1985.

Ratzsch, Del. *The Battle of Beginnings.* Downers Grove, Ill.: InterVarsity Press, 1996.

_____. *Science & Its Limits: The Natural Sciences in Christian Perspective.* 2nd ed. Downers Grove, Ill.: InterVarsity Press, 2000.

Reid, Thomas. *An Inquiry into the Human Mind*, edited by Timothy Duggan. Chicago: University of Chicago Press, 1970.

_____. *Thomas Reid's Inquiry and Essays*, edited by Keith Lehrer and Ronald E. Beanblossom. Indianapolis: Bobbs-Merrill Company, 1975.

_____. "The Philosophy of Common Sense." In *The Portable Enlightenment Reader*, edited by Isaac Kramnick. New York: Penguin Books, 1995.

Richardson, Alan and John Bowden, eds. *The New Dictionary of Christian Theology.* London: SCM Press, 1983.

Robertson, O. Palmer. *The Christ of the Covenants.* Phillipsburg, N.J.: Presbyterian and Reformed Publishing, 1980.

Rorty, Richard. "Solidarity or Objectivity." In John Rajchman and Cornel West, eds. *Post-Analytic Philosophy.* New York: Columbia University Press, 1985.

Ross, Andrew, ed. *Science Wars.* Durham and London: Duke University Press, 1996.

Rushdoony, Rousas John. *The One and the Many.* Fairfax, Va.: Thoburn Press, 1978.

Ryle, Gilbert. *The Concept of Mind.* Chicago: University of Chicago Press, 1984.

Sagan, Carl. *Cosmos.* New York: Random House, 1980.

Schaeffer, Francis A. *True Spirituality.* Wheaton, Ill.: Tyndale House, 2001.

_____. *The Complete Works of Francis A. Schaeffer: A Christian Worldview.* 5 vols. Wheaton, Ill.: Crossway Books, 1982.

Schaff, Philip. *History of the Christian Church.* Vol. 5. Grand Rapids, Mich.: Eerdmans Publishing, 1907.

Schilpp, Paul Arthur, ed. *Albert Einstein: Philosopher-Scientist.* Living Philosophers, Vol. 7. New York: MJF Books, 2001.

Scruton, Roger. *Kant: A Very Short Introduction.* Oxford: Oxford University Press, 2001.

Shea, William R. "Galileo and the Church." In *God & Nature: Historical Essays on the Encounter Between Christianity and Science*, edited by David C. Lindberg and Ronald L. Numbers. Berkeley: University of California Press, 1986.

Schreiner, Susan E. *The Theater of His Glory: Nature and the Natural Order in the Thought of John Calvin.* Grand Rapids, Mich.: Baker Books, 1991.

Spiegel, James S. *The Benefits of Providence: A New Look at Divine Sovereignty.* Wheaton, Ill.: Crossway Books, 2005.

Sproul, R. C. *Not a Chance.* Grand Rapids, Mich.: Baker Books, 1994.

Stafleu, M. D. "The Idea of Natural Law." *Philosphia Reformata* 64 (1999): 88.

Suppe, Frederick. *The Structure of Scientific Theories.* 2nd ed. Urbana, Ill.: University of Illinois Press, 1979.

Torrance, Thomas F. *Theological Science.* Edinburgh: T&T Clark, 1996.

Van Til, Cornelius. *The Defense of the Faith.* Philadelphia: Presbyterian and Reformed Publishing, 1972.

Van Till, Howard J., Davis A. Young, and Clarence Menninga. *Science Held Hostage.* Downers Grove, Ill.: InterVarsity Press, 1988.

Veith, Gene Edward, Jr. *Postmodern Times: A Christian Guide to Contemporary Thought and Culture.* Wheaton, Ill.: Crossway Books, 1994.

Voltaire, Francois-Marie Arouet de. "On Bacon and Newton." In *The Portable Enlightenment Reader*, edited by Isaac Kramnick. New York: Penguin Books, 1995.

Warfield, Benjamin B. *Evolution, Science, and Scripture*, edited by Mark A. Noll and David Livingstone. Grand Rapids, Mich.: Baker Books, 2000.

_____. *The Inspiration and Authority of the Bible*, edited by Samuel G. Craig. Philadelphia: Presbyterian and Reformed Publishing, 1967.

Watson, James D. *The Double Helix,* edited by Gunther S. Stent. New York, London: W. W. Norton Company, 1980.

The Westminster Standards, Larger Catechism. Philadelphia: Great Commission Publications.

Wilson, Edward O. *Consilience: The Unity of Knowledge.* New York: Random House, 1999.

Wolters, Albert M. *Creation Regained.* Grand Rapids, Mich.: Eerdmans Publishing, 1985.

Wolterstorff, Nick. *Thomas Reid and the Story of Epistemology.* Cambridge: Cambridge University Press, 2001.

Yates, Francis A. *Giordano Bruno and the Hermetic Tradition.* New York: Random House Vintage Books, 1964.

Zuidema, S. U. *Communication and Confrontation.* Toronto: Wedge Publishing, 1972.

Index